SOCIOLOGY AS METHOD

CRITICAL ESSAYS ACROSS EDUCATION
Volume 1

Series Editors

Alan J. Bishop, *Monash University, Melbourne, Australia*
Thomas Popkewitz, *University of Wisconsin-Madison, USA*
Ole Skovsmose, *Aalborg University, Denmark*

Scope

This new book series aims at providing readers with a set of monographs dealing with current educational issues from a research and theoretical perspective. In dealing with the many problems besetting our increasingly globalised world, education remains one of the most critical professions, with educational research and theorising being one of the most potent vehicles for comprehending and informing future policies and practices. Thus *Critical Essays across Education* intends to provide academics, policy-makers, research students and concerned general readers, with critical reflections on up-to-date ideas from the international research field of education. In particular this series will reflect the growing trend for borderland crossings in education, whereby cross-discipline research is creating new and important theoretical pathways.

Much theoretical and research-based writing in educational texts tends towards the inaccessible end of the readability dimension. So the brief for intending authors in this series will be to reflect on their research, and those of others, in such a way as to help educate the generalist, as well as the specialist, readership

Sociology as Method
Departures from the Forensics of Culture,
Text and Knowledge

By

Paul Dowling
Institute of Education, University of London, UK

SENSE PUBLISHERS
ROTTERDAM / TAIPEI

A C.I.P. record for this book is available from the Library of Congress.

ISBN 978-90-8790-811-9 (paperback)
ISBN 978-90-8790-812-6 (hardback)
ISBN 978-90-8790-813-3 (e-book)

Published by: Sense Publishers,
P.O. Box 21858, 3001 AW Rotterdam, The Netherlands
http://www.sensepublishers.com

Front cover photo by Paul Dowling.

Photo of author on back cover by Kimiko Takase.

Printed on acid-free paper

In grateful memory of my mother, who taught me to read, and my father, who taught me mathematics

TABLE OF CONTENTS

Preface: Inside the Cave   ix

Acknowledgements   xi

List of Figures   xvii

1. From Forensics to Constructive Description   1

2. Analysing Texts: The idea of an organisational language   15

3. Mustard, Monuments, Movies and Media: A pastiche   45

4. Treacherous Departures: Bernstein and Dowling framed   69

5. A Timely Utterance   109

6. Quixote's Science: Public heresy/private apostasy   125

7. Pedagogy and Community in Three South African Schools:
   An iterative description (with Andrew Brown)   149

8. Knower's Ark/A Ship of Fools? (with Soh-young Chung)   193

9. Sociology as Method   227

Appendix I: A Shooting in Hiroshima   253

Appendix II: Eyeless in Ginza   257

Postface: Inside Another Cave   265

Glossary   267

References   281

Index   291

PREFACE

Inside the Cave

I'm inside a dark cave, but I'm looking out into the light, not at shadows on the back wall.

An elderly woman shambles out of the bathhouse.

"*Domo arigatou*", she drawls as she hands bottles of body wash and shampoo to the attendant hiding in the kiosk. She moves to her shoes that have been waiting for her, glancing back at me. She thinks about a greeting, thinks better of it and shambles out. A young couple hurry in. Bolder, the girl bows and the boy mutters,

"*Konnichiwa*." And they hurry up the stairs to their room. A sporty team of boys step shyly inside the door. They enquire at the kiosk, take their bottles and shuffle into the bathhouse. Not much later, dampened, they shuffle out again, asking the way to the station (how did they get here, I wonder).

Two boys and a dog, a woman with an umbrella (it's quite sunny out), a man with a briefcase and a traffic of cars and vans and scooters glide past without so much as a glance.

A middle-aged woman appears to say '*tombo*'—dragonfly—on her way out of the bathhouse; perhaps I've missed a syllable or two or, more likely, adjusted a couple of consonants.

Then a young American man, wearing shorts, stands in the doorway, looking at me, and asks,

"What kind of place is this?"

"It's an *onsen*."

"Excuse me?"

"It's a hot spring bathhouse and hotel. You pay at the kiosk."

"Cool", he says and wanders off.

But it's not cool at all. In fact it's very, very hot—too hot—and very public. Which is why I'm sitting in the lobby and waiting for my friends and not in the bath.

Are you interested in all this? I guess the answer might depend on where it's going. Well, it's not going anywhere, right now.

ACKNOWLEDGEMENTS

Over breakfast at the house in Tosashimizu, I've just been watching a TV programme on which the main feature was the eighty-eight-year-old *manga* artist, Yanasei Takashi. It appears that Yanasei-san doesn't like formal speeches at awards ceremonies and so forth, preferring to offer a *karaoke* performance instead. Participants at a Japan Cartoon Association event happily clapped along and took mobile phone photos; he was a real star. What on earth did he think he was doing? Surely, awards ceremonies are about the award winners and their supporters. They are also about the awarding institution, of course, but that function, too, is best served by a celebration of the excellence of the competition and not by yet another opportunity for the adulation of the already notorious guest of honour. I think that it's a general rule that formal presentations are never about the one giving the presentation, but, on the contrary, they properly subordinate the presenter to the alliance that has staged the event and, in particular, to its central contributors on this occasion. The formal speech is a key strategy in the maintenance and fostering of the alliance and, in this respect, can work however dull its content, however lacklustre its delivery. The acknowledgements section of a book is a bit like a formal speech.

The alliance that I want to celebrate is, of course, virtual, but no less for that. The ideas in this book have arrived over pretty much the whole period of my twenty years (and, currently, still going) tenure at the Institute of Education, University of London. It is an immense privilege to work in this place: it has its irritating aspects, of course (what doesn't), but for a fair amount of the time I am allowed to sit in my office receiving visits from very clever people who bring me fascinating stories and complex thoughts and who also pay me the honour of listening—really listening.

I have been particularly fortunate in my present group of (sole and jointly supervised) doctoral students, many of whom are able to meet together every fortnight during the term time. I have benefited, I'm sure, at least as much as they from these meetings and from our individual meetings; they have all introduced me to worlds of which I had been completely ignorant. It seems inadequate simply to list them in alphabetical order, but to do otherwise would run the risk of the acknowledgements becoming another book. Sincerest thanks to Jeremy Burke, Soh-young Chung, Russell Dudley-Smith, Jaamiah Galant, Samuel Haihuie, Yuko Hashimoto, Dermot Kelly, Colin McCarty, Joanne Metivier, Mary Rees, Atsuko Suzuki, Yueh-Lin Tu—Irene—and, now quite recently graduated, Darryll Bravenboer—who has extended my thinking into philosophy of education—Rod Cunningham—aspects of whose work are used in Chapter 7—and Natasha Whiteman. Natasha's thesis (Whiteman, 2007) deploys and develops my organisational language and combines this with her own approach in a fascinating and highly original study of online fan communities. Dialogue with her on this project has been immensely formative in the development of much that is in this book; she initially continued to provide inspiration and education as a postdoctoral fellow and co-teacher on some of the programmes that I'm involved with and now holds a permanent position at the University of Leicester. The fortnightly meetings are often joined by others, including, quite regularly, Pinky Makoe and Claudia Lapping, a colleague on the Institute staff—my thanks to them for productive contributions.

A former colleague once asked me, in relation to another publication, why I had chosen to be publicly critical of the work of another colleague. I was naïvely surprised, 'but this is a university; we're not supposed to agree with each other, but, well, equilibrate, maybe even hegemonise.' I will not simply exchange narratives with colleagues, or others, whose work is worth reading and worthy of engagement. So I am grateful for the academic and professional leadership of Gunther Kress, but also for the substantial developments in my own work that have arisen out of my misreading of his.

My position at the Institute has also provided numerous opportunities to work overseas and these activities have often led to periods of accelerated theoretical and empirical development. The work in South Africa (Chapter 7) was made possible by a UK Overseas Development Agency (ODA) funded link between myself and Andrew Brown, of the Institute, and the Universities of Cape Town and the Western Cape. I am particularly indebted to Paula Ensor and Joe Muller, of the University of Cape Town, and Cyril Julie, of the University of the Western Cape, for supporting this link. Andrew and I also benefited substantially from meeting and working with Zain Davies and Jaamiah Galant, at that time, both of the University of Cape Town. Intellectual and academic engagement with these and other South African colleagues in the course of the ODA link was immensely productive. Jaamiah and Ursula Hoadley both offered critical comments on an earlier version of Chapter 7 and also agreed to append some footnotes offering some clarification and contextualisation; the result has been a considerably improved chapter.

Chapters 2 and 3 in part originated as presentations that I gave in Seoul and I am grateful to Soh-young Chung and Yun-chae Noh for their hospitality, for generative conversation, and for introducing me to their colleagues and students at Sogang and Yonsei Universities, where the presesntations were given.

Japan has been an important element in my personal and academic life since around the turn of the millennium and this is visible at various points in the book, notably in the two Appendices, but elsewhere as well. My western cultural expectations never cease to be astonished by Japan's. Unlike the two main protagonists of *Lost in Translation*, however, I have been neither repelled back to a life that I thought I wanted to escape from, nor have I been enthralled into an attempt at 'going native'. Japanese and western culture co-exist, for me, in pastiche, with Japan serving as a deforming technology, iteratively revealing more, not so much about itself, but about me; it also, I hope, remains uninstructed by my response. So I am grateful to Kimiko Takase for teaching me Japan and, of course, for a good deal more and grateful also to her family, particularly her sister,

Mitsuki; Japanese generosity and close attention to the needs, even the whims, of its guests, though not everywhere apparent, are surely unsurpassable, where they are.

There are a small number of others who have had, in very different ways, a major impact on the form and content of this book; I shall mention them in the reverse of the order in which I met them.

Most recently, but, nevertheless, for most of this decade, I have been lucky enough to have been the teacher, student and friend of Soh-young Chung. She has already appeared twice in this section and will make another major appearance as my co-author in Chapter 8. Though first my student on a masters programme and then as a doctoral student, Soh-young already had a doctorate in English Literature, had held academic posts in South Korea; she is one of the sharpest thinkers whom I have ever met and, though it is not her first language, she writes far better English than I do. She came new to sociology as I came new to literature; I can only say that I hope she has gained and will continue to gain as much as I have in the relationship.

Jeff Vass and I have conversations to die for. Conversations that last whole train rides (once we even acquired an audience *en route*), whole days, whole weekends. Quite apart from Jeff's superb intellect and prodigious knowledge, that he seems to aim at openness and I at closure entails that we can never step into the same discussion twice. Irony is always the subtext of our literal talk; the literal always gushes from even our most extravagant ironic play. At the end of a session I feel as if my IQ has been boosted by twenty points; it's a lot of fun as well. I fear that I've objectified Jeff, somewhat, where he appears in this book. This is perhaps inevitable—he's too big for the book—but his impact on the rest has been very considerable.

Andrew Brown and I started at the Institute on the same day in 1987. Since that day we have worked together, not continuously, but frequently and extensively in research and in writing and teaching at the Institute and in numerous institutions around the world. It has frequently been noted, in respect of our public presentations, that we work extremely well together and much of our published material had its first outings in teaching. This is how it should be; why give the students secondhand stuff? Andrew is able to do most of the things that I can do at least as well. But he can also do most of the things that I never seem to be able to do. Andrew's contribution to this book extends far beyond the co-authored Chapter 7, indeed, I wonder how much of my nominally sole-authored work would have been produced at all without the intellectual energy of our work together and his work on his own. Thank you, Andrew.

I met Basil Bernstein a year or so before I joined the Institute. He has had a tremendous impact on my work, but I will defer my tribute to him until Chapter 4.

Parin Bahl collaborated with Andrew Brown and myself in the research that is represented in Chapter 7, but she had been my partner and advisor for some years by that time. It was Parin who first introduced me to sociology and who, in the early days (and some of the later ones) would offer stinging criticism that always jolted me into doing better. I wonder what I would be doing now had it not been for Parin; not this, that's for sure.

***

There are other acknowledgements that are of a different nature, but nevertheless crucial. Firstly, I am grateful to Alan Bishop for his role as series editor at Sense and also for initially suggesting that I approach Sense with the proposal for this book. I am also gratefult to Peter de Liefde for making the publication process painless and for running a publishing house that looks forward rather than backward.

Madonna in Maestà, tempera on wood panel by Cenni di Pepo Cimabue is reproduced as Figure 2.1. The original is in the *Galleria degli Uffizi*, Florence and is reproduced here *su concessione del Ministero dei Beni e delle Attività Culturali*. No further reproduction of this image from this book is permitted without the permission of the Ministry.

Deposizione di Cristo, painting on canvas by Giotto di Bondone, is in the *Capella degli Scrovegni, Padova* and is reproduced as Figure 2.2 with the permission of *dell'Assessorato ai Musei Politiche Culturali e Spettacolo del Comune di Padova*.

The first section of Chapter 4 was originally published as Dowling, P. C. (2001). Basil Bernstein: prophet, teacher, friend, in *A Tribute to Basil Bernstein 1924-2000*, Sally Power, Peter Aggleton, Julia Brannen, Andrew Brown, Lynne Chisholm and John Mace (Eds.), pp. 114-116. ISBN 978-085473-651-5, Institute of Education, University of London, and is reproduced here with the permission of the Institute of Education.

Figure 4.3 is a re-drawing of Figure 9.3 that appeared on page 175 of Bernstein, B. (1996). *Pedagogy, Symbolic Control and Identity*. London, Taylor & Francis and is published here with the permission of Taylor & Francis Books (UK).

Figures 5.6, 5.7 and 5.9 include an image of the Institute of Education, University of London homepage (www.ioe.ac.uk) as it appeared in February 2005. This image is reprinted with the permission of the Institute of Education, University of London.

Chapter 6 was originally a contribution to an edited collection that had been requested by Bill Atweh—thanks for that, Bill, and thanks for the continuing interest in my work. The chapter appears in Atweh, B. *et al* (Eds). (2007). *Internationalisation and Globalisation in Mathematics and Science*. Dordrecht: Springer. pp. 174-198, copyright by Springer Science and Business Media and is reprinted here, with some minor amendments with the permission of Springer Science and Media. Figures 1-15 in the original version are reprinted here as Figures 6.1-6.15 and Figures 16 and 17 are reprinted here as Figures 3.2 and 3.1 respectively. Figures 6.1-6.14 were originally sourced from the Trends in International Mathematics and Science Studies (TIMSS) website at http://www.iea.nl/iea/hq/ and are reprinted here with the permission of the copyright holder, the International Association for the Evaluation of Educational Achievement (IEA).

Figure 8.4 is a modified version of Figure 3.1 that originally appeared on page 54 of Maton, K. (2006b). On Knowledge Structures and Knower Structures. *Knowledge, Power and Educational Reform: Applying the sociology of Basil Bernstein*. R. Moore, M. Arnot, J. Beck and H. Daniels. London, Routledge and is published here with the permission of Taylor & Francis Books (UK).

LIST OF FIGURES

Figure 2.1	Madonna in Maestà by Cimabue	30
Figure 2.2	Deposizione di Cristo by Giotto	31
Figure 2.3	Structure of Hodge's and Kress's Analysis	36
Figure 2.4	Comparison of Analytic Strategies	40
Figure 3.1	Modes of Interactive Social Action	46
Figure 3.2	Modes of Authority Action	53
Figure 3.3	Modes of Authority and Some Signalling Texts and Practices	57
Figure 3.4	The Dynamics of Authority Strategies	58
Figure 4.1	Classification and Framing	77
Figure 4.2	Schema for Constructive Description	85
Figure 4.3	Bernstein's Discursive Map	88
Figure 4.4	The Dual Modality of Practice	94
Figure 4.5	Practical Strategic Space	95
Figure 4.6	A School Mathematical Investigation	101
Figure 4.7	Equivalent Patterns	102
Figure 4.8	Primitive Bubble Arrangements	103
Figure 4.9	A Complex Bubble Arrangement	104
Figure 5.1	Elephant 1	111
Figure 5.2	Elephant 2	111
Figure 5.3	Elephant 3	112
Figure 5.4	Examples of Textual Modes	113
Figure 5.5	Textual Modes	114
Figure 5.6	The Institute of Education WWW Homepage as at February 2005	115
Figure 5.7	The Institute of Education WWW Homepage Framed in a Browser Window	116
Figure 5.8	The Institute of Education WWW Homepage on My (Old) Computer Screen	117
Figure 6.1	TIMSS (USA) Home Page	131
Figure 6.2	'Explore Your Knowledge' (NCIS Site)	133
Figure 6.3	TIMSS Test Item for Grade 4 Science 1	134
Figure 6.4	TIMSS Test Item for Grade 4 Science 2	134
Figure 6.5	TIMSS Test Item for Grade 4 Science 3	135
Figure 6.6	TIMSS Test Item for Grade 8 Science 1	135
Figure 6.7	TIMSS Test Item for Grade 8 Science 2	136
Figure 6.8	TIMSS Test Item for Grade 8 Science 3	136

Figure 6.9   TIMSS Test Item for Grade 4 Mathematics 1   137
Figure 6.10 TIMSS Test Item for Grade 4 Mathematics 2   138
Figure 6.11 TIMSS Test Item for Grade 8 Mathematics 1   138
Figure 6.12 TIMSS Test Item for Grade 8 Mathematics 2   139
Figure 6.13 TIMSS Answers Page   140
Figure 6.14 Information about International Performances on Selected
             TIMSS Test Items   141
Figure 6.15 3/4 + 3/4 = ?   141
Figure 7.1   Classroom Layout in Mont Clair Geography Class   157
Figure 7.2   Student/Teacher Identity   181
Figure 7.3   Regulatory Strategies   183
Figure 7.4   Leader/Follower Identity   189
Figure 8.1   Mary Douglas's 'Cultural Theory'   201
Figure 8.2   Domains of Action   206
Figure 8.3   Grammatical Modes   207
Figure 8.4   'Legitimation Codes of Specialisation'   219
Figure 8.5   Modes of Legitimation   220
Figure 8.6   Modes of Authority Action   221
Figure 8.7   Schema of Interpretation   224
Figure 9.1   Domains of Action at 2 Levels of Analysis   235
Figure 9.2   Domains of Action at 3 Levels of Analysis   236
Figure 9.3   Competing Discourses   237
Figure 9.4   Public Domain Contested by 5 Discourses   238
Figure 9.5   Delimiting and Expanding Strategies   240
Figure 9.6   Discursive Comportment   241
Figure 9.7   Modes of Nostalgia   242
Figure 9.8   Suturing and Rupturing Identification   243
Figure 9.9   Distribution of Subjectivity in Pedagogic and Exchange
             Relations   244
Figure 9.10 Perspective/Value Schema   246
Figure 9.11 Aesthetic Modes   246
Figure 9.12 Acquirer Strategies   248

FROM FORENSICS TO CONSTRUCTIVE DESCRIPTION

>> I sometimes wonder why you want to continue to address some of the
>> audiences you do.
>>
>
> because I want to rearrange the deck chairs on the titanic; what else is there
> to do?
>
> --> join the orchestral ensemble?

I don't like the music.

This is a representation of an email conversation between Jeff Vass (the first speaker) and myself. It subsequently occurred to me that the response, though accurate, was not entirely complete. It is true, I do want to rearrange the deck chairs, but I first want to demonstrate that we are sinking without hope of salvation. Only then can we feel comfortable playing musical chairs.

As I am writing this, the Intergovernmental Panel on Climate Change (IPCC) has just published a report following a meeting in Brussels. This report does indeed seem to indicate that we are sinking. Professor Michael Parry, co-chair of the working group that authored the report outlined its findings.

> "What [scientists] have done now is finally establish at the global level there is an anthropogenic, a man-made, climate signal coming through on plants, animals, water and ice," he told reporters. "This is the first time, at the international level, and for the IPCC that there has been confirmed this signal."

We are not entirely without hope yet, though, it seems: Parry's speech included reference to conclusions to the effect that we may still be able to attenuate or delay the impact of our destructive activities. But what precisely is the origin of the 'signal' that is 'coming through'?

A while ago, Soh-young Chung—my co-author in Chapter 8—gave me a working paper titled 'Towards Methodology' (Chung, 2005). She began the paper by juxtaposing extracts from two poems, one by Samuel Taylor Coleridge, the other by Wallace Stevens. The distinction that she made between them comes very close to addressing the question about the origin of the 'signal' and very close too to the transition that I am trying to establish in this book. Chung selected an extract from Coleridge's *Dejection: An Ode*—well chosen, because the Aeolian lute—the poet himself—played by nature is presented in contradictory duet with Stevens' guitarist. But I'll replace it with a section from *The Nightingale*, only because it seems to demand less in terms of knowledge of poetry.

> And hark! the Nightingale begins its song,
> 'Most musical, most melancholy' bird!
> A melancholy bird? Oh! idle thought!
> In Nature there is nothing melancholy.
> But some night-wandering man whose heart was pierced
> With the remembrance of a grievous wrong,
> Or slow distemper, or neglected love,
> (And so, poor wretch! filled all things with himself,
> And made all gentle sounds tell back the tale
> Of his own sorrow) he, and such as he,
> First named these notes a melancholy strain.
>
> (www.online-literature.com/coleridge/642/)

'Nature as it really is' is for Coleridge, potentially tarnished by subjectivity, which must be eliminated if nature as it really is, in all its glory, is to shine through to us. Stevens strikes a different chord in *The Man with the Blue Guitar*.

I

The man bent over his guitar,
A shearsman of sorts. The day was green.

They said, "You have a blue guitar,
You do not play things as they are."

The man replied, "Things as they are
Are changed upon the blue guitar."

And they said then, "But play, you must,
A tune beyond us, yet ourselves,

A tune upon the blue guitar
Of things exactly as they are."

II

I cannot bring a world quite round,
Although I patch it as I can.

I sing a hero's head, large eye
And bearded bronze, but not a man,

Although I patch him as I can
And reach through him almost to man.

If to serenade almost to man
Is to miss, by that, things as they are,

Say it is the serenade
Of a man that plays a blue guitar.

(www.writing.upenn.edu/~afilreis/88v/blueguitar.html)

For Stevens, it is precisely the poet's imagination that produces the poetry. Professor Parry probably meant to index the signal of science—he was, after all, celebrating an agreement, forged out of hard, all-night (he hadn't changed his clothes since the day before), international bargaining and the initially cacophonous strumming of mutually antagonistic guitars, resplendently decked in their respective national colours. But for this signal to have its intended political impact, the orchestrated version would have had to be claimed to be playing at least roughly in tune with the planet. The scientific signal would have to be pointing at somethings as they are and, more importantly, at the culprits who/that have made things as they are as they are; this is what I am calling *forensics*. So, too, Coleridge and Stevens, though privileging different voices, both retain the idea of 'things as they are', undisturbed by subjectivity.

Parry himself seemed to be producing a discourse that would mediate that of science, something closer—despite the graphs and tables—to everyday language, what we might (and I shall) call the *public domain* of science. He didn't get it quite right. As I recall from the BBC World live broadcast, for example, at one point Parry was unsure whether it was a build up of 'carbonic' or 'carbolic' acid that was being generated by the dissolving of CO_2 in the sea. Nevertheless, Parry's *public domain* discourse would seem to be a necessary mediation, because natural scientists often seem to generate rather unnatural ways of talking about the world. This is how at least one group of astrophysicists looks at the night sky:

> Photometric redshifts can be routinely obtained to accuracies of better than 0.1 in Deltaz/(1 +z). The issue of dust extinction, however, is one that has still not been well quantified. In this paper the success of two template-fitting photometric redshift codes (IMPZ and HYPERZ) at reliably returning A_V in addition to redshift is explored. New data on the 2nd Canadian Network for Observational Cosmology (CNOC2) spectroscopic sample of $0.2 < z < 0.7$ galaxies are presented. These data allow us to estimate A_V values from the observed Balmer decrements. We also investigate whether the empirical value of gamma= 0.44, the ratio between gas- and star-derived extinction, as determined by Calzetti, is necessarily the best value for this sample. (Babbedge *et al*, 2005, p. 1 of pdf version)

This looks more like (what I shall call) the *esoteric domain* of science and will certainly need mediating for many people. As I understand the situation, though, there is definitely a forensics of the universe going on here.[1]

Let's look at it like this. For the most part, we routinely and earnestly engage in everyday discourse about our surroundings. This everyday discourse is generally quite loosely defined, quite context dependent—I will develop this general idea in Chapter 4. The physicists and climate change scientists have effected a sceptical separation from this everyday discourse via generally quite extended apprenticeships into their respective esoteric domains. These domains, in the case of the natural sciences, may be presumed to be strongly *institutionalised*. That is to say, we might expect there to be a high degree of regularity in their deployment within any given field; Bernstein (2000) describes these fields as characterised by 'hierarchical knowledge structures'; I will also engage with this in Chapter 4. Further, these domains also incorporate instruments or, as Latour and Woolgar (1979) famously described them, 'inscription devices', that mediate (or construct) scientists' perceptions of the world. This strong *internal* institutionalisation of the scientific esoteric domain discourse and the claimed (as it has to be) reliability of its inscription devices entail the claim of the elimination of subjectivity—a claim that, as I shall argue in Chapter 6, is also strongly made in the area of school science. These are instruments that, played by any competent musician, will each always produce consistent melodies. This, perhaps, is the music of Coleridge: each Aeolian lute acting selectively, but not otherwise transformatively on nature.

Many areas of the natural sciences are imbricated into diverse state and commercial institutions and practices within society including, for example, health care, engineering, the military and funding by the state and other sources for 'big science' is clearly very substantial compared with, for example, funding for the social sciences and the humanities. It is also worth pointing out that the mediated, public domains of the natural sciences, whilst far more weakly institutionalised, are nevertheless very widely and frequently elaborated in the mass media as well as on the school curriculum. This constitutes a strong *external* institutionalisation of the natural sciences.

So, the strong internal and external institutionalisation of the esoteric and public domains of the natural sciences has effected the making of our most secure truths about the world. There is a sense in which we cannot think beyond them. Yet at the heart of our most secure truths, there are fractures. We need alternative (and, at least in part, contradictory) discourses of physics for the everyday (classical mechanics and electromagnetic theory), the very small (quantum mechanics) and the very large (general relativity) (see Penrose, 1997). It seems also to be the case that many medical procedures performed routinely are not actually backed up by scientific 'knowledge' and are quite often ineffective (see The *Guardian*, 7th April 2007). The position that asserts that that which is true is that which is socially institutionalised as true is often referred to as 'social realism'. But truths are always

---

[1] See Dowling (2006, cc. 4 & 5) for my interpretation (not authoritative) of what's going on here and in this article.

open to challenge on the basis of at least three strategies. Firstly, shifting between discourses, as my reference to the alternative discourses of physics illustrates, but more radical redescriptions would result from a move from physics to, say, sociology. Secondly, shifting between levels of analysis. We can also use the physics example here: quantum mechanics might be interpreted as a consistent discourse; physics inconsistent. The third shift entails demanding elaboration: there would probably be general agreement on the statement that defenestration from a twenty-first floor apartment is likely to prove fatal, but there are innumerable ways to re-textualise this 'truth'.

What holds together these various and often contradictory truths is generally some kind of claim to the fixity of 'things as they [really] are'; at the centre of all forms of realism is a longing for the unobservable. Let me illustrate with a description of the game, 'Mastermind', an online version of which can be found at www.irt.org/games/js/mind/.[2] The original game consisted of a rectangular plastic board with rows of (four or five—I can't remember) holes that would accommodate coloured pegs. The row at one end of the board was or could be concealed by a screen. Behind the screen, the first player would arrange a row of coloured pegs. The second player—would guess the arrangement and fill the first row at the opposite end of the board with an arrangement of coloured pegs. The first player would 'mark' the second player's guess by indicating how many pegs in the second player's arrangement were both of the correct colour and in the correct position and how many were of the correct colour but in the wrong position. On the basis of the new data from the first player, the second player would fill their second row, which would, in turn, be marked by the first player, and so the game would proceed until either the second player made a correct guess, in which case they would win, or the board filled up, in which case the first player would win: a clear example of a forensic challenge.

I used to play a variation on this game with Parin Bahl. In our version, one of us would think of a five-letter word and the other would try to 'guess' the word via a similar process of trial and response. Following the first move, which would, generally, be a simple guess, the second player would deploy one of two strategies; I'll illustrate with an example. Suppose Parin had thought of the word, QUARK and suppose that my first guess was MESON. Parin would inform me that there were no correct letters correctly placed, nor, indeed, were there any correct letters, wherever placed. At this point, I would know that none of the letters in my initial guess were correct. I could formulate my second move by producing a 'theory', which is to say, a guess that is consistent with the totality of the information that I had. An example of a theory would be LIGHT, though this would yield another null response. If the rule is that a theory has to be a recognisable word, then my

---

[2]   Interestingly, Austin (1975) describes how players generally—deliberately or otherwise—misrecognised the rules of this game as originally marketed. Of even greater fascination was the finding that, when the rules as published were changed in an attempt to match those that it was thought players were actually applying, most players continued to deviate from the rules that were packaged with the game.

options have become considerably limited, because I have only A, U and Y left as possible vowels. I could, of course, continue to formulate theories. But I might decide to try an 'experiment'. The word, GLEAM, for example, has four letters that I know are incorrect, so trying this word will tell me if the letter A is in the target word. As it happens, QUALM would be a better experimental word, but I know this only because I'm playing against myself! In any event, the second player would continue to offer a sequence of theories and experiments until the target word was identified; sometimes the sequence of theories and experiments was quite extended, especially if the first player had chosen a word that was unknown to the second. In principle, though, the target word will always be found.

Suppose that we extend the game. Suppose that we imagine this entire book as the target 'word'. Now, I think I'll assume that this book accommodates all twenty-six letters of the English alphabet, but do we tell the second player how many words it contains? Whether or not we do, playing the game has now become something resembling another game involving a sufficiently large number of monkeys, each with a typewriter and having a sufficiently extended period of time to produce the works of Shakespeare (I'm not comparing my writing with that of Shakespeare in any other sense). But the book also contains some Japanese and Greek and mathematical expressions and various forms of emphasis and punctuation, diagrams, images, and so forth. In principle, these might all be coded and digitally rendered (as, presumably, my wordprocessor does for me) and the whole produced as a single binary number. I'm now wondering what number it would be! I'm also wondering whether turning the book into a number would make the game easier or more difficult and what the answer might tell us about language and numbers.

The presentation of statistical information about the book (how many words, how many pages and so forth) or its coding as a binary number are forms of textualising that are, in some sense, equivalent to the quantification of the heavens by Babbedge et al. Attempts to 'guess' the book in its original form would be more 'qualitative' in nature. In all cases, however, the game is constructed as a closed system that also incorporates *the* truth and a mode of interrogating *the* truth that will yield perfectly valid, forensic information about it. The theories and experiments produced by Babbedge et al operate within a system that is open because it cannot include the pre-coded universe, which is unobserved/unobservable.

Nevertheless, the proponents of realist approaches find it necessary to attempt in some way to capture the unobserved/unobservable. A particularly sophisticated realist approach and one currently much in vogue is *critical realism*, the principal exponent of which is Roy Bhaskar (1997, 1998). Bhaskar distinguishes between the ontological *intransitive dimension* of knowledge and the epistemological *transitive dimension*. The conflation of these two dimensions is what Bhaskar refers to as the *epistemological fallacy* and is tantamount to taking what we 'know' (transitive) to be what really is (intransitive). It is the separation of these dimensions that puts the 'critical' in critical realism: we must always maintain a degree of scepticism about what we 'know', however secure it may seem to be in terms of making predictions. Indeed, for Bhaskar, prediction itself is problematic, even in the natural sciences. Bhaskar's reality consists of three levels. The 'real' consists in 'structures' and 'mechanisms' that give rise to 'events' in the natural world and 'relations' that give rise to 'behaviours' in the social world. Events and behaviours constitute the 'actual' and produce our 'experiences' in the 'empirical'. Here, it is important to note that the events of the 'actual' are produced whether or not they are experienced, so the answer to old question of whether a sound is made by a tree falling in the forest when no one is around to hear it is, 'yes'. Bhaskar claims that the real world is generally 'open', so that regularities in events and behaviours are not generally produced; they may occur locally in the natural world, but not at all in the social world. Thus reliance on the 'constant conjunction' of events and the inference of laws on the basis of regularity is inappropriate and prediction, certainly in the social world, is not possible.

Now this last point may sound a bit strange and susceptible to the same kind of jibe that Alan Sokal has made in inviting relativists to jump from his twenty-first floor window (see Chapter 8). After all, I can predict pretty reliably that a whole bunch of students will turn up at my institution on the first day of term. But, of course, this is focusing entirely on the transitive dimension in dealing with the knowable; it isn't getting anywhere in terms of what actually 'exists', the structures, mechanisms and relations of the 'real', to assume that it is, is to commit the 'epistemological fallacy'. This kind of criticism is also applied to quantitative forms of research. In general terms, quantification must presume qualitative regularity (the word count for this book treats all of the words as the same kind of entity) and so, in a sense, presumes what the 'real' does not generate. Social constructionist approaches that understand reality to be constructed socially also, quite clearly, commit the epistemological fallacy in failing to recognise the need to investigate the underlying structures, mechanisms and relations. 'Triangulation' is an approach that is consistent with critical realism. Here, different strategies are combined in order to reveal some of the limitations of each.

This is very clever stuff. However, to insist on its relevance to my project would seem to entail a tacit claim that I am doing philosophy and I want to insist that I am not. Not everyone would agree; this is from an introduction to critical realism:

> A good part of the answer to the question 'why philosophy?' is that the alternative to philosophy is not *no* philosophy, but *bad* philosophy. The 'unphilosophical' person has an unconscious philosophy, which they apply in their practice—whether of science or politics or daily life. (Collier, 1994, p. 17)

Now I've had this kind of argument before with the exponents of 'ethnomathematics'. These are educationalists, such as Paulus Gerdes (1985,1988), who seem to believe that anybody doing anything that can be described in mathematical terms—such as building a traditional African house—is actually doing mathematics and that, furthermore, revealing this to them is an act of emancipation. This is what Gerdes suggests:

'Had Pythagoras not ... *we* would have discovered it'. The debate starts. 'Could our ancestors have discovered the "Theorem of Pythagoras"?' 'Did they?' ... 'Why don't we know it?' ... 'Slavery, colonialism ...'. By 'defrosting frozen mathematical thinking' one stimulates a reflection on the impact of colonialism, on the historical and political dimensions of mathematics (education). (Gerdes, 1988, p. 152)

And here is the mechanism of emancipation:

The artisan who imitates a known production technique is—generally—not doing mathematics. But the artisan(s) who discovered the techniques, *did* mathematics, *developed* mathematics, was (were) thinking mathematically. (Gerdes, 1985, p. 12)

As I argued in Dowling (1998), Gerdes is constructing the practices of those he observes as the public domain of his gaze that is a mixture of European school mathematics (Pythagoras), Fordist production techniques (production is imitation), and European historiography (technologies are the inventions of 'great men'). He is also prescribing his own version of conscientisation therapy. What he is not doing is allowing the African cultures that he surveys to stand as values in and of themselves and with their own voice: they are not doing mathematics, they are making their own culture. Similarly, I am not doing philosophy just because what I do can be described in philosophical terms. To claim otherwise is to engage in what I refer to as *mythologising*: treating the public domain as if it were 'real'. But it's not, it is recontextualised practices. I am not doing what Roy Bhaskar seems to think that I ought to be doing. I am quite unashamedly operating in his epistemological 'transitive domain'. However, I deny the charge of epistemological fallacy on the grounds that I am not looking for or claiming to have found truths or real mechanisms, structures and relations. Rather, I am attempting to build a culture and this entails producing some kind of regularity in the same ways, in some respects, as the builders and designers of other artefacts: I am a theory/research engineer, providing an organisational language that potentially allows people to see the world in new ways that may be of interest or may be productive for them. I use the tools of sociology and methodology because they are the ones I have to hand and I have developed a small fluency with them—they are a part of my language, philosophy, in the sense of its problematics that span millennia, is not.

My position is explicitly anti-realist, but not in the naive sense ridiculed by Sokal and other realist critics of postmodernism that are discussed in Chapter 8. Indeed, I strongly suspect that earnest adherence to naïve realism generates an empty set, at least within the academic field. I don't deny the existence of Bhaskar's ontological, intransitive domain, I simply do not feel that faith in it has any clear implications for what I do. I suppose I lack the conviction that science or society are, in any clear and general sense, improving, though local 'improve-ments' (and deteriorations) are palpable. I guess I can just work on the arrangement of my little corner of the world without the need to be sure that I am doing something of ineffable, but certain value. Walking past the cemetery near where I (sometimes) live in Yokohama, my friend noted that her brother had stated quite explicitly that he did not want any of the Japanese, Shinto-Buddhist pomp and ritual performed after his own death, but rather wished his ashes to be simply scattered, Hindu-style (he didn't mention running water, so this didn't seem to signal an actual conversion). My comment was to the effect that death rituals were for the living, not for the dead and it was not really his place to dictate the preferences of others. Unless, that is, he had an ontological commitment in some kind of afterlife or other after-death mechanisms, structures or relations that would justify his intrusion into the grief of those who survived him. Personally, I find the cemetery a rather attractive, peaceful place to get away from the traffic and to remember. If all I'm building is a cemetery, that's fine by me—I guess this bears some similarities with rearranging the deck chairs on the Titanic.

So, anti-realism does not necessarily entail a direct challenge to either the *esoteric* or *public* domains of natural science knowledge. All that it must do is reject the need to dwell in the mythical land of the unobservable. It is my contention that, at best, the insistence on the existence of a state of 'things as they are' is a political or marketing strategy. Indeed, Robert Alan Jones (1999) describes Émile Durkheim's 'social realism' as precisely a political strategy. It provides an alibi for errors and contradictions, by positing an ideal state of perfect knowledge, unobtainable, but something that we are all trying to close in on. In respect of the natural sciences, the success of their predictions is often understood as evidence of precisely this, whereas their failures to predict are generally allowed to fade (or not published in the first place).

Unfortunately, realist pronouncements can have more damaging effects, limiting reflective thinking and debate. The constitution of the dual realms of knowledge and reality allows the bigoted debater to hop between two stools in an argument, thus, in response to a sociological analysis,

"But that's not the way the world works."

"How do you know?"

"Science tells us."

An alternative example would be the attempt to hold on simultaneously to both modes of legitimation of anthropological commentaries that are offered by Clifford Geertz (1988): 'being there' and 'being here'. 'Being there' legitimates statements on the grounds that the anthropologist has lived in the setting about which they write; 'being here' grounds legitimation on the anthropologist's apprenticeship into the anthropological discourse, a discourse of the university—'here'. As Geertz elegantly points out, the nature of 'having been there' is of course constituted by having 'been here' (see Chapter 8). You cannot have your cake and eat it, but the attempt is precisely what I want to avoid. I find it pervades so much of the discourses of the social sciences and educational studies, in particular. We might speculate that it is precisely the comparatively weak internal and external institutionalisation of these discourses that allows their infection by the virus of everyday naïve realism and, perhaps, contributes to their failure to develop strong institutionalisation.

So, what I mean by demonstrating that we're sinking without hope of salvation is that we must not depend on a real real—'things as they are'—as a lifebelt (or, if we encounter it as an iceberg, then were really sinking). Having established this—to my own satisfaction, at least—I can concentrate on rearranging deck chairs, or on my performance on my blue guitar. As Chung (op. cit.) has pointed out, Stevens aims at something beyond mere blueness. This extension is precisely Stevens/my subjectivity. There is more than one option. I might work to produce fiction. I might stay close to the weakly institutionalised, analogue discourses of the everyday and play with the empirical. Alternatively, I might engage in intertextual dialogue with other fiction and treat the empirical with a degree of abandon—some social theory seems to operate like this. I will not choose either of these options, though I share with both fictive forms the initial assertion that my (any) work is only a (re)textualising of perceptions: this is precisely the critical dimension of my discourse. I share with the first option the concern to engage with the empirical. I share with the second the concern to dialogue with, shall we say, the theoretical. I am concerned to establish a degree of pedagogic potential in my discourse and so I need to make its central principles explicit—as explicit as possible. This might ease, but certainly not ensure, its institutionalisation beyond the academic activities of myself and my students.

The pedagogy may not be easy or quick, however. Here is an extract from another Stevens poem, my use of which also follows Chung:

One must have a mind of winter
To regard the frost and the boughs
Of the pine-trees crusted with snow;

And have been cold a long time
To behold the junipers shagged with ice,
The spruces rough in the distant glitter

Of the January sun; and not to think
Of any misery in the sound of the wind,
In the sound of a few leaves,

Which is the sound of the land
Full of the same wind
That is blowing in the same bare place

For the listener, who listens in the snow,
And, nothing himself, beholds
Nothing that is not there and the nothing that is.

(Stevens, 2001, p. 11)

The snow man acquires the gaze of winter after a long time in the cold, shedding the everyday apparatus that shivers against it. My metaphor, here, is the winter as my own discourse, that—simple and inadequately developed as it may seem—has been a long time in the making and has arisen out of dialogue and discussion with interlocutors and with texts and cultural settings. The result is neither closed nor complete, of course, but, more particularly, it is not realisable as a linear programme of development. All of this is the case with any culture capable of more than trivial descriptions and the failure to recognise these features of cultural systems permits mythologisings such as the school curriculum, with its steady developmental structure.

So this book has not been arranged as a developmental curriculum, other than in the inclusion of this introduction, a concluding chapter (Chapter 9)—that I hope is more than a summary—and the positioning of Chapter 2 before Chapters 3 to 8. Each chapter is its own departure—Chapters 2 and 3 depart from the same point, the former to the introduction of the idea of a sociological analysis of text, the latter to the presentation of aspects of and commentaries produced by my organisational language. Each chapter has arisen out of and is constructed as a conversation with one or more key figures, ideologies, texts, or places. They were all written with the current project in mind, though most can be traced back to more local events and one—Chapter 6—has been published elsewhere in a slightly different form.

The central figure with whom I am dialoguing is Basil Bernstein, my former mentor. This dialogue has been ongoing since 1986 and is the point of departure for Chapter 4—in more ways than one, the central chapter in this book. The chapter incorporates its own history, so I'll not elaborate on this further here. The chapter is an attempt to mark out the key points of departure of my constructive description from Basil's forensics. The dialogue with Basil is extended in Chapter 8 in which Soh-young Chung and I engage with some recent (and some not so recent) work that has sought to develop Bernstein's sociology of knowledge. This chapter has its origins in my involvement in Soh-young's work in the sociology of literary studies and also in my own methodological work, in particular, in the production of a module for a Master of Research degree for the University of London external programme (Dowling, 2006).

Chapter 5 and also Chapter 2 include parts of an important (to me) dialogue with my colleague Gunther Kress. Here, I engage in some practical textual analysis in attempting to establish the points of departure of my constructive description and sociological organisational language, on the one hand, and Kress's linguistically motivated approach. Chapter 5 has its origins in a presentation that I gave at the European Systemic Functional Linguistics Conference and Workshop, held at King's College London in August 2005. Some of the text analysis in Chapter 2—including the analysis of a work by the Florentine, Cimabue—began with a workshop on text analysis that I ran as a part of the pre-conference proceedings at the Southern African Association for Research in Mathematics and Science Education conference in Cape Town in January 1995, I used it again in a presentation at the University of Lisbon in 1999.

Chapter 6 began as, first a seminar that I ran as a part of a masters programme in 1988 and then as a chapter in an edited collection (Dowling, 1991a). Here, it constituted a dialogue with the discourse of technological determinism—I would say a dialogue with the ideology of technological determinism, but I am summoned by the utterance by Deleuze and Guattari, 'There is no ideology and never has been' (1987, p. 4)—this discourse is distinctly forensic in nature. In Chapter 6 I have picked up this dialogue and developed it into a critique of critique (I suppose). This chapter, in a slightly different form, is also an invited contribution to an international collection on mathematics and science education (Atweh *et al*, 2007).

Chapters 2, 3 and 7 and also Appendices I and II dialogue, in different ways, with places and cultures. I have begun both Chapter 2 and Chapter 3 with the same anecdote that stands as a dialogue with India, though the chapters themselves move swiftly away from their starting points. Chapters 2 and 3 were both initiated as presentations that I gave at Yonsei and Sogang Universities in Seoul in the autumn of 2003. Chapter 7 is a more substantial dialogue with the Western Cape region of South Africa. The chapter is an original presentation and re-analysis of an empirical study carried out by Andrew Brown and myself in the mid-nineteen-nineties. The two appendices are of a different nature from the other chapters, perhaps more in the public domain. They stand as representative of an ongoing dialogue with Japanese culture. As is the case with all of these chapters dialoguing with places and cultures, they are not constructed, primarily, as commentaries on these places and cultures, but rather the products of transactions between a method and cultural texts that serve as much to introduce and develop the method as to relay their own tales.

Chapters 3 to 8 all include relational spaces that establish various strategic modes. For example, Chapter 3 introduces a fourfold strategic space constituting a modality of interaction and Chapters 3, 6 and 8 all deploy a space constituting a modality of authority action. All of these relational spaces have emerged out of the constructive description of empirical texts (though not necessarily the texts introduced in this book). Chapter 4 includes my schema for constructive description itself that was first introduced in Dowling (1998). The particular form that the constructive description takes is sociological and by this I mean that I am understanding the sociocultural terrain to consist in the formation, maintenance and destabilising of alliances and oppositions through strategic, autopoietic action. It is the transaction of this foundational proposition with diverse empirical texts that generates the strategic spaces that I shall introduce and their commentaries on the empirical texts.

This chapter and Chapter 9—not begun at the time of writing this—bookend the main chapters in the book and, are intended to mediate them in respect of the central line of argument of the book as a whole. I shall not anticipate Chapter 9 here other than to say that it will include some speculative developments and additions to my organisational language. I began the present chapter with a snatch of a(n ongoing) conversation between myself and Jeff Vass about audiences and the deck chairs and orchestral ensemble on the Titanic, pointing out that I don't like the music of the latter. That music is the music of forensics, of dualisms.

Michael Parry's presentation of the IPCC report on climate change opens a dualism in respect of the origin of the signals that it identifies: is this the voice of science, or is it the voice of the planet. Similarly, are Babbedge *et al* presenting the voice of science or the voice of the universe. In a discourse of the social sciences, Clifford Geertz articulates the same category of forensic dualism: is anthropology legitimated by being here (in the university) or by being there (in the field)? In the arts, Coleridge longs for the voice of nature, Stevens for the voice of the poet. We seem quite easily to be able to recognise the dualisms of the social sciences and the humanities as themselves constituting legitimate fields of contestation. The internal institutionalisation of these discourses tends, of course, to be quite weak, having nowhere a strong grip on language. Their external institutionalisation—their public domains—are even less strongly instititutionalised; how many general readers have any clear idea of the commentaries generated by sociology or by educational studies? The natural sciences are different. Here, we might speculate that the strong external institutionalisation of their discourses supports their already strong internal institutionalisation (though perhaps this was less the case in the days of the amateur man [sic] of science).

The strong dual institutionalisation of the natural sciences seems to conceal its own dualism, so that science and nature seem naturally to be singing from the same hymn sheet. But the ventriloquising of the voice of the natural world by the voices of human discourse—what Hayles refers to as 'the platonic backhand' (see Chapter 2) and what I refer to as forensics—always creates a doubled space where finding an alibi for incomplete theoretical development is always possible. I have presented the game, Mastermind, as an ideal type for scientific investigation. Here, experiment and theory are meaningful because the game itself incorporates its own solutions as, in a sense, does science, which, in a sense, makes the world that it investigates. This, incidentally, is not a cynical voice—quite the contrary.

I am cynical, though, about the forensic postulation of 'things as they are'. But this cynicism is not a challenge to philosophies such as critical realism. It is a challenge to the hegemony of philosophy. I am no more doing or dependent upon philosophy than is the engineer, the architect, the watchmaker or the novelist. I am doing sociology and, from time to time, think of myself as a theory engineer—a maker of theoretical machines. I start with the assertion that the sociocultural consists in the autopoietic formation, maintenance and destabilising of alliances and oppositions as a theoretical installation. I proceed via the transaction of this installation with culture, text and knowledge as pointers to empirical settings. The outcome is the generation of commentaries of these settings—constructive descriptions—and, at the same time, the development of an organisational language, currently (until Chapter 9) referred to as social activity theory. Philosophy may participate in dialogue in a kind of a pastiche arrangement, but may not hegemonise my discourse (see Chapter 3).

I am attempting to address a very diverse audience, including those for whom the central message of this chapter is not news, but also the forensic sociologists and educationalists, whom Jeff Vass thinks I may as well ignore. I am also addressing the antitheorists (a more difficult audience, perhaps). At a recent (successful) viva of one of my doctoral students, one of the examiners asked what the point might be of all this technical language, why couldn't the thesis be written in a language that would be intelligible in the settings investigated. But, of course, if the thesis had been in any meaningful sense intelligible in these settings, then it could not have stood meaningfully within an academic discourse—it should have failed! Some antitheorists operate a different version of forensics, a monism rather than a dualism. For them, 'things as they are' are transparently available to us. These are the precisely the critics of Stevens's guitarist. Other antitheorists, perhaps, favour fiction and 'playing with the empirical'. I'll address them anyway.

In another conversation with Jeff Vass (as it happens, the other examiner of the very same thesis) I suggested that it occurred to me that theory is very often regarded much as are the biscuits passed round on a plate at committee meetings: delicious or not, it is/they are no part of the real business of the university. Perhaps I'll ignore those who think in this way.

As for the others, part of the message that I want to address to you concerns the importance of focussing on the matter at hand—constructive description, commentary, and organisational language—and avoiding mythical transport to the discourse of the real (whether or not you are a believer). The other part of the message consists of a marketing strategy. I am presenting you with a technology—an organisational language—and some illustrations of how it might be deployed and developed and also of what it is capable of producing in transaction with the empirical; the resulting commentaries are presented as what I hope are new perspectives on a whole range of settings. In presenting all of this I am, of necessity, having to adopt a pedagogic tenor, but, at the end of the day, the evaluation is yours: it's really a matter of whether or not you find tuneful my particular style of blues guitar.

ANALYSING TEXTS

The idea of an organisational language

Picture a scene in rural Rajasthan in December. A narrow, roughly metalled road divides fields of mustard plants. The road is sparsely lined with trees, foliage a darker, greyer green than the emerald mustard leaves. A tourist coach chugs along the road passing, every now and then a village of grey-brown low dwellings, men in drab walking or cycling along dirt paths. Women are working in the fields, resplendent in their brightly coloured saris, each one different. Now: how do you read this visual text?

***

Some years ago I took a coach tour in northern provinces of India. The fields of green mustard leaves behind the trees sparsely lining the road between Agra and Jaipur were radiant against the pale blue mountains in the distance.

"Look at the women in the fields," prompted one of my fellow tourists, "aren't their saris beautiful." And indeed they were. Though quite a distance away and mainly bending down, working in the leaves, the women dazzled in purples and blues and reds, each one different, jewels in Rajasthan's own vast emerald silk sari. The other passengers on the coach agreed and cooed and photographed and felt happy in the warm sun and the mild intoxication of beer at lunchtime. As a sociologist I felt obliged to speak.

"What about the men?" I asked.

"What do you mean, there aren't any men; we haven't seen any men?"

"Yes you have, you saw them in the villages that we've driven through. What colours were they wearing?"

"Well, mainly drab khakis and greys."

"So you probably wouldn't notice them even if they were in the fields."

"No."

"Tell me, in an agricultural environment in which people work spread out over a large area that is pretty much monochrome, what do you think is the best way to ensure that you can keep control of your women and still be free to get up to whatever takes your fancy?" My colleagues were aghast.

"You've ruined our afternoon." And so I had, and perhaps mine as well. Jeremy Bentham could not have designed a more efficient rural panopticon; the vivid markings of this particular beast now merely warned of the sting in its tail; idyllic culture had been stripped of its lustrous garment to reveal the hard core of the social structure that wears it as a veil: sari-technology. Tourist discourse was a cutaway to an idyllic dream; sociological discourse here, a beauty's awakening, but I was no Prince Charming.

AN AMERICAN IN HAITI

In this chapter I am concerned with the analysis and with the mythologising of text and its meaning. The object text in the case of my Rajasthan example—what Barthes (1981) might have described as the text-as-work, the unread text—is no more than an assemblage of clips that we as un-self-conscious editors cut seamlessly together to constitute our text-as-text, the text that is read. We know what the text says because we know what game we are playing—I was playing my game in the wrong playground. Oddly, we audience real film in a similar way even though the titles and credits—not to mention our own commonsense—make it quite clear that a great deal of authorship has gone into the construction of the movie. We have no difficulties at all installing ourselves in impossible observer positions, hitching onto the plot *en route* to the denouement, achieving so much more than Coleridge's (1817) suspension of disbelief. Even where there is an apparently deliberate attempt to disrupt our smooth ride, the ideal mythologised narrative form is the pattern against which our walk through the scenes is revealed as random. These playgrounds are well organised and at the corner of every street. Stranger still, where a text does not declare its authorship we seem to have an irrepressible urge to install one—God, patriarchy, whatever.

Not all playgrounds are as apparently uncontested. To invoke Roland Barthes once again, we might recall his French soldier on the cover of *Paris Match* (1973). But I'll use a soldier of my own, this one American (see Brown & Dowling, 1998, p. 85, also Dowling & Brown, 2009).[3] The soldier is suppressing a Haitian. The soldier is a very powerful man, rendered almost monumental by the camera angle. He is armed with a fearsome weapon, which he is prepared to fire—his finger clearly rests on the trigger. The soldier is vigilant, on the watch for further trouble. Yet this is a benevolent soldier. Although he holds a deadly weapon, it is pointed downwards and not at anyone. He holds the Haitian down with his knee—a minimum amount of force.

The Haitian contrasts starkly with the soldier. He appears physically small—a feature exaggerated by the foreshortening effect of the camera angle. He is weak and easily suppressed by the soldier who does not need to use his gun. A stick lies on the ground. This might have been a weapon dropped by the Haitian as the soldier pinned him down—a primitive weapon for primitive people. There are two groups of Haitians in the background. One group, on the left, seems to be engaging in a brawl. The members of the other group, in the top right, appear indifferent to the action. Behind the soldier, lies a pile of rubble. Behind him and to his left, a media sound recordist is recording the action for the news.

Clearly, some interpretation has already taken place in this description of the text. The stick might not, after all, be a weapon, for example. This interpretation

---

[3] To see this image, create an account on the Associated Press website at www.apimages.com and search for image I.D. 9409290609.

has been guided by an orientation to another level of description that I want to make, that of the 'mythical' figures constituted in and by the image. The USA—signalled by the soldier—is a powerful, but benevolent state. This state takes on an altruistic responsibility for other, less developed nations, protecting primitive societies from self-destruction. Haiti is precisely such a society, characterised by criminality, apathy, and low-level technology; and already lying in ruins. The press, represented by the sound-recordist and by the photographer of the image (in the place of the observer), is shown as a neutral organ, telling it as it is.

Now the question you have to ask yourself is, does it matter where the photograph appears? If it appears on the cover of *Time* magazine, then we may well feel that the above reading is appropriate. Suppose, however, that it appears on the cover of *Living Marxism*. In this case we would probably reject the celebration of America and the disparaging of the Third World state. Rather, we would probably interpret the text as ironic: this is how America thinks of itself and of its neighbours and this is precisely the problem in contemporary global politics. After all, the gaze of the soldier resembles nothing so much as the optimistic gazes of the blond youths in so many Nazi images. In fact, the text is taken from the front page of *The Guardian*, a UK newspaper with a broadly centre-left editorial orientation. Here, perhaps, the text signifies the journal's own neutrality in the play between the literal and ironic readings of the photograph.

To take another example: the city-as-work, how do we constitute it as text. I tend to village London according to the occupations and routine journeys and occasional visits of my own life history and these differ somewhat both from the historical, London-as-accretion-of villages and the zoning of new housing development, and from the sociological London-as-social-class-map. Each of these and all other readings hypertextualise the city to form unholy allegiances between boroughs, buildings, streets. In order to get their licence, London cabbies must 'do the knowledge':

> All licensed taxi drivers in the capital must have an in depth knowledge of the topography of London, 'The Knowledge'. For would be All London or 'Green Badge' holders, this means that they need to have a detailed knowledge of London within a six mile radius of Charing Cross. This is based on 320 routes (or 'runs') as set out in the Public Carriage Office "Guide to Learning the Knowledge of London" (the 'Blue Book') They also need to know the places of interest and important landmarks on the route and within a quarter mile radius of both start and finish points. (http://www.the-knowledge.org.uk/main/ (last accessed 06/03/07))

London is less an alliance of villages and more a library of narratives.

HAPPENINGS AND THEIR TEXTUALISINGS: BOUNDING THE TEXT

My examples are intended to point at two questions that confront us when self-consciously embarking on textual analysis, questions that must be addressed yet that defy security in response (as any good question must). The first question invites us to specify the text. Barthes' methodological (if I may call it that) distinction between text-as-work and text-as-text is helpful, but to operationalise it is to forget that the text-as-work has already been established as a text-as-text at the point of its naming. The book on the library shelf—whether or not it has been opened—is already a part of a larger text-as-work which we might establish as a text-as-text by calling it the library, or the institution or practice that houses or sponsors or manages it, and so forth. This issue of text and context (con-text) is clearly a problem that is raised by my consideration of the photograph of the American soldier. Allan Kaprow turns things around somewhat and might be taken to imply that, insofar as it aspires to art, the book shouldn't be in the library in the first place:

> ... the better galleries and homes (whose decor is still a by-now-antiseptic neoclassicism of the twenties) desiccate and prettify modern paintings and sculpture that had looked so natural in their studio birthplace. [...] artists' studios do not look like galleries and [...] when an artist's studio does, everyone is suspicious. I think that today this organic connection between art and its environment is so meaningful and necessary that removing one from the other results in abortion. (Kaprow, 2003, p. 85)

For Kaprow, habitat is vital:

> The place where anything grows up (a certain kind of art in this case), that is, its "habitat." gives to it not only a space, a set of relationships to the various things around it, and a range of values, but an overall atmosphere as well, which penetrates it and whoever experiences it. Habitats have always had this effect, but it is especially important now, when our advanced art approaches a fragile but marvelous life, one that maintains itself by a mere thread, melting the surroundings, the artist, the work, and everyone who comes to it into an elusive, changeable configuration. (*Ibid.*, p. 85)

The habitat is the atelier, presumably, which must house the artist's entire developing corpus (is it OK for a piece to be moved from the easel to allow work to proceed on the next) and anyone who wishes to experience it. Is it more than coincidence that Kaprow's article was originally published in 1961, the same year as Joseph Heller's *Catch 22*? Kaprow escaped the catch by containing his art temporally as well as spatially as 'Happenings'. The first of these events, '18 Happenings in 6 Parts' was performed in October 1959 in the Reuben Gallery, New York. Clear, plastic walls divided the space into three rooms and the audience were sent 'props' and told that they would participate in the work and given tickets that showed individual timetables in terms of specified seats in particular rooms at specified times. Events included an orchestra playing toy instruments, a girl squeezing oranges and drinking the juice and actors reading placards whilst moving through the rooms. We might interpret '18 Happenings in 6 Parts' as an attempt to detextualise art. In a sense there is no art-as-work. It can be planned, even scripted, but the participation of the audience—however limited this might actually have been in practice—accentuates the spontaneity of the live theatre and weakens even if only slightly the distinction between author and audience; the Happening is authored and audienced at least in some degree simultaneously. Further, no one at all sees all of the Happening, not even Kaprow, its originator, who may nevertheless hope to benefit from its mythologising:

> To the extent that a Happening is not a commodity but a brief event, from the standpoint of any publicity it may receive, it may become a state of mind. Who will have been there at that event? It may become like the sea monsters of the past or the flying saucers of yesterday. I shouldn't mind, for as the new myth grows on its own, without reference to anything in particular, the artist may achieve a beautiful privacy, famed for something purely imaginary while free to explore something nobody will notice. (*Ibid.*, p. 88)

Did his 'beautiful privacy' entail another catch, I wonder.

The performance artist, Jack Bowman, includes Kaprow's Happenings as examples of performance art.

> When I did my first major performance art piece at the Cleveland Performance Art Festival on April 9, 1993, I handed out a flyer with the performance of Jack's Theorem and the Primal Thought. On this flyer I wrote "The Act is TRUTH. Nothing that was ever recorded is truth. Nothing that was ever said is truth. Only the ACT." This is the best definition that I am aware of for performance art. (Bowman, 2001/2006)

Bowman's 'definition' neatly effaces the term 'truth' (nothing, including the definition, can be pronounced as true in speech or writing) and, together with it, any recourse to a meaning lying behind the performance. Homer Simpson put it perfectly, at the end of a family discussion on the possible moral of the story in the episode:[4]

Lisa: Perhaps there is no moral to this story.

Homer: Exactly! Just a bunch of stuff that happened

Marge: But it certainly was a memorable few days.

Homer: Amen to that!

And the bunches of stuff that comprised Kaprow's happenings and Bowman's performances were also (it would seem) memorable, having left traces in the memories of participants and audiences and also in museums and video and image archives and in print publications and also distributed across the internet. The question is, has the art been detextualised in the sense that '18 Happenings in 6 Parts' never was and still is not a text-as-work. Well, it has in this sense. But then

---

[4]   Extract from 'Blood Feud' episode written by George Meyer, Directed by David Silverman. Text at http://www.snpp.com/episodes/7F22.html (last accessed 06/03/07).

this is precisely the condition of all text, which is to say, that it is always authored in its reading; the text-as-work is merely an analytic placeholder that reminds us that we need to be clear about just exactly where we are starting from. '18 Happenings in 6 Parts' is not the only object of interest that is unavailable as a prototype; this is also the case with my holiday trip through Rajasthan as with all other temporally contained objects. It is also the case with spatially contained objects that are unavailable for reasons of the social and geographical striation of space. Let's say, then, that such happenings cannot in themselves become the direct objects of textual analysis. But we can have access to what I earlier described as an assemblage of clips, mnemonic or more tangible derivatives of the postulated prototype; in other contexts, this assemblage might appropriately be described as data.

My first question requires the specification of the text for analysis. The answer must delineate the assemblage, the dataset. In the case of the photograph of the American soldier, I must be clear on whether the text is comprised solely by the photograph—or a part of it—or whether it includes other information, for example, a verbal description of the scene including the location and nationalities of the figures, the Associated Press photographer's note that was appended to a slightly different shot taken at the same time, the caption that appeared with the photograph, the name of the journal and where it was placed and so forth. I refer to this practice as *bounding the text*—establishing its extent.

In *Doing Research/Reading Research: A mode of interrogation for education*, Andrew Brown and I (Dowling & Brown, 2009, see also Brown & Dowling, 1998) proposed that a research process might begin with the establishing of an analytical distinction between *theoretical* and *empirical fields*. The former consists of *general* claims and debates connected to the sphere of interest. This field will include the conclusions of previous research and other documentation that might be construed as commentary. It will also include theoretical positions and debates that bear on the general theoretical line that is to be adopted by the researcher. At the most sharply defined point of the theoretical field we placed the research question or hypothesis. On the other side of the divide, the empirical field consists of *local* practices, experiences, utterances and so forth. In order to address the research question, we must construct an *empirical setting* in which to conduct the research. We do this through the processes of research design—for example, deciding whether the research is to be exploratory or experimental or some combination of the two—and decisions on sampling and on data collection and analysis techniques. When we have completed the research, we will have compiled, firstly, a set of *findings*. These are *local* statements about the empirical setting and are the sharpest end of the empirical field. The extent to which the findings adequately represent the empirical setting is a measure of their *reliability*. Secondly, we will have an answer to the research question, which may now be reformulated as a conclusion. The extent to which the findings address the research question as local instances of it is a measure of their *validity*.

Let me take an example. Suppose that I am concerned with the gendering of cultural practices in rural Rajasthan. The manner in which I have stated this interest suggests a sociological or anthropological approach, so my theoretical field will include sociological and anthropological and possibly demographic literature and so on, relating to Rajasthan. I may be adopting a particular theoretical interpretation of gender; my off-the-cuff analysis on the tourist coach might suggest a general interest in a socialist or radical feminist approach and there is clearly a wealth of potentially relevant literature here. Unless I was to be adopting a strongly experimental line, I would expect my research question to develop over the course of the research. As a starting point, however, I might consider, 'how do men and women recruit visible cultural practices such as dress in the reproduction of and opposition to dominant patterns of gender relations?'

Now I will return to the scene at the start of the chapter. This clearly suggests a possible setting for the research, at least in terms of location. What I now need to do is to generate one or more *texts* for analysis. Let's suppose that the setting consists of a coach ride through Rajasthan on 29th December 1993 or, rather, the view from the window of the coach. This setting is spatially and temporally contained in the same way as are Kaprow's Happenings. Like '18 Happenings in 6 Parts', even as a participant at the time—in my case, as a passenger on the coach— my experience of the setting is partial. There is, in this sense (and in others) no setting as such that does not invite an authorship, an omniscient God, perhaps, so that to capture the setting would be to attain God's view. So, I refer to my own recollections of the scene—under other circumstances these may have included fieldnotes, photographs, even interviews with other passengers as observer-informants and with local people, had the coach stopped to allow it—the totality of this assemblage is to constitute my text.

Can I get closer to God by enlarging my text? No: if we insist on enumerating texts or their possible component parts, then the total number is always infinite and I can deal only with a finite number; any finite number as a fraction of infinity is zero. But this is only part of the answer, because it rests on the nature of my answer to my first question posed in engagement with textual analysis, the question, 'what is the text?' The second question is perhaps a little more subtle, 'what is the text an instance of?' Answering this question is, essentially, what I am attempting to do in the whole of this book.

PLATO'S TENNIS: REFERRING THE TEXT

If we stay on the coach in Rajasthan we will recall that at least two answers to my second question were advanced: the text—a view from the window of the coach as experienced by a given individual—is an instance of idyllic, rural beauty; the text is an instance of patriarchal oppression. The choice depends not on which window we're looking from, but on what game we are playing, on whether we are tourists out to enjoy the day or whether we are sociologists of a particular kind—and there are many kinds, of course. Now there's nothing really very surprising about this; we're well used to the idea that beauty and ugliness lie in the eyes (or should it be the transactional gaze) of the beholder, especially after having learned well the lessons of poststructuralism. But what is surprising is that the language of so much academic utterance, as well as utterances in other regions of discourse, seems difficult to reconcile with even the mildest of relativisms. Here, for example, is Lev Manovich:

> What follows is an attempt at both a record and a theory of the present. Just as film historians traced the development of film language during cinema's first decades, I aim to describe and understand the logic driving the development of the language of the new media. [...]
>
> Does it make sense to theorize the present when it seems to be changing so fast? It is a hedged bet. If subsequent developments prove my theoretical projections correct, I win. But even if the language of computer media develops in a different direction than the one suggested by the present analysis, this book will become a record of possibilities heretofore unrealized, of a horizon visible to us today but later unimaginable. (Manovich, 2001, pp. 7-8)

Manovich's theory of the present must clearly constitute a transformation of the present—it is other than his record, which, itself, must be a selection. This is fine. But he then claims that this will potentially provide access to a driving logic, the engine of media language development. He further seems to suggest that this will enable him to produce testable propositions that will, ultimately, be put to the test of time. Even if they fail as predictions, his propositions will nevertheless constitute a transparent window on today for the future. The text, it seems, is an instance of its referential setting, the present, whether it is looking forward or backwards. Manovich's move here stands as an illustration of the forensics that I introduced in Chapter 1 and, perhaps, what Katherine Hayles has tagged the 'platonic backhand':

> The Platonic backhand works by inferring from the world's noisy multiplicity a simplified abstraction. So far so good: this is what theorizing should do. The problem comes when the move circles around to constitute the abstraction as the originary form from which the word's multiplicity derives. Then complexity appears as a "fuzzing up" of an essential reality rather than as a manifestation of the world's holistic nature. (Hayles, 1999, p. 12)

Pierre Bourdieu makes a similar point:

> The science of myth is entitled to describe the syntax of myth, but only so long as it is not forgotten that, when it ceases to be seen as a convenient translation, this language destroys the truth that it makes accessible. One can say that gymnastics is geometry so long as this is not taken to mean that the gymnast is a geometer. (Bourdieu, 1990, p. 93)

To recognise that beauty lies in the eye of the holder is to admit that the text is an instance not of some external source, but of the system of categories and relations that are brought to bear by the analyst: a gymnastic performance is an instance of geometry, but only when viewed by a mathematician *qua* mathematician (albeit one with a penchant for metaphor—see Chapter 8). This is not to say that the viewer can only ever see what they have seen already. An encounter with a text is a point of the potential reformulation of the observer. Previously (see, for example, Dowling, 1998), I have used Piaget's (1995) equilibration metaphor—the reading of a text is ultimately describable as a process of a coming to a state of equilibrium. This metaphor is consistent with Piaget's grounding principle of autoregulation or homeostasis. There is a problem with equilibration however in that it constitutes equilibrium as a property of the equilibrating system, either as an edenic or utopian state. Crudely, the system has to be able to 'know' which direction to move in (Dowling, 1998). It is not at all obvious that this is a helpful assumption; a poetic engagement with a text, for example, does not stand in any obvious relationship to equilibrium, neither do the rhizomes proposed by Deleuze and Guattari (1987). As alternatives, I shall make pragmatic use of *autopoiesis* or *emergence* depending upon where I am positioning myself as authorial voice. Hayles (1999) associates these terms with the second and third 'wave' of cybernetics respectively and homeostasis predominantly with the first. I shall use *autopoiesis*—self-organisation—where I am identifying with the analyst and *emergence* where I am describing the formulation and reformulation of a system from outside of it, as it were; we might think of de Certeau's (1984) two views of the city: walking through the streets; viewed from above.

My use of the term, *autopoiesis*, derives from the second order cybernetics of Humberto Maturana (see Hayles, 1999), but I am deploying it pragmatically and without general epistemological pretensions. The concept enables me to think about the internal organisation of the audience as (analytically) distinct from the structural coupling of the audience and text that enables the latter, shall we say, to surprise the former but not to communicate the meaning of the surprise. The latter is determined by audience self-organisation, which may involve greater or lesser equilibrium or stability, shall we say.

Both tourist and sociologist responses to the Rajasthan text exhibit a fair degree of stability to the extent that they are unsurprising to an observer who plays both games. Of course, there are likely to be variations in response between tourists and between sociologists, but it is nevertheless plausible to construct a stability in the respective discourses at some sufficiently high level of analysis. I shall refer to the extent of this stability is a measure of the *institutionalisation* of the discourse. The limits to the delicacy of the institutionalisation are revealed in empirical differences in response within the discourse, so that the delineation of such differences is really establishing the level of analysis at which institutionalisation is being described.

The way that I have described it suggests that the institutionalisation of a discourse or practice might be interpreted as the product or language of an *alliance* of subjectivities. Then the differentiation of discourses—tourist and sociologist, say—marks an *opposition* of subjectivities. I should make clear at this point that the term 'subjectivity' here refers to the subject or 'speaker' of the discourse and may be defined at any level of analysis so that an individual human subject, having been apprenticed into diverse discourses and practices, is appropriately interpreted as an articulation of subjectivities. Thus *oppositions* and *alliances* may be inter- or intra-subject.

At a higher level of analysis, we can interpret institutionalised discourses and practices as *emergent* epiphenomena on the play of structural couplings that constitute the formation of oppositions and alliances of authors and audiences. The distinction between author and audience merely directs our attention to the particular utterance or action that is of current interest. Viewed from within a system, autopoiesis looks like the acquisition or recruitment or deployment or construction or dismantling of an *organisational language* or, in its tacit form, a habitus (cf. Bourdieu, 1990), perhaps. From outside of the system, such organisational languages and habituses appear as epiphenomena or, perhaps, as ideologies—cultural practices in relation to social structure. Thus the transmission and acquisition of a discourse or practice, which is to say, pedagogy (whether tacit or explicit) may, from outside of the system, be interpreted as cultural reproduction emergent on the expansion of an alliance (social reproduction).

The decision as to whether we are within or outside a system is simply a question of the level of analysis at which we are operating, whether I am constructing or expositing my theory or considering its status. For example, I may think of my thoughts as the product of my consciousness (autopoiesis) or I may think of my consciousness as epiphenomenal in relation to, say, evolutionary or biological action. Crucially, as I have constructed them here, the languages of autopoiesis and emergence are isomorphic: structural coupling and organisational language correspond directly to social structure and cultural practice. Insofar as the language that I develop is able to sustain this isomorphism, the method will exhibit a fractal quality. That is to say, its deployment is independent of the level of analysis at which it is deployed and indeed, as I have suggested, the method may also be deployed in the analysis of itself.

A brief dismantling of a familiar metaphor may assist in the stabilising of my own organisational language; the metaphor is that of camera as observer. The camera is certainly structurally coupled to the world around it, principally (or ideally) through the medium of light. The camera automatically and through the agency of the photographer selects its subject and adjusts for focus, exposure, white balance and so forth and writes a record to film or digital memory. But there is no autopoiesis involved here in the sense that I am deploying the term. The inscription of the record—the photograph—is simply the structural impact of one part of a system on another; the camera has no organisational language. So there is no transmission of information as such. Information is constituted only at the point at which the photographer views the inscribed image, either in the viewfinder or on the film or LCD display and activates a photographic or tourist or domestic organisational language.

I am now in a position to return to my second question concerning the analysis of texts, that is, 'what is the text an instance of?' I can now say that the structural coupling between text-as-work and its audience (or, alternatively, the author of its reading as a text-as-text) is that which establishes the possibility of the text-as-text. However, the nature of the text-as-text will be given by the organisational language—the strongly or weakly institutionalised discourse or practice—that the audience deploys. The text, then, can only be construed as an instance of that organisational language; any alternative would entail the reification of the text-as-work. As I have established, the latter is purely a placeholder; there can be no such thing as a text that stands outside of an audience's reading of it; the unobserved falling tree, in other words, is not a text.

MYTHOLOGISING THE TEXT/CONJURING THE REAL

The language that I am constructing here has the advantage—for my purposes—of coherence and consistency, but the general claim that I am making here is widely recognised, at least; we might say that although there are counters to it, the claim is strongly institutionalised in academic writing in the social sciences. The question that this raises, then, is why is it so widely ignored? I have offered one illustration of this ignoring in the claims made by Lev Manovich who will certainly not be unaware of relativist epistemologies (if this is not an oxymoron), yet he is content to set his own work within the context of a naive realism—in this case, the postulation of generative structures that are, at least potentially, accessible. Here is Dick Hebdige responding to texts by Jean Baudrillard and others:

> Whatever Baudrillard or *The Tattler* or Saatchi and Saatchi, and Swatch have to say about it, I shall go on reminding myself that this earth is round not flat, that there will never be an end to judgement, that the ghosts will go on gathering at the bitter line which separates truth from lies, justice from injustice, Chile, Biafra and all the other avoidable disasters from all of us, whose order is built upon their chaos. And that, I suppose, is the bottom line on Planet One. (Hebdige, 1988, p. 176)

We can certainly add a whole lot more 'avoidable disasters' since 1988. What seems to be disturbing Hebdige is that some people are having fun writing academic papers or making advertisements or kitsch watches whilst others are having somewhat less fun and that the one is entailed in the other in some kind of a master-slave dialectic. I feel inclined to point Hebdige in the direction of a story about a wealthy young man who wanted to know what he had to do in order to attain salvation (he can find a discussion of it in Chapter 3 and in Dowling, 1998); but I'm sure that the good Professor's activities in film studies and art studio are, at this very minute, bringing practical relief to the suffering all over the world. Here is Stuart Kauffman setting the scene for his theory of order in the universe:

> If the universe is running down because of the second law [of thermodynamics], the easy evidence out my window is sparse—some litter here and there, and the heat given off by me, a homeotherm, scrambling the molecules of air. It is not entropy but the extraordinary surge towards order that strikes me. Trees grabbing sunlight from a star eight light-minutes away, swirling its photons together with mere water and carbon dioxide to cook up sugars and fancier carbohydrates; legumes sucking nitrogen from bacteria clinging to their roots to create proteins. I eagerly breathe the waste product of this photosynthesis, oxygen—the worst poison of the archaic world, when

anaerobic bacteria ruled—and give off carbon dioxide that feeds the trees. The biosphere around us sustains us, is created by us, grafts the energy flux from the sun into the great web of biochemical, biological, geologic, economic, and political exchanges that envelopes the world. Thermodynamics be damned. Genesis, thank whatever lord may be, has occurred. We all thrive. (Kauffman, 1995, p. 10)

I am quite astonished at what Kauffman seems to be able to see from his window. Most of it seems to be composed of the constructs of the natural sciences. It is interesting, though, that when he gets to the social sciences, he sees economic and political order where Hebdige sees chaos. It is not entirely without relevance that Hebdige's comment appears at the end of his paper and Kauffman's is in the introductory chapter of his book. They stand as accessible metatheoretical postscript and preface to the substantive achievements of their respective works. What both appear to be doing is, firstly, making very strong claims on the existence of a reality that is independent of the observer; Kauffman's window is very similar to my own, no doubt, and I only have to look out to confirm his facts prior to voting with him on the issue of the second law of thermodynamics. Secondly, both are painting the scenery with colours selected from very particular paintboxes. Kauffman recruits substantially from the natural sciences, but there is no shortage of tropic language—grabbing trees, sucking legumes, ruling bacteria. Hebdige establishes a chain of identification between sociological and commercial fun-loving tricksters to which he opposes sorry media eventalisings with janusian ghosts in-between. Both fine, prime-time examples of Hayles' Platonic Wimbledon—forensics. The depictions offered by each author is a construction of their respective organisational languages, but their authorship is, here, hiding in the blinding light of their verbal virtuosity to emerge elsewhere in their more measured presentations of their analysis. The text-as-work—the potential view from the window, as it were—is a mythologised world; the transparency of the window passes unchallenged. In each case, the mythologising is a *point de capiton* that fixes an a alliance with those of the rest of us that have a need to believe that there is a reality out there that we really can reach, and predict, and control, and change.

There is another kind of mythologising:

We used to think of texts as being made out of words and sentences; now under the conjoined influences of postmodern theory and electronic writing technologies, we think of texts as being made out of text. The loom is still needed to weave the individual elements (unless they are 'found objects', lifted from other texts), but organization and linearization is now a two-stage process, the virtual text produced by the first stage serving as input to the second. While the writer remains responsible for the microlevel operations, she may bypass the macrolevel stage, thus offering *du texte* as a freely usable resource to the reader, rather than *un text* structured as a logical argument aiming at persuasion. (Ryan, 1999, p. 100)

Composition after Duchamp is idea-generative, not product-oriented. As data-interaction, its only directive: Take whatever data is recorded (call them, perhaps, these 'having become') and from them make a tracing. If three-dimensional objects give off a two-dimensional shadow, writing is now conceived of as a three-dimensional shadow of a fourth-dimensional process of becoming. (Sirc, 1999, p. 195)

These extracts—both from the same volume edited by Ryan (1999)—far from mythologising the text-as-work, etherealise all text. Just as Marcel Duchamp established, in his 'readymades', the act of the artist's selection as the degree-zero of all art, so Marie-Laure Ryan and Geoffrey Sirc celebrate the action of the writer. Ryan's author is the weaver of a gift to be admired briefly, or not, and to be unpicked and rewoven, in whole or in part, by the next weaver. Sirc's composer is rather more Nietzschean. In either case, it is now the author rather than the text that is mythologised. Ryan and Sirc are seeking different alliances, perhaps, alliances with authors rather than the audiences that Hebdige and Kauffman are intending to impress. Because it is authorship itself that they are celebrating, Ryan and Sirc have no need to establish a metatheory as such, they can simply theorise.

We might think of the mythologising of the authors whom I have mentioned here—Manovich, Hebdige, Kauffman, Ryan and Sirc—as marketing strategies. It might even be useful to pin labels to their respective target markets: naïvely realist audiences in the case of the first three listed; and let's say, for the time being, constructivist audiences in the case of the last two. The names aren't crucial, here, they are merely potential strapline markers. They serve what Basil Bernstein (2000) might have described as 'classificatory' functions, distinguishing between categories, allowing the nature of what goes on within the categories—'framing'— to be elaborated elsewhere.[5] But the work of classification is not fully achieved simply by the marking out of categories. Naïve realists will also need to choose between Hebdige's semiotic mode of analysis and left-political interest, and Kauffman's natural science mode and his focus on biology. Constructivists may prefer Ryan's weaving to Sirc's becoming or the other way around. In other words, whilst the marketing or classification of a work may or may not appear to be separated from the work itself as packaging, such demarcation is never really possible. Nevertheless, authors do have strategic decisions to make in relation to marketing strategies. In my experience, packaging is a useful strategy if you have very little in the way of a product; if you do, then you run the risk of a clash, or of attention being focused on the package rather than the product. Unless, of course, the package is wholly consistent with the product, in which case, 'packaging' is probably the wrong term—it is perhaps more accurate to speak in terms of the public face of the product itself. My own preferred strategy, then, is to go for a product—and it will be recalled that I am referring to an organisational language here—that incorporates its own marketing.

---

[5]   See Chapters 4 and 8 for critical engagements with this categorising and with other Bernsteinian work.

A FLORENTINE CASE STUDY

The organisational language that I shall be introducing is concerned with the analysis of text. I have already introduced two of its key aspects in terms of questions, which I shall now state in the form of principles:

- The text as object of analysis is to be bounded.

- The text is to be understood as an instance of the organisational language that is deployed in its analysis.

In order further to pave the way for the introduction of my organisational language, I shall provide contrasting analyses of a specific text. The text that I have chosen is shown in Figure 2.1. It is a thirteenth century Italian painting, *The Madonna in Maestà*, by the Florentine, Cimabue, painted around 1280. I have chosen this particular image because it has already been subject to a careful and sociologically relevant analysis by Robert Hodge and Gunther Kress (1988). A contrasting of this earlier analysis with my own will enable me to illustrate a number of the general features of the approach that I am taking that I take to be crucial. I shall first introduce and discuss the approach to the analysis that is taken by Hodge and Kress. In the course of this introduction I shall need also to provide some background on, as well as my own interpretations of some of, some of the work that they cite.

Hodge and Kress construct the basis for their 'diagnostic social semiotic' reading of the Cimabue work by generating a number of propositions from a discussion of sociological and sociolinguistic theory. In this discussion, they draw on a number of key theoretical antecedents including Émile Durkheim's categories, organic and mechanical solidarity. These concepts are central in Durkheim's work, *The Division of Labour in Society* (1984). In what was his doctoral thesis, Durkheim wanted to ask how it was that, if human beings could be characterised in terms of the destructive will proposed by Schopenhauer, human societies did not destroy themselves. He answered the question by proposing a modality of social solidarity. Certain societies are characterised by a simple division of labour and a segmental structure, that is, communities within society are essentially interchangeable with each other. The coherence of such societies—mechanical solidarity—depended upon a powerful state, repressive law, and a collective conscience. The latter established allegiance to a unifying idea such as a religion. As the division of labour becomes more complex, the collective conscience becomes increasingly difficult to sustain, but is replaced by interdependence within a society that can no longer be described as segmental. The responsibility of the state moves to the maintenance of restitutive law. This more evolved form was referred to as organic solidarity and was seen by Durkheim as an ideal. However, its development was inhibited by pathological forms including, for example, forced division of labour and the anomic form described in Hodge's and Kress's analysis. I should point out that Hodge and Kress do not actually cite *The Division of Labour in Society*, but Durkheim's work, *Suicide* (1951). Their analysis also involves a discussion of suicide drawing on this work.

Hodge and Kress align Durkheim's organic and mechanical solidarity with a classification of speech types that they refer to as 'high' and 'low' languages which apparently correspond to Bernstein's (1971) 'elaborated' and 'restricted' speech codes—Bernstein's categories will be discussed in Chapter 4. Social organisations that exhibit organic solidarity and high languages are characterised, they claim, by 'hypotaxis', that is, hierarchical organisation. On the other hand, mechanical solidarity and low languages are characterised by 'parataxis', that is, they lack hierarchical organisation. Thus, they argue that hypotaxis and parataxis, which are linguistic categories, are 'transparent signifiers' of organic and mechanical solidarity, respectively.[6] Hodge and Kress also draw upon work (influenced by Halliday's sociolinguistics) on schizophrenic language, which is found to be markedly discohesive in terms of senseless syntagmatic connections, senseless references, and non-congruous relations between speakers. In view of this, 'schizophrenia is interpreted as a transparent signifier of breakdown in the social order' (Hodge & Kress, 1988, p. 110). This is summarised, in the sixth of seven propositions, as:

Absence or disruption of hypotactic and paratactic structures is a transparent signifier of the repudiation of kinds of social order and belonging: that is, of Durkheimian 'anomie'. (Hodge & Kress, 1988, p. 111)

In fact, the association between, for example, hypotaxis and organic solidarity may be less than 'transparent'. Such transparency as might be apparent to another reader is probably contingent upon their acceptance of Hodge's and Kress's characterisation of organic solidarity as a 'hierarchically ordered social structure'. However, there is, as far as I can see, nothing in Durkheim's *Division of Labour in Society* (1984) that encourages this. Durkheim describes organic solidarity as established by cooperation and mutual dependence and law is predominantly restitutive, that is, facilitating. Hierarchical organisation is comparatively weak as Durkheim proposes:

---

[6] In the appendix to their book Hodge and Kress gloss 'transparency' and its opposite, 'opacity', as follows: 'Sign systems function most economically in producing meaning if there is a clear link perceived between signifiers and signified by all users of the signs. However, negative and hostile relationships within the semiosic plane motivate the opposite tendency, an inaccessible link between signifiers and signifieds, leading to systematic distortion of such links. Signs can therefore be ranged on a continuum between transparent and opaque, in terms of how clearly the link between signifier and signified is perceived by a class of semiotic participant' (Hodge & Kress, 1988, p. 262).

Figure 2.1. Madonna in Maestà, tempera on wood panel by Cenni di Pepo Cimabue. Original in the Galleria degli Uffizi, Florence. No further reproduction without the permission of the *Ministero dei Beni e delle Attività Culturali.*

Figure 2.2. Deposizione di Cristo, painting on canvas by Giotto di Bondone.
Original in the Capella degli Scrovegni, Padova.

To the extent that segmentary organs fuse together each social organ becomes larger in volume, and this all the more so because in principle the overall volume of society increases simultaneously. Practices common to the professional group thus become more general and abstract, as do those common to society as a whole, and consequently leave the field more open for particular divergences. Likewise the greater independence enjoyed by the later generations in comparison with their elders cannot fail to weaken the traditionalism of the profession, and this makes the individual still freer to innovate.

Thus not only does professional regulation, by its very nature, hinder less than any other form of regulation the free development of individual variation, but moreover it hinders it less and less. (Durkheim, 1984, pp. 243-244)

In mechanical solidarity, there is a necessity for repressive law to sustain the unitary collective conscience. Under these circumstances, some form of hierarchy would seem to be a pre-requisite. This is the reverse of Hodge's and Kress's description of these categories.

In drawing on Bernstein's work, Hodge and Kress claim that:

> Elaborated codes position participants at a distance from each other and from the world of referents, and hence must be explicit. Restricted codes can be implicit because they are context-bound, close to a context which links speakers and hearers in a common bond. So restricted codes express high solidarity, and elaborated codes the opposite. (Hodge & Kress, 1988, p. 109)

This does not sit easily with either Durkheim's or Bernstein's sociology in the sense that these categories refer to modes rather than degree of solidarity, in the case of Durkheim, nor is it clear that Bernstein's speech codes ordinalise solidarity. Hodge and Kress also introduce Bernstein's early work on the classification and framing of educational knowledge. They describe, in particular, collection and integrated curriculum codes. In his introduction to Volume 3 of *Class, Codes and Control* (1977), Bernstein seems to be quite clear that the codes are derived from the more fundamental concepts, classification and framing, which I have already mentioned above. In Bernstein's conception: 'classification' refers to the strength of boundary between contents and derives from the distribution of power within society; 'framing' refers to the organisation of relations within categories and derives from principles of control. It seems odd, perhaps, that Hodge and Kress mention 'classification' once (in parentheses appended to their own term, 'grid' (possibly a tacit reference to Mary Douglas (1970, 1996a), see also Chapter 8) and do not refer to 'framing' at all. Furthermore, whilst they appear to have acknowledged the paradox that Bernstein identifies towards the end of his paper, they have removed any reference to Durkheim. Bernstein's description reads:

> ... the covert structure of mechanical solidarity of collection codes creates through its specialised outputs organic solidarity. On the other hand the overt structure of organic solidarity of integrated codes creates through its less specialised outputs mechanical solidarity. And it will do this to the extent to which its ideology is explicit, elaborated and closed and effectively and implicitly transmitted through its low insulations. Inasmuch as integrated codes do not accomplish this, then order is highly problematic at the level of social organisation and at the level of the person. Inasmuch as integrated codes do accomplish such socialisation, then we have the covert deep closure of mechanical solidarity. This is the fundamental paradox which has to be faced and explored. (Bernstein, 1971, pp. 224-225; 1977, p. 110)

Hodge and Kress recontextualise:

> ... the 'integrated' [code] is characterised by low boundaries and weak boundary maintenance, so that the form of the code is characterised by cohesion of the whole, though the whole that coheres in this way is

formidably complex, and only an elite could grasp it. So we have a contradiction between the meaning of this code as transparent signifier of solidarity and cohesion, and its function, to differentiate between an elite and the rest. Similarly, the 'collect' code, with its high boundaries, signifies the individuation of knowledge and society. But 'collect' codes declare and enforce the lack of power of the learner, because of a hierarchy of knowledge in which beginners have strict limits, while at the top specialists are excluded from a grasp of the whole. (Hodge & Kress, 1988, p. 110)

Bernstein relates his concepts to the more fundamental concepts of organic and mechanical solidarity, which Hodge and Kress also want to use. However, Bernstein's paradox challenges the 'transparency' of the signifying relationship between code, measured in terms of classification and framing, and social structure. Bernstein later resolves this difficulty via the notion of an 'invisible pedagogy' (1977). Hodge and Kress resolve the problem by dispensing both with the derived status of the knowledge codes and with Bernstein's own language, specifically, classification and framing. They also omit all reference to the relationship of Bernstein's work to Durkheim's modes of solidarity, despite the fact that they were discussed in the paragraph immediately preceding the introduction to Bernstein's sociolinguistics.[7] Hodge and Kress retain Bernstein through the recontextualisation of his speech codes as transparent signifiers for mechanical and organic solidarity (the terms are reintroduced after the discussion of Bernstein has been completed). The trace of his classification and framing work is to be found in their second proposition:

High or emphatic boundaries in the syntagmatic or the paradigmatic plane are transparent signifiers of solidarity and cohesion (within groups) and non-solidarity and discohesion (outside groups); and low, weak boundaries signify the opposite. (Hodge & Kress, 1988, p. 111)

'Boundaries' are thus operational indicators that are 'transparent' signifiers for the concepts of solidarity (within and between). The exposition on Bernstein and Durkheim seems intended to establish both the theoretical concepts and the validity and reliability of the concept/indicator link—the relationship between social solidarity and boundary strength—which appears to be presumed by the term 'transparent'. The seven propositions that they present are the terminal level of Hodge's and Kress's theoretical discussion before moving onto the analysis of the painting. It is not necessary to my purpose here to discuss them all as I need only to raise the question of the relationship between the inputs from sociology—principally, Durkheim and Bernstein—and the analytic framework that Hodge and Kress develop and deploy. I shall return to this issue later. For the time being, it is

---

[7] Bernstein's recruitment of Durkheim itself entails a recontextualising of the latter. Specifically, whilst Durkheim's types are related diachronically, Bernstein employs them to differentiate, synchronically, within a configuration. In Bernstein's case this does not constitute a problem because he has adequately re-theorised the concepts in establishing his own coherent system.

enough to point out that, rather than the sociological theory motivating the semiotic analysis, it may be more appropriate to describe the apparatus of linguistic tools, including terms such as, syntagmatic, paradigmatic, hypotaxis and parataxis, as constituting an organisational language for the recontextualisation of the sociology.

Hodge and Kress describe the Cimabue painting in the following terms:

> The text itself is marked by strong boundaries on the syntagmatic plane. The frame around the painting is emphatic, a simple angular shape covered in expensive gold leaf. Within this frame, the concern with boundaries continues. Haloes around the saints and angels not only enclose each in their own sacred space but separate their heads from their bodies. The chair the Madonna sits in is a massive barrier, and the saints below her are enclosed by architectural niches. The drawing style is linear, using lines rather than shading to indicate gradations in shape and mass. The represented social relations are similarly shown as fragmented. The society of angels has no internal structure: each relates loosely to the Madonna, or turns away. The saints below have no unambiguous relationship to anyone. The Madonna does seem to be aware of the presence of the Christ child on her knee, but this awareness is not reciprocated. (Hodge & Kress, 1988, p. 113)

In terms of the 'paradigmatic plane', Hodge and Kress remark on the very limited range of colour, mainly flat and homogenous and close to the primaries. The social world is sharply divided into sacred and profane, the latter being excluded from 'the presented world'. Other oppositions are male/female and human/angel with members within categories being hardly differentiated from each other. The symmetry of the painting, left-right, and 'upper-lower dominance' are paratactic rather than hypotactic and 'the angels are strung vertically like beads on a string'. Overall:

> The effect of the emphatic boundaries, added to the paratactic organisation, is incoherence in the picture as a whole. In Durkheim's terms, it signifies a strongly anomic, egoistic and fragmented form of society. (Hodge & Kress, 1988, p. 113)

The authors support their reading by offering a brief description of late thirteenth-century Florence as 'a city-state in turmoil'. They do not attempt an explanation as to why the dominant classes of a chaotic state would be expected to sponsor the production of chaotic cultural artefacts.

My reading of the painting is somewhat different. The throne does indeed constitute a powerful boundary, but it is marking a simple division of labour. The fundamental division is between Heaven (the Madonna, Child and angels) and Earth (the saints). The angels frame the Madonna and Child in a halo that, like the halos around all of the figures, bespeaks the sacred quality of the haloed. Indeed, the haloed/hallowed status of the figures is itself a style-marker, an emblem. The geometry of the painting is, in fact, very far from paratactic. The throne is a pyramid with its vertex at the head of the Madonna. The inclination of the Madonna's head and the direction of her right hand draw the observer to the real focus of the picture, which is the head of the Child, with his most elaborately embellished halo. The hierarchical ordering of the painting is clear. The angels and saints gaze in all directions, signifying, perhaps, the omniscience of God. But the gaze of the Madonna and of the Child is directly out of the frame at the observer. The Madonna's hand is raised in a gesture that offers the Child to the world as its salvation. The Child's hand is raised in the very act of the Benediction, blessing the observer.

The angels and the saints certainly lack individuality, but this, surely, seems inconsistent with the 'cult of the individual', which characterises egoistic society. The frame of the picture as a whole signifies the segmentation of the social within a simple division of labour. At its focus, the Word, in front, the World, the observer who, her/himself, is being offered the Word. This is precisely the simple division and unifying Idea of mechanical solidarity. The Idea, furthermore, which is emblemised in the central icon of Christianity, the icon that is formed by the heavy vertical line from the heavenly head of the Madonna to the two central, earthly saints and the line, which joins the heads of the two lowermost angels: the sign of the cross.

A crucial difference (among others) between my sociology, on the one hand, and the sociologies of Durkheim and Bernstein, on the other, is that whilst they are concerned primarily with social structure and its cultural realisation, I—despite occasional appearances to the contrary—prioritise strategic social action and, shall we say, structuration (Giddens, 1984). I, therefore, interpret mechanical solidarity as a form of activity that constitutes a simplification of the division of labour rather than being simply constituted by it. Maximum complexity would differentiate between each individual and even differentiate within individuals in respect of context. Contemporary commercial advertising might be taken, in general, as a strategy operating in this direction. Mechanical solidarity strategies simplify. They also privilege the unification of beliefs and sentiments. Such an activity must, clearly, construct markers of this unity. To describe thirteenth-century Florence as not very cohesive is hardly the point. If we make a general claim that all societies are constituted in and by the formation of emergent alliances and oppositions, then our analyses will always reveal strategies that are directed at the establishing, maintenance or destabilising of these. Insofar as the Church is constituted as an institutionalised alliance, then its official texts will be recognised as those given official sanction and tending to maintain the status quo. In everyday language, one might reasonably expect the Church authorities (who patronised Cimabue) to attempt to maintain their authority *vis-à-vis* the masses; whether or not they succeeded is neither here nor there.

Giotto di Bondone was a Florentine painter of the next generation (and was probably Cimabue's pupil). Hodge and Kress do not offer an analysis of one of his paintings. They do, however, state that Giotto varied the 'logonomic rules' that they say characterise Cimabue's painting. It is for this reason that he is regarded as a significant painter. It is certainly the case that Giotto produced very different paintings as is apparent from the briefest of glances at his *Deposizione di Cristo*, Figure 2.2. Christ, posthumously returned to his mother's arms, is surrounded by apostles and others. Hands are being wrung, even the angels are agonised in their expressions and their contortions. The simple geometry of the Cimabue work is gone; colours are more diverse. The simple division of labour between heaven and earth remains, however. This time, it is marked out by the hard line of the rock. But this line also participates in the essential icon of the cross, which again forms the fundamental organising structure of the painting. This time up-ended, its earthy foot penetrates the heaven. Christ—sent down to earth by God—and his mother are at its head and its cross-piece is represented in the line of individuals forming the diagonal at the bottom lefthand of the painting. The cross motif is repeated in the agonised acts of symbolic crucifixion by the angels and by one of the apostles at the centre of the painting. The unhaloed—the 'observer' is now included by Giotto in the painting itself—are carefully positioned at the three points of the cross, again receiving the offer of the benediction even at this moment of tragedy. The Giotto represents a markedly different style of painting, but the social semantics are the same: simple division of labour; unifying Idea, emblemised by the cross and the benediction—again, strategies of mechanical solidarity.

I want now to consider the semiotics of the analyses themselves. I have organised them structurally in Figure 2.3. In my description of their text, Hodge and Kress have first discussed antecedent work, the first explicit structural feature of their analysis, and I have focused, in particular, on the sociological contents, Durkheim and Bernstein. In the third column of the table I have indicated that this constitutes a *selection* (in the case of Hodge and Kress, part of their selection) from a theoretical field. The theoretical field itself is a *construction*, although it remains a tacit construction in Hodge's and Kress's analysis. They move on to construct their organisational language which comprises seven principles, two of which I have referred to explicitly here. This language includes both linguistic and sociological terms as well as less technical, but important analytical terms such as

Structural Feature	Contents	Action
Theoretical Field	General Statements	Construction
Antecedents	Durkheim, Bernstein	Selection
Organisational Language Analysis	Linguistics/Sociology	Construction
Text	Paintings (Cimabue, Giotto)	Selection
Setting	13-14th Century Florence	
Empirical Field	Local Practice & Experience	Construction

Figure 2.3. Structure of Hodge's and Kress's Analysis

'boundaries.' I have described their setting as a selection from an empirical field of practice and experiences and they have divided this into a text—the Cimabue painting—and the historical setting within which it originated. Again, the empirical field of practice and experience is a construction that is tacit in this part of Hodge's and Kress's work.

Now Hodge's and Kress's book is titled *Social Semiotics*, which suggests—and this is borne out by the content—that they are placing their emphasis on their organisational language rather than on any particular analysis or on any specific setting; they are not, in particular, writing a treatise on 13th-14th Century Florence nor, indeed, on Byzantine or any other form of painting. However, it seems to me that their overt strategies tend to establish a unitary space comprising the structural features of their analysis. In demonstrating this I shall establish a logic of their text rather than its linear sequence in print. They do not, here, explicitly make reference to broader theoretical or empirical fields, so that their selections are simply points of entry into their text. They then work to establish a more or less seamless, deductive line from their antecedents—here, Durkheim and Bernstein—and their organisational language (their principles). Correspondingly, the tacit empirical field comes to meet them via claims about their setting—the kind of place that Florence used to be—and the presentation of their text as an instance of that setting. Having, so to speak, discovered their text, their organisational language goes to work on its analysis, which happily bears out their definitive claims about the original setting. Essentially, they cast out to the world beyond themselves, finding Durkheim, Bernstein and Cimabue and weave them together with their linguistic apparatus in a dexterous demonstration that they are all in agreement.

These are the more explicit strategies. Implicitly, however, they are locating authority for their construction outside of that construction, in the real world. The concurrence between Durkheim and Bernstein and Cimabue and common knowledge (or, at least, easily verifiable knowledge) about Byzantine Florence is itself that which underwrites, well, itself. The value of their organisational language lies in its facility to reveal this to us. Kauffman will deploy similar strategies, though in his case he will start with a dissonance between the second law of thermodymanics (a condensation of Ludwig Boltzman and others) and the view from his own window. This is the semiotics of conjuring: we know about hats and rabbits and we know that the former cannot at the same time be empty and contain the latter—abracadabra! One problem with conjuring is that, as generations of magicians and academics have shown, almost anything can be pulled from inside almost anything else including, I'm sure, hats from rabbits. So, were we to notice the barriers and lack of obvious hypotactical organization of Piet Mondrian's *Broadway Boogie Woogie*[8] we may be inclined to read it as a transparent signifier of a strongly anomic New York at a time (1942-3) when one might have imagined the powerful unifying ideology of patriotism to be holding sway. There is also the slight problem presented by Giotto. Whilst my reading of

---

[8]   See http://www.ibiblio.org/wm/paint/auth/mondrian/broadway.jpg (last accessed 10/03/07).

his painting constructs similarities with Cimabue's, the suggestion of fundamental difference by Hodge and Kress suggests that Florence managed to resolve its anomie in pretty short order—the paintings were produced only about twenty years apart. Not a problem for the conjuror as such, for whom alternative outcomes to their wand-waving can only add spice, but perhaps a little sticky for the sociologist.

A second difficulty with the conjuring approach is that there is always the danger that someone will uncover the trick. This, of course, has been the point of my challenges to Hodge's and Kress's interpretations of Durkheim and Bernstein. What in effect they have done is to establish a cut in the discursive field, placing Durkheim and Bernstein in one hand and Cimabue in the other, then selected the metonyms, boundary, strength (of solidarity) and hierarchical organisation, from the discourses of the antecedent authors and from simple descriptions of Byzantine Florence and Cimabue's painting and tied these string-ends together using their own linguistic categories; just blow on my hands and, hey presto, the string is whole again. We can always find metonymic chains linking any two concepts (see Eco, 1984, and his illustrations in Eco, 1989). This is a very common strategy in the social sciences, we simply make someone else's work say whatever we want it to say; either we make it support our own line or we use it as a fall-guy in our own line of repartee—ventriloquism either way.

There is a third problem with conjuring to the extent that the secrets of the trick are not revealed in the performance. This is a problem because then we are left with rabbits hopping about all over the stage chewing on bits of string. Some conjurors—some of those mentioned here—do try to convince us that we really do need rabbits and bits of string, but insofar as academic work claims to be methodologically constructive—not to mention, teachable—then we really do need to see the method. Hodge and Kress do not hide behind a magic circle. Rather, they provide details of their organisational language, exemplified in (but not limited to) the seven principles that they apply to Cimabue. The difficulty here is not in the visibility of the language but in the overall incoherence of the attempt to deploy linguistic language to the analysis of a painting in order to reach sociological conclusions. Furthermore, their description of Byzantine Florence renders the whole reliant upon an unexplored transcendental move wherein the ravaged state of social relations are synthesised by the painter and, presumably, by the churchmen who allow the exhibition of such icons. Despite their attempts to establish a unity in the structure of their analysis, indeed because of the way in which they have gone about this, their structural features are isolated from each other, strung out like beads on a chain, or like the haloed heads of angels and, within the halo, their language stands pristine; we just have to have faith.

My own strategy of course includes elements of conjuring and ventriloguism, not to mention realist language. What I am attempting to do, however, is mark out a method via the strategic alienation or at least damping down of these elements even as they appear in my own writing. My starting point is in the middle of the structural features, with an always already existing organisational language that constructs and selects from theoretical and empirical fields in autopoietic action. My concern here is to market the organisational language by apprenticing my audience into it. Key features, then, must be explicitness and coherence and, of course, distinctiveness. In my analysis of the painting I am acting constructively and selectively on its features, constituting them as semiotic resources that are translatable into my own language. Here, that language includes a recontextualisation of Durkheim's mode of solidarity as a strategic mode. I will not retain this feature in the further development of the language throughout the rest of this book, but it serves as a useful transit stage. I have placed the boundary around my object text—the Cimabue painting—so as to include certain details of its origination and placement in Byzantine Florence. But rather than claim the painting as an instance of an absent real world, I have constituted it as an instance of my organisational language. Similarly, I have described the theoretical antecedents in terms of my organisational language. For me, these antecedents include Hodge and Kress.

I can summarise my description of their analysis alongside my description of my own diagrammatically as in Figure 2.4. Clearly, insofar as my introduction of autopoiesis is intended as a general description of the engagement of an audience with a text, then the two columns might be expected to be identical. However, my claim is that whilst I am attempting to align my textual strategies, as far as is possible, with my description of autopoiesis in keeping with the proposed fractal nature of the organisational language, Hodge and Kress do not attempt this. Indeed, there is no reason why they should since they are marketing their own work and not mine. To put it in the simplest possible terms, whilst I claim that both analyses entail the analysts seeing what they want or are able to see in the objects of their gaze, Hodge and Kress must assume some kind of input or feedback into their organisational language in order to locate the authority for their argument outside of it in a supposed independent world which is potentially available to all for verification. Their column therefore describes their textual strategies rather than their substantive actions.

FROM MYTHOLOGISING TO ORGANIZING

This work—or any part of it—stands between two regions of myth just as Stuart Kauffman's window stands between himself and the world outside. Behind my text, so to speak, I stand as author, as originator: in front of it stands the world to which my text provides access or, alternatively, which grants the world access to me and, through me, access to itself in an infinite loop. Or is it, perhaps, a hermeneutic helix: read my text, know me to understand my text better, better to understand yourself to understand my text better and so forth. Similar constructions are, of course, a part of everyday interaction—though possibly without the perpetual motion around a single utterance. But they are also institutionalised features of academic writing. In order to obtain a PhD a candidate must demonstrate that they have produced an original contribution to knowledge in the relevant field and that this is their own work (at least, this is the case in my own

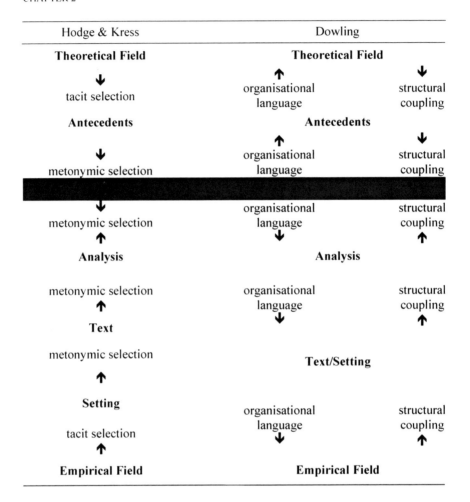

Figure 2.4. Comparison of Analytic Strategies

institution). The thesis, authored by the candidate, illuminates and enhances the field. Strange that such ritual persists even in areas where the work of Barthes, Derrida, Eco, Foucault, Lacan *et al* are standard, even regarded as texts by revered authors (itself, of course, an irony). My former mentor, Basil Bernstein once asked me whether I thought that it was possible to produce a postmodern thesis. Never one to be daunted by the rhetorical nature of a question, I offered, 'yes, but in order to succeed it would have to fail.' I was perhaps rather naïve over the divergences between the official and local practices of thesis examination. Nevertheless, insofar as the academy must reify its knowledge—which it must celebrate—its faculty—

whom it must venerate—and its students—whom it must graduate, there is no official defense of a thesis that undermines either authorship or field.

Institutionalisation reins and commodifies originality, which must always be established within the context of the academic regime of myth. But yearning for a de-schooled, convivial society (Illich, 1973) is no more than an appeal to another utopia, another myth. I am taking a different line here, a pragmatic line. I cannot hedge every potentially mythologising utterance, place every word under erasure (and of course place the erasure under erasure). Rather, I want to recruit institutionalised language in the construction and presentation of what Basil Bernstein (2000) and I, following him, referred to as a language of description. Here, I have introduced the expression, *organisational language*, which I feel is more consistent with, in this case, itself. Since I have introduced the term 'pragmatic', I should perhaps point out that my 'organisational language' is not the same thing as Rorty's (1989) 'final vocabulary' and indeed is inconsistent with it, though there are resonances and I would certainly describe the position that I am adopting here as ironic or, at least, stereoscopic (see, for example, Bann, 1995). From my authorial perspective—albeit a self-reflective authorial perspective—my organisational language is that which constructs texts-as-texts out of texts-as-work that are structurally coupled but informationally decoupled. There is no original text-as-work in the sense of an information-transmitting object. The organisational language develops in a process of autopoiesis—self-organisation. Perhaps it is also worth pointing out at this point that, because my attention is sustained on a particular organisational language, it is unhelpful to inscribe in it any indelible predicate that belongs to another. This particular organisational language is for the construction of orderly and explicit description rather than for the evaluation of its descriptions in political or empathic terms; however my other organisational languages may function, here, I can accept Rorty's irony, but not, as part of my organisational language, his liberal sentiment.

In the opening sections of this chapter I introduced two questions that seem to me to be invoked in any embarking on textual analysis. These may be glossed as: i) 'what is the text in question?' and ii) 'of what is the text an instance?' I have referred to the process of answering the first question as bounding the text—putting a boundary around it, so to speak. So, I am given an image of a sunset over the sea. I am entranced by its steely blues and greys and yellows, by the plays in line and form above and below the horizon and the movement that invites me into the suns gravitational well only to be pushed away in a gleeful *fort da* game, like the waves themselves, massaging the sand, I am intrigued by the islands—pebbles on the horizon. Then I'm told it's a photograph and I wonder about exposure and white balance settings—are sunsets ever really that colour? Then I'm told the name of the photographer—a close friend—and I think fondly of her shambling along the beach, arm-in-arm with her husband who smiles as she giggles as the sun goes down over the cool waves, she pauses to record the gorgeous moment on her miniature digicam and, later, a twinge of disappointment—the colours were so much more than that. There can be no absolute answer to the question—I have to decide. And to give myself room to manoeuvre I'll generally leave the answer to this question just a little fuzzy, but I must always be aware that even this fuzziness has implications.

I have spent rather more time on the second question. I have argued that the text is always and only an instance of the organisational language that is deployed in its reading. As I push the boundaries of my sunset over the sea text I find that my organisational language shifts from, shall we say, my aesthetic language, to a photographic language to a language of creative play with emotionally charged memories. These languages vary in their level of institutionalisation. The play of memories is perhaps closest to an idiolect although it nevertheless recruits from film and other media images—I have never seen my friend in this kind of setting with or without her husband (though I have seen them together in other settings). The aesthetic language is still unschooled, but it recruits in a slightly more regulated way via its recognisable (to some) but undisciplined (to the cognoscenti) reference to Freud. The photographic language may or may not pose the right questions, but they do at least derive directly from my reading of the user's manual for my newest digital SLR. The key issue is the decision as to whether this text is an instance of aesthetic experience or photographic practice or personal reverie; it can be all and more, but none of these languages facilitates translation into any of the others. In other words, the organisational language that is activated constructs the objects of which it speaks and there must always be, to a greater or lesser extent, an incompatibility between languages. Hodge's and Kress's linguistics will not, unless fundamentally re-organised as a sociological language, speak about the social and not even Durkheim and Bernstein can otherwise provide them with secure footbridges—they'll have to make do with magic wands. All of this is a somewhat roundabout way of saying that my organisational language should construct objects that it is actually interested in and not simply project objects-at-hand into the unknown and thereby, unknowable, reified, mythical—forensics.

The basis of my own organisational language entails that it is not transmittable, that there is a sense in which it must remain idiolectical. However, the nature and extent of the structural coupling between human interlocutors entails, perhaps, that co-autopoiesis can potentially allow the negotiation or emergence of a functional methodological alliance; this sole authored book does, after all, include two co-authored chapters. So, I shall proceed in pedagogic mode and this will entail making the organisational language as explicit as possible, using rhetorical devices where this seems to be helpful. Because the action of the language is the construction of orderly and explicit description, order or coherence must be a characteristic and its development must involve the enhancing of coherence and, indeed, the enhancing of its relational coherence. Since the language does not specialise the range of texts that it can address, it must operate independently of level of analysis, that is, it must exhibit a fractal or zoom quality. In particular, it must be capable of describing itself so that there is no effective distinction between, shall we say, theory and metatheory; there is no space for an epistemology as such. To summarise the principles of text analysis and the criteria that are to be applied to my organisational language that I have introduced in this chapter:

The Text

1. The text must be bounded even if the boundary remains, for operational purposes, a little fuzzy.
2. The text is to be understood as an instance of the organisational language that is deployed and that develops in the analysis.

The Organisational Language

3. Structurally linked to the text-as-work but informationally decoupled from it.
   - So the text-as-work is a convenient placeholder, not to be mythologised.
4. Constructs the objects about which it speaks.
5. Should be as explicit as possible.
6. Should be as coherent as possible.
   - Should be as relationally complete as possible.
7. Should exhibit a fractal or zoom quality.
   - Must be able to take itself as object.
   - No detached epistemology.

I shall have cause—particularly in Chapter 5—to depart somewhat from item 6—too much coherence is necrotising—but structural linking with a succession of new texts should entail that the complacency of undue coherence is never achieved.

As for the limited details of the organisational language that I have introduced thus far and that I will augment just a little here, I have started with the proposition—introduced, in part, in Chapter 1—that the sociocultural consists of the strategic formation, maintenance, and dismantling of oppositions and alliances, which describe emergent regularities of practice. Alliances define subject positions as what I shall refer to as *subject avatars* in terms, for example, what may be said or done by whom. Clearly, an alliance defines opposition avatars as objects. The human subject might be understood as a complex of subject avatars grounded in the human body as singular (another myth, of course). Focusing attention on an alliance emphasises a regularity of practice and on identities constituted in and by this regularity. Focusing attention on the human subject emphasises subjectivity and the construction and deployment of organisational languages in alliance/opposition forming, maintaining, dismantling strategies.

To return to my own response to my opening text: I could have played the game and attempted to maintain my membership of the alliance of tourists on the coach. This would have given me a range of options including, perhaps, the introduction of contrasting or resonating narratives from previous holidays (being careful, of course, not to claim too much in the way of expertise or travel experience by the use of appropriate hedging). I chose, however, to oppose the tourist alliance by invoking a discourse that was alien to my companions. This gave me almost free rein on what I could say. The outcome may have been one of enthusiasm whereby one or more of my audience switched languages to take up the position of apprentice to my teacher thus forming, potentially, a new alliance. That this did not happen should have come as no surprise.

CHAPTER 3

MUSTARD, MONUMENTS, MOVIES & MEDIA

A pastiche

(I am starting this chapter from the same point of departure as Chapter 2)

MUSTARD

Some years ago I took a coach tour in northern provinces of India. The fields of green mustard leaves behind the trees sparsely lining the road between Agra and Jaipur were radiant against the pale blue mountains in the distance.

"Look at the women in the fields," prompted one of my fellow tourists, "aren't their colours beautiful." And indeed they were. Though quite a distance away and mainly bending down, working in the leaves, the women dazzled in purples and blues and reds, each one different, jewels in Rajasthan's own vast emerald silk sari. The other passengers on the coach agreed and cooed and photographed and felt happy in the warm sun and the mild intoxication of beer at lunchtime. As a sociologist I felt obliged to speak.

"What about the men?" I asked.

"What do you mean, there aren't any men, we haven't seen any men?"

"Yes you have, you saw them in the villages that we've driven through. What colours were they wearing?"

"Well, mainly drab khakis and greys."

"So you probably wouldn't notice them even if they were in the fields."

"No."

"Tell me, in an agricultural environment in which people work spread out over a large area that is pretty much monochrome, what do you think is the best way to ensure that you can keep control of your women and still be free to get up to whatever takes your fancy?" My colleagues were aghast.

"You've ruined our afternoon." And so I had, and perhaps mine as well. Jeremy Bentham could not have designed a more efficient rural panopticon; the vivid markings of this particular beast now merely warned of the sting in its tail; idyllic culture had been stripped of its lustrous garment to reveal the hard core of the social structure that wears it as a veil: sari-technology.

I (re)recount the story not simply to point to yet another hiding place of patriarchy—that's commonplace—but to illustrate the potential in the establishing of dualisms, here by dehiscing the sociocultural. In forcing its traversal, the dehiscence—on one side, a structure of social relations and, on the other, a set of cultural practices—warns us against undue celebration of culture. By allowing a carefully regulated suturing, it will also, potentially, allow us to escape the determinism—social or technological—that my example might suggest. In the context of a pastiche of diverse texts and practices, this is what I hope to illustrate in this chapter. Here, the dehiscence will be afforded by the organisational language that I have been developing for some time, part of which I will introduce in this chapter in organising its pastiche—if that's not a contradiction in terms.

FROM HEGEMONY TO PASTICHE

I want to begin with a simple re-statement of my general field of interest, which is, firstly, with patterns of *relations* between *positions*. These patterns comprise (exclusively) *alliances* and *oppositions*; this is the social. Secondly, alliances and oppositions are to be construed as established, maintained, and destabilised only in social *action*, the visible forms of which are cultural *practices*. I shall postulate that alliances may be formed between *similars* or between *disimilars* and that interactive social action may be concerned with closure or with openness at the level of discourse. This postulate provides me with two variables each a binary nominal scale. I can never resist a cross-product, so here it is in Figure 3.1.

Alliance	Target of Discursive Action	
	Closure	Openness
Similars	*equilibration*	*exchange of narratives*
Disimilars	*hegemony*	*pastiche*

Figure 3.1. Modes of Interactive Social Action

Now, beginning with the lower left cell, *hegemony* might describe what we expect to see within the traditional pedagogic encounter. Teacher and students confront each other as disimilars. Insofar as the game is one of acquisition, then success is a measure of the extent to which the teacher's discourse prevails over that of the student. *Equilibration*—shall we say, debate lifted clear of the authority entailed in hegemony—is the rhetoric of the academic community. But this is a community that is itself transacted by lines of alliance and opposition. My own experience of conferences etc has often resembled more closely the telling of anecdotes—the *exchange of narratives*—over drinks in the bar. On another holiday—in Mombassa, this time—I remember indeed sitting in the bar and engaging in a lively conversation exchanging tales of previous vacations with new friends. At one point I made an analytic intervention concerning the ways in which we were all using our hands to make plays for and keep and yield the floor. The ensuing silence was, as they say, deafening—not hostility, anomie—until a brave soul pitched in with the next story making absolutely no reference whatsoever to my analysis. Closure entails a degree of risk; analysis, if we allow it to touch us, burns. So we listen politely to each other's papers and give encouraging plaudits ensuring that questions are confined to matters of chronicle and contextual detail and never encroach on the heart of the matter. The alliance of similars is sustained by the recontextualising of all contributions as narratives; insofar as they relate to localised experiences, narratives cannot be gainsaid.

The final cell involves discursive openness in the context of an alliance of disimilars. The young Japanese girls photographing each other in front of the memorial to Sasaki Sadako in Hiroshima's Peace Memorial Park (see Appendix I). They all make 'victory V' signs that they'll refer to, if asked, as signifying peace. But the sign is the automatic response of young Japanese girls to a camera lens whatever the circumstances—cool, not hot. A little farther up the delta, in front of the scaffolded ruin of the A-bomb dome a young Japanese father is taking a photograph of his family—the obligatory tourist shot. The mother is holding her baby in her arms.

"*Chotto matte*"—"wait"—yells her other child, a boy of maybe five or six. He crouches slightly with one foot thrust forward and the other back and carefully aims the toy rifle that he is holding directly at his father.
"Shoot."

Here, the ironic pastiche of an earnest plea for world peace (or is it the construction of the Hiroshima corporate image—either way) and its ludic or negating recruitment into the tourist snapshot is held open by a lack of interactivity in the Museum site. There is only me to object—and I don't and, anyway, my Japanese probably isn't up to it. This recruitment of a silent partner in pastiche is perhaps a little timid, but it does enable us to see its workings. Jerome McGann (2001) picks up Emily Dickinson's suggestion of reading poems backwards and Galano dela Volpe's approach to interpretation in his proposal for critical work as 'deformance':

> Interpretation is the application of scientia to poiesis, or the effort to elucidate one discourse form in terms of another. Furthermore, the effort is not directed toward establishing general rules of laws but toward explaining a unitary, indeed a unique, phenomenon. A doubled gap thus emerges through the interpretive process itself, and it is the necessary presence of this gap that shapes della Volpe's critical thought. We may usefully recall here that when poets and artists use imaginative forms to interpret other such forms, they pay homage to this gap by throwing it into relief. (McGann, 2001, p. 127)

McGann prosecutes his practice in a technologically supported game—'The Ivanhoe Game'—in which players adopt explicit schemas to make moves in the space opened up by a novel or a corpus or an archive and responding to each other's moves according to their respective schemas which are archived but, until the game's conclusion, private. Alternatively, random distortions of a digitised Rossetti painting—*The Blessed Damozel*—in Photoshop reveal a structural resonance between the figure of the damozel and the background of heavenly embracing lovers, thus revealing her radiant spiritual meaning (McGann, n.d., 2001). By textualising his interpretation—Rossetti's painting as consistent with his/John Ruskin's pre-Raphaelite philosophy—McGann points at the 'doubled gap' which I interpret as that between scientia (digital technologies) and analysis and between analysis and poiesis (the painting as text). I will pick this up again in Chapters 7 and 8. Katherine Hayles (1999) constructs a different kind of pastiche in her articulation of a scholarly account of the development of cybernetics with literary analysis of science fiction maintained as pastiche and evading hegemony largely via the device of chapter boundaries and to a large extent allowing radiance of her third element to remain unspoken, pending the authorship of her audience. The productivity of the pastiche is to open up the possibility of something else without the negation of that which is initially juxtaposed.

I want to construct another mode of pastiche that resonates gently with both McGann's and Hayles' strategies. I want to begin with a second analytic frame that might be recognised as a form of deformance of the first. The juxtaposition of this with its objects of analysis will be constituted as one dimension of my pastiche. The assembling of a diverse array of objects will be the second. My intention is to provide an organising of texts and practices that will cast a light on the dynamic of current transformations in media technologies that I hope will exhibit just a little more delicacy than the well-rehearsed modern/postmodern opposition. Before I begin, though, I shall make a brief diversion to make a few comments on the nature of analysis.

A NOTE ON ANALYSIS

Clearly, analysis entails the establishing of divisions. A great deal of epistemological thinking has been concerned with the subject/object division. Crotty (1998) draws attention to three dominant lines, objectivism, which proposes that knowledge arises from the nature of objects, constructionism, holding that knowledge is constructed via a subject-object transaction of some form, and subjectivism which, regards knowledge as the independent construction of a mind—the subject. I am not, however, concerned with epistemology, but with poiesis—construction or making. Nevertheless, I find it helpful to make a distinction—a pragmatic distinction—between what I bring to analysis (and which, I hope, develops in the engagement) and what I take to be the object(s) of my analysis (my understanding of which will, I hope, also develop). I have used different terms to catch at this distinction. In Dowling and Brown (2009) (see also Brown & Dowling, 1998) we refer to a dehiscence in the cultural that establishes a theoretical and an empirical field (I also used this term in Chapter 2). We use this initial division as the first organising principle in developing our 'mode of interrogation' for educational research. The schema in Dowling and Brown (2009) derived from my conceptualising of my general methodology that I refer to as *constructive description* (Dowling, 1998). I will review this conceptualising in Chapter 4. Here, as I announced in Chapter 1, I shall refer to an organisational language—part of the theoretical field in the former convention and a central component of constructive description—and a text or texts—part of the empirical field. More generally, though, any empirical analysis (any analysis that establishes some kind of distinction between its own subjectivity and its objects) might be considered to comprise: i) a theoretical framework and/or a method; ii) one or more objects of its gaze; iii) a commentary on and/or arising out of a consideration of these objects. I want to propose that this suggests two questions that we might put to any analysis that may be offered to us:

- What limits or boundaries are placed on the object? Addressing this question is first analytic strategy introduced in Chapter 1.

- What is the relationship between the constructions of the method/theory and those of the commentary? This is a reformulation of the second analytic strategy introduced in Chapter 1.

I do not propose to answer these questions here in any detail in respect of analysis produced by other authors. However, it does seem to me that a very common approach in the area of text analysis entails, firstly, a silence on the precise limits of the data that constitute the text in question. For example, it is sometimes not entirely clear whether or to what extent aspects of the empirical author of the text are to be included in the data or whether these are to be related to the details of the context in which the text was produced as a work, etc. By this I mean that the implication of authorship in this sense often varies without any clear rationale. This kind of openness, of course, provides a handy escape route in the face of critical reinterpretation of what is presented on any given occasion. Secondly, analysis frequently seems to involve the effective dissociation of theory/method, on the one hand, from the objects that are constructed in the commentary that is produced as the principal outcome of the analysis.

It seems to me that, in particular, these characteristics are often found in work that proceeds on the basis of a linguistic theoretical apparatus to pass comment on the social and political, which is generally entirely untheorised. In Chapter 1 I suggested that this was a problem for Hodge's and Kress's (1988) analysis of the Cimabue work. Fairclough (1995, see also Chouliaraki & Fairclough, 1999) achieves this fragmentation of his theoretical field—a break between the theorised and the untheorised—via the detachment of the categories of *genre* and *discourse* from his otherwise highly systematic theory. Effectively, what may count as a genre or a discourse is whatever Fairclough claims as such, thus:

> There are no definitive lists of genres, discourses, or any of the other categories I have distinguished for analysts to refer to, and no automatic procedures for deciding what genres etc. are operative in a given text. Intertextual analysis is an interpretive art which depends upon the analyst's judgement and experience. (Fairclough, 1995, p. 77)

As far as it goes, this seems reasonable. However, insofar as the generic and discursive organisation of cultural texts and practices is taken to be the principal purpose of the analysis, we might want to ask precisely what is the highly elaborate linguistic apparatus for; to stand as an alibi for untheorised motives, perhaps. We might refer to such approaches as theoretical dualism. They divide the theoretical into two regions that are effectively dislocated whether or not they are equally theoretically developed. As a result, they can present the appearance of X-ray vision: one region of theory (generally the more theorised one) is presented as penetrating the empirical text so as to reveal the other theoretical region (generally undertheorised) lying behind it, a marvellous ventriloquy indeed—forensics.

My approach here is as openly 'interpretive' as is Fairclough's. However, my aim is not to reveal, for example, power relations. On the contrary, this being a sociology, power—here, the constitution of subjectivity—is implicated in my theoretical constructions themselves and, indeed, is implied in the rhetorical form of this book—there is, as I hope my analysis below will demonstrate as well as exhibit, no getting away from it. Rather, my analysis consists, firstly, of an initial partitioning of my field of vision into, on the one hand my organisational language and, secondly, my object text or texts. The ensuing dialogue generates a second partitioning via the production of my commentary—the textualising of the object text, as it were. Thereafter, my autopoietic work proceeds as a productive dialogue between these three constructions; a dialogue that develops all three in respect of, at least, their internal coherence and correspondence of form. As is commonly the case, the final product—this book, for example—tends to elide the dialogic and developmental nature of its production.

MONUMENTS AND MOVIES

I shall begin the introduction of the next aspect of my developmental language with two keynote (object) texts that bear a superficial similarity to each other, but which must be read as radically different. The texts are Piero Manzoni's *Socle du Monde* (1961, Herning Museum) and Rachel Whiteread's *Monument* (2001, originally in Trafalgar Square). A caveat: my treatment of both pieces as conceptual is arguably a greater deformance of the Whiteread than it is of the Manzoni. As I have indicated, however, deformance or recontextualisation is what I am setting out to achieve in this pastiche and I will offer no apologies, though interested readers may refer, for example, to the review by Searle (2001) for a contrasting (though not necessarily contradictory) approach.

Manzoni's piece consists of an upturned plinth, which establishes the world as the work. As with Marcel Duchamp's 'readymades' (though Manzoni is perhaps somewhat more flamboyant), we can interpret the *Socle du Monde* as identifying the essential quality of art as the act of selection of the artist who thereby lays claim to authorship and originality. This is the case even with a mass-produced bottle rack or urinal because the artist establishes their choice as a singular event, which is simply recorded iconically and symbolically (in the catalogue and gallery notes) in the museum. The act of artistic production, then, constitutes an authored singularity—a *charismatic* singularity—in an entirely open field of practice; anything, even the world, even a mass-produced bottle rack, may be transformed into something unique and, of course, potentially saleable. The authority invoked here is a Nietzschian form, divested of traditional imperatives. Elsewhere we glimpse it in the architecture of Le Courbusier (return to the (unique) plan) and in the literature of Philip K. Dick who can work seriously with the concept of a small-scale organ manufacturer setting out to reproduce the American Civil War by building perfect simulacra of every participating individual from Abraham Lincoln on down (Dick, 1972). If we go to the movies we might watch Spike Jonze's *Being John Malkovich* (1999), but we will certainly want to pay attention to the titles and credits; similarly, we might be drawn to check the by-line of a newspaper report— certainly, the name of the newspaper—before putting too much faith in it.

The mode of authority strategy that I am marking out here is close, but not identical, to Max Weber's (1964) 'charismatic' form. Here I am defining it as a closing down of authorship in the context of a potentially open field of practice. If I buy into this mode then, whilst I won't be able to hang Manzoni's *Socle du Monde* on my wall, I will certainly be looking for something singular, a unique piece by a very particular artist.

Whiteread's sculpture is a clear resin cast of the fourth plinth in Trafalgar Square, London, which it occupied between June 2001 and May 2002. This plinth has until recently been unoccupied, the others celebrating famous generals and King George IV on a horse (a statue commissioned by the king himself). Whiteread's cast was placed inverted on top of the plinth recalling, perhaps, Manzoni's inverted plinth. Forty years on from Manzoni and with the benefit of Baudrillard's insight, it is now possible to read this work as a questioning of the artist. It inverts Manzoni's plinth (technically I suppose it is not Manzoni's plinth that is upsidedown, but the viewer) as the mirror image of the plinth on which it stands and which precedes it as the condition of existence of Whiteread's work qua art. The transparency of the work also reveals the physical condition of existence of the plinth itself, which is the space that it consumes[9]. Whiteread's work signals a system of monumentalising practices that always precedes the monument and that simulates it as production rather than as merely reproductive of the practice of monumentalising. The now—at the time of writing—again empty plinth (or the sign in the gallery informing us that the painting normally occupying this space has been taken away temporarily for cleaning) does the same, but with rather less force. Monumentalising as a practice is established as a system of differences (following Saussure) that enables certain constructions and locations to be recognised as for, which is to say simulating, art.

Anything can now be placed on the plinth (hung in the gallery) and anyone can put it there (although it may be 'legitimately' removed by officials), so that production and exchange-value, in Marx's terms, is revealed as 'ideological', which is to say, as constituting an alibi for the 'real' activity of reproduction (of the system of monumentalising and the broader sociocultural system of which it is a context). Whereas we might see Manzoni as establishing exchange-value within a 'commodity law of value' (Baudrillard, 1993), value now takes a symbolic form within the 'structural law'. Baudrillard challenges Marx's fixating on the use-value/exchange-value nexus and interprets the base-superstructure model as the

---

[9] And so marks out this mode of monumentalising from the other that is prevalent in Trafalgar Square (and elsewhere in Westminster) that is eloquently spoken to by Mark Wallinger's piece, *Ecce Homo*, that was the first work to appear on 'the empty plinth'.

mirror-image of society: the superstructure now constitutes the base as its alibi. My deformance of Whiteread's work reveals the 'base' of artistic production—her inverted, transparent plinth—as the alibi for the superstructural (in Marx's terms) plinth (the concrete one), which is where symbolic value is to be recognised. In other words, it is the system of monumentalising that simulates artistic production.[10]

The postmodern challenge to modernist charismatic authority approximates to Weber's bureaucratic form. In my configuration the specificity of authorship is now open. Practice is now closed because authority itself resides in or is claimed on behalf of a prior system, which defines the practice. Schlock art and schlock literature are established as art and literature not in and of themselves, but through their installation as such in locations that establish and are established for art and literature. My personal response to *Monument* was dominated by its aesthetic appeal—that's OK too, as long as it's on the plinth, which points to the established system of practice. What makes a film is not the specificity of director or cast, but the existence of systems of narrative and generic structure. Some films of, course, draw our attention to this: one thinks of *Pulp Fiction* (Dir. Tarantino, 1994), *The Usual Suspects* (Dir. Singer, 1995), and the archetypal, Robert Altman's *Short Cuts* (1993). At a different level of analysis, the system of film production, marketing and distribution will also draw our attention as will the system of news production that establishes the mundane as extraordinary.

In my constructions, here, Whiteread, Tarantino, Singer, Altman are all charismatic authors producing charismatic singularities. But these singularities index the bureaucratic form of authority; correspondingly, the work of Manzoni may well be regarded as schlock. Specific texts may also be read in different ways. *Forrest Gump* (Dir. Zemeckis, 1994) may with some justification be interpreted as a schmaltzy celebration of the American Dream of a land in which anyone—even a poor boy with learning difficulties—might achieve anything. A charismatic dream, perhaps: *you* are the author of your own destiny. Yet the opening scene behind the titles suggests an alternative.[11] A feather, drifting down from the heavens touches the shoulder of a hurrying businessman who brushes it away irritably. It lands at the feet of Gump, sitting erect and immaculate—shirt buttoned all the way up to the neck (there's nothing to distinguish one button from another). Gump picks up the feather and places it carefully between the covers of a book inside his orderly attaché case. Gump's only ambition is to be 'normal'. But he's anything but that. His route to normality is to take everything at face value, to attend scrupulously to the minute detail of what is immediately to hand. His achievements come to him

---

[10] Strolling through Shin Yokohama Station recently I passed a young woman wearing a tee bearing the legend, 'The seed comes before the harvest'. Wrong: this is not just a replay of the chicken and egg paradox (itself easily sidestepped via a simple model of evolution). The seed and the harvest are not of the same nature (unless the latter is serving as no more than a plural of the former). It is of course the cultural practices of harvesting that motivate the seed *qua* seed. The harvest clearly comes before the seed.

[11] See also Durães (2001) for further discussion of *Forrest Gump* along these lines.

undreamt yet far outstretch the wildest dreams of the other characters in the film. Their lives are tragic or mundane. President Kennedy shakes hands with and puts the same dumb question to a group of athletes—'How does it feel to be an All American'. Gump provides the relief, 'I gotta pee'. The dreams of other characters are only ever realised through Gump's agency and never through their own endeavours. Gump's own dream is spoiled—he gets the girl, but she dies. But he is quite satisfied with the son she gives him. Yet we can identify with any of the characters in the film except Gump whose naivety provides its humour. We laugh at him, we are not he, the American Dream is a myth, what we see is all there is and that's as good as it's going to get because no matter what we do we can only reproduce the bureaucratic system.

If we buy into bureaucratic authority then the value attributed to the pictures on our walls might be attributed not to their unique qualities or those of the artist, but to their position in a collection. For collectors, we might suppose, the drive towards completeness is paramount. This cool, *obsessive*, bureaucratic approach to art contrasts with the hot, *hysteria* of the charismatic mode. Their definition, however, has opened up further possibilities; this is, of course, a crucial function of theory. The charismatic and bureaucratic modes of authority strategy have been defined as, respectively, closed and open authorship and open and closed field of practice. As with the schema presented in Figure 3.1, we have two variables each a binary nominal scale. The cross product now gives rise to the frame in Figure 3.2.

	Field of Practice	
Category of author	Open	Closed
Closed	*Charismatic*	*Traditional*
Open	*Liberal*	*Bureaucratic*

Figure 3.2. Modes of Authority Action

The schema presents the charismatic and bureaucratic modes as opposites, but also reveals another pair of opposites that differ from each of the first pair on only one variable. For the mode exhibiting closure of authorship and practice I have recruited Weber's third term, traditional authority, my definition again resonating but not coinciding with his category. The closure of authorship and practice are achieved together in alliances and oppositions that both define membership and regulate the rules of the discourse. Art and literature here are canonical. If, as William Morris claimed, 'You can't have art without resistance in the materials' (quoted by McGann, 2001, p. 54) then not only Morris himself, but Carl André's *Equivalent 17* and much of the work of Barbara Hepworth amongst many others are there to reveal some of this resistant quality to us. Picasso exemplifies (and charismatically inaugurated, amongst other categories) cubism, Magritte, surrealism, and so forth. Here, though our focus shifts from charismatic originality and bureaucratic structure to cultural content and its authorised spokespeople. In evaluating film I am concerned with verisimilitude in relation to the setting or perhaps, in the case of an adaptation, with the canonical novel that is constituted as the source of the screenplay; in reviewing *Emma* (Dir. McGrath, 1996) I am drawn to compare it with Austen's novel, but I am also, perhaps, paying attention to the American Gwynneth Paltrow's English accent; I am concerned about the introduction of an American actor in the lead of *Possession* (Dir. LaBute, 2002) and at the exclusion of most of Byatt's poetry that was integral to her novel (1991). Here, I am claiming 'traditional' expertise in the evaluation of aspects of these films against the basis of that expertise—knowledge of literature or English dialects.

When I open the newspaper I am now at last focusing on the news content and may be puzzled as to why an earthquake in Hokkaido should get more coverage in the British press than in Korea and why the death of Hugo Young at least as much attention in *The Guardian* as does that of Edward Said; the structures of news production may speak, but they pass unheard here. Indeed, the 'serious' newspaper must construct its reportage as disinterested so that the front page photograph, discussed in Chapter 2, of a U.S. soldier, pinning to the ground with his foot a Haitian—who may or may not have been a rioter and who may or may not have been justified—whilst gazing vigilantly out of the frame, may mythologise the American saviour of a country in ruins or the American imperialist primarily responsible for the ruins in the first place; no commentary, just the caption, 'Gun Law'—the reader will decide on the basis of the facts brought to them by the newspaper, 'traditionally' authorising itself as the legitimate and unbiased purveyor of news.

In 'traditional' mode, my walls and bookcases are dressed with representations of the canon—whether 'high' or 'low' culture—I display the legitimacy of my taste (and, therefore, of myself) by example. Here is the domain of the rule of discourse, the rule of subject as subject to. The pathology of 'traditional' authority is *depression*.

Finally, the 'liberal' mode is constituted as the opposite of tradition: open authorship and an open field of practice. In this strategy, authority is relinquished by the author, handed over to the audience. Art as such is difficult here precisely because the author can have no voice—interactive art, perhaps, the art of the kaleidoscope. Kaprow's 'happenings' discussed in Chapter 2 will not do insofar as the audience was scheduled. Forrest Gump would serve well here as a role model: attend to what is at hand. But *Babette's Gæstebud* (Dir. Axel, 1987) works perfectly:

> Here, the elders of the dour Protestant community can share with the gourmet general a table prepared by the finest chef de cuisine ever to delight Paris and all can depart sated by the certain knowledge that their principles have been upheld, that they have righteously abstemiously or rightfully indulgently or right creatively possessed the feast and, in doing so, denied no one. The feast, of course, was—at least subsequent to its preparation—inanimate and so

indifferent to possession. There was, furthermore, quite enough to go around. (Chung, Dowling & Whiteman, 2004)

This is the field of the scrapbook or, nowadays, the blog. If I'm displaying artwork then it's the children's drawings magnetically pinned to the fridge. This is the field *par excellence* of self-authoring, self-making, the autopoiesis of second order cybernetics, discussed in Chapter 2, in which the observer (at any level of analysis) is an informationally closed system immune to pedagogic authority (Hayles, 1999). But the absence of feedback proposes *anxiety* as the pathology of this mode: do what you like, but you'll never know how you'll have been received.

AUTHORITY IN RELIGION AND EDUCATION

To consolidate the picture generated by my authority schema I will take two fields and run them round the cells of Figure 3.2. The first field is that of religion. We might begin with *The Bible* in the Christian tradition and, in particular, the New Testament. I will take a story from St Matthew's Gospel (see Dowling, 1998). A young man had approached Jesus and asked what he must do in order to achieve salvation. Jesus recited the commandments to him, whereupon:

20　The young man saith unto him, All these things have I observed: what lack I yet?

21　Jesus said unto him, if thou wouldest be perfect, go sell that thou hast, and give to the poor, and thou shalt have treasure in heaven: and come, follow me.

22　But when the young man heard the saying, he went away sorrowful: for he was one that had great possessions.

23　And Jesus said unto his disciples, Verily I say unto you, it is hard for a rich man to enter into the kingdom of heaven.

24　And again I say unto you, It is easier for a camel to pass through a needle's eye, than for a rich man to enter into the kingdom of God.

25　And when the disciples heard it, they were astonished exceedingly, saying, Who then can be saved?

26　And Jesus looking upon *them* said to them, With men this is impossible; but with God all things are possible.

(*The Holy Bible, the revised version*, Oxford: OUP; Matthew, 20, 16-26)

The young man had approached Jesus in an attempt to look behind the simulacrum of goodness constructed by the Commandments. But he was not offered an option in verse 21. To be perfect is to be God: '*One* there is who is good' (*Ibid.*, verse 17; my emphasis). The rich man cannot become that which he is not, but this neither gives nor denies him access to heaven. What he lacked was not poverty, but faith and no strategy is offered for the achievement of either. God, here, seems to be in the place of Forrest Gump as a wholly exteriorised other, which may nevertheless impact upon our lives. But the imperative is not simply to pay attention to matters at hand, rather it is to attend to the commandments—a very specific set of practices. These practices are privileged by the Christian Church, an alliance that also establishes the legitimacy of authors.

The Koran by contrast elaborates the Old Testament, very strongly inserting God as author and The Prophet as his legitimate relay.[12] There is also a degree of arbitrariness introduced into the practices in the sense that they might have been otherwise and changes have been made (for example between the respective dietary rules for Judaism and Islam) but that the command is nevertheless absolute under the unique and total authority of God. In this analysis, *The Koran* moves the field of religion from the traditional to the charismatic mode.

The bureaucratic mode establishes a position for religion in the sociocultural field. However, that which is practiced is determined solely by that which occupies this position. To this extent, then, all religions are commensurable and it becomes possible for *Star Trek's* (TV, 1987-1994) Captain Jean-Luc Picard to announce that he respects the beliefs of all religions: it doesn't matter what's preached in the Temple, it's religion. Insofar as religion must establish pedagogic authority either in terms of authorship or practice or both, the liberal mode is anathema.

The second field that I will illustrate, briefly, is Education (and see, also, Chapter 6). The traditional school curriculum centres on subject disciplines taught by specialist teachers. In terms of educational theory, traditional authority is established by the approach of situated cognition (Lave & Wenger, 1991), which constitutes apprenticeship as a career from legitimate but peripheral participation in a practice to central participation. In this scheme the practice itself seems not under negotiation, but this shifts somewhat with Wenger's (1998) later reconfiguration. The concept of scaffolding, commonly associated with Vygotskian approaches (1978, 1986) is also consistent with the traditional mode. Here the focus of pedagogic action is placed in advance of that which the learner can achieve unaided at a level at which they can demonstrate success with support. The regulating discourse establishes the basis upon which the necessary directionality might be established under this approach. In the social sciences and humanities, at least, in Higher Education, the closed door of the traditional doctoral tutorial and the comparatively open choice of examiners in many fields and institutions suggests scope for charismatic authority as the voice of the supervisor, potentially at least, is able to dominate the field. This certainly describes my own experience as a doctoral student; I'll let my own students speak for themselves.

In England and Wales, official education at all levels has been coming under bureaucratising pressures, as is discussed in Chapter 6. In the school this has taken the form of standardised curricula and tests (see Dowling & Noss, 1990; Flude & Hammer, 1990), standardised school inspections, the publication of school test and examination results and so forth. In Higher Education it has taken the form of the modularisation of courses, the vetting of some programmes by state agencies, quality assurance inspections and so forth. In my institution as well as in many others a currency was devised rendering comparable all academic work from

---

[12] I have access only to the English translation of *The Koran*, N.J. Dawood (trans.). 2003. London: Penguin.

teaching to research to administrative responsibilities.[13] In fact, all curricula are to some degree bureaucratising strategies insofar as they institutionalise principles of

Charismatic	Traditional
Authorship: closed	Authorship: closed
Practice: open	Practice: closed
Texts	Texts
Socle du Monde (Manzoni)	*Equivalent 17* (Carl André)
Being John Malkovich (Jonze)	*Emma* (McGrath)
We Can Build You (Dick)	*Possession* (LaBute)
Film	Film
Titles & Credits	Verisimillitude
Journalism	Journalism
Bylines	News content
Religion	Religion
The Koran	*The Bible*
Education	Education
'Traditional' PhD	Traditional subject-based
Liberal	**Bureaucratic**
Authorship: open	Authorship: open
Practice: open	Practice: open
Texts	Texts
Interactive art	*Monument* (Whiteread)
Kaleidoscope	*Pulp Fiction* (Tarantino)
	Short Cuts (Altman)
	Usual Suspects (Singer)
	Forrest Gump (Zemeckis)
Film	Film
Babette's Gæstebud (Axel)	Narrative & genre structure
Forrest Gump (Zemeckis)	Production & Distribution
Journalism	Journalism
Scrapbooks & blogs	The simulation of news
Religion	Religion
Atheism	All religions comparable
Education	Education
Piaget	Standardised curricula
Student-centred curriculum	Modularisation
	Quality assurance

Figure 3.3. Modes of Authority and Some Signalling Texts and Practices

---

[13]   This currency is now defunct, though new workload measures are currently being devised.

selection, sequencing, pacing and so forth, they reduce the authority of the discourse in favour of the system. We might speculate that bureaucratising can happen only in the context of the relative weakening of traditional alliances. Perhaps this is visible in the shifts in the structure of the clubs that we call the learned journals, now far more *ad hoc* than associated with traditionally institutionalised practices.

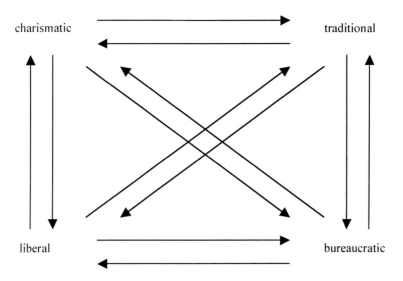

Figure 3.4. The Dynamics of Authority Strategies

Liberal education is, essentially, the educational theory of Jean Piaget (1995) and the student-centred curriculum. For Piaget, the introduction of pedagogic authority of any form is inhibitive of the processes of equilibration whereby the individual constructs their own knowledge. Equilibration is associated with homeostasis and feedback.[14] In this sense, Piaget does not constitute the learner as a closed system and predates the second order cybernetics that I (following Hayles, 1999) have linked to this mode of authority. But appropriate feedback is always non-authoritative and authority is a socially constituted pathology so that Piaget's ideal pedagogy is also consistent with the liberal mode. A variation on Vygotsky's concept of the zone of proximal development that does not entail developmental directionality, as such, would be to consider a learning network (alliance) in confrontation with a problematic situation that the network cannot immediately resolve, but where the resources for its resolution are potentially available within the network itself and where resolution entails an equilibrating adjustment

---

[14] Piaget's original field of study was zoology.

(accommodation/assimilation) of the network itself. This interpretation is consistent, in general terms, with Piaget's own genetic epistemology[15] though not entirely with my use of the expression in the relational space defined in Figure 3.1, because the learning network may be constituted as an alliance of similars or of disimilars. In any given empirical instance, it may be possible to constitute a liberal mode at the level of the network-problem. However, dropping down a level of analysis to consider action within the network itself, we might expect to find evidence of pedagogic authority strategies that might be described in terms of the other modes presented here, so that the interactions might be more appropriately labelled, in my terms, hegemony rather than equilibration.

I have summarised my analysis schematically in Figure 3.3 and also pointed forward to the next phase of my discussion in Figure 3.4. Here I shall be concerned with the use of the framework in organising the dynamics of authority strategies.

A NOTE ON METHOD

The schemas that I have introduced in Figures 3.1 and 3.2 construct ideal-typical spaces. By this I mean that the categories that they constitute are ideal-types rather than empirical realities. Any empirical instance is to be described in terms of the ways in which it may be construed as illustrating or incorporating or dominated by one or more of the strategies. As we shift our attention between levels of analysis—between an individual work of art and the museum that displays it and so forth—or move within a text of practice the pattern of authority strategies that we use to describe it is likely to shift as well. To this extent, Figure 3.3 may be somewhat misleading. This is illustrated by the appearance of *Forrest Gump* in two of the cells. Indeed, the character Gump is clearly constructed by other characters as a charismatic authority in at least the part of the film in which he decides to run across America (a decision not taken all in one go, of course). We could therefore legitimately place the film in the charismatic cell as well. I have borrowed Jerome McGann's term (though not, perhaps, precisely his use of it) to describe the action of my schema, which does not seek to capture a text or practice or even to represent it, but rather to re-present it, to recontextualise the text or practice in an action of principled *deformance*. In Chapter 4, I shall use *treachery* and *heresy* and in Chapter 8 the terms *misreading* and *misprision*. The theoretical scheme becomes a description machine, a part of the organisational language that I adumbrated in Chapters 1 and 2. Its use-value is measured by the extent to which it allows us to establish a degree of organisation on our observations that show the objects of our analysis in a new but consistent light. If pushed, I might argue that all analysis that deploys explicit schemas is of the same form, though sometimes rather more grandiose claims are made for it—but more will be said of this in Chapter 8.

The diagram in Figure 3.4 constructs a logical, relational space by which we might map moves or transformations between authority strategies within any given

---

[15] See, for example, Piaget (1972, 1980, 1995).

activity. It does not entail that all moves will be observed; this is another facility of theory, it has the potential to make silences speak. I have already mentioned one of the moves, that is, the bureaucratising of the traditional school and university curriculum. The move from traditional to charismatic authority describes attempts of members of an alliance to establish a unique position within the field. If they succeed, then sooner or later their work is likely to become canonised and recruited to traditional strategies. To conclude this chapter I want to consider, in the terms of this dynamic, developments that might be described as the formation of new alliances between technological and traditional practices.

MEDIA

Firstly, digital technologies have long had a foothold in the field of academic production. I suspect that, for some time now, few manuscripts have been produced with the aid of a pen or a typewriter. Furthermore, the UK academic network, JANET, has been in place for more than two decades now so that many academics in most fields will have been using electronic mail for a significant proportion of their careers; I have used it as my main medium of distance (and not so distanced) communication since 1987. These technologies have far wider applications than this, of course, but their exploitation entails considerable investment in terms of time and often finance. In the context of an academic environment dominated by traditional authority strategies there is no clear return on this investment. However, this does open up a potential space for charismatic strategies. We see this in the hybrid work of Jerome McGann, whom I have mentioned, and also in the work of Janet Murray (1997) and Katherine Hayles (1999, 2002), both authors having dual backgrounds in literature and science or technology. The hybrid is clearly a potentially effective charismatic strategy, the more so to the extent that the fields that are thus brought together are, in the context of the traditional field, strongly classified with respect to each other. As I have suggested, the presence of digital technologies as everyday tools within literary studies and other non-technological fields is particularly helpful to these hybrid forms.

Another hybrid charismatic move has perhaps greater significance. This is the alliance of literature and technology in the form of hypertext. Here, the work of Aarseth (1994, 1997, 1999), Bolter (2001), Douglas (1998, 2001), Joyce (1992, 1995, 1998, 1999, 2001) Kaplan (2000), Landow (1997), McGann (2001), Miles (2001) and Moulthrop (1995, 1999) are outstanding examples. Much of the hybridising work concentrates on the technical limitations of print technology. This approach resides predominantly in the liberal mode and operates to reduce some of the purely technical limitations to autopoiesis, to eliminate friction. Bolter, for example, suggests that:

> What all media and media forms have in common for our culture is that promise of immediacy. Transparent media promise to disappear and leave us in contact with the unmediated world, although it is a promise that they can never entirely fulfull. Hypermediated media give up the attempt to present a

world beyond themselves; instead they offer themselves as immediate experiences. When one medium sets out to remediate another, it does so by claiming to do a better job. It can claim to be better at transparency. For example, virtual reality promises to be the ultimate transparent medium, better than painting or photography, because the viewer in virtual reality can actually step into the world viewed. Or the medium can promise a more elaborate hypermediacy, as World Wide Web sites do in combining painting, photography, graphic design, film, audio, and video into a sort of popular *Gesamtkunstwerk*. In either case the new medium is trying to convince us that it offers greater immediacy than its predecessors. Because our culture today is saturated with media, claims of greater immediacy are constantly being made, as new and older media vie for our attention. (Bolter, 2001, pp. 25-26)

Jerome McGann argues that his 'Rossetti Archive'[16] provides a far more usable resource than the traditional critical edition. In particular, it can handle multimedia or, to use Gunther Kress's (2003) term, multimodal texts, which is particularly crucial in the case of an artist whose corpus includes both written text and images. Indeed, McGann stresses that all texts are modally complex:

For the truth is that all textualizations—but pre-eminently imaginative textualities—are organised through concurrent structures. Texts have bibliographical and linguistic structures, and those are given by other concurrencies: rhetorical structures, grammatical, metric, sonic, referential. The more complex the structure the more concurrencies are set in play. (McGann, 2001, p. 90)

For McGann, the fact that digital technology can handle the presentation of multimodal texts rather more effectively than print (which can't handle sound at all) is part of the gain. But, crucially, sophisticated markup protocols can potentially at least enable far more complex search and retrieve strategies in the context of texts organised through multiple and overlapping concurrent structures. Perhaps even more fundamental is the fact that a digital archive located in active memory is never definitively complete nor necessarily under a restricted authorship. This last feature is in part the basis for McGann's 'Ivanhoe Game' that I have referred to above.

McGann underplays authority and postulates a technological advance within the context of what is effectively an idealised liberal environment. Other hybridising work focuses attention on the shifting game of authority. Marie-Laure Ryan points towards the shift proposed by these hybridisers, re-quoting (see Chapter 2):

We used to think of texts as being made out of words and sentences; now under the conjoined influences of postmodern theory and electronic writing technologies, we think of texts as being made out of text. The loom is still needed to weave the individual elements (unless they are "found objects,"

---

[16] Accessible at http://www.rossettiarchive.org/index.html (last accessed 06/02/09).

lifted from other texts), but organization and linearization is now a two-stage process, the virtual text produced by the first stage serving as input to the second. While the writer remains responsible for the microlevel operations, she may bypass the macrolevel stage, thus offering *du texte* as a freely usable resource to the reader, rather than *un text* structured as a logical argument aiming at persuasion. (Ryan, 1999, p. 100)

'Postmodern theory and electronic writing technologies' seems to capture the specificity of the hybrid. The point to note, however, is the construction of the electronic hypertext as attenuating, in my terms, the charismatic or traditional or bureaucratic authority of the text. They are no longer imposing a unique or conventional argument, rather they are offering a 'resource' to the reader in a shift towards liberal strategies.

J. Yellowlees Douglas (1998) also describes the move in terms of a 'problem' with conventional text technology:

The cruel irony of reflexivity is that the conventional linearity of print rhetoric drives even the most rigorous reflexive relativist-constructivists through the exact same gyrations as the sociologists they are busily attempting to discredit. One of the chief problems with linearity is that it generally leads to something singular. (Douglas, 1998, p. 151)

Douglas is locating the disingenuousness of the sociologists in their linear text technology. As is the case with much of the hybridising work, Douglas is, presumably self-consciously, ironically deploying precisely the same technology in her own discrediting. She might have attended to Bourdieu (1991) for whom it is clear that the power of language lies outside of it, symbolically in the skeptron that grants authority to speak. In my schema, the skeptron may be in the gift of the discourses of relatively stable alliances that characterise traditional authority. Alternatively, it may be in the non-discursive system of alliances and oppositions characterising bureaucratic authority. Or it may be grasped by a charismatic seeking to capitalise on an instability in discourse or system. The solution offered by Douglas and other hybridisers lies in hypertext technology, which may be applied both to academic writing and literature. In general, the claim proposes a liberalising of authority.

Jay David Bolter describes hypertext reading as 'performance', Adrian Miles describes the hypertext link as risky both for author and reader. Michael Joyce describes his interpretation thus:

The reader of a hypertext not only chooses the way she [sic] reads but her choices in fact become what it is. The text continually rewrites itself and becomes what I term the constructive hypertext: a version of what it is becoming, a structure for what does not yet exist. (Joyce, 1998, pp. 179-180)

What is being offered here is quite clearly a liberal image of reader authority. This is an environment that seems to suit Geoffrey Sirc (1999) admirably. As I noted in Chapter 2, following Duchamp, Sirc wants to dissolve rather than entrench, to choose rather than make. The problem for his readers is that his choosing hardly lends itself to further selection. It is too context dependent, tied too tightly to its illustrations and sources. This signals a fatal flaw in the liberalising work of the hybridisers. One may claim authority for oneself, but only as a reader. To claim authority as a writer—even as a writer on behalf of someone else—is to shift right back into one or more of the authoritative strategies, the traditional, charismatic or bureaucratic modes. We always did have authority as readers, although Bolter, McGann and others may very well be correct in claiming that this authority is more efficiently elaborated within hypertextual technologies than in conventional print. The real test comes when the reader attempts to go public. Whiteread's art, despite its apparent simplicity, involves highly technical craft skills, maybe I can't compete there. I certainly can (and regularly do) produce an unmade bed, though, but no one's going to nominate *me* for the Turner Prize for it.[17]

Douglas (2001) must sense this problem in her performance of Michael Joyce's hypernovel, *Afternoon: a story* (1992). 'Just tell me when to stop' is the title of her chapter. Her performance involves four readings of the novel after which she feels that she has solved the puzzle posed by the novel at its start. But this is not enough; there is a real sense in which she is looking for a hypertextual equivalent of a final page. She locates it in two lexias that she claims occupy key positions in the novel's topography. It is the location of these lexia combined with her grasp of narrative denouement that stimulate her sense of completion. It seems, though, that

> ... fundamentally, what she has done in this auto-ethnography is to find a way of returning to the author of the novel—in this case, Michael Joyce—an authorial voice that may otherwise be lost in the celebration of open readings. (Chung, Dowling & Whiteman, 2004)

Joyce, it would seem, has written a mystery and hidden the keys to its solution inside the complex structure of his novel; this would seem to be pretty much in line with traditional authorial authority.

Johndan Johnson-Eilola provides a glimpse of something nearer to a liberal reading in his observation of children playing computer games (which also deploy hypertextual technology):

> This emphasis on taking action and representing knowledge across broad, flat surfaces is a repudiation of historical distinctions between appearance and true content, a hallmark of postmodernism. Children learn here to deal tactically with contingency, multiplicity, and uncertainty. Where modernists are compelled to understand the rules before playing a game—or at best, must be able to discern simple, clear rules by trial and error—postmodernists are capable of working such chaotic environments from within, moment by moment. Their domain is space rather than time. They exist with time,

---

[17]   The reference is to Tracy Emin's work, *My Bed*, that was nominated for the Turner Prize in 1999 and subsequently sold for £15 000.

dancing across it, rather than being subordinated to it. (Johnson-Eilola, 1998, pp. 195-196)

Of course, we don't know the nature of the alliance that the children under observation here were establishing, maintaining or dismantling, but it seems likely that they were doing something rather different from Douglas's practice in performing *Afternoon*. Computer games such as *Tomb Raider II*,[18] for example, are not stand-alone texts. Indeed, playing the game to its conclusion (by which I mean making all the pickups, getting to the end sequence and so forth) would be difficult in the extreme were this to be the case. It's not clear, for example, that a player would spontaneously come up with the notion that there might be an invisible bridge across an otherwise uncrossable chasm unless: i) they make the connection with one of the Indiana Jones movies (I forget which one); ii) they read about it in a relevant game player magazine; iii) they visit a walkthrough site on the internet; iv) they are part of a formal or informal community of players that reproduces such knowledge; v) they have previously played another game that included such a device; vi) in frustration, they dive the avatar into the abyss at precisely the right place and discover it by accident.

Essentially, the game is associated with a diverse network of texts and practices, including other games, which borrow and recontextualise from each other facilitating the accumulation of a repertoire of tactics by the avid game player. Also built into this game and many others are 'cheats' which, for example, enable the player to gain access to all of the weapons that are potentially available if you can find them. Another cheat enables the avatar, Lara Croft, to do a handstand, another will blow her up and, of course, the internet has plenty of saved games that you can download if you want to start somewhere other than at the beginning. We are, then, dealing with a central text that is made available to multiple modes of use—performances. When I played the game I started off with the intention of 'playing by the rules'. However, I failed to get past the very first hurdle which involved getting out of the first setting. So I searched the internet for a walkthrough.[19] I then proceeded by trying things out for myself first and checking with the walkthrough if (when) I got stuck. I also checked the walkthrough before making an irreversible move to ensure that I hadn't missed anything vital. Doubtless my strategy would not win me many plaudits from games enthusiasts. I have, though, also watched children playing the game. What I saw was repeated acts of avataricide as Lara was made to jump from high buildings, drowned, blown up, shot and so forth with no attempts to advance the game at all in the way that I had been playing it.

What facilitates liberalisation here is the move from authorship to readership. We may speculate that if the companies producing computer games wish to

---

[18] *Tomb Raider II: The dagger of Xian*, 1997, Core Design, Eidos. See Sunnen (2000) for an analysis of this game, which deploys other elements of the theoretical framework that is introduced in this paper.

[19] http://www.tombraiders.net/stella/

maximise their sales, they will want to facilitate the widest possible range of modes of use. Games players will doubtless invent further modes. Provided they remain in the position of readers, their authority is paramount. Any move towards authorship must entail the reintroduction of an alternative authority strategy. Of course, I am doing precisely this in recruiting my own game playing into academic writing. Hypertext technology does facilitate, even suggest alternative forms of reading and writing to those commonly (not exclusively) deployed in print technology. It may generate more efficient reading and writing in many different ways. As technology in and of itself, however it cannot be answerable for the authority strategies that are deployed through it. These strategies are always directed towards the establishing, maintenance or destabilising of sociocultural alliances and oppositions. The liberal mode is viable only where social action ends.

A PASTICHE

In Chapter 2 I presented an approach to the analysis of text that places emphasis, firstly, on a need to be clear as to the empirical extent of the text, to place a boundary around it. Secondly, the approach constitutes the text as an instance, not of some absent structure that is, in and of itself, unobservable (more of this in Chapter 8), but of the organisational language that is being developed and/or deployed in the analysis itself. So the relational spaces in Figures 3.1 and 3.2 are introduced as a components of my organisational language, hitherto referred to as Social Activity Theory (Dowling, 1998); I may need to amend this label, especially as it is sometimes used to designate other approaches that are linked to Vygotsky and Leont'ev[20], but I'll defer the decision until the concluding chapter of this book. The organisational language begins with the proposition—introduced in Chapter 1—that the sociocultural consists of the strategic formation, maintenance and destabilising of alliances and oppositions. This proposition defines my theoretical object of study, the sociocultural, conceived in this way. In the terms of Figure 3.1, this chapter has presented a pastiche of dissimilar (perhaps somewhat tacitly bounded) objects and regions of practice and, in effect, this fundamental proposition of my organisational language, together with the space introduced in Figure 3.1. Figure 3.2 has, by contrast, emerged out of a consideration of the objects and regions of practice. This particular emergence is an artefact of the production of this chapter: the space in Figure 3.2 originally emerged from an analysis that I conducted, in the context of a teaching session on the doctoral programme at the Institute of Education, of a letter that had been circulated within the Institute.[21] Of course, Figure 3.1 emerged in similar circumstances—as I recall,

---

[20] As is my approach, but in a far more detached way, see Dowling (1998) and becoming further detached in this work.

[21] I have always constituted my teaching as providing opportunities for theoretical and empirical development and have encouraged my students to do the same; that the schema in Figure 3.2 has proved useful (and will reappear in other chapters in this book) far beyond its origin as a pedagogic example came as no surprise to me whatsoever.

in the course of a doctoral supervision tutorial—though I have presented it here in a more *a priori* mode.

It has been my intention to make no attempt to foreclose on the analysis of any of the objects or regions of practice that remain available for further or alternative analysis. Rather, to reveal the potential productivity of the transaction, as deformance, between an organisational language and its empirical objects in terms of both the development of the language and the constructive description of the objects. The production of the organisational language is a necessary condition for this constructive description in enabling different—in this chapter as elsewhere in this book, very different—objects to be described in the same way and so bring them, seen in this way, into a certain state of commensurability. Seeing the objects in this way, does not capture the objects, it maps them only in the terms of the gaze.

This chapter (and most of the rest of the book) is substantially *pedagogic* in form. By this I mean that I, as author, am deploying strategies in writing (providing definitions, constructing a linear form of argument and so forth) that seek to claim control over the principles of evaluation of my text, here, in terms of its meaning. I am seeking to claim pedagogic authority with respect to my audience mainly in traditional mode—by, for example, occasionally making explicit my knowledge and understanding of canon works that appear in my bibliography and by including myself in this bibliography—and in charismatic mode—by attempting to introduce an approach that has originated with me (insofar as any approach can originate with an individual). To the extent that the chapter/book is effective in this pedagogic mode, I am producing a hegemonic form of pedagogy *vis-à-vis* my audience. Ideally, this pedagogy will enable my audience to determine for themselves whether and to what extent and in what ways the organisational language and analysis that I am presenting might be of some value to them in their own projects. In this latter respect and at this point, I am operating in liberal mode and the text is constituted as what I refer to as an *exchange* text: control of the principles of evaluation of the text—here in terms of its use—is delegated to the audience. I shall take up this distinction between *pedagogic* and *exchange* modes again in Chapter 4 and throughout this book.

I began this chapter, as I began the last, with the story of my trip through Rajasthan—a story that has doubtless become mythologised in my mind in its frequent re-telling. The difference in inflection between my fairly standard (sociologically) analysis of the patriarchal 'sari technology' and my putatively Durkheimian analysis of the Cimabue work in Chapter 3, on the one hand, and the analysis of monuments, movies and media presented in this chapter is the leitmotif of the book as a whole. In the former approaches I seem to be presenting the outcome of a forensic investigation that has led to the identification of a social force—patriarchy, mechanical solidarity—as the culprit of cultural action. My departure from this forensic sociology is to avoid pointing the finger of blame—there is, for me, no reason why the social is as it is; it just is, 'it's just a bunch of stuff that happens', as Homer Simpson might have said (see Chapter 2). Rather, I want to construct a description and, in doing so, construct an organisational language. To the extent that my descriptions become institutionalised, then the sociocultural will have changed, though not, I'm absolutely sure, in a manner over which I will have had any control.

TREACHEROUS DEPARTURES

Bernstein and Dowling framed

A TRIBUTE TO A PROPHET, TEACHER AND FRIEND[22]

In the field of social thought and research Bernstein was a prophet. His activities organised the field into sets of friends and enemies, colleagues, critics and acolytes that may well have been more or less equinumerous though not necessarily disjoint; that is what prophets do. There will, quite rightly, be no shortage of tributes to Bernstein the prophet from leading figures in the field.

A few of us were able to work closely and individually with him as his students. Oddly enough, whilst we may well be divided in our responses to his work proportionately to the divisions of the field as a whole, we are, I am sure, united in our recognition of the astonishing good fortune that brought us under his supervision.

As was the case with a number of his doctoral students, I was summoned by Professor Bernstein to discuss the possibility of research registration on the basis of something that he had identified in my masters dissertation (although reviewing the work now, I have to confess to being somewhat unclear as to what this 'something' might have been). Embarking on work on my thesis I found myself to be cast into a situation in which every aspect of my sociological knowledge—however well established its pedigree—every epistemological presupposition, every tentative offer of empirical justification came under such vigorous and detailed interrogation that I felt as if I was experiencing the intellectual equivalent of the osteopath's table: I was being taken apart, ossicle by ossicle. Furthermore, no region of the sociocultural terrain (and what else is there) was immune from the Bernsteinian analytic gaze. Whatever took our attention in our weekly meetings would be minutely disassembled, reconfigured and ultimately recontextualised in a manner that inaugurated (although Basil would say revealed) the sententious in the mundane. What specialised sociology was not its object, but its privileging of relations and, in this, Basil was a true student of Marx.

Early on my writing would always begin with an extended contextualising trip around what I perceived to be the relevant theoretical background. 'Where does it begin?' Basil would say as he flicked impatiently through ten pages that had taken several times as many hours to produce. 'At last', on page 11, 'some data, let's see

---

[22]   Originally published as Dowling (2001b).

what sense (if any) you've managed to make of it'. The ensuing display of theoretical coherence and analytic virtuosity was, initially, dazzling. But my career—managed and encouraged by the master—from the peripheral position of observer to the central one of active, even principal participant was (with deference to Jean Lave and Etienne Wenger) the quintessence of academic apprenticeship. Basil was not only a prophet, he was a teacher.

And, of course, there was more. Producing a doctoral thesis can be (almost inevitably is) a traumatic experience under any conditions. However stern his intellectual criticism, in the personal—I might say pastoral—context, Basil was thoughtful, considerate, concerned. When Basil asked 'How are you today?' I knew that he was genuinely interested in my answer—sympathetic and supportive in the troughs, celebratory at the peaks. The lunches that generally succeeded (although never truncated) the business part of our meetings continued and extended the wide ranging social and cultural analyses that had characterised our earliest sessions before my work had developed its peculiar focus. I shall treasure these as amongst the most entertaining and warm social occasions that I have experienced in any context.

Even in its early stage of development—as instanced in my doctoral thesis—and most definitely now, my own work stands epistemologically and methodologically in a dialogic, which is of course to say a critical relationship with Basil's and I reject the epithet 'Bernsteinian' as a descriptor of my position. Nevertheless, it is clear to me that his intellectual products and productivity have informed and shaped it in a manner the diversity and extent of which becomes increasingly apparent even at my present distance from the original thesis. Once, on re-reading one of his papers that I had previously referenced in 1986 I noticed a marked resonance with a position that I had been establishing some five years later. Intellectual arrogance directed my knee jerk response and I remember thinking at first and with smug satisfaction that I had influenced him—until I looked at the date of publication.

First and foremost, however, what I hope Basil has given me (and what I know he has given to many others) is precisely the facility to develop coherence and systematicity in my own theoretical and methodological constructions. That my own route contrasts with his has, delightfully, enabled me to continue my dialogic apprenticeship to him well beyond the supervision of my thesis and even beyond his death. I shall end this tribute by quoting from my acknowledgement to him in the thesis itself:

> The supervisor of this research was Professor Basil Bernstein. Basil brought to the supervision the stunning power of his own thought and work and an often devastating, but always constructive criticism of mine. This was combined with a level of commitment, in terms of time and care, that I cannot imagine being surpassed. The impact of this supervision upon the intellectual productivity, conceptual clarity and, indeed, the readability of this thesis is immeasurable, but immense.

Goodbye, Basil, and thank you.

THE FRAMING OF BASIL BERNSTEIN

In the autumn of 1999 I was invited to give a talk on the work of Basil Bernstein to the Education Department at King's College, London. I agreed on the condition that a critical rather than expository or celebratory approach would be acceptable; it was. Now, it had been in the nature of my many hours of conversation with Basil that we would rarely discuss his own work other than in pedagogic mode, he the teacher and I the student (oddly and despite my protestations of (genuinely felt) ignorance, he would often spontaneously adopt the opposite role whenever mention was made of certain other theorists, Michel Foucault, for example). Basil would occasionally inform me of the limitations of my language of description: it was unable to handle interaction; I was dealing only with textual rather than empirical subjects. These deficiencies, it seemed (though this was not generally made explicit), would be overcome were I to bring my language into alignment with his, but it was, of course, my thesis and, in any event, the deficiencies would not prove fatal, just limiting. I believed him to be wrong, of course. I considered that the 'deficiencies' were apparent only from his general methodological position, which was inconsistent with mine. I suspected that our ways of experiencing the world were, in some respects, opposites and that we compensated for our respective one-dimensionalities in the construction of our theory. Basil experienced the world existentially, I thought, I always feel outside of it. Basil theorised an objectivity; I projected my theoretical avatar into my discursive dolls' house. I would need to switch avatars in order to 'experience' interaction and these avatars were, of course, all textual—*il n'y eut pas de hors-texte*. On the other hand, as is common in realist methodologies, Basil's subjects were *dei ex machinis*. So, what with one thing and another, whilst I felt uncomfortable with Basil's theoretical framework, I had quite deliberately avoided formulating an explicit critique. I decided to use the King's presentation as an opportunity to do so.

As is my usual practice with public presentations, I produced my critique as a paper from which I then made lecture notes (with teaching I often work the other way around—I find both to be productive). I delivered the presentation, shortly before the end of the autumn term, and then wondered what, if anything, to do with the paper. It certainly hadn't been written with a specific publication in mind, but I asked one or two colleagues who thought that the *British Journal of Sociology of Education* might be interested, as much of the work that I had cited had, at one time or another, appeared in this journal. I posted the paper on my website (where it remains) and also sent it to a former research student of mine who had passed her viva only six months earlier. As I recall, my former student made few or no comments on the paper, but did suggest that I should send it to Basil before attempting to publish it. I remembered that, in a very early conversation with Basil, he had bemoaned what he believed to be the current practice of publishing critiques without first presenting them to the author criticised for their observations. I agreed that, if this represented the common practice, then this was indeed a regrettable state of affairs. My former student had a point. But there was a problem, two problems, in fact.

A year or two before the King's presentation Basil had sent me a rather aggressive letter asking me to explain an observation that I had made in the hearing of a mutual colleague—he apparently felt insulted by the comment. I remember thinking that the colleague must have inadvertently misrepresented what I had said by removing it from the context in which it had actually stood as praise of my former supervisor. I replied to Basil informing him of this and suggesting that perhaps we might meet for lunch but that I was in no mood for a telling-off. Basil never acknowledged my reply and we had had no communication since (apart from a Christmas card that I sent him that he apparently resented because it contained no message apart from a greeting and a signature). The second problem was Basil's health, which had been deteriorating for some time and he was now seriously unwell. I wasn't sure whether a communication from me—especially in the form of a critique—would be welcome or helpful. Nevertheless, I held my former students' case to be sound, at least on ethical grounds, and I sent Basil the paper together with a short note regretting his poor state of health and explaining that I would be very grateful to receive his comments and that I would be submitting the paper— with amendments, if necessary—to the *British Journal of Sociology of Education* in due course. I received a one-line email reply: 'Thank you for your paper.' This was in January 2000 and was the last communication that I ever received from my mentor; Basil Bernstein died on September 24th that year.

I have absolutely no evidence that Basil had any involvement with the refereeing of my paper (unless one counts his assertion—to the same mutual colleague who had unwittingly caused our estrangement—that he had had nothing to do with its refereeing, as suggestive that he had in fact been involved). Whatever, the paper was roundly rejected as uninteresting and misguided. It was a simple matter to infer the identity of the referees (and why should they remain anonymous anyway), each individual being, in different ways, connected with Basil (one, another former student, the other a hagiographer). One of them suggested that the paper did not advance my own work beyond that already published. A stock expression used for rejections. It is clearly a matter of opinion or debate as to whether or not the paper constituted an advance in my previously published work, but I strongly doubt that this particular individual had read very much of it. The other claimed that I would not have made such criticisms of Bernstein's work had I been familiar with work in the field of the sociology of science; he cited Fleck as an example—presumably Ludwik Fleck whose epistemology of science in the 1920s and 1930s (1981) was re-discovered by Thomas Kuhn (1970). Kuhn's and other work on the sociology of scientific knowledge is clearly of great interest, but neither this work nor that of Fleck could in any sense that I could see gainsay my criticism of the lack of any empirical basis for Bernstein's characterisation of scientific knowledge, nor do either Fleck or Kuhn introduce the kind of empirical work that would be needed in order to establish the claims that Basil makes (and Basil didn't cite Fleck anyway). So the paper never made it into *BJSE*, but it is still on my website in its original location[23] and on my updated site.[24] But this is not quite the end of the story.

In 2004 a colleague of mine attended the Third International Basil Bernstein Symposium, which was held at Clare College, Cambridge. At the conference my colleague discovered that Basil had in fact written a reply to my paper. However, rather than send it to me as, in a sense, I had requested, he entrusted it to a number of individuals with instructions that it be published in the event of the publication of my paper, but not otherwise. My colleague was unable to determine how many individuals had received this bequest, he did, though, identify two of them. One of them is apparently the very former student of mine who had advised me to send the paper to Basil in the first place. This former student, now a full professor at a South African University has, interestingly, never informed me of the existence of the reply (nor has anyone else before my colleague discovered it)—perhaps she also advised Basil to send the paper to me. I have not, at the time of writing, seen the reply nor had any indication of its content. Indeed, the only hint that I have is an inference from two passages in what appears to be a hastily written introduction to the second edition of *Pedagogy, Symbolic Control and Identity* (Bernstein, 2000). I quote from this introduction in the chapter below and shall not do so here, in advance. Suffice it to say that the passage that I shall cite might be taken as a hint to the effect that Basil had accepted the validity of at least part of my critique. Then again, Basil was never one to eschew irony and, after all, this song might not be about me at all, I'm not so vain as to insist that it must.

AN EPILOGUE

This chapter was born 1999 (following a period of gestation of some fifteen years or so), when the first version was completed. The first section above was written and published in 2001 and the first draft of the second section and main body of the chapter in its present form were written and published on my website in late 2005. In June 2006 the former student, mentioned above, and a colleague of hers (also a friend not seen for a long time) paid a visit—*en route* back to South Africa from the US. Basil's reply was mentioned. My former student stated her belief that Basil had not accepted my critique, but felt that I should see his response to my original paper—she said that she would consult with others. She did so and mailed the paper to me in mid July 2006, shortly after the Fourth Basil Bernstein Symposium, held at Rutgers-Newark. Another of my students, who had attended the conference, told me that there had been an informal enquiry to determine who had been a recipient of Basil's original email, distributing the response.

So I now have the response and have read it. What do I do about it? In a sense, the ethical problem that I might have in mounting a response to the response is rendered irrelevant because most of Basil's comments concerned the first part of the original paper, that I cut from both the 2005 and final versions, and the

---

[23] http://www.ioe.ac.uk/ccs/dowling/kings1999/index.html
[24] http://homepage.mac.com/paulcdowling/ioe/publications/kings1999/index.html

comments about the part that remains, in modified form, do not persuade me to alter it. Indeed, it seems to me that they serve to underscore the contrast between our general approaches. With a single exception, therefore, I have decided to edit the final version of the main body of the paper for this book as if I had not read the response to the original version.

The single exception is in respect of the origins of the category, 'framing'. On the basis of my conversations with Basil, I had inferred that these rested with Goffman's use of the term. Basil's framing is clearly not the same as Goffman's, but they do resonate strongly with each other. In his response to my original paper, Basil points out that Goffman's *Frame Analysis* (1974) was published after his own first use of the term. This may or may not be telling. However, it was not a major point in my argument and I am content to let it lie; I have adjusted the chapter accordingly.

I have included this and the above two sections in this chapter as the place of departure for my journey through the inspirational work of Basil Bernstein to my own sociology as method. Their principal interest may appropriately lie less in their exposition of my own development than in what they may say about the relationship between one of the key figures in educational studies in the twentieth century and one of his students. Nevertheless, these sections serve my own purpose as well. In Chapter 3 I recruited Jerome McGann's term 'deformance' to catch at a fundamental aspect of my method: the point is not to dig into a text in order to uncover the true meaning that supposedly lies hidden within it (forensics), but to engage with it in order to present the text in a new light, to make new meaning. The same may be said of the way in which we approach our theoretical antecedents—our teachers. In this chapter I shall use the term 'heresy' to describe my engagement with Bernstein's work and, in Chapter 8, I will use the terms 'misreading' and 'misprision', making reference to Harold Bloom. There is a development in theoretical precision in the move from deformance through heresy to misreading/misprision. The first term seems to signal any kind of distortion— McGann, after all, illustrates his own deforming action by reference to random mutations of a digitised painting via the use of Photoshop filters. Heresy suggests a fundamental assault. Misprision refers more productively, I suppose, to the birthing of a new work and the necessary pain that this brings to its parent (and, indeed, to its author). The harsher 'heresy' will do for now. Basil himself spoke from the other side of heresy, using 'misrecognition' to frame his critics.

THE FRAMING OF PAUL DOWLING

Misrecognition

Misrecognition takes a few lines but its exposure takes many. In this detailed case study of misrecognition I shall, perforce, have to explicate what Harker and May (1993) have silenced. (Bernstein, 1996, p. 182)

Bernstein's use of the term 'misrecognition'—also used in the title of his chapter—is interesting. It presumably entails a challenge to Harker's and May's principles of recognition. Yet principles of recognition must always be tacit because to render them explicit would be to produce principles of realisation, in other words, to re-elaborate one's own discourse. In Bernstein's case, this would take very many lines indeed, but it cannot expose that which is tacit. Harker and May (1993) have certainly acted selectively and transformatively on Bernstein's writing, but this must be true of any commentary, including that of Bernstein himself in respect of his own work. The question is, simply, does he or does he not approve of the result. In the case of Harker's and May's critique, the answer would appear to be that he does not. Indeed, his disapproval was emphatically realised in the delight with which he received the desktop shredder containing the partially shredded copy of Harker's and May's article that my colleague, Andrew Brown, and I gave him on the event of his seventieth birthday. Each guest at his birthday party was individually treated to the witnessing of a few more millimetres of gleeful destruction. We were members of an alliance that deferred to Basil on the admission of new members. Nevertheless, we would still need to distinguish between, say, ironic and literal recognition so, to put the situation another way:

The unconscious is that part of the concrete discourse, in so far as it is transindividual, that is not at the disposal of the subject in re-establishing the continuity of his conscious discourse. (Lacan, 1977, p. 49)

Thus we might describe as the unconscious the regularity of the practice that is established in and that establishes the alliance, which is to say, the tacit principles of recognition of its own instances. Naturally, the alliance may be described at any level of analysis, so that, in particular, we may wish to replace Lacan's 'transindividual' with 'transsubjective' and interpret 'subjective' in the linguistic sense that allows us to regard human subjectivity as a multiplicity of identity avatars: the unconscious establishes and is established by the unity of the human subject as well as that of inter-individual alliances.

The accusation of misrecognition is a strategy that establishes not an alliance, but an opposition. In this chapter I am also seeking to establish an opposition in the creation of the basis for an alternative alliance. In a cryptically reflexive moment, Bernstein chooses different terms for this kind of move:

Independent of failures in their empirical power, all theories reach an inbuilt terminal stage when their conceptual power ceases to develop. This is when the generating tension of their language fails to develop more powerful sentences. I am inclined to believe this is when the possibilities of the initiating metaphor is [sic] exhausted. And some metaphors get exhausted sooner than others. At this stage of inner termination, defensive strategies are often employed: disguised repetition, concern with technicalities becomes a displacement strategy, omnipotence to preserve a position acts as a denial strategy, restricting the intellectual 'gene' pool by controlling disciples. This is only a temporary strategy as it leads eventually to the enlargement of the 'gene' pool through dissent (or treason?) (Bernstein, 2000, p. xiii)

This is the introduction that I referred to earlier and is cryptic to the extent that he might have been anticipating the eventual publication of some of the argument in this essay, which he had already seen in the paper that I sent him (Dowling, 1999a). In this earlier work I described as 'disciples' some of the recruiters of Bernstein's theory (and, as a result, upset at least one of them—obviously not a politically sound move from a position of relative weakness) and I used the term 'heresy' for my own engagement with him—a strategy that Donna Haraway (1991) reminds us is to be distinguished from apostasy (though I don't suppose that that was much consolation). I am, however, not wholly opposed to accepting the label 'treason,' but I'll replace it with treachery; I wouldn't want to nationalise him.

The particular form that my treachery will take will be to take three points of departure from his theory in order to work towards my own. In each case I shall arrive at, or at least pass through, my own (treacherous) interpretation of the category, recontextualisation; it was my early encounter with this term in reading Bernstein that inspired a great deal of what was to come.

Collapsing the walls

There is no point in beating about the bush, so I shall begin with the two fundamental Bernsteinian concepts of classification and framing: I make extensive use of a concept of classification, but rarely refer to framing.[25] Why is this?

The origins of these concepts contribute to the specialising of Bernstein's own heresy. Classification has its roots in the work of Émile Durkheim and both this category and framing seem to have emerged in the course of—which is not to say because of—a dialogue with Mary Douglas. I shall refer again to this dialogue in Chapter 8. In Bernstein's work, the two categories carry, respectively, the principles of power and control, which is to say:

> ... briefly, control establishes legitimate communications, and power establishes legitimate relations between categories. Thus, power constructs relations *between*, and control relations *within* given forms of interaction. (Bernstein, 1996, p. 19)

---

[25] In fact, I now use the term *institutionalisation*, though I originally retained 'classification'.

Within Bernstein's work, the concepts are associated with opposing sets of terms as illustrated in Figure 4.1.

Classification	Framing
power	control
space	time
between	within
what	how
voice	message
recognition rules	realisation rules

Figure 4.1. Classification and Framing

For example:

> Whereas the recognition rule arises out of distinguishing *between* contexts, the realization rule arises out of the specific requirements *within* a context. We know that the principle of the classification governs relations between contexts, and that the principle of the framing regulates the transmission of appropriate practice *within* a context. (*Ibid.*, p. 107)

Framing is defined as follows:

> Framing is about *who* controls *what*. What follows can be described as the *internal logic* of the pedagogic practice. Framing refers to the nature of the control over:
> - the selection of the communication;
> - its sequencing (what comes first, what comes second);
> - its pacing (the rate of expected acquisition);
> - the criteria; and
> - the control over the social base which makes this transmission possible.
>
> Where framing is strong, the transmitter has explicit control over selection, sequence, pacing, criteria and the social base. Where framing is weak, the acquirer has more *apparent* control (I want to stress apparent) over the communication and its social base. Note that it is possible for framing values—be they strong or weak—to vary with respect to the elements of the practice, so that, for example, you could have weak framing over pacing but strong framing over other aspects of the discourse. (*Ibid.* p. 27)

Consider an example, which is based on Mark Warschauer's (1999) observation of an English non-fiction writing course at an American university. Warschauer's interest was in the ways in which the teacher's and students' practices changed as the medium changed between face-to-face (f2f) and computer mediated communication (CMC). In particular, he found that the teacher tended to operate in a didactic lecturing mode in the f2f situation. CMC was described as more 'democratic', which is to say, the teacher intervened far less and with more open questions than in the f2f mode and it was the students rather than the teacher who apparently directed the discussions. Now in terms of the above definition, it would seem that the change in practice between the two modes constitutes a weakening of frame. Classification, however, has remained constant insofar as there has been no change in respect of the degree to which this class is to be distinguished from other classes. However, consider this statement by Bernstein:

> In the case of invisible pedagogic practice it is as if the pupil is the author of the practice and even the authority, whereas in the case of visible practices it clearly is the teacher who is author and authority. Further, classification would be strong in the case of visible forms but weak in the case of invisible forms. (Bernstein, 1996, p. 12)

Now the CMC mode looks very much like an invisible pedagogy, which here is described as exhibiting weak *classification* with no reference being made to framing. Elsewhere in Bernstein's book there is a virtual exclusion of the category 'framing' in favour of classification; I noted only a single instance of it in Chapter 3, for example.

The source of the confusion, for me, resides in the fact that, as Bernstein himself notes (p. 19), power and control and so classification and framing operate at different levels of analysis. A crucial feature of power relations, for Bernstein, is the construction of boundaries or insulation, thus:

> The distinction I will make here is crucial and fundamental to the whole analysis. In this formulation, power and control are analytically distinguished and operate at different levels of analysis. Empirically, we shall find that they are embedded in each other. Power relations, in this perspective, create boundaries, legitimize boundaries, reproduce boundaries, between different categories of groups, gender, class, race, different categories of discourse, different catefories of agents. Thus, power always operates to produce dislocations, to produce punctuations in social space.
> [...]
> But I want to argue that the crucial space which creates the specializations of the category—in this case the discourse—is not internal to that discourse but is the space between that discourse and another. In other words, A can only be A if it can effectively insulate itself from B. In this sense, there is no A if there is no relationship between A and something else. The meaning of A is only understandable in relation to other categories in the set; in fact, to all the categories in the set. In other words, it is the insulation between the categories of discourse which maintains the principles of their social division of labour. In other words, it is silence which carries the message of power; it

is the full stop between one category of discourse and another; it is the dislocation in the potential flow of discourse which is crucial to the specialization of any category. (*Ibid.*, pp. 19-20)

In the formulation of this argument in Dowling (1999a) I made reference to John F. Kennedy's speech at the Brandenburg Gate. This was the speech in which the President asserted that the proudest thing a man could say was 'I am a doughnut' (*'Ich bin ein Berliner'*—he should, of course, have said, simply, *'Ich bin Berliner'*). This was by way of introducing the Berlin Wall as a plausible example of a boundary and I had, indeed, taken a piece of the wall to the presentation as a visual aid ;-). Now the wall was certainly implicated in the establishing of distinct political regimes—implicated, but not imbricated. The substance of the wall is suitable for its purpose solely by virtue of its sharing of a predicate with that which it keeps apart. Specifically, the wall and the people on either side of it are mutually impervious. That is to say, in the constitution of a 'division of labour'—the differentiating of political regimes—the function of the wall is to assert a sameness, not a difference. The same, incidentally, is true in respect of insulation. The plastic material surrounding domestic electrical cable shares the predicate of 'electrical conductance' with bodies that it separates.[26] Again, the introduction of the boundary constitutes an assertion of sameness. To take a symbolic example, a full stop—or its spoken analogue, an intonational fall—again asserts that the same kind of grammatical object is (or is potentially, in the case of a termination) to be found on either side.[27]

To state the situation in terms of fundamental principles, a boundary is of necessity a moment in the precise region of a system in which it is constituted as a boundary. Classroom walls, then, create punctuations of space not curricular subjects. How do we move from a strongly classified physical space to a strongly classified curriculum? Not simply by labelling the doors—such labels are merely addresses and addresses are like boundaries insofar as they assert participation in the same system. A strongly classified curriculum is not in any sense predicated upon a strongly classified physical space, although the former may well recruit the latter in sustaining its classification, just as an existing political system recruited the Berlin wall in sustaining its classification.

Rather, the strongly classified curriculum is achieved by strategies that—at any given level of analysis—specialise the various contents. Specialising always takes place *within*; the *between* is always established in terms of intertextuality. Minimally, this may be established in terms of negativity: in mathematics we use symbols that are *not* used in geography, and so forth. Walls are, of course, no barriers to intertexuality.

---

[26] In this case, the insulation must have a low value of conductance in order to separate two bodies having high conductance. In this sense, insulation is a negative kind of wall.

[27] It would seem that this is a general rule for punctuation marks. Questions marks, for example, that appear to stand in breach of the rule are not, *qua* question marks, boundaries. That which follows a question mark may or may not be a question. What is asserted, however, is that it will be another sentence.

Bernstein is correct only to a very limited extent in claiming that what is classified may be realised in different ways, specifically, in different interactional modes. The CMC classroom is plausibly one in which very strong classification is realised.[28] Suppose, for example, that the teacher is completely silent, or 'lurks'. S/he can, nevertheless, review every contribution made by the student, which might then be graded according to highly specialised principles and pass lists subsequently published. The problem for the student, of course, would be gaining access to the principles. Arguably, this is not a pedagogic situation, in Bernstein's terms, because there is no transmission. The teacher may transform the situation into a pedagogic one by employing either weakly or strongly framed strategies— open questioning or lecturing, say. However, open questioning can remain open only insofar as the principles to be transmitted are weakly specialised or, rather, only in respect of those regions or aspects of the discourse that are weakly specialised. The panopticon (Foucault, 1977) might be construed as the archetype of weak framing.[29] However, as with the teacher-lurker in the CMC environment, this can work only where the prisoner already possesses the principles of evaluation of their behaviour and that would not be a pedagogic situation, in Bernstein's terms, because, again, it would entail no transmission. In terms of the construct introduced in Chapter 3, a *pedagogic relation* would not be in place because there is no mechanism whereby the author (teacher-lurker, warder in the tower) seeks to maintain control over principles of evaluation. The introduction of, say, a reward and/or punishment regime to complement the panopticon technology would establish pedagogic strategies—this is the technology of the road speed camera.

Essentially the situation is as follows. Where that which is classified is the privileged content (that which is to be transmitted) in a pedagogic situation, then the strength of framing of interactions must coincide with the strength of classification. Only where that which is classified is decoupled from this privileged content can classification and framing vary independently. An example of the latter would be, 'you can do anything you like so long as you do it in this room'. Strong classification/weak framing, yes, but only because they do not refer to each other.

The problem can be resolved once we recognise that it can be traced to Bernstein's original decoupling of space and time. Such decoupling is, of course, characteristic of various strands of structuralism and has been challenged in each of them; Derrida (1978) in respect of Saussure; Baudrillard (1993) in respect of Marx; Lacan (1977) in respect of Freud; Bourdieu (1977) in respect of Lévi-Strauss; and so forth. Bernstein and Piaget—the great educational structuralists—have remained substantially immune, to date (although see Dowling, 1996a, 1998, in respect of Piaget). Essentially, a space-time decoupling can be sustained only to the extent

---

[28] I have taught masters modules and other courses on CMC employing CMC as the pedagogic environment.

[29] Or, in a schooling context, Samuel Wilderspin's use of cherry trees in the playground (see Hunter, 1994; Dowling, 1998).

that we ignore a shuffling between levels of analysis and that we keep our distance from the empirical.[30]

A consequence of the resolution of the problem is that of the four concepts, power, control, classification and framing, three are redundant. I propose to retain a concept of classification and, in the construction of my own language, dispense with the other three. In my own language I use the term *institutionalisation* to refer to the extent to which a practice exhibits an empirical regularity that marks it out as recognisably distinct from other practices (or from a specific other practice). Thus, I propose that activities—say school mathematics—be construed as strategic spaces whereby subjects are positioned and practices distributed. In particular, specialising strategies constitute practices that are strongly institutionalised with respect to those of other activities. Pedagogic action must entail the transmission or attempted transmission of these specialised practices. In order to achieve this, the transmitter must constitute a discourse that is accessible to the acquirer. This in turn is achieved when the transmitter—as a subject of the activity in question, say mathematics—casts a gaze beyond mathematics and recontextualises non-mathematical practice so that it conforms to the principles of specialised mathematical practice. Recontextualising is achieved by localising strategies, thus, the purchase of a loaf of bread in a supermarket becomes a local instance of specialised arithmetic.[31]

The effect of these strategies is to constitute a region of school mathematical practice that is weakly institutionalised with respect to the non-mathematical. This is the *public domain,* which contrasts with the *esoteric domain* that comprises practices that are strongly institutionalised with respect to the non-mathematical.[32] I shall move on to a consideration of my recontextualising of recontextualisation in Bernstein in the next section of this essay.

Recontextualising recontextualisation

It is of course obvious that all pedagogic discourse creates a moral regulation of the social relations of transmission/acquisition, that is, rules of order, relation, and identity; and that such a moral order is prior to, and a condition for, the transmission of competences. This moral order is in turn subject to a recontextualising principle, and thus this order is a signifier for *something other than itself.* (Bernstein, 1990, p. 184)

---

[30] This issue of space-time decoupling will also come up in Chapter 8.

[31] In another context, the purchase of a loaf of bread might become the localised instance of specialised domestic science and would be recontextualised to quite different effect.

[32] In Dowling (1998 and elsewhere) I measure strength of classification (now to be re-termed, institutionalisation) in respect of content and expression separately, thus generating a two dimensional space. The esoteric and public domains refer to those regions for which content and expression are both strong or both weak, respectively. The other two possibilities give rise to the descriptive and expressive domains. The full schema is presented in Chapter 8.

My concept of 'recontextualisation' is also heretical in respect of Bernstein's work. Bernstein's use of the term refers to the creation of imaginary discourses from real discourses according to the 'recontextualising principle' that is 'pedagogic discourse' via the embedding of an 'instructional discourse' in a 'regulative discourse'. Instructional discourse refers to specialised skills and regulative discourse to a moral order. By way of examples, Bernstein offers the recontextualising of carpentry—a 'real discourse'—as 'woodwork'—an 'imaginary discourse' and the recontextualising of university physics as school physics. My concern is that Bernstein's theorising is constituting, for me, an unnecessary priority and not a little confusion. In order to demonstrate this, I shall need to work towards Bernstein's higher-level concept, the pedagogic device. My point of departure is the above extract, which is from *Class, Codes and Control volume 4*.

The mode of expression has been modified in the revised version of this chapter (see Bernstein, 1996, c. 3)—it is, apparently, no longer quite as 'obvious'. The theoretical formulation is retained, however, and the regulative (moral) discourse remains 'the dominant discourse' (Bernstein, 1996, p. 46) *vis-à-vis* the discourse concerned with the transmission of competences (the instructional discourse). However, in the 1996 version, the distinction between regulative and instructional discourse is analytic or, perhaps, ideological:

> In my opinion, there is only one discourse, not two, because the secret voice of [the pedagogic] device is to disguise the fact that there is only one. Most researchers are continually studying the two, or thinking as if there are two: as if education is about values on the one hand, and about competence on the other. In my view there are not two discourses, there is only one. (Bernstein, 1996, p. 46)

There is only one, yet one of them is dominant. A little further on:

> ... *pedagogic discourse is a recontextualizing principle*. Pedagogic discourse is constructed by a recontextualizing principle which selectively appropriates, relocates, refocuses and relates other discourses to constitute its own order. In this sense, pedagogic discourse can never be identified with any of the discourses it has recontextualised.
>
> We can now say that pedagogic discourse is generated by a recontextualizing discourse [...]. The recontextualizing principle creates recontextualizing fields, it creates agents with recontextualizing functions. These recontextualising functions then become the means whereby a specific pedagogic discourse is created. (*Ibid.*, pp. 47-48)

The apparent confusion here is, so far as I can determine, the result of a failure by Bernstein to use key terms consistently and to invent neologisms when *and only when* they are needed.

Bernstein is clearer when providing an example.

... the authors of textbooks in physics are rarely physicists who are practising in the field of the production of physics; they are working in the field of recontextualization.

As physics is appropriated by the recontextualizing agents, the results cannot formally be derived from the logic of that discourse. Irrespective of the intrinsic logic which constitutes the specialized discourse and activities called physics, the recontextualizing agents will select from the totality of practices which is called physics in the field of production of physics. There is selection in how physics is to be related to other subjects, and in its sequencing and pacing (pacing is the rate of expected acquisition). But these sections cannot be derived from the logic of the discourse of physics or its various activities in the field of the production of discourse. (*Ibid.*, pp. 48-49)

Bernstein may well be correct in his claim that school physics textbook authors are not generally practising physicists. However, this rather misses the point. The authors of university physics textbooks generally are practising physicists, yet there are many important differences between university textbooks and, say, research papers (see Myers, 1992, also Dowling, 1998). The downplaying of the relevance of the logic of the discourse of physics in its recontextualised form is also open to some challenge. In an associated field, for example, the development of the 'modern' school mathematics in the nineteen fifties and sixties was heavily influenced by the Bourbakiist principle of mother structures (see Dowling, 1989, 1998, 2007; Dowling & Brown, 2006; Moon, 1986 and also Chapter 6 of the present work). It is also questionable whether the 'field of production' is the only or even the dominant object of the gazes of recontextualising agents. The nature of integral calculus in advanced level mathematics, for example, certainly attests to this: at high school students seemingly endlessly practice integration by standard methods only to discover that the university mathematics department finds little interest in any function that is integrable. I shall refer to this example again later.

Essentially, Bernstein is making empirical claims and providing quasi-empirical illustrations in order to bolster his theoretical apparatus. The productivity of the more esoteric regions of this apparatus is difficult to imagine. In an earlier formulation, the instrumental and expressive orders constituted schemes through which the school might be and indeed was analysed (see King, 1976—an analysis critical of Bernstein—and its criticism in Tyler, 1978; also Power *et al*, 1998). Now 'there is only one discourse'.

Jean Lave and Etienne Wenger agree that school physics is very different from university physics. They suggest that the decoupling may be even greater than Bernstein seems to imply:

... in most schools there is a group of students engaged over a substantial period of time in learning physics. What community of practice is in the process of reproduction? Possibly the students participate only in the reproduction of the high school itself. (Lave & Wenger, 1991, p. 99)

In my conception, the school as a site is to be conceived as a moment of a sociocultural system (Baudrillard, not Parsons). In terms of interaction, all such sites are characterised by a specific form of articulation of the two modes of social action that I specified in Chapter 3. *Pedagogic* action constructs an author, an audience, and a privileged content in respect of which the principles of evaluation of texts or performances resides with the author. In *exchange* action the principles of evaluation are located with the audience. We might say that strongly classified—or formally institutionalised—content is likely to be elaborated under pedagogic relations; weakly classified—or informally institutionalised—content is likely to be elaborated under exchange relations. The distribution of these relations constitutes or, at least contributes to differentiation within the school.[33]

I have now made tacit reference to all three dimensions of Bernstein's pedagogic device: distribution, recontextualisation, and evaluation. The device—presumably, the 'something other than itself' for which pedagogic discourse is a signifier—is a somewhat heretical recontextualising of Chomsky's language acquisition device, with Bernstein explicitly adopting a Hallidayan rather than a Chomskian methodology (no problem here, of course). Bernstein argues:

> Both the language device and the pedagogic device become sites for appropriation, conflict and control. At the same time, there is a crucial difference between the two devices. In the case of the pedagogic device, but not in the case of the language device, it is possible to have an outcome, a form of communication which can subvert the fundamental rules of the device. (Bernstein, 1996, p. 42)

But, of course, these devices cannot become sites for any such thing. They are not, in fact, sites at all because they are not, ultimately, empirically operationalisable. The pedagogic device is a very high level theoretical object and we must descend through multiple layers of theory before we ever get to something that we might validly refer to an empirical text. The pedagogic device is a part of Bernstein's 'internal language':

> Briefly, a language of description is a translation device whereby one language is transformed into another. We can distinguish between internal and external languages of description. The internal language of description refers to the syntax whereby a conceptual language is created. The external

---

[33] Some elaboration is needed here. Pedagogic and exchange action are not to be interpreted as achievements—a teacher (author) may fail dismally in their attempts to teach (tell me about it!) Rather, they are strategic actions. In the pedagogic mode, the audience's performance may be evaluated according to visible pedagogic content. In exchange mode, performance may be evaluated in the same way, but the underlying evaluative principles are invisible (cf. 'invisible pedagogy' in Bernstein, 1977) and this gives rise to a potential contrast between the audience performance—which the audience themselves may evaluate—and their competence as assessed by the author. A visible rendition of the latter situation (though in a perhaps confusingly different language) is a school report in which a student is graded 'A' for effort and 'E' for achievement; a not altogether uncommon finding in my own experience as a school teacher.

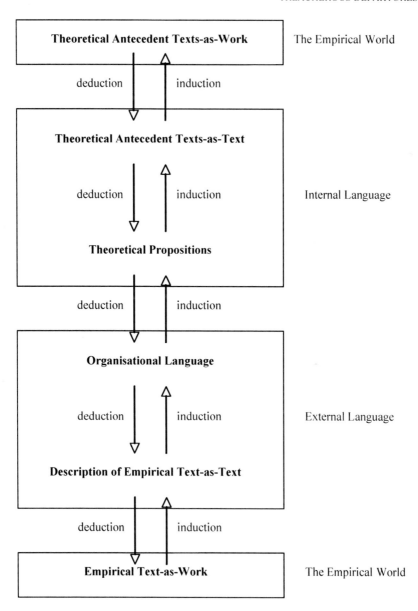

Figure 4.2. Schema for Constructive Description

> language of description refers to the syntax whereby the internal language
> can describe something other than itself. (Bernstein, 1996, pp. 135-136)

Bernstein's own work has a strong tendency to reside in the internal—I shall again make reference to this in Chapter 8. It is left to others to generate external languages. By and large, these tend to be very thin, commonly making reference to boundaries and insulation and so forth, which often carry serious theoretical problems (see Dowling, 1999a).

My formulation of my own general methodology—*constructive description*—is illustrated in Figure 4.2. This schema conceives the empirical world as being divided by the analyst to constitute theoretical and empirical texts. The nature of this division is institutionalised only up to a point. In particular, there seems to be a greater limitation on what might count as a theoretical text than there is on what might be taken as an empirical text. Thus, as will be discussed in Chapter 8, Rob Moore and Karl Maton (2001) take (not without problems) a work of literary studies by Frank Kermode (1967) as a key empirical object. Under other circumstances, such a work might well form part of the theoretical field. It is unlikely, however, that the empirical texts described in Chapters 2 and 3— agricultural settings, photographs and paintings, movies, monuments—would be considered legitimate theoretical texts, certainly not in sociology, though one might imagine some interesting developments upon making such a move.

The distinction, in Figure 4.2, between text(s)-as-work and text(s)-as-text (introduced in Chapter 2) is from Roland Barthes (1981). Essentially, the text-as-work is a purely imaginary category referring to the book on the library shelf or the potential view from the bus window etc prior to being noticed. Once the text has been noticed, theorising has begun on the basis of more or less explicit theoretical propositions or a more or less explicit organisational language. To put this in another way, 'only theoretical objects may be discovered; an empirical object is merely encountered' (Dowling 2007, p. 191fn.). Figure 4.2 also distinguishes between deduction and induction such that the former refers to moves from the theoretical side of the division to the empirical and the latter to moves in the opposite direction. This suggests something about the nature of the original division that is consistent with the tendency for paintings and movies etc to be restricted to the empirical side—deduction seems to require language. I shall introduce the term *discursive saturation*, below, to formalise this distinction.

The two central boxes in Figure 4.2 seem to approximate to that, which in Bernstein's formulation, are the internal and external languages of description. It is important to note that the principal theoretical and empirical achievement—such as it is—of my work takes place in the area signified by the box corresponding to Bernstein's external language. That is, at the point of interface between the theoretical and the empirical. Bernstein seems to want to produce a theoretical system that is a model of what might metaphorically be described as the consciousness of society. My own project is rather less ambitious. I am simply trying to manufacture a machine that will help me to organise what I see. In order to move between levels of analysis—say between the analysis of a conversation and the analysis of school practices (move 1) and the analysis of state policy (move 2), and so forth, I simply reapply the same conceptual framework, generating indicators that are appropriate to the new level. The method has, in this respect, the fractal quality that I mentioned in Chapter 2. Recontextualisation, in my language, is far more generalisable than it would appear to be in Bernstein's. I define it as the subordination of the practices of one activity to the principles of another. It is precisely the empirical analysis of the productivity of recontextualisation that enables the constructive description of the recontextualising activity.

The categories, classification and framing also exhibit a fractal quality. Their disadvantage lies, as I have argued, in that they do not themselves occupy the same level of analysis. A good deal of Bernstein's theory (and here he is certainly not alone) is fixed in terms of its referent level. It may be that this is associated with his preference, following Halliday, for network analysis. This is an approach that fixes levels of analysis in relation to each other as one moves between levels of the network. I would describe a network as an analysis that has been terminated at a stage prior to the full development of theory. Bernstein has similar reservations about ideal types:

> Classically the ideal type is constructed by assembling in a model *a number of features* abstracted from a phenomenon in such a way as to provide a means of identifying the presence or absence of the phenomenon, and a means of identifying the 'workings' of the phenomenon from an analysis of the assembly of its features. Ideal types constructed in this way cannot generate other than themselves. They are not constructed by a principle which generates sets of relations of which any one form may be only *one of the forms* the principle may regulate. (Bernstein, 1996, pp. 126-127)

My feeling is that it is inappropriate to crystallise a method in this way. In Chapter 1, I presented the game, Mastermind as an ideal type for scientific investigation and, in Chapter 3, I explicitly described my own organisational language as employing ideal types. However, my approach is to make a group of modes conceptually coherent to the point that they participate in the same theoretical system. *Pedagogic* and *exchange* actions constitute a case in point: they are defined in relation to each other in terms of the variable, 'location of the principles of evaluation'. The application of an empirically driven network analysis does not encourage theorising to this level; the development of a theoretically driven network does not encourage empirical operationalisation, or productive dialogue between the theoretical and the empirical—more of this in Chapter 8.

Vertigo and verticality

Bernstein's networks are commonly theoretically driven, hence his resistance to the accusation of having produced ideal types. The empirical is not absent in his theory building, but appears, shall we say, hazily. His description of vertical and horizontal discourses is illustrative. The network (Figure 4.3) is beautifully clear in terms of its oppositions: vertical/horizontal, between/within, strong/weak, explicit/tacit. The difficulty arises when we try to assign empirical instances to locations in the network. There are two modes of vertical discourse:

A vertical discourse takes the form of a coherent, explicit, systematically principled structure, hierarchically organized, *or* it takes the form of a series of specialized languages with specialized modes of interrogation and specialized criteria for the production of texts. (*Ibid.*, p. 171)

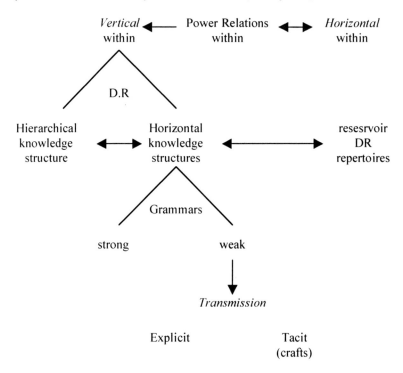

Figure 4.3. Bernstein's Discursive Map (from Bernstein, 1996, p. 175)

The natural sciences are offered as characterised by the former mode (hierarchical knowledge structure) and the humanities and social sciences by the latter (horizontal knowledge structures). Now my question is, where does the essential quality of the knowledge reside? Is it in the day-to-day working practices of practitioners, or in the structure of learned journals, in the lexicon of specialised terms, in the activities of research funding agencies, in models of apprenticeship of new practitioners? I could continue. Having some experience of higher education in both the natural and social sciences, my suspicion is that any discipline will exhibit variations in terms of horizontality and hierarchising as we shift attention between these and other contexts. In any event, both Bernstein's original claim and my suspicion raise empirical questions that remain to be addressed.

Bernstein's descriptions of knowledge structures came at the very end of his career. However, it seems clear that their origins lie in his very earliest work on speech codes and orientations to meaning. Ruqaiya Hasan presents in sociolinguistic terms the problem of inequality of access in schooling, which was Bernstein's concern.

> ... in the everyday register repertoire of the dominating classes, there are some discourse types which are much closer to the social domains introduced in the pedagogic system. This prepares children from the dominating classes to receive the discourses of educational knowledge with much greater readiness. In addition to this, the semantic orientation of the dominant classes is congruent with the required semantic orientation for the (re-) production of 'exotic,' uncommonsense knowledge. The discourses of education, thus, present little or no threat to the habitual ways of meaning and saying which children from the dominant classes bring to the school. (Hasan, 1999, pp. 72-73)

The problem being that the same cannot be said of the ways of meaning and saying that the children from the subaltern classes bring to the school. This was a problem for teachers which, a quarter of a century earlier, Bernstein had famously framed as follows:

> If the culture of the teacher is to become part of the consciousness of the child, then the culture of the child must first be in the consciousness of the teacher. (Bernstein, 1971, p. 199)

Driving home his critique of so-called 'compensatory education', Bernstein followed this aphorism with:

> It is an accepted educational principle that we should work with what the child can offer: why don't we practise it? The introduction of the child to the universalistic meanings of public forms of thought is not compensatory education—*it is education.* (*Ibid.*)

In another chapter in the same collection, Bernstein elaborates on what he means by 'universalistic meanings':

> ... we might be able to distinguish between two orders of meaning. One we would call universalistic, the other particularistic. Universalistic meanings are those in which principles and operations are made linguistically explicit, whereas particularistic orders of meaning are meanings in which principles and operation are relatively linguistically implicit. If orders of meaning are universalistic, then the meanings are less tied to a given context. The meta-languages of public forms of thought as these apply to objects and persons realize meanings of a universalistic type. (*Ibid.*, p. 175)

The culturally acquired orientations towards speech variants realising, respectively, universalistic and particularistic meanings are the well known *elaborated* and *restricted codes.* Bernstein introduces various examples of these speech variants, some taken from empirical work conducted by himself or colleagues and some that seem to be imaginary. One example 'constructed' by a colleague, Peter Hawkins, 'as a result of his analysis of the speech of middle-class and working-class five-year old children' (*Ibid.*, p. 178) involves two short stories. The children in Hawkins' research had been shown a series of pictures showing, firstly, boys playing football, then the ball going through a window, a woman looking out of the window and, finally, a man making 'an ominous gesture' (*Ibid.*, p. 178). The two stories are as follows:

1. Three boys are playing football and one boy kicks the ball and it goes through the window the ball breaks the window and the boys are looking at it and a man comes out and shouts at them so they run away and then that lady looks out of her window and she tells the boys off.
2. They're playing football and he kicks it and it goes through there it breaks the window and they're looking at it and he comes out and shouts at them because they've broken it so they run away and then she looks out and she tells them off. (*Ibid.*, p. 178)

The use of 'constructed' or imaginary illustrations is quite common in Bernstein's work. Another example appears in his analysis of knowledge structures:

> With this definition in mind, I wish to consider a fictitious community operating only with horizontal discourse. (Bernstein, 1999, p. 159)

This approach to the empirical sometimes raises problems, as I shall argue later. It is not entirely clear why, in the footballers case, he chooses not to introduce two stories that were actually produced by children participating in the research. Nevertheless, the manufactured stories do adequately illustrate his categories. Essentially, whereas the second story makes frequent direct references to the pictures, the first does so only once ('that lady'). Bernstein argues that the reader of the first story does not need to have access to the pictures because the meanings are made explicit and are universalistic, whereas the reader of the second story does need the pictures because meanings are implicit and particularistic. I shall return to these stories later. For the moment, though, I want to outline—in very general terms—Bernstein's argument in relation to social class, codes and schooling.

Firstly, and although the relationship is not simple or by any means determinate, Bernstein claims that the tendency is for primary socialisation in working class families to privilege restricted codes and therefore orientation to particularistic meanings and for that in middle class families to provide greater access to elaborated codes and therefore orientation to universalistic meanings; as Bernstein summarises: 'One of the effects of the class system is to limit access to elaborated codes' (Bernstein, 1971, p. 176).[34] Secondly, Bernstein argues that the potential for

---

[34]   Collins (2000) also raises the question of the gendering of coding orientations.

change in the principles of a practice and of reflexivity in respect of the bases of socialisation is greater in the case of elaborated than restricted codes:

> Elaborated codes are less tied to a given or local structure and thus contain the potentiality of change in principles. In the case of elaborated codes the speech can be freed from its evoking social structure and it can take on an autonomy. A university is a place organized around talk. Restricted codes are more tied to a local social structure and have a reduced potential for change in principles. Where codes are elaborated, the socialized has more access to the grounds of his [sic] own socialization, and so can enter into a reflexive relationship to the social order he has taken over. Where codes are restricted, the socialized has less access to the grounds of his socialization and thus reflexiveness may be limited in range. (Bernstein, 1971, p.176)

How often do we hear academics insisting on the material effectiveness of their own ideology?

Thirdly, Bernstein contends that because schooling is oriented towards the 'universalistic meanings of public forms of thought', schools that are not adequately geared to the introduction of these universalistic meanings to children having limited access to elaborated codes are likely to induce failure in these children, thus:

> What is made available for learning through elaborated and restricted codes is radically different. Social and intellectual orientations, motivational imperative and forms of social control, rebellion and innovation are different. Thus the relative backwardness of many working-class children who live in areas of high population density or in rural areas may well be a culturally induced backwardness transmitted by the linguistic process. Such children's low performance on verbal IQ tests, their difficulty with 'abstract' concepts, their failures within the language area, their general inability to profit from the school, all may result from the limitations of a restricted code. (Bernstein, 1971, p. 151)

Now I should emphasise that Bernstein's theory is highly complex and develops within each of his major books—all of which are collections of papers originally written separately—and between them (Bernstein, 1971, 1977, 1990, 1996, 2000). I have, of necessity, had to simplify here. It is also important to mention that there is a great deal of empirical work that is associated with this early sociolinguistic theory and with his later work.[35] Nevertheless, it is possible, on the basis of what I have been able to introduce, here to raise some critical issues, which do, I believe, have more general validity.

Firstly, referring back to the two stories about the footballers, not only is it a dubious claim that most readers of the second story would need access to the

---

[35] For example, see Adlam (1977), Bernstein (1973), Bernstein *et al* (2001), as well as the references in Bernstein's own writing.

pictures (or descriptions of them) in order to make sense of the story, but the first story is perhaps better described as vague rather than universalistic. It is not clear how we might interpret it unless we have further information about the context of its telling: is it a report of an experience, an interpretation of a scene, an academic example, etc? Precisely what would one be able to conclude about what was going on upon overhearing just this amount of the conversation? Bernstein is able to refer to the first story as more universalistic than the second only because he has prioritised specifically linguistic markers of context of which there are more in the second story than the first. The teller of the first story can produce such a vague utterance only because their audience shares the immediate context. On overhearing the second story, I would suggest, one would actually have more clues to enable one to make sense of the situation. This is not to deny the kind of distinction that Bernstein is making—it is a crucial one, as I shall argue later. However, my intention is to challenge, heretically, his interpretation of the nature of the difference.

In their work with American teenagers from upper and middle class backgrounds, Gee, Allen and Clinton (2001) find that, indeed, teenagers do use different styles of language to 'fashion themselves' with respect to quite distinct worlds:

> The working class teens ... use language to fashion their identities in a way that is closely attached to a world of 'everyday' ('lifeworld') social and dialogic interaction .... The upper middle class teens ... use language to construct their identities in a way that detaches itself from 'everyday' social interaction and orients more towards their personal biographical trajectories through an 'achievement space' defined by the (deeply aligned) norms of their families, schools, and powerful institutions in our society. In addition, the upper middle class teens often seem to use the abstract language of rational argumentation to 'cloak' (o[r] 'defer') their quite personal interests and fears, while the working class teens much more commonly use a personalized narrative language to encode their values, interests, and themes. (Gee *et al*, 2001, p. 177)

As the authors recognise, it would be easy to apply the labels of elaborated and restricted code to these two forms. However, they argue that this would be to fail to recognise that each style is highly dependent upon interpretive frames that are generated by their specific and material life conditions. Furthermore, they claim that neither group seems able to reflect consistently or critically about society. Neither group, in other words, seems able to generate the kind of reflexivity for which Bernstein sees potential in elaborated codes.[36]

---

[36] Cheshire describes differentiation in narratives recounted in peer groups by young teenagers. She concludes that 'for the boys the telling was the more salient aspect of a narrative whereas for the girls it was the tale' (Cheshire, 2000, p. 258). Like Gee *et al* she grounds the differentiation in a social base, in this case in the gendered patterning of peer relations.

Put another way, Bernstein's suggestion that 'a university is a place organised around talk' is stunningly asociological in its apparent ignoring of the patterns of social relations that enable meaning to be attributed to university talk as discourses and as strategies in the establishing, maintenance and dismantling of the alliances and oppositions that constitute these relations. As Pierre Bourdieu (1991) has argued, the power of language comes from outside of it; Bernstein was handed the authorising skeptron of an academic chair rather early in his career. Even so, he should have known better, being a master player of the power game himself. Here is part of one of his footnoted references to me; as someone he considers, no doubt quite rightly, to be a junior player, I can only ever aspire to footnoted appearances:

> [Dowling] shows successfully how the texts constructed for these 'ability levels' incorporate, differentially fictional contexts and activities drawn from the Public Domain in the classification and framing of mathematical problems ... (Bernstein, 1999, p. 170)

In my work I have explicitly rejected the concept of 'framing'—a fact of which he was certainly aware. Here I am, nevertheless, being installed as a faithful Bernsteinian.[37]

Bernstein's early work on speech codes and his mature work on knowledge structures fail, in my heretical view, by fetishising different domains of cultural practice. The speech codes work detaches the linguistic from the social by dealing hastily (or not at all) with the empirical observation of linguistic production. The characterising of knowledge structures does much the same thing in fetishising knowledge or ideas—more of this in Chapter 8. A neat link is found in the reference to the university as 'a place organised around talk', a claim that was uttered in the earlier phase. It is worthy of mention, in passing, that Bernstein's characterisation does indeed seem consistent with Ludwik Fleck's (1981) 'thought collectives', but that hardly addresses my criticism. Bernstein wants to catch at the real, but attempts to do so by ignoring the phenomenal forms that, in his own methodology, might enable his real to speak to him. As I have indicated here and in earlier chapters, I have no interest in fabricating a subjacent real. But my constructions must at least in part derive from a preliminary organising of the kinds of phenomena that I am designing them to structure. Ultimately, these must include the micro-actions relating to the formation, maintenance and destabilising of oppositions and alliances upon which social structure and cultural practice are to be seen as emergent.

Nevertheless, the kind of distinction that Bernstein is making is, as I suggested above, potentially highly productive. Drawing on this and on a whole set of other attempts at establishing roughly corresponding oppositions (see Figure 4.4), I have formulated a distinction between two strategic modes—as distinct, of course, from knowledge forms and from orientations to universal or local meaning. Actions,

---

[37] In this extract, Bernstein also presents a misrepresentation of my category, *public domain*. This term refers to already recontextualised practice—shopping under the gaze of school mathematics, not shopping as such—see below and Chapter 8.

then, can be considered in terms of the extent to which they tend to realise the principles of an activity in discursive form. Texts that exhibit this feature are said to exhibit a high *discursive saturation* (DS$^+$). On the other hand, texts that tend to render the principles in non-discursive form are described as low discursive saturation (DS$^-$). Incorporating this variable in the system that I have been

Author	Abstract Context-independent Generalisation DS$^+$	Concrete Context-dependent Localisation DS$^-$
Bernstein	elaborated code	restricted code
	vertical discourse	horizontal discourse
Bourdieu	formal/theoretical logic	practical logic
De Certeau	strategies	tactics
Foucault	programmes	technologies
Freud	ego	id
Lévi-Strauss	science	bricolage
Lévy-Bruhl	modern thinking	primitive thinking
Lotman	rule-governed practice	repertoire of exemplary texts
Luria	abstract thinking	situational thinking
Piaget	sociocentrism/egocentrism	technique/sensori-motor
	science/reflective thought	
Sohn-Rethel	intellectual	manual
Vygotsky	conceptual thinking	complex thinking
Walkerdine	formal reasoning	practical reasoning

Figure 4.4. The Dual Modality of Practice[38]

---

[38] The table refers to the following work: Bernstein (1977); Bourdieu (1977, 1990); De Certeau (1984); Eco (1976, regarding Lotman); Foucault (1980); Freud (1973); Lévi-Strauss (1972); Luria (1976, and regarding Lévy-Bruhl); Piaget (1995); Sohn-Rethel (1973, 1975, 1978); Vygotsky (1978, 1986); Walkerdine (1982).

developing in this book, I produce the practical strategic space shown in Figure 4.5. The distinction between specialising and generalising corresponds to that between localising and articulating; the former category in each pair operates to delimit the range of application of the practice, whilst the latter extends it.

| | Institutionalisation | | Pedagogic Strategies | Non-Arbitrary Pedagogic Resource |
	Formal (I^+)	Informal (I^-)		
DS^+	*discourse*	*idiolect*	Specialising	Principles
			Generalising	
DS^-	*skill* (competence)	*trick* (performance)	Localising	Exemplars
			Articulating	
	Pedagogic	Exchange		
	(Re)producing Activity			

Figure 4.5. Practical Strategic Space

I want to raise the claim that my approach facilitates both theoretical development and the analysis of empirical technologies, texts and sites. In order to do this I shall illustrate the application of the practical strategic space by quite briefly telling the stories of two educational activities of which I have quite extensive professional and academic experience. Firstly, I shall consider the teaching of educational research methods and methodology at postgraduate level, including the supervision of doctoral students. Here, I will draw on my experience as the student of Basil Bernstein as well as that as a teacher and supervisor, myself, and as an author, both of research papers and of texts directly addressing research methods (for example, Brown & Dowling, 1998; Dowling & Brown, forthcoming; Brown, Bryman & Dowling, forthcoming). Secondly, I shall focus on the teaching of mathematics at secondary education level. My own student experience in this area is rather too far in the past to be reliably recalled, but I do have fifteen years experience as a professional teacher of mathematics followed by several further years in initial teacher education and have published research in the field of mathematics education (in particular, Dowling, 1998, but also see Chapter 6 in the present volume). The insertion of this brief *curriculum vitae* is intended, of course, to establish one foot in the empirical or phenomenal textual graveyard (texts-as-work/texts-as-texts). To plant both feet would be to submit, I think, to naïve empiricism, an alternative to the theoreticism of the dematerialised soul. Nevertheless, I should confess to being, here, not quite as close to the empirical as I would like; in its formulation, analysis should allow the phenomenal text voice if it is itself to speak (even if only transiently) about something other than itself, if it is to learn (a tenet frequently uttered, though less frequently followed by my former mentor).

THE FRAMING OF RESEARCH METHODS

Those of us whose authority often rests, in traditional mode, on an attributed facility with academic research may tend to represent it as exhibiting a strongly institutionalised, DS^+ form. In the terms of Figure 4.5, this would be to deploy a strategy of *discourse*. This is certainly the mode of much of the presentation of my written work on methodology and, indeed, in most other written work that I have come across. Approaches to data collection and so forth are marked out (*specialised*) and brought under a single logic (*generalised*). Terms are defined in the production of a self-referential *esoteric domain* that is taken to be research methodological knowledge. Elements of this 'knowledge' are then recruited in the writing-up and presentation of research reports and papers, research questions are (usually) clearly stated, research designs and sampling strategies are clearly identified, and measures of validity and reliability offered. In terms of its public face, research methodology—whether quantitative or qualitative in emphasis—is generally presented as highly principled and strongly regulated—indeed, to allow any weakening of the institutionalisation of methodology would be to weaken the authority of the author. Clearly, the reproduction of the *discourse*—the teacher-student encounter—is *pedagogic*.

But the principles that are laid out in research methods texts do not generally operationalise all that readily. The first inkling of this that occurs to the teacher is in the appraisal of students' coursework. The apparent acquisition of the methodological 'knowledge' does not, in itself, facilitate the production of an acceptable review of a research paper.[39] The notion of an academic argument, for example, is implicit in the system of methodology and is strongly institutionalised, which is to say, the teacher can readily recognise when an adequate argument is presented and when one is not. For example, there is, in my experience, generally a high probability of agreement between teachers; my co-markers and I rarely disagree on initial marking of more than ten percent of coursework and then almost always only by a single grade or inflection and our disparities are quickly resolved (one way or the other) in discussion. Yet, whilst the students can generally formulate and commonly deploy the definitions of methodological terms, the production of an argument in a review seems far more tricky and unreliable. This is because, as I have suggested earlier, the principles of recognition of an academic argument are largely tacit and there are no—arguably, there can be no—explicit principles of realisation. The approach to be adopted by the teacher, here—again pedagogic—is likely to be the deployment of *localising* and *articulating* instances of *skill*, most effectively, perhaps, through the presentation of *exemplars* of recognised good practice. But the focus, here, tends not to be on the specific

---

[39] The production of a critical review of a research paper is the main component of the coursework for an MA module in research methods that I am associated with at the Institute of Education.

instance of skill, but rather on the development of a generalisable *competence* on the part of the student precisely because the practice—the visible form of the skill—is strongly institutionalised.

The esoteric domain of research methodology and the recognition and realisation of academic arguments together constitute the strongly institutionalised, visible face of research. Much of the doing of research, however, is not visible and so less likely to be strongly institutionalised; strong institutionalisation would have to depend upon a strongly maintained (but largely unpoliceable) ethic or collective conscience. It will be apparent that from my general methodological perspective, a collective conscience must stand as the projected construct of the commentator rather than as a generative structure; projections onto private domains are mere mythologisings. Just how does one go about analysing hundreds of pages of interview transcripts or fieldnotes? Well, the supervisor of one's thesis can help, again via the production and articulating of local instances of analytic skill, though they can't do it all.[40] Precisely because of the privatised and, indeed, individualised nature of the task, the emphasis must be placed on the *performance* rather than on any underlying competence. The latter, of course, is to be rendered accessible by assessment practices that may find their way into the *viva voce* examination (or may not; in the UK the viva is itself still a pretty private affair). But here we have moved back to the public face of research methods, insofar as the thesis itself is publicly accessible. Insofar as the actual enactment of analysis—the deployment of *tricks*—tends to be private, its performances are achieved in *exchange* mode.

Now presenting one's work generally entails some kind of claim to originality. There are, of course, numerous ways in which this might be attempted, but they will all involve territorialising in respect of one or more of the three aspects: theory, methodology and empirical setting. The marking out of a specific empirical setting on the basis of opportunity—a common feature of work carried out for masters dissertations—involves a localising strategy that lays claim to originality in respect of a specific trick, which is to say, the performance of this particular legitimate access. This is my strategy here in making reference to my experience as a teacher and student of research methods in establishing the empirical setting for these remarks. I might, of course, have deployed some of the discourse of research methods in introducing specific illustrations pointing, for example, to my sampling strategy (why this particular example) and I may feel inclined to introduce some discussion of research ethics in justifying the use of data deriving from my professional teaching activities, but I have chosen not to do so here. Where originality is claimed in terms of the development of new methods or new theory, then it is likely—certain, in the latter case—to be necessary to produce an analogue of principled discourse that is, by very virtue of its originality, weakly institutionalised. Indeed, the institutionalisation may be limited to the singular instantiation of the methodology or theory. This would be an *idiolect* strategy. Insofar as my own theoretical and methodological constructions have been

---

[40] Especially if, as is commonly the case at the Institute of Education, the data is in a language spoken by the student, but not the supervisor.

published and cited elsewhere, I may claim to a degree of institutionalisation that aspires to discourse. The reader may care to consider whether terms such as 'elaborated description', 'epistemological paradox' and the specific definitions of 'localising' and 'generalising' that originated (as far as I am aware) in *Doing Research/Reading Research* (Brown & Dowling, 1998) are appropriately construed as discourse or idiolect. New theory and methodology, then, is idiolectical unless and until it becomes institutionalised within the esoteric domain of the academic field in which it participates. Until that time, it must accept the imposition of audience principles in respect of its evaluation; its reproduction, such as it may be, is exchange mode.

This brief analysis of research methods establishes a public/private division in the activity. The comparatively strongly institutionalised public region consists of books, reports, papers, presentations and so forth that are taken to materialise the esoteric domain discourse of educational research methods and methodology (as well as the specific regions of educational research—sociology of education, applied linguistics, and so forth—that the respective documents represent). The regularities of form exhibited by this documentation also facilitate the communication of competence in the form of the deployment of tacit principles of recognition and realisation of legitimate academic argument. This public region is emergent upon a private region of relatively weakly institutionalised actions by individual researchers in the construction and marketing of their research. This construction and marketing, though privately elaborated, is conducted within the context of the emergent discourse and skills as a background and as a target as researchers aspire to feature in the discourse.

An interesting collateral result lies in the plausible contrast between at least some approaches to quantitative as distinct from qualitative research. So, to the extent that, for example, survey data collection and analysis is at least potentially carried out in public through the availability of survey instruments and raw data, then these aspects of quantitative research are appropriately interpreted as discourse. That is to say, they are strongly institutionalised and explicitly principled. Scope for private performance is then to be found in, for example, the production of individual questionnaire items; scope for idiolect is to be found in the attempted development of new statistical theory. With qualitative research, the actual practice of data collection and analysis are, in my experience, often amongst the most privately performed actions. This was, for example, the case in the fieldwork carried out for the research reported in Chapter 7—we have certainly never made our interview tapes or fieldnotes available to anyone else. There is a resonance between the kind of public/private distinction that I am marking here and that which I shall present in Chapter 6, the point here being that the really important decisions are often only ever taken in private.

THE FRAMING OF SCHOOL MATHEMATICS

School mathematics also establishes a public/private distinction but, partially, at least, in a slightly different way. The public region of the practice is perhaps most evident in textbooks and other published curricular material, including syllabuses and curricula; this region exhibits a partitioning, often realised as a dichotomy. As I have illustrated elsewhere (Dowling, 1996b, 1998, 2001a), 'high ability' is constructed, textually, as meriting access to the explicit principles of the *esoteric domain* of school mathematics. As I have indicated above, I define the esoteric domain of a practice as that region in which both content and forms of expression are most strongly institutionalised. In school mathematics, this region is substantially—though not exclusively, as I shall illustrate below—constituted by high discursive saturation strategies. 'High ability' is therefore constructed as meriting entry into mathematical discourse. 'Low ability', by contrast, tends to be constructed as demanding residence in the *public domain*. The public domain is the product of the casting of a mathematical *gaze* onto non-mathematical practices, *recontextualising* them via a redescription in terms consistent with mathematical principles, that is to say, consistent with the principles of the esoteric domain.

Now, firstly, it will be apparent that, insofar as the principles of the redescribed practices constituting the public domain are not themselves available within the public domain, then an audience that is textually limited to that domain is presented with practices that are, in effect, tacitly principled.[41] Here is an example of such a public domain task.

Here are two packets of washing powder. The small size contains 930g of powder. It costs 84p.
The large size contains 3.1 kg of powder. It costs £2.56.
(a)   How many grams do you get for 1p in the small size?
(b)   How many grams do you get for 1p in the large size? (Remember you must work in **grams** and **pence**.)
(c)Which size gives more for your money?
(*SMP 11-16 Book G7*,[42] p. 2)

The procedure for completing tasks that are all very similar to this one is given in the text. However, this is formulated in localised, public domain terms, so that no access is provided to the generalised, esoteric domain mathematical principles relating to, in this case, direct proportion. It is these esoteric domain principles that facilitate the general deployment of such strategies. It should also be noted that the mathematical recontextualising of, for example, shopping practices generally entails that the procedures offered in textbooks are radically inconsistent with those deployed by shoppers (see Dowling, 2001a; Lave *et al*, 1984). This establishes an intertextual tension between school mathematical strategies and what we might call, following de Certeau (1984), everyday tactics. Such tensions may help to explain the social class patterning of school mathematics performances described by Cooper and Dunne (1999). However, the point to be made, here, is that the

---

[41]   I should emphasise that this is a textual limitation. There is no insistence here that an empirical audience may not infer principles that will enable successful completion of public domain tasks, simply that the text itself may not provide access to those principles.
[42]   Published by Cambridge University Press.

exclusion of high discursive saturation strategies in textbooks constituting 'low ability' audiences presents as skills practices that, within the context of school mathematics generally, are more appropriately understood as discourse (access to which is a textual condition for the generalisation of public domain procedures). In everyday terms, these practices are more likely to be recognised as tricks in that their elaboration is generally privatised.[43]

As I have suggested, not all of the school mathematics esoteric domain is constituted by high discursive saturation practices. I will give one brief example from my own (albeit somewhat distant) experiences as a mathematics teacher. This example—the one that I indexed earlier in this chapter—relates to the teaching of standard techniques in the topic, integral calculus. I want to suggest that, whilst the techniques themselves—for example, integration by substitution—are presented discursively, the principles of their application—the principles of recognition that generate the selection of the particular approach to be used in a particular case— generally are not. The student must acquire what is probably best described in my schema as a skill. This is not wholly dissimilar to the acquisition of competence in academic literacy as discussed earlier. It is of further interest that the use of such techniques has little or no use-value in the study or application of mathematics and related fields above school level, other than in school mathematics teaching, of course. This skill, then, stands merely as a shibboleth for entry into such fields.

In the 1980s—around the time of the publication of the Cockcroft (1982) report on school mathematics—an interest burgeoned in developing an investigative approach to mathematics (see, for example: ATM, 1979; Bloomfield, 1987; Mason, 1978, Mason *et al*, 1982). The concern was to shift emphasis from the transmission of techniques to the production of mathematical knowledge that would be, in some sense, original, at least to the students producing it. The general idea involved the deployment of the kind of heuristics articulated by George Polya (1946) in new situations. Figure 4.6 is an example that I found in various forms in use in school texts and classrooms. The kinds of heuristic techniques that might be deployed on this task are publicly and discursively available in Polya's and more recent publications. As is the case with integration techniques, the principles of their deployment is given only by published exemplars (for example, Mason *et al*, 1982) that might or might not be sufficient to enable students to make a start on the 'investigation' in Figure 4.6. 'Investigating', then, involves skills and, perhaps, tricks. I will make a start on the task in Figure 4.6 to illustrate how it might be approached.

---

[43] Many of the examples presented in Lave (1988) and Lave *et al* (1984) give the impression of being both idiosyncratic (tricks) and very imaginative.

Bubbles

These are *bubbles*

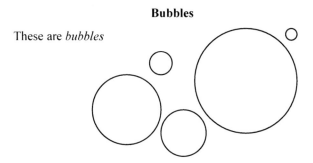

Bubbles can be enlarged or shrunk and can be
placed next to each other, like this:

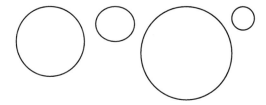

Or bubbles can be placed inside each other, like
this:

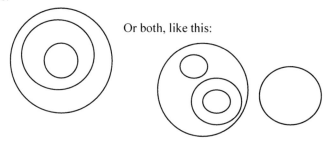

Or both, like this:

Bubbles cannot intersect. Investigate.

Figure 4.6. A School Mathematical Investigation

Firstly, I need to understand my problem (Polya, 1946). In this case, this means
to make some decisions as to what features of bubble arrangements I want to be
concerned with. I am going to decide that I am concerned only with differences
relating to the two operations, putting bubbles alongside each other and putting one
bubble inside another. That is, the actual location of one bubble relative to another
on a page is only to be considered in terms of whether it is: i) outside, but not
containing the other; or ii) outside and containing the other; or iii) inside the other.

This is an arbitrary decision in the sense that I might have decided to take account of, say, the size of a bubble or its location on the page in terms of a coordinate system. The decision that I have taken entails that, for example, the two arrangements in Figure 4.7 are to be regarded as equivalent. It also entails that all bubbles are equivalent (ie irrespective of their sizes). It will be apparent that, in the context of this 'investigation', there is an openness in the interpretation of the heuristic, 'understand the problem'. Its method of deployment—though not the delineation of the resulting 'understanding'—is certainly achieved via strategies of low discursive saturation. In my case, the decisions that I have taken might be regarded as a skill, because I have chosen to establish equivalence to mean topological equivalence, that is to say, I have adopted an aspect of an established mathematical language.[44]

Pattern 1

Pattern 2

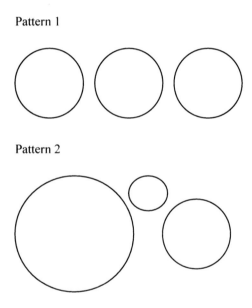

Figure 4.7. Equivalent Patterns

---

[44] 'Topology is concerned with those properties of geometric figures that are invariant under continuous transformations. A continuous transformation, also called a topological transformation or homeomorphism, is a one-to-one correspondence between the points of one figure and the points of another figure such that points that are arbitrarily close on one figure are transformed into points that are also arbitrarily close on the other figure. Figures that are related in this way are said to be topologically equivalent. If a figure is transformed into an equivalent figure by bending, stretching, etc., the change is a special type of topological transformation called a continuous deformation.' *Columbia Encyclopedia.* http://www.bartleby.com/65/to/topology.html.

I notice that deploying either of my two operations successively generates a particular mode of arrangement. I shall call these kinds of arrangement, respectively *serial* and *concentric*; see Figure 4.8.

'serial' pattern

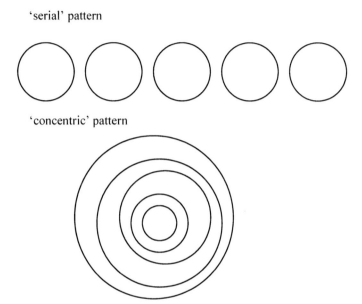

'concentric' pattern

Figure 4.8. Primitive Bubble Arrangements

Mathematics is concerned with the exploration of the general properties of formal systems. As things stand, my only way of representing my system of bubbles involves the use of diagrams. These are limiting because each diagram represents only a topologically equivalent set of bubble arrangements. I need a notation that will allow me to develop an algebra, to represent general states. I shall do this by using the variable, x, to represent 'bubble' and defining two operations on the basis of the two moves that are to be used in arranging bubbles, thus:

1. $x \oplus x$ means place one bubble outside but not containing another bubble.
2. $x \otimes x$ means place one bubble outside and containing another bubble (or bubbles).[45]

---

[45] I have defined this operation as placing one bubble *outside* rather than *inside* another bubble because this enables me to 'enclose' several bubbles in another—I cannot, unambiguously, place one bubble inside a bubble arrangement such as that in the lower righthand of Figure 4.6 or the arrangement in Figure 4.9, but I can uniquely specify the arrangement whereby a bubble is placed outside and containing either arrangement, or outside and not containing either arrangement.

The 'serial' and 'concentric' patterns in Figure 4.8 may now be represented as

$$x \oplus x \oplus x \oplus x \oplus x \text{ or } 5x \text{ and}$$
$$x \otimes x \otimes x \otimes x \otimes x \text{ or } x^5 \text{ respectively.}$$

This notation gives me a way of representing any legitimate pattern, however complicated. Thus the pattern in Figure 4.9 is rendered as

$$4x \oplus 2x^2 \oplus x^3 \oplus x^4$$

Someone well drilled in school mathematics may be inclined to rush headlong into factorisation and presume an equivalence between this expression and something like

$$x(4 \oplus 2x \oplus x^2 \oplus x^3).$$

However, this would be an error, both because the order in which we perform the operations matters and the number, 4, on its own, has no value in this system.

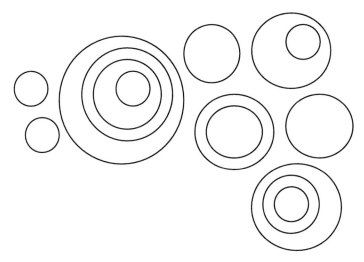

Figure 4.9. A Complex Bubble Arrangement

I shall not take this 'investigation' further, here, as I have done enough to be able to illustrate the points that I want to make. Essentially, the 'investigative' approach to school mathematics introduces new areas for low discursive saturation strategies and tactics—skills, tricks—in a discipline that is apparently dominated by high discursive saturation strategies. Indeed, a general preference for the latter is illustrated by my rationalising of my move from the diagrammatic (low discursive saturation) to the algebraic (high discursive saturation) representation of my bubbles problem. Here, the principles of deployment of heuristics are, to recall Bernstein's language, far more context dependent than is the case with other areas of mathematical practice. I have suggested above that my recruitment of topological principles in 'understanding my problem' suggests that that aspect of my 'investigation' is more of a skill than a trick, associating mathematics with what Bernstein describes as a 'craft' (see Figure 4.3). However, insofar as I have chosen to develop a notation and (potentially, at least) explore the system in that way, I am perhaps deviating from the approach that one finds more commonly adopted with 'investigations', that is to count, in this case, the number of patterns for each number of bubbles—see the discussion on the NRICH site at http://nrich.maths.org/askedNRICH/edited/503.html, for example. In this sense, my strategy might be considered more of a trick and associated more with Bernstein's 'horizontal discourse'. Certainly, the particular form of notation that I have deployed is (as far as I know) not entirely standard in work in topology and might be considered ideolectical.

The boards on the NRICH site and on the multitude of other websites concerned with school mathematics as well as conventional journals written for and by teachers and mathematics educators, such as *Mathematics Teaching* and *Mathematics in School*, constitute public forums in which strategies and tactics such as those deployed here are shared and discussed. Many tactics generated in classrooms may appear once at most. Others may develop a higher level of institutionalisation and eventually find their way into school mathematical discourse. What is clearly the case is that it is not appropriate to identify school mathematics or, as I have illustrated earlier, educational research methods, as unitary in the sense of either horizontal or hierarchical knowledge structures, or even vertical or horizontal discourses.

The fetishising of knowledge—or indeed of discourse—as an entity or entities that have an existence that is in some sense independent of the actual practices with which it or they are being associated may be a helpful initial organising move in thinking about cultural regularity. It seems to me, however, to be a very unhelpful move if we have any interest in engaging with the empirical. Bernstein takes possession of the empirical only to enable him to ignore its voice. Similar strategies have been adopted by some (though by no means all) other sociologists of knowledge, see, for example, Beck and Young (2005), Maton, 2000, Moore and Muller (1999, 2002), Moore and Young (2001a); some of this work is discussed in some detail in Chapter 8. Bernstein's structure in Figure 4.3 is necrotising in its anti-empirical pigeonholing. My schema in Figure 4.5—ironically resembling far more closely an array of pigeonholes in a school staffroom—provides a language that originates in a theoretical-empirical dialogue, that has subsequently been rendered analytically coherent, and that is now available for organising the empirical from the particular perspective provided by two polarised concepts— *level of institutionalisation* and *level of discursive saturation*. Such organisation enables the regionalisation of an empirical practice, it renders visible trajectories and, potentially, mechanisms of differentiation and, ultimately social and cultural production and reproduction, that is, the formation, maintenance and destabilising of the alliances and oppositions that constitute the social as emergent upon autopoietic cultural action. In terms of its potential in informing pedagogy, the schema—and the others that I and colleagues have generated—provides a basis for exploring, and potentially engineering, the alignment between proposed pedagogic action and the competences and performances that are to be fostered. The fetishising of knowledge can never achieve this precisely because the very act silences both teacher and student.

CONCLUSION (THOUGH NOT YET AN ARRIVAL)

At the start of this essay I pointed out that Bernstein had accused his critics, Harker and May of misrecognition. Doubtless he would have accused this essay—at least in large part—of much the same thing. Here, I have chosen to describe my reading of Bernstein as treachery and as heresy. My sociology arises from a *deliberate* misreading of Bernstein; deliberate, in the sense that I am fully aware of the radical irreconcilability of our respective general approaches. Bernstein's existential experience stands—it seems to me—opposed to his mode of objectification of the sociocultural, establishing him inside trying to get out. My objectivist experience inaugurates the opposite kind of lack: I am outside trying to get in. Had Bernstein been less concerned with policing his academic legacy (always a lost cause) and more concerned with simply doing his sociology, he might have referred to Harker's and May's misrecognition as a recontextualisation. But, to do justice to such a classification, he would have had to engage in some sociological analysis of their empirical text; the rhetorical approach would not have served well such a purpose.

Recontextualisation is the central theme of this chapter. The schema established by classification and framing is viable only to the extent that the sociocultural chronotope is recontextualised as consisting of mutually independent synchronic and diachronic planes, or where contiguous levels of analysis are recontextualised through their collapse onto a single level. My recontextualising of Bernstein's schema generates a single category, level of institutionalisation, that points to emergent structure to be recruited by autopoietic action and not subjacent structure that is generative of it. My recontextualising of Bernstein's recontextualisation results in a general method—*constructive description*—that pushes towards the necessity of an inaugural constitution of and subsequent dialogue between the theoretical and the empirical. Here, crucially, the dialogue must be such as to permit the theoretical to learn and the empirical to be organised (and, indeed, reorganised). This is the outcome of my recontextualisation of the major strand in Bernstein's corpus that begins with restricted and elaborated speech codes and ends with vertical and horizontal discourses and hierarchical and horizontal knowledge structures. From this strand, as well, I have generated a second key category in my own work, that of *discursive saturation*. The recontextualisings thus establish my own analytic space that, as a component of my general organisational language, stands in dialogic relation to, in this chapter, research education and school mathematics, which have themselves become the objects of analytic recontextualisation. It may (or may not) be that the I/DS, practical strategic space has reached its terminal point of development. The dialogue, though, is present in an openness of the language as a whole to new structure—new categories and new analytic spaces—that re-contextualises that which precedes it. The productivity of all of this engagement lies in the facility of the new language to stimulate new insights into the modes of formation, maintenance and destabilising—which is to say, the emergence—of alliances and oppositions.

We might speculate that all treachery entails the resistance of a becoming subjectivity to the restriction to being imposed in the very pedagogic relations that inaugurated that subjectivity. I am in absolutely no doubt at all that none of my work would have been possible without the work and indeed pedagogic action of Basil Bernstein. But I have had other teachers as well—many of whom I will never meet, many of whom are misread in this book, and doubtless, there are many more of whom I remain regretfully unaware or forgetful. Basil could have taken pride in his own achievements and in the legacy of work that has been and is to be accomplished by those inspired by him. But the proudest claim that he might have made in respect of at least one of these, is that he is not a Bernsteinian.

CHAPTER 5

A TIMELY UTTERANCE

Every self-conscious act or utterance imagines itself the kiss of creator and created, structure and event, *langue* and *parole*, competence and performance (but which is which?) And there is anxiety: is this the kiss of my lover, or of Judas; does it wake me, or am I forever dream(t/ing)/betray(ing/ed)? All too often I sense that it's the kiss of Midas the necrophiliac. None of this is new, but it overtures the interrogation of our tribalisms, our alliances and oppositions and, as such, it is one of several points of departure, which is to say, points of entry into our discourse, where it functions also as a semantic shibboleth. Once under way, we may look around for alternatives. Halliday and Mathiessen (2004), for example, introduce the relationship between climate and weather as a metaphor for that between linguistic system and linguistic text. This is fine, so long as we recognise that system and text are already seeds of doubt for a faithless Orpheus. Geoffrey Hartman (from whose object and title I borrow my own) seems to want to distinguish between intertextual field and sense-experience:

> I have offered a mildly deconstructive reading: one that discloses in words 'a "spirit" peculiar to their nature as words' (Kenneth Burke). Such a reading refuses to substitute ideas for words, especially since in the empiricist tradition after Locke ideas are taken to be a faint replica of images, which are themselves directly referable to sense-experience. One way of bringing out the spirit peculiar to words, and so, paradoxically, making them material 'emphasizing the letter in the spirit' is to evoke their intertextual echoes. Ideas may be simple, but words are always complex. Yet the construction of an intertextual field is disconcerting as well as enriching because intertextual concordance produces a reality-discord, an overlay or distancing of the referential function of speech, of the word-thing, word-experience relation. Even though the fact of correspondence between language and experience is not in question (there is a complex answerability of the one to the other), the theory of correspondence remains a problem. (Hartman, 1987, pp. 159-160)

The production of an intertextual field is always autobiographical, always retrospective, always a synchronising of departed sense-experiences.

Gunther Kress wants to distinguish between speech/writing and image:

> The two modes of writing and of image are each governed by distinct logics, and have distinctly different affordances. The organisation of writing—still leaning on the logics of speech—is governed by the logic of time, and by the logic of sequence of its elements in time, in temporally governed arrangements. The organisation of the image, by contrast, is governed by the

logic of space, and by the logic of simultaneity of its visual/depicted elements in spatially organised arrangements. To say this simply: in speaking I have to say one thing after another, one sound after another, one word after another, one clause after another, so that inevitably one thing is first, and another thing is second, and one thing will have to be last. Meaning can then be—and is— attached to 'being first' and to 'being last', and maybe to being third and so on. (Kress, 2003, pp. 1-2)

Yet, if we concur with Heidegger (1962)—or, for that matter (and *mutatis mutandis*), Ong (1982)—that temporality is the mode of our being, then simultaneity—I shall say synchronicity—might be understood as a way of covering our tracks. I recall the rather cute (if not entirely original) device in the film, *Truly, Madly, Deeply* (Minghella, 1991). Here, bereavement (a dead lover) could not be closed in the diachronic, being arrested by persistent nostalgia that, in effect, established an edenic synchronicity. The cute device consisted of a move in the diegesis whereby the synchronic rotated onto the diachronic (the appearance of the lover's ghost) allowing the mythical eden to be dismantled, upon which achievement the rotation was reversed. Synchronicity is always edenic (or utopian) and this applies to the synchronicity claimed in the inscription of an image or writing—including autobiographies—the work being presented in its entirety to facilitate any order of reading. It also characterises the poetic devices that facilitate synchronicity in oral cultures (Ong, 1982). Referring to this latter point, we might say that in terms of its form, poetry (whether spoken or written) has a tendency towards greater synchronicity than does prose, though anaphora or cataphora in either is synchronising, mythologising. Having made something of an encampment here, I shall initiate my own mythologising with a structuring of textual mode, beginning, as seems most apt, with some analysis by my colleague, Gunther Kress.

In a recent seminar contribution to a masters course that I run, Kress showed two transparencies showing what he referred to as 'signs', both relating to the world's largest land mammal. I don't have his slides, so I'll replace them with my own (I hope he won't mind) in Figure 5.1 and Figure 5.2. In the seminar, Kress compared the signs along the following lines:

The imaginative work in writing focuses on filling words with meaning—and then reading the filled elements together, in the given syntactic structure. In image, imagination focuses on creating the order of the arrangement of elements which are already filled with meaning. (Kress, 2003, p. 4)

He also made the point, introduced in the earlier extract, about the temporal and spatial basis of the logics of writing and image respectively. Now, it seems to me to be unhelpful to my own ends to refer to Figure 5.2 as a 'sign'. This is because I want to reserve that term for a moment [46] of an already established (that is, mythologised) system. Rather, I want to refer to Figure 5.2 as a *text*. In this case, it

---

[46] See Laclau and Mouffe (1985) for a resonant discussion on differentiating between the categories, *moment* and *element*.

is a unique articulation of selections from a relatively *weakly coded repertoire*, which includes the range of my facility in the use of a marking pen.

ELEPHANT

Figure 5.1. Elephant 1

Figure 5.2. Elephant 2

But Figure 5.1 was also produced as an articulation of selections. It was created in MS Word as the result of a sequence of selections from menus. First I selected the Comic Sans MS font, then its point size, then upper case, then the letters comprising the word, ELEPHANT. Described thus, it seems clear that Figure 5.1 should also be regarded as a text. The distinction between these two texts is that Figure 5.1 was authored via the deployment of selection principles operating on a relatively *strongly coded* (which is to say, highly reliable) *register* or *registers*, whereas Figure 5.2 was authored via the deployment of realisation skills enabled by a relatively *weakly coded repertoire*. I would tend to place Figure 5.3 closer to Figure 5.2 than to Figure 5.1, in this schema, even though it is still in written mode. Reading—I shall say audiencing—the three texts in the way I would expect (to the extent that authoring entails the prediction of audience response) would be described in the same way. Thus reading Figure 5.1 would entail principles of selection from a strongly coded register or registers, whereas reading Figure 5.2 and Figure 5.3 would involve, in this case, recognition skills enabled by a weakly coded repertoire. It is important, at this point, to stress that I realise that the prediction of audience response in this way is very far from being an infallible science. All three of these texts need to be written (authored/audienced) and it may be useful to refer to this process as 'filling with meaning' (though I shall not use this expression in my own formulation). However, the distinction that Kress needs to make, whilst helpful in starting me on my own way, is possible only by constituting them as signs rather than as texts.

Figure 5.3. Elephant 3

The temporal/spatial distinction that Kress makes is also helpful, but his particular formulation steers me a little too close for comfort to the language of essentialism and, indeed, to the decoupling of time and space that I rejected in Chapter 4. Instead, I want to propose that we may seek to identify, in the authoring/audiencing of texts, strategies that emphasise the diachronic and strategies that emphasise the synchronic. A *diachronising strategy* will tend to highlight a sequence. The organising of printed text in a novel and the arrangement of letters in the wordprocessed or handwritten word, 'elephant', entail diachronising strategies. A *synchronising strategy* will tend to make multiple elements of a text available at the same time. An image, such as that in Figure 5.2 deploys synchronising strategies, although Kress and van Leeuwen (1996) might want to argue that the left-to-right orientation of the drawing signals a direction within a western semiotic system (and, in this respect, the drawing is operating as a sign as well as a text).

Poetic devices such as rhythm and rhyme as well as anaphoric and cataphoric references in prose and poetry also operate as synchronising strategies and synchronicity is, of course, the mode of operation of memory. There is clearly a sense in which texts cannot be authored/audienced purely in the diachronic. Nevertheless, we might usefully differentiate between categories of text in pointing at the different strategies that they foreground (or, rather, that we might foreground in their analysis). This is illustrated in Figure 5.4, which includes examples of textual forms that seem to privilege the respective textual strategies: 'print'/strongly coded diachrony, a 'roadmap'/strongly coded synchrony, 'handwriting'/weakly coded diachrony, 'drawing'/weakly coded synchrony.

This is not an essentialising analysis. We might illustrate this by considering the category, film. The medium clearly presents us with a digital sequence of images, generally experienced as an analogue[47] diachrony. In respect of the specifics of the images, we might describe the film as a sequenced realisation (authoring) or selection (audiencing) from a weakly coded repertoire. These strategies place the

---

[47] That is, continuous as opposed to digital. The material of the film is, of course, constructed as a sequence of discrete images, but generally experienced as an analogue stream.

film in the top righthand cell of Figure 5.4. However, films may deploy strategies that synchronise. This is particularly apparent in the film *Timecode* (Figgis, 2000), which consists of a single take on four synchronised cameras displayed on a split screen. This aspect of the film would locate in the bottom righthand cell of Figure 5.4. Stronger coding might apply where we attempt to locate a film within a specific genre (action, film noir, western, etc) and a consideration of the sequencing of shots (close-up, mid-range, long-shot) would shift back into the diachronic so that these strategies would operate in the lefthand bottom and top cells respectively. All films will deploy all of the strategies, but are likely to weight them differently in different aspects. Because of its unfamiliarity, *Timecode* seems to foreground weakly coded synchrony, whilst *Russian Ark* (Sokurov, 2002)—also shot in a single, unedited take, but using a single camera—foregrounds weakly coded diachrony.

Chronotopic Strategy	Register/Repertoire	
	Strong Coding	**Weak Coding**
Diachronising	*print*	*handwriting*
Synchronising	*roadmap*	*drawing*

Figure 5.4. Examples of Textual Modes

Kress bases his theorising of mode on its materiality. Here, he refers to the physical qualities of the mode, again invoking the space-time differentiation:

> The logic of space leads to the spatial distribution of simultaneously present significant elements; and both the elements and the relations of the elements are resources for meaning. The logic of time leads to temporal succession of elements, and the elements and their place in a sequence constitute a resource for meaning. (Kress, 2003, p. 45)

Thus space-based and time-based modes exhibit different 'affordances'. Appropriately, in a materialist theory, he also places the body in a central position:

> The affective affordances of sound are entirely different to those of sight or those of touch; sound is more immediately tangibly felt in the body than is sight, but certainly differently felt. (Kress, 2003, p. 46)

I'm not sure that this differentiation resonates with my own experiences. To me, sound and visual stages feel very similar to each other, whether in the background or foreground of my attention, and extremes in either perceptual channel generate the same kinds of pain. Certainly, sight and sound can signify physical distance in a way that touch, taste and smell do not, though this may be more semiotic than physical, given that all involve material contact of some form.[48]

Kress makes interesting empirical observations, here. However, for my purposes, the limitation of the theory lies in its empiricism and, in the above pair of extracts, its risk of unsutured dualism—the affordances of the material of the text/the affordances of the perceptual apparatus; empiricism seems particularly problematic when dealing with the perceptual apparatus itself. We may restart with a more analytic theory on the basis of the following observation: no authoring or audiencing, and so no text, is possible in the absence of some synchronising apparatus. As I have indicated above, the synchronising apparatus that is always present is that of memory. As Hayles (1999) points out, a theory of text that ignores its materiality is inadequate, but this materiality must address, in some form at least, the embodiment of the text, which is to say, its embodiment in memory. This being the case, we might differentiate texts on the basis of their mnemonic facilities, but the resulting analysis would not coincide with Kress's space-based/time-based modes. Rhyming and rhythmic spoken poetry may be highly mnemonic as, in some sense, is a novel (the whole of the book is generally present for backwards and forwards reference); a visual text may vary in respect of its mnemonic properties, different features of regions being more or less strongly marked out, etc. I do not choose to establish my own organisational language as a theory of memory or as a dualistic theory of matter and perception, but as a sociology. As a point of entry into it, however, I have chosen the analysis of textual modes introduced in Figure 5.4 and reproduced in Figure 5.5 using general terms, rather than exemplars, for categories of textual mode.

	Register/Repertoire	
Chronotopic Strategy	Strong Coding	Weak Coding
Diachronising	*printing*	*scribing*
Synchronising	*mapping*	*painting*

Figure 5.5. Textual Modes

I shall describe textual mode as a complex—organised in Figure 5.5—of cultural strategies. Now, I want to go further than to produce a typology of cultural strategies. Kress has similar ambitions in associating the advancement of multimodal representation with actual and potential shifts in relations of power between author and audience. Referring to the WWW homepage of the Institute of Education, he points out that:

---

[48] Sight involves material contact with electromagnetic radiation or photons, hearing with sound waves (or so we are led to believe). In each case, subject and object are materially 'connected'.

… there are eleven 'entry points', which themselves respond to or perhaps reflect the interests of potential 'visitors' [...] The significant point [...] is that 'reading' is now a distinctly different activity to what it was in the era of the traditional page. Reading is the imposing of the reader's order on this entity, an order which, while of course responding to what is here, derives from criteria of the reader's interest, disposition and desire. This is reading as ordering. Even when I have decided to enter via a category on the menu, it is my choice which category I choose to enter. (Kress, 2003, p. 138)

Figure 5.6. The Institute of Education WWW Homepage as at February 2005

This contrasts with the 'traditional page', which, in English, conventionally, has a single point of entry, the top lefthand corner. Kress's book includes an image of the homepage that was current in 2002. Figure 5.6 shows the equivalent page at the time of writing the original version of this chapter (February 2005)—it hadn't changed much. In fact, Kress has rather misrepresented the page, which is always framed in a browser window, which will often include additional 'entry points', as in Figure 5.7. I can go even further by pointing out that the browser is framed by a computer 'desktop', for example as in Figure 5.8 and, indeed, the computer is

Figure 5.7. The Institute of Education WWW Homepage Framed in a Browser Window

framed by the physical and social context in which it is being viewed. At the point of Figure 5.8, I am in much the same position with the IoE page as I would be with this page in Microsoft Word, which is currently active on my screen. I may re-enter my authoring (or audiencing) at any point on this page, that is, at the beginning or end of any character or space or by highlighting any single block of text, or by selecting from the menu options in the header or by selecting a word from the dictionary pane or typing into its search field. Alternatively, I may select another open window, including the image of the IoE page, though the browser is currenly offline as I am on the front seat of the upper deck of a London Bus (which has now broken down, so I have had to transfer to another, which move has inspired another entry out of linear sequence). Then, of course, I might close my computer and select another item from my bag or look out of the window or at my fellow passengers and so forth. In other words, as I pointed out in Chapter 3, authoring and audiencing have always been very open activities. Furthermore, the 'traditional page' has a single conventional entry point only if it is a page of a very particular kind, say a novel. This is a common generalisation (see Kaplan, 2000), but one that is not necessarily appropriate. Telephone directories, diaries, shopping lists, restaurant menus, bus timetables and so forth have been around for quite a while and I would imagine that the Domesday Book was probably rarely read and not intended to be read from beginning to end in a linear fashion. The linearising aspects in some texts are often diachronising strategies, to be sure, but they do not determine audiencing and may indeed facilitate navigation as is the case in the ordering in a dictionary—in this case, linearity is a synchronising strategy and not a blueprint for reading.

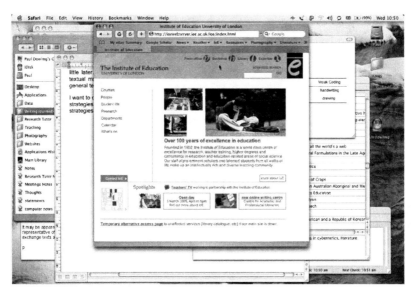

Figure 5.8. The Institute of Education WWW homepage on my (old) computer screen

My question is not concerned with whether authoring/audiencing is open or closed—both have always been open—but with what the authoring/audiencing activity is about, what is it for. From a sociological point of view—my sociological point of view—linguistically-oriented theory—and this certainly includes Norman Fairclough's Critical Discourse Analysis (Fairclough, 1995; Chouliaraki & Fairclough, 1999) as well as Kress's treatment of multimodality—has a tendency to begin in the wrong place. Unlike Fairclough (see Dowling, 2004), Kress is careful not to claim to be able to read social relations of power from cultural texts after the fashion of scientific marxism. On the other hand he is unashamedly optimistic about the potential transformative 'affordances' of the new modes of communication:

> The combined effects on writing of the dominance of the mode of image and of the medium of the screen will produce deep changes in the forms and functions of writing. This in turn will have profound effects on human, cognitive/affective, cultural and bodily engagement with the world, and on the forms and shapes of knowledge. *The world told* is a different world to *the world shown*. The effects of the move to the screen as the major medium of communication will produce far-reaching shifts in relations of power, and not just in the sphere of communication. Where significant changes to the distribution of power threaten, there will be fierce resistance by those who presently hold power, so that the predictions about the democratic potentials and effects of the new information and communication technologies have to be seen in the light of inevitable struggles over power yet to come. It is already clear that the effects of the two changes taken together will have the widest imaginable political, economic, social, cultural, conceptual/cognitive and epistemological consequences. (Kress, 2003, p. 1)

It is difficult to see around the marketing—framed in the language of technological determinism—particularly in the final sentence. Sociologically, such a position has long been seen as untenable (see, for example, Dowling, 1991a). I should also add that I find the treatment of power as something that is held rather than something that is constitutive of subjectivity is unhelpful, particularly in the absence of any further theorising of this category.

For me, though, the central problem lies in the fetishising of the text as a cultural product, or even as a cultural process. We can, after all, see multimodal, multi-entry-point texts in all kinds of activities and they are not all (if ever) appropriately associated with a shift of authority from author to audience. The US government TIMSS website at http://nces.ed.gov/timss/, for example, provides a great deal of information that is open to exploration following diverse routes and links. None of this exploration, however, allows any alternative authoring of the official discourse of what I shall refer to, in Chapter 7, as mathematicoscience. On the contrary, its very openness and accessibility substantially contribute to the globalising of the accountability of public education to what is, basically, curricularised onanism; multimodalised mathematicoscience certainly offers no direct or indirect lines of access to the reauthoring of the global order. Even 'unofficial' popular culture hypermedia sites exhibit strong authorial authority *vis-à-vis* their audience-contributors. Silent Hill Heaven, for example, is a site for fans of the 'horror survival' video game series, *Silent Hill*. Although the site includes forums in which fans may sound-off their criticisms of each version of the game, the site clearly serves the marketing interests of the game's manufacturers by providing both free market research and sustaining the fan community. Furthermore, rigorously enforced rules impose strong principles of classification on what can be posted, where, and by whom. I might also add that, despite its multimodal form, a diachronising feature that requires gamers to return repeatedly to a central room in the game space in version 4 of the game is the source of considerable dismay amongst many of the fans. Natasha Whiteman (2005, 2007) has produced an original analysis of some of these aspects of the game and, indeed, some development of the organisational language that is being introduced in this book. The IoE website is certainly far more facilitative than the printed prospectus in respect of audience navigation. What this might be expected to achieve, however, is the maximal accessibility of the institution's academic products; no amount of information will enable a potential student to re-write that institution's offer, nor a past student to re-author the grading of their examination.

Simply providing a typology or grammar of multimodal texts will not generate a sociology—we need to look somewhere else. The schema that I have introduced in Figure 5.5 is about textual mode, but it organises these as strategic resources that may be deployed in the formation, maintenance and destabilising of social relations in the form of oppositions and alliances; any sociologically adequate language must get closer to this territory. The schema in Figure 5.5 is a small part the organisational language being introduced in this book, part of which structures answers to the question, *how* are these oppositions and alliances formed, maintained and destabilised in terms of autopoietic action. As I have indicated in earlier chapters, the language sets out to describe what strategies are available to authors in constructing communicative acts in which they seek to retain the principles of evaluation of audience performances—pedagogic relations—or in which they delegate authority over these principles to their audience—exchange relations.

In general terms, we might describe the IoE site from the author's perspective as exhibiting pedagogic relations in terms of content (which is clearly non-negotiable) and exchange relations in terms of navigation. In keeping with this description, textual mode on the site shifts to printing (strongly coded, diachronising) mode at those points that are directly concerned with content, such as the printed text under the heading, 'Over 100 years of excellence in education'. Mapping mode (strongly coded synchronising) in headings and the search engine[49] hand over control to the audience in respect of the sequencing of content. The images (painting)—for example, the long shot of the IoE building, a woman (student, staff, member of the general public) reading on the grass in the sun, another (probably) looking at a computer screen, activities in what might be teaching rooms—in fact do not seem to me to convey much in the way of meaning at all in relation to the academic activity that contextualises them, but are, in contrast to the verbal text, vague, to say the least. They all seem to present activity of a form that is consistent with (but no more than this—what's she reading: Nietzsche or Mills and Boone?) the intellectual, but, further than that, make of them what you, as audience, will; exchange relations/synchronic, but weakly coded mode; not all images are the same.

My description of autopoietic action—the *how* in relation to the formation, maintenance and destabilising of oppositions and alliances—is always constituted from (my construction of) the perspective of the author. This also includes the

---

[49] The search engine is strongly coded in the sense that it will accept only standard characters and synchronising in the sense that it gives simultaneous access to all pages containing the input string.

active reading by the empirical audience, in circumstances in which this is available as text. I describe the answer to the question, *what* oppositions and alliances are formed, maintained and destabilised, as structure that is emergent upon autopoietic action. I am interpreting this structure as emergent rather than generative, so that it looks different from different perspectives. Structural synchronising, nevertheless, is what we, as temporal be(com)ings do to the sociocultural, constituting regularities that are thereby available for recruiting in and by autopoietic action. Halliday's and Mathiessen's weather/climate metaphor is quite apt, here. There is, of course, always going to be play between the constructions of emergent climate or of emergent alliances and oppositions from different perspectives and this is the basis of dynamism in the system as a whole.

I have described the photographs on the IoE homepage (Figure 5.6) as weakly coded. In discussion, Soh-young Chung—my co-author in Chapter 8—suggested that these images were typical of the kinds of images to be found in the prospectuses and on the websites of universities, so that, in effect, they conveyed no meaning at all apart from the identification of the IoE as a university school. She was, here, deploying a recognition skill that is enabled by a weakly coded repertoire, itself emergent upon her history of autopoietic action in audiencing such texts. The extent to which this reading is generalisable is an empirical question that addresses the level of its institutionalisation, which is one aspect of emergent structure. I have referred to another aspect of emergent structure as its level of discursive saturation. This category relates to the intellectual/manual character of the division of labour and is defined as a measure of the extent to which the principles of a practice are available within discourse. Whether or not my colleague's reading of the IoE website is strongly institutionalised, it seems clear that its principles are more likely to be tacit than explicit, so that any elaboration would be likely to be limited to listings of (or pointings to) equivalent images rather than principled definitions. With these two categories, I have the basis for the practical strategic space that I introduced in Chapter 4 (see Figure 4.5).

I have described my colleague's practice as the deployment of a skill, which is to say, the realisation of an attributed competence—attributed, that is, in and by the establishing of an emergent regularity of practice. We may consider the level of institutionalisation at any level of analysis. We might, for example, consider the reliability of her responses—to what extent are repeated readings self-similar. A high level of reliability would indicate strong institutionalisation at the level of the individual. Alternatively, we might consider the extent to which readings by different individuals are self-similar. Here, a high level of self-similarity within a specific category of individuals would indicate strong institutionalisation within that category and may lead us to postulate the existence of an alliance of some form (alliances, in my conception, may be alliances of identification and need not necessarily be explicitly organised). Where a form of reading is reliable with respect to an individual, but does not generalise to a broader category, then the practice is clearly not institutionalised above the level of the individual. In such cases, the reading would be interpreted by a general audience as an idiosyncrasy, a performance rather than an expression of competence; I use the term trick to refer to such instances.

As I stated in Chapter 4, both skills and tricks are characterised by low discursive saturation (DS⁻) and are differentiated by their degree of institutionalisation above the level of the referent subject (often, the level of the individual). My own organisational language is weakly institutionalised to the extent that it is available, as a functional language, to—in comparison with, say, Basil Bernstein's language—a relatively small number of individuals, who are my own students, colleagues and readers of my earlier publications and who may (or may not) recruit the language in ways more or less consistent with my own (they may, quite legitimately, as far as I am concerned, produce heretical readings). My intention in this book, as in previous work, is to render the principles of the language explicitly available within discourse, to constitute it as high discursive saturation (DS⁺). Thus, it might be referred to as idiolect and, as with a DS⁻ trick, it is likely to be widely regarded, in terms of its specificity, as a performance rather than as an expression of competence.[50] Systemic Functional Linguistics (SFL), by contrast, is now well established, which is to say, strongly institutionalised, internationally and is clearly DS⁺ as is readily apparent from even an amateur's perusal of Halliday's and Mathiessen's book (2004). We may legitimately refer to SFL as a discourse in its own right and, for example, papers accepted for presentation at its international conferences are legitimately regarded as (potential) expressions of competence in this discourse.

The categories of emergent structure and autopoietic action that I have now introduced are summarised in Figures 5.5 and 4.5. I need to introduce a caveat before concluding. I have, here, introduced the category coding as a strategic option in the authoring and audiencing of texts. It clearly relates to the category institutionalisation, but they are distinct in that the latter, as an emergent feature, serves as a resource for coding. I can make a text using potato printing, selecting characters from a set of embossed potato-halves painted with powder colour. Such a strategy clearly exhibits strong coding, but is weakly institutionalised not least by virtue of its extreme localisation in time and space (especially in the summer). I might also add that, to the extent that a primary school student is permitted unconstrained to make their own embossings, then the lesson might, in this respect, anyway, be regarded as exhibiting weak framing in a Bernsteinian analysis.

My organisational language—of which the schemas introduced in this and other chapters form a part—attempts a sociological rather than a linguistic analysis of texts. The organisational language is sociological because it foregrounds social relations, which is to say, it is centrally concerned with the formation, maintenance

---

[50] Interestingly, perhaps, the extent to which my interpretation of the work of other authors whom I cite matches the received interpretations that are reproduced on undergraduate courses might be used as a measure of my competence. To the extent that an outcome is the pronouncement of my authorship as incompetent, then this would evidence a disciplinary drag (spun otherwise, a form of quality control) on the progression of idiolect towards discourse. As a member of the staff of a postgraduate institution, I have never taught undergraduates.

and destabilising of oppositions and alliances of social actors and with the realisation and recognition of these oppositions and alliances in cultural practices as instanced in cultural texts. I have described the text that is this book as I^- and DS^+. It is clearly strongly coded and the various relational spaces constituted in and by the key tables—Figures 5.5 and 4.5, in this chapter—are clearly synchronising strategies; the work is, at least in part, a mapping. How, then, does it resist betrayal as or by necrophiliac, faithless mythologising? Well, of course, it does not, entirely. But Judas, Midas, Orpheus were all denied that which they most desired, which is to say, their diachrony, their becoming, their lives, precisely because their utterances of grief were not timely, but synchronising in a lost or imagined perfection. My language has no Edens and no Utopias and, though synchronising, is no more than an instrument on which to play. That music will always be diachronising, will always be performance and, so long as it is not repeated too often, may at least offer timely relief from stultifying institutionalisation.

APPENDIX: THE GARDEN OF FORKING PATHS

I have described the synchronising strategies that construct Edens and Utopias as, ultimately, necrotising. We can see just how just how fatal they are if we push them as far as they will go in a nihilistic reading of Jorge Louis Borges' 'Garden of Forking Paths.' Here is the central problematic, explained by the main protagonist in the story:

> In all fictions, each time a man [sic] meets diverse alternatives, he chooses one and eliminates the others; in the work of the virtually impossible-to-disentangle Ts'ui Pen, the character chooses simultaneously all of them. He creates, thereby, 'several futures,' several times, which themselves proliferate and fork. (Borges, 1998, p. 125)

Now, this kind of fiction operates on the basis of some concept of causality. There are nodal points at which decisions must be made and what follows is dependent upon the decision, hence the proliferation of the garden of forking paths. This works rather well in fiction because what fiction does is rarify the nodal points—only certain points in the fiction entail decisions, so that the resulting garden is highly labyrinthine, but imaginable, even if not realisable. In practice, the author makes choices on behalf of his/her characters in suggesting a storyline (fabula). The problematic of Borges' story is that the plot (sjuzhet) does not unambiguously index a storyline. Although the plot appears to follow a single trace of choices, inferences made about the storyline seem to suggest that this trace is not unbroken. It is as if the short story that has been presented has been compiled from different possible stories, different paths in the garden. The denouement seems to propose that it is the linearity of time that limits us to a single choice at each node. The short story is a kind of narrative equivalent of one of M.C. Escher's engravings, which seem to say something similar about space.

In what we might care to describe as reality, of course, there is no limitation on the proliferation of nodal points; at every point on the continuum of our lives—

let's say, at least, our waking lives—we might have acted otherwise. In effect, this consideration proposes an infinity of synchronic planes, each constituting the instantaneous state of a universe at a given point on a particular time line. Thus, each plane might be said to carry its own history—a switch to another plane is a switch to an alternative history. The hypersystem that is the system of all synchronic planes consequently subsumes the temporal and effectively eradicates time; all that there is is a field of all possibilities that is defined relationally—a kind of super-langue, there is no parole; all that we are is static nodes. Time and space are inaugurated by the relational nature of the hypersystem; we have no past, no future, there is no we, me, you, nothing at all; the big bang becomes a big puff. Of course, we may not care to take this particular path.

QUIXOTE'S SCIENCE

Public heresy/private apostasy

At this point they came in sight of thirty forty windmills that there are on plain, and as soon as Don Quixote saw them he said to his squire, "Fortune is arranging matters for us better than we could have shaped our desires ourselves, for look there, friend Sancho Panza, where thirty or more monstrous giants present themselves, all of whom I mean to engage in battle and slay, and with whose spoils we shall begin to make our fortunes; for this is righteous warfare, and it is God's good service to sweep so evil a breed from off the face of the earth." (Miguel de Cervantes)

El Don Quixote was right, of course, windmills in Cervantes' Europe were monstrous giants, though wrong (as he eventually discovered) in his chivalrous crusade. If the enhanced performance of this new technology over hand milling didn't persuade the locals to pay the miller's fee, then the destruction of their querns by or on behalf of the wealthy mill owners—local lords or the church—would chivvy them into the new era.[51] Did the introduction of windmills change people's lives? Even this brief account points in the direction of a division of labour.[52] There are entrepreneurs, shall we say (the owners of the mill), there are millrights (employed by the entrepreneur), there is the miller, and there are producers of grain, there are the henchmen who take a hammer to household handmills in a kind of Luddism in reverse. The millright's skills had been developing for half a millennium before Quixote took exception to them, but, essentially, all of these positions were in place, *mutatis mutandis*, before the building of the first mill. The appearance of the giant on the landscape signalled an enhancement in the organisation of this division of labour that effected a movement in the demarcation of the public and the private; the deterritorialisation of domestic flour production and its reterritorialisation as a publicly available (at a

---

[51] See 'The history of flour milling' at www.cyberspaceag.com/kansascrops/wheat/flourmillinghistory. htm.

[52] Perhaps the term 'division of labour' is somewhat unfashionable in educational studies, these days. I retain it both to acknowledge a residual debt to Marx (and another to Durkheim)—a debt of the same character, perhaps, as that acknowledged by Foucault (I forget where)—and because it is now sufficiently anachronistic to stand out and thus allow me to avoid a neologism for that which brings together definable (and, of course, hierarchically organised) social groups with specific regularities in practice the articulation of which activities is constitutive of the sociocultural order. As I have been asserting throughout this book, this is here being interpreted as an emergent structure.

cost) service.[53] So, people's lives changed, but the change constituted and was constituted by a developing sophistication in the division of labour of which the windmill stood as a material sedimentation. Quixote's error was in mistaking a signifier for the social organisation that it signalled, though his lance would never have been a match for either.

This, essentially, was the line of argument that I offered in Dowling (1991a), although in that essay I was concerned not with 'the windmill', but with 'the computer' and, nearly two decades later, I might want to replace the latter by 'the internet' which, of course, I can access via my mobile phone or my TV as well as my MacBook Pro and which can be imagined as a very visible sedimentation of the globalised division of labour. That is to say, I am conceiving of *technology* as a more or less strongly institutionalised regularity of practice; the kind of regularity, indeed, that enables us to recognise the internet as such. This regularity is emergent upon the autopoietic formation of diverse oppositions and alliances that we can think of as social action and that carries on at all levels of analysis from state activity down to the strategies and tactics of individual players. This is the fundamental position that I have been presenting throughout this book.

A curriculum is a technology. It exists in at least two forms, an official or general form and its realisation in local instances (cf Bernstein, 1996/2000). A technological determinist kind of argument might conceive of the local curriculum, in its enactments—in classrooms and lecture theatres—as only relatively autonomous with respect to the official form. In this conception, emphasis would be placed on the effects on local practices of changes in the official form as well as, perhaps, the nature of and limitations upon the autonomy of the classroom. Consider, though, the push for modern or new mathematics in many parts of the world in the 1960s (see Cooper, 1983, 1985; Moon, 1986; Dowling, 1990). Here, the crucial bourbakiist message was ultimately dissipated as the central organising language of set theory was recontextualised as a pedagogic resource in the primary classroom (hoops and chalk circles for organising objects) and as merely another topic on the secondary curriculum.[54] The strong classification in the division of labour between mathematicians and school mathematics teachers survived, quite intact, the intervention of the former in the activities of the latter.

Similarly in Higher Education, being required (by quality assurance scrutineers) to provide explicit lists of intended learning outcomes for postgraduate seminars results merely in the production of an official, local curriculum and has little impact on the local, local curriculum in which the professor is still established as

---

[53] The terms, 'deterritorialisation' and 'reterritorialisation' are from Lacan via Deleuze and Guattari (1984) (see also Holland, 1999), whose position is not entirely inconsistent with my own in this chapter, though it grates rather more elsewhere in this book.

[54] Bourbakiism refers to the philosophy and activities of a group of mathematicians that was active in the formulation of the 'modern' or 'new' mathematics programmes referred to here. In terms of the influence of this group, the key characteristic of these programmes was the constitution of set theory as their central organising language. This characteristic was very substantially attenuated, if not annihilated, in the actual teaching of these programmes.

author rather than relayer of knowledge, albeit within a tradition of discourse, a discipline, perhaps. Here, the division of labour closely associates the person of the professor with the institutionalised practice of the discipline so that they may claim what I have referred to in Chapter 3 as traditional authority (see Figure 3.2). This mode of authority action is most likely to be effective under conditions of relative stability. Thus, back in school, in a period of healthy supply of mathematics graduates, those appointing mathematics teachers are in a position to stipulate that a degree in mathematics is a requirement for a successful application. Such a stipulation brings together a particular category of person and a particular technology (the mathematics curriculum) in authorising its appointee who may, of course, teach mathematics, but not science, which is the exclusive territory of graduates in that field. But, as an 'expert', the qualified mathematics teacher may claim a degree of authority over the mathematics curriculum giving rise to the dominance of the local over the official, the private over the public.[55]

In 1970s London the supply of mathematics graduates wanting to enter teaching had fallen below demand to such an extent that the possession of a mathematics degree was more of a rarity than a requirement for a mathematics teacher. Indeed, I was appointed as a teacher of mathematics despite having only a degree in physics and no professional or academic teacher education. I was appointed head of department less than three years later. The crisis continued throughout that and much of the next decade and teachers from all sorts of academic backgrounds found themselves teaching mathematics. As head of department I found myself working with physical education specialists, language teachers and geographers as well as a fair number of fellow natural scientists. Clearly, authorising strategies had reined back on the specificity of the author—the teacher. However, many schools in London began adopting a student-centred scheme of school mathematics called SMILE.[56] This was a workcard-based scheme that had been designed specifically in response to the shortage of specialist mathematics teachers. That which was principally demanded of the teacher was skill in classroom management and administration. In addition, local meetings at which workcards would be revised and new cards produced would also function as in-service training for the teachers. The effect was the constitution of an official curriculum over which individual teachers may be disinclined to claim individual authority. Rather, their role would be, to a substantial extent, defined by the curricular technology so that the authority would reside in the role or practice rather than in the person. This is the bureaucratic authority strategy from Chapter 3. Naturally, with the weakening of the autonomy of the teacher, this mode of authority action is likely to be associated

---

[55] Those teaching in England in the 1970s and 1980s may remember the 'mode 3' public examination syllabuses which were under the control of teachers and could even be established at the level of an individual school.

[56] Secondary Mathematics Learning Experiment—later, 'experiment' was replaced by 'experience' in the title. This was a teacher-led response to the changing situation, particularly in London; the state response was somewhat slower.

with an assertion (or reassertion) of the dominance of the official over the local, the public over the private.

Now in Dowling (2001c) I offered some examples of current trends in the development in the division of labour that entail the production of disembodied analogues of competence in what I am referring to as technologies. The unification and codification of school curricula in England and Wales (see Dowling & Noss, 1990; Flude & Hammer, 1989) and the development of national qualifications frameworks here and elsewhere are examples as are spellcheckers and other software developments such as Adobe Creative Suite which (amongst a great deal more) allows me—a sociologist, not a photographer—to produce quite acceptable digital images from the rather amateur RAW files captured on my Canon 5D (its predecessor, as far as I was concerned, the 10D, was obsolescent less than four years after its unveiling and has now itself been replaced by a 5D Mark II and 1D Mark III). These bureaucratising technologies are emergent upon the weakening of the esoteric control of the traditional expert over the form of institutionalisation of the practices to which they relate. The digital codification of these practices operates rather like the mass media, which, as Becker and Wehner (2001) point out, serve as 'reduction mechanisms', rendering their messages accessible to the public.

What appears to have happened is not that technologies have been invented that are able to achieve this—the technologies still have to be acceptable to their audiences—but that changes in the division of labour have effected a shift in the mode of relationship between (certain) categories of traditional 'expert' and their audiences. With the 'expert' exercising traditional authority, this relationship is pedagogic, which, to reprise, means that the author in an interaction retains, or seeks to retain, control over the principles of evaluation of their utterance. The kind of change that I am describing here gestates as this authority strategy becomes increasingly ineffective and the 'expert' is increasingly held to account for their actions. The relationship takes on more of the character of an exchange mode, whereby the principles of evaluation are devolved to the audience. The bureaucratic technology that facilitates this, through its 'reduction mechanisms', signifies the presence in the division of labour of a mediating or competing authority—the state, in the case of curricula and qualifications frameworks, software houses etc in the case of spellcheckers. The significance of such developments is that to some extent (perhaps to an increasing extent) the voice of the expert may be heard only in terms of the public forms of their practice that are codified in and by the technology. I will return to this in the closing of this chapter.

In the UK, the change in the field of education was signalled when, in 1962, the then Minister of Education referred to the school curriculum as a 'secret garden' (see Kogan, 1978). The invasion of this garden by politicians and capital over the ensuing forty years established the curriculum as a national park. The mathematical region of this park has been discussed in Dowling and Noss (1990).[57] However,

---

[57] Though this was published at a time when we had to rely on paper publication of the National Curriculum.

with corresponding public spaces opening up in other national systems and being freely available on the internet, the impact of each national government's policies becomes comparable in terms of a further 'reduced', international curriculum. A key representative of this technology is to be found in the series of comparative *Trends in International Mathematics and Science Study* (TIMSS) carried out under the auspices of the International Association for the Evaluation of Educational Achievement (IEA).[58] The results of this study and diverse reflections on the performances of participating nations[59] are available globally for recruitment in struggles relating to the bureaucratising of education at national level. This is how it is put on the National Center for Educational Statistics (NCES) website:

> With the emergence and growth of the global economy, policymakers and educators have turned to international comparisons to assess how well national systems of education are performing. These comparisons shed light on a host of policy issues, from access to education and equity of resources to the quality of school outputs. They provide policymakers with benchmarks to assess their systems' performances, and to identify potential strategies to improve student achievement and system outputs.
> (http://nces.ed.gov/surveys/international/IntlIndicators/)

Given the trend towards the globalising of English (see Crystal, 2003), what we have in this technology is a globally visible public educational discourse; the secret garden has blossomed into a world heritage site.

The first point to note about this discourse is that its subject focus establishes mathematics and science as the global public face of schooling, relegating most other areas to a relatively private sphere. It is easy to see why this is bound to be the case. As the exponents of ethnomathematics and ethnoscience (see, for example, D'Ambrosio, 1989; Davison & Miller, 1998) have been energetic in pointing out, mathematical and scientific knowledge has long been appropriated by the dominant and self-styled 'developed' nations as their own.[60] At the same time, most other areas of school knowledge—such as history and art—are closely and enthusiastically allied with individual national identities. A study entitled, Trends in International Poetry and Painting would present engaging methodological as well as political problems and Trends in International History would certainly provoke belligerent uproar.[61] Comparative literacy rates are clearly of political interest (see, for example, the Progress in International Reading Literacy Study

---

[58] See http://www.iea.nl/iea/hq/, also http://timss.bc.edu/ and http://nces.ed.gov/timss/

[59] See, for example, Symonds (2004) on the US and Wolf (2002) on Chile, both referring to poor performances on TMSS.

[60] See Dowling (1998) for a discussion of these claims in respect of ethnomathematics. D'Ambrosio (1985) described ethnomathematics as the mathematics that is practised in professional and cultural groups

[61] See, for example, the furore in South Korea and China over a Japanese school history textbook that, it is claimed, downplays Japanese militarism and war crimes committed by Japanese troops http://news.bbc.co.uk/2/hi/asia-pacific/4678009.stm

(PIRLS), also an IEA study[62]), but they do not (and, at the moment could not) specify the language (what with English, Spanish, Arabic and Chinese all legitimately vying for global hegemony). Perhaps sport comes closest to exhibiting the global status of (western) mathematics and science, but really only at the level of elite performance, which is clearly not the primary concern of formal schooling. This observation is consistent with, at the global level, a *public* curricular sphere consisting of mathematics and science in which context other curricular areas are relegated to a national, which is to say comparatively *private* sphere; there is an important exception to this division to which I will return later.

Stanley Fish localises in time and place the hegemony of science:

> ... in our culture science is usually thought to have the job of describing reality as it really is; but its possession of that franchise, which it wrested away from religion, is a historical achievement not a natural right. (Fish, 1995, p. 72)

Now I do not, in any case, subscribe to a theory of natural rights—here, at least, I am a happy (perhaps unhappy) positivist[63]—and so I will certainly go along with Fish in understanding western science as a cultural arbitrary.[64] This particular cultural arbitrary, however, is now constituted as one key element in a global hegemony. Furthermore, the contrast in modes of authority that are deployed by religious and scientific practices, respectively, is also consistent with the public ownership of the latter at the expense of the relative privatising of the former. Specifically, religious practices commonly involve the development of a traditional and/or charismatic priesthood in one form or another (see Chapter 3). The developments in science and mathematics curricula that I am referring to here, on the other hand, facilitate bureaucratic authority which tend to render individuals interchangeable: we can all be scientists to the extent that we can have public access to the principles of evaluation of scientific texts; but only a Catholic priest may hear a confession.[65]

Rather than tilt at my windmill, I want to explore it further to determine just what kinds of relationships (between author and audience) and practices it privileges. As my empirical object I shall take the US government TIMSS website at http://nces.ed.gov/timss/ (see Figure 6.1).[66] I do not propose to conduct a detailed analysis of this site. Rather, I shall use aspects of it to illustrate the points

---

[62] See http://www.iea.nl/iea/hq/

[63] See Crotty (1998) for a discussion of naturalist and positivist philosophies in the fields of research and law.

[64] 'Arbitrary' in the sense of Bourdieu & Passeron (1977).

[65] There is a corresponding contrast between the modes of authority deployed as, in Western culture, science replaces literature as the apogee of erudition. The origins of the humanities in British universities was predicated upon a sense of embodied literature and other artistic faculties as the necessary prerequisite of a cultivated English gentleman.

[66] All screenshots were made in September 2004. URLs and some of the text on this site have now changed, but there seems to be little point in updating them as they are likely to change again before too long.

that I want to make. Firstly, concerning the form of the technology, this is fairly conventional hypertext site, so that each page consists of a set of common elements—a standard header, a menu to the left (including links to the parent NCES site), page-specific text (which may or may not contain links) to the right, below all of this are plain text links to the NCES site, and above are links to a site map, the US Department of Education site, the NCES site, and a search engine. The righthand section of the home page contains a graphic link (a cartoon frog) to some of the questions used in TIMSS, 'For Students!' Below this are two windows, one showing 'What's New' and the other 'International Fast Facts', the content of which changes when the page is refreshed, apparently on the basis of a random selection from a file of 'facts'.

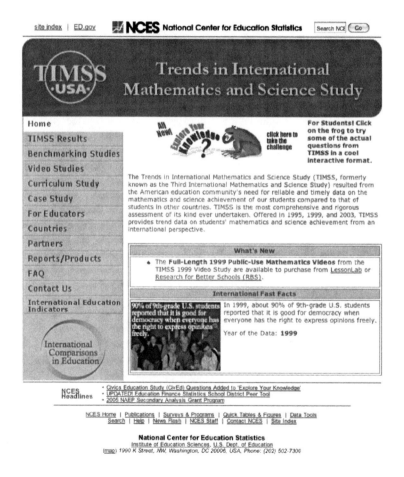

Figure 6.1. TIMSS(USA) Home Page

This design presents, on each page, the key claims to bureaucratic authority—established by the links to other government sites in the page header and footer[67]—and the structure of the site—principally in the menu—which consistently frames the page-specific content. On this site the page-specific content is generally linear, discursive text. In addition, this page-specific content is, in most cases, marked, which is to say that it carries one or more links. These links are generally to other pages in the same site or the parent NCES site.[68] The design conforms to what Michael Joyce (1995) has described as an 'exploratory' rather than a 'constructive' hypertext. James Sosnoski succinctly describes the difference as follows:

> The exploratory (or expository) hypertext is a 'delivery or presentational technology' that provides ready access to information. By contrast, constructive hypertexts are 'analytic tools' that allow writers to invent and/or map relations among bits of information to suit their own needs. (Sosnowski, 1999, p. 163)

In my terms, the site establishes pedagogic relations between its author and audience; this is unsurprising, of course, in a government publication. It is, however, worth pointing out that even were the site to include multiple links to other, non-governmental sites, this would itself remain a pedagogic action insofar as it is a privileging of marked over unmarked text; the TIMSS site asserts a stronger pedagogic claim by additionally retaining control over the targets of links to marked text. Unmarked text is, of course, open to interrogation—any term or terms may be copied into a non-governmental search engine. However, such alternative readings are privatised by the TIMSS site. Similarly, the reader may formulate alternative structures for the site—this is essentially what I am doing here.[69] Again, though, such strategies are privatised by the pedagogic site, which deploys bureaucratic authority strategies and essentially privileges an explicit taxomony and marked text over contingent organisation and unmarked text. So, the educational technology that I have been discussing signals—which is to say, is emergent upon—the establishment of a public/private partitioning of educational discourse that locates mathematics and science and strongly institutionalised modes of reading within the public sphere and other areas of knowledge and alternative modes of reading in the private.

The next question to be considered relates to the nature of the public mathematical and scientific knowledge. In order to address this I will click the frog link on the TIMSS homepage (Figure 1). This takes me to a page on another site parented by NCES, the 'Students' Classroom' (http://nces.ed.gov/nceskids/index).

---

[67] The authority action is bureaucratic because government *per se* is bureaucratic insofar as its authority is taken to reside in the office (practices) rather than in individuals. Of course, other modes of authority may be deployed in establishing the legitimacy of government.

[68] Although it is possible to exit the NCES site by following some of the links as I will illustrate below.

[69] My access to publishers prepared to publish my work is, of course, a move towards re-publicising of this particular privatised reading, but even this leaves my reading in a comparatively weak—which is to say, comparatively privatised—position *vis-à-vis* the TIMSS globally public reading.

The particular page is titled 'Explore Your Knowledge' (http://nces.ed.gov/nceskids/eyk/index and see Figure 6.2). The page gives access to assessment items from the TIMSS study and also from the Civic Education Study (CivEd) to which I shall return later. From the page in Figure 2 I select my subject, grade and the number of questions (5, 10, 15 or 20) and am presented with the required number of test items; examples of these are shown in Figures 6.3-6.12. After making my selections from the multi-choice radio buttons I can click 'show me the answers' and my page is replaced with an answers page including a score given as a percentage—Figure 6.13 shows part of an answer page. Clicking on the globe button—one is given for each item—opens a pop-up window (Figure 6.14) showing the US national performance and the international average for the item; buttons in other country locations on a world map[70] will replace the US flag and performance with those of the relevant country.

Figure 6.2. 'Explore Your Knowledge', NCIS Site

Before proceeding to look at some items, I will briefly make two preliminary observations based on the description thus far. Firstly, the provision of the world

---

[70] The full list of TIMSS participating countries is given at http://nces.ed.gov/timss/countries.asp. Each information map shows only a small selection, though the US is always included (it being a US site).

map and clickable international comparisons (Figure 6.14) is a good illustration of my point that we are talking about global public discourse here, even if only in its larval stage. Secondly, the combination of multi-choice radio buttons and definitively 'correct' answers is a particularly effective privatising of alternatives by a strongly pedagogic technology. The multi-choice test item (and the pre-coded questionnaire and countless other digitisings) is a technology that is emergent upon a drive to render all commensurable, all accountable to a public discourse via the exclusion of the private.

2. **Some children were trying to find out which of three light bulbs was brightest. Which one of these gives the best START toward finding the answer?**

○ "One bulbs looks brightest to me, so I already know the answer."

○ "All the bulbs look bright to me, so there cannot be an answer."

○ "It would help if we had a way to measure the brightness of a light bulb."

○ "We can take votes and each person will vote for the bulb he or she thinks is the brightest."

Figure 6.3. TIMSS Test Item for Grade 4 Science 1

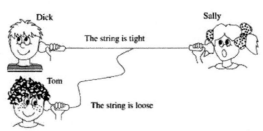

14. **The picture shows Dick and his friends playing with a string-telephone. Sally is speaking. Dick and Tom are trying to listen. Which of them can hear her speak?**

○ Both of them can hear equally clear.

○ Neither of them can hear.

○ Only Tom can hear clearly.

○ Only Dick can hear clearly.

○ Both of them can hear equally faintly.

Figure 6.4. TIMSS Test Item for Grade 4 Science 2

The TIMSS test items construct scientific and mathematical knowledge in a familiar way, perhaps. Firstly, they constitute formal modes of expression (see Figure 6.6) and content (see Figure 6.7, which invokes a taxonomy) that represent what I am referring to as the esoteric domain (see Chapters 4 and 8) of mathematical or, in these cases, scientific knowledge. The esoteric domain consists of discourse, which is strongly marked out from other areas of practice and contrasts with the public domain, which is weakly marked out.[71] Thus, contrasting with Figures 6.6 and 6.7, the item in Figure 6.4 refers to a children's game using a tin can phone—a public domain setting. The item in Figure 6.10 also employs a public domain setting and it is significant to note that the term, 'probability' is substituted by 'chance'. This is consistent with my findings in my analysis of a major British textbook scheme that the theme of probability was (at least at that time and in that place) very substantially taught within the public domain (Dowling, 1998).

16. Four children can feel and smell an object inside a bag, but they cannot see it. Which of the following is NOT an observation about the object?

○ "It is flat at one end and round at the other."

○ "It smells like peppermint."

○ "It has a bump on it."

○ "I hope it is candy."

Figure 6.5. TIMSS Test Item for Grade 4 Science 3

17. Alexander Fleming noticed that bacteria growing on a plate of agar did not grow next to a mold that was growing on the same plate. He wrote in his laboratory report: "The mold may be producing a substance that kills bacteria." This statement is described as:

○ an observation

○ a hypothesis

○ a generalization

○ a conclusion

Figure 6.6. TIMSS Test Item for Grade 8 Science 1

School science and, especially, mathematics constitute esoteric domains that are strongly institutionalised. This is to say that scientific and mathematical language are deployed with a high degree of regulation—far more so than in most other areas of the curriculum. If I may gloss mathematics, as such, as the study of formal systems, then it is clear why its esoteric domain must be strongly institutionalised. Science, then, might be thought of as the study of partially- or to-be-formalised systems and its esoteric domain language emerges out of (induction) and is projected onto (deduction) the systems that are to be formalised. Science too, then,

---

[71] I have been referring, throughout this chapter, to public/private divisions. This use does not correspond to the esoteric/public domain distinction that I am making here and throughout this book, although there is clearly some relation between them. For the sake of clarity here it is best to think of 'public domain' as a single term rather than an adjective-noun pair.

is predicated upon a strongly institutionalised esoteric domain. However, public

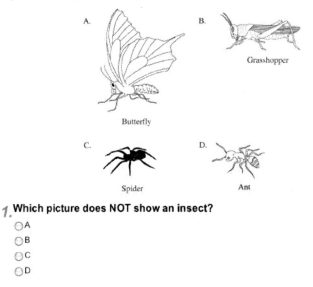

1. **Which picture does NOT show an insect?**

○ A
○ B
○ C
○ D

Figure 6.7. TIMSS Test Item for Grade 8 Science 2

13. **Two open bottles, one filled with vinegar and the other with olive oil, were left on a window sill in the Sun. Several days later it was observed that the bottles were no longer full. What can be concluded from this observation?**

○ Vinegar evaporates faster than olive oil.

○ Olive oil evaporates faster than vinegar.

○ Both vinegar and olive oil evaporate.

○ Only liquids containing water evaporate.

○ Direct sunlight is needed for evaporation.

Figure 6.8. TIMSS Test Item for Grade 8 Science 3

domain text renders invisible the esoteric domain structuring that makes a task mathematical or scientific rather than something else. In the item in Figure 6.5, the response, 'I hope it's candy' is indeed an observation about the object in the bag,[72] but not in the scientific sense which must exclude the subjective. 'Intensity' has been replaced by 'brightness' in the item in Figure 6.3; which bulb is 'brightest'

---

[72] The statement may be reformulated as, 'the object in the bag is something that I hope is candy', thus making the object in the bag the subject of the principal clause.

may well relate to colour (frequency) as well as to intensity and so call for a subjective response; again, subjectivity must be excluded from formal school science. The item in Figure 6.8 is particularly interesting in that the most likely public domain response—someone has been making salad—is not offered as an option. There is a sense in which this item might be thought of as teaching rather than assessing.

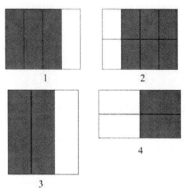

9. **Each figure represents a fraction. Which two figures represent the same fraction?**

◯ 1 and 2
◯ 1 and 4
◯ 2 and 3
◯ 3 and 4

Figure 6.9. TIMSS Test Item for Grade 4 Mathematics 1

Some of the mathematics test items (Figures 6.9-6.12) may be interpreted as tending to undermine esoteric domain mathematics and science. The Figure 6.9 item represents a standard teaching metaphor, which may be glossed as 'a fraction is a piece of cake'. The correct answer is the first one on offer because both diagrams 1 and 2 conventionally represent the fraction $\frac{3}{4}$. However, as I have previously pointed out (Dowling, 1990), this metaphor pedagogically challenges the esoteric domain constitution of a fraction as a number—that is of $\frac{3}{4}$ as a number between 0 and 1. Thus, if we use diagram 1 from Figure 6.9 to illustrate the sum $\frac{3}{4} + \frac{3}{4}$ as in Figure 6.15, then a perfectly reasonable (though, of course, mathematically incorrect) answer would be $\frac{6}{8}$.[73] The 'correct' response to the item

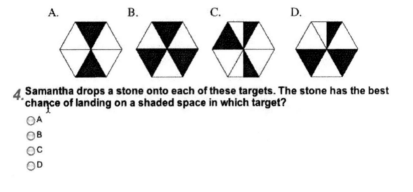

A.   B.   C.   D.

4. **Samantha drops a stone onto each of these targets. The stone has the best chance of landing on a shaded space in which target?**

○ A

○ B

○ C

○ D

Figure 6.10. TIMSS Test Item for Grade 4 Mathematics 2

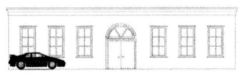

14. **The car is 3.5 m long. About how long is the building?**

○ 18 m

○ 14 m

○ 10 m

○ 4 m

Figure 6.11. TIMSS Test Item for Grade 8 Mathematics 1

in Figure 6.11 is the second radio button, 14 m. However, this appears to discount the width of the car (and its distance from the building). If the visible side of the car is a little under 2 m from the building, then a viewpoint 7 m away from the car in line with the rear of the car and the lefthand end of the building would make the

---

[73] This is because the metaphor, 'a fraction is a piece of cake', invites the student to take the number of shaded pieces to be the numerator and the total number of pieces to be the denominator. It is also the case that the total amount of shaded cake in Figure 6.15 is $\frac{6}{8}$ or $\frac{3}{4}$ of the total amount of cake. That we frequently find students making this error does not affirm that they are interpreting the diagrams as I have suggested, but their error is at least consistent with this interpretation.

first option—18 m—a better answer. The item appears to be testing estimation skills, but the public domain simulation renders it ambiguous.[74] The item in Figure 6.12 appears to be an esoteric domain text. However, there is a unique answer only if we qualify 'relation' with the term 'linear'. If the nature of the relation is not specified then there is no limitation on what might replace the question mark in the table. We may take the reference to a 'missing number' as indicating that the relation is between two numerical variables, but, even so, all five offered answers are equally acceptable, mathematically. Here, it is not the construction of a public domain setting that has generated the ambiguity, but a reduction of the complexity of the esoteric domain.[75]

x	y
2	5
3	7
4	?
7	15

18. The table represents a relation between x and y. What is the missing number in the table?

○ 9
○ 10
○ 11
○ 12
○ 13

Figure 6.12. TIMSS Test Item for Grade 8 Mathematics 2

This brief analysis of ten test items[76] suggests that mathematics and science—and the difference between them, here, is not as great as one might suppose—are constructed as laboratorised or, shall we say, laboratorising practices. These

---

[74] South Africa—quite easily the lowest scoring country in both mathematics and science—scored 26% answers correct on this item as compared with the 74% international average. It would be interesting to see which responses dominated in South Africa (and, of course, to ask the respondents why).

[75] A feature that is particularly common in texts directed at lower performing students as is the prevalence of public domain settings (Dowling, 1998).

[76] The site notes that there are about 130 items available, presumably these cover ninth grade civics as well as fourth and eighth grade mathematics and science.

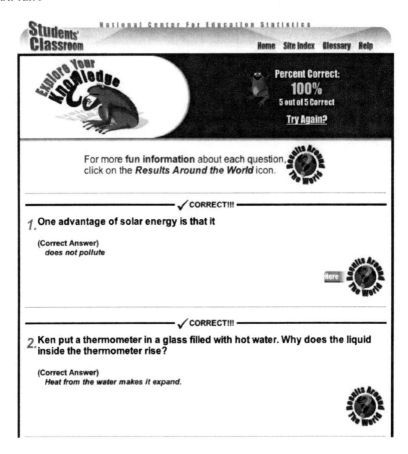

Figure 6.13. TIMSS Answers Page

laboratorising practices operate on the phenomenal world in much the same way as a hypertext author operates on text, which is to say, by marking that which may legitimately be operationalised; the unmarked, extraneous, subjective regions of the text are methodologically excluded. In both mathematics/science and hypertext, this marking may often be invisible. In hypertext, however, we are well practiced in scanning the text with the cursor so as to reveal the links. No similar divining rods are to be found in mathematics or science and that is why, of course, my revealing of the ambiguities introduced by the public domain contexts does not challenge the items as suitable for their purpose—I obtained 'correct' answers on my first attempt on all of the items, despite my recognition of their 'flaws'. This is presumably consistent with my standing as a physics graduate and, more to the point, one-time teacher of high school mathematics and science.

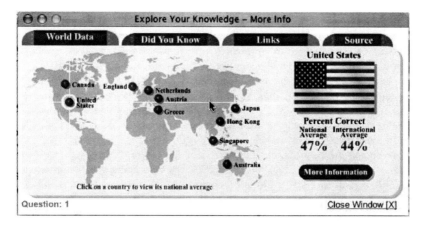

Figure 6.14. Information about International Performances on Selected TIMSS Test Items

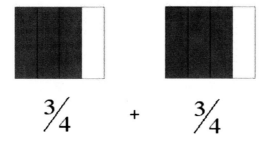

Figure 6.15. $\frac{3}{4} + \frac{3}{4} = ?$

So my point is not to criticise the validity or reliability of the test items, but to illustrate the kind of practice that hegemonises the global public educational discourse.[77] To the extent that mathematics and science exhaust this discourse, then

---

[77] Indeed, critics of multi-choice test items tend to limit their criticisms to issues of face and content validity. However, to the extent that the authors of the test have established a strong measure of convergent validity of these items with respect to, shall we say, measures derived from clinical interviews, then there is no reason why they should not be used in large scale surveys, such as TIMSS. In their exploration of Piagetian stages, Shayer *et al* (1992) precisely did take steps to affirm the convergent validity of their experimental tests in relation to clinical interviews of the type used by Piaget himself. This precaution was ignored by Donaldson's (1987) much cited challenge to Piaget's findings. I have not studied the validity tests used by the TIMSS authors, because the point,
(continued)

we might infer that they define, firstly, the legitimate mode of relationship to the empirical and, secondly, the legitimate form of argumentation. In both cases, legitimacy is established by principles of exclusion that are governed by the esoteric domains of mathematical and scientific practice that exclude, in particular, the subjective and the contingent, thus relegating them to the private sphere. As I have suggested above, we may tentatively distinguish between the two esoteric domains by referring to science as a formalising discourse and mathematics as a formalised discourse.[78] Given this distinction, we might speculate that science takes the dominant role in respect of the constitution of the legitimate mode of the relationship to the empirical, and mathematics in respect of the legitimate form of argumentation. The blurring of the distinction between mathematics and science in their high school forms also blurs this division of discursive labour. In any event, mathematics and science taken together do seem to define the legitimate form of rational action so defining, on a global stage, the bureaucratic public voice,[79] so I'll refer to the public global technology as *mathematicoscience*.

Now, clearly, mathematicoscience is not the only public forms of discourse. However, apart from the operational matrix[80] of the internet itself, it is arguably the principal form of discourse for which globalised regularity or institutionalisation might be claimed and this is signified by its prominence in the global curricular technology to which I have been referring. Insofar as there is a globally prevalent aspiration for universal schooling and insofar as mathematicoscience, more or less as I have described it here, territorialises the globally public content of schooling, the significance of this discourse should not be understated.

---

in this chapter, is to examine the workings of this global public discourse and not its convergence with local forms of assessment.

[78] I am reminded here of Foucault's comment on mathematics:

> ... the only discursive practice to have crossed at one and the same time the thresholds of positivity, epistemologization, scientificity, and formalization. The very possibility of its existence implied that [that] which, in all other sciences, remains dispersed throughout history, should be given at the outset: its original positivity was to constitute an already formalized discursive practice (even if other formalizations were to be used later). Hence the fact that their establishment is both so enigmatic (so little accessible to analysis, so confined within the form of the absolute beginning) and so valid (since it is valid both as an origin and as a foundation); hence the fact that in the first gesture of the first mathematician one saw the constitution of an ideality that has been deployed throughout history, and has been questioned only to be repeated and purified; hence the fact that the beginning of mathematics is questioned not so much as a historical event as for its validity as a principle of history: and hence the fact that, for all the other sciences, the description of its historical genesis, its gropings and failures, its late emergence is related to the meta-historical model of a geometry emerging suddenly, once and for all, from the trivial practices of land-measuring. (Foucault, 1972, pp. 188-189)

[79] This seems to be consistent with Max Weber's (1968) remarks on the increasing prevalence of *zweckrationalitat*.

[80] I define 'operational matrix' as a technology—a regularity of practice—that incorporates, non-discursively, the principles of its own deployment: a supermarket and the World Wide Web would both be examples.

So what are the implications? Well we might begin by considering this chapter. I am certainly laying claim to both bureaucratic and traditional authority. My affiliation to the Institute of Education, University of London establishes that I hold an office that authorises me to speak academically about educational matters. This is a very weak claim, however, as the practice of peer review (or clubbing, as I tend to think of it), for example, ensures that the *ex officio* authority of academics is limited, generally to that which they may hold over their students. My recruitment of what I may hope is a familiar academic style and my deployment of familiar academic terms also constitutes a bureaucratic action in the way that I (*pace* Max Weber) have defined it: I am, in this sense, allowing (or pretending to allow) the discourse to ventriloquise me. Traditional authority is claimed in terms of my yellowing PhD thesis and also through the community of celebrated academic authors to which I affiliate via my egocentric bibliography (clubbing in the imaginary, perhaps).

But I am clearly trying to do more than that. Bureaucratic and traditional authority strategies both invoke institutionalised, which is to say, stabilised practices. Such strategies are appropriate in the context of schooling insofar as the authority of the teacher or of the curriculum rests on training or on a construction that has already been completed. In this respect, at least, schooling is structurally conservative as is illustrated by the recontextualising of set theory, which I mentioned earlier.

The authority of the academic, on the other hand, is established dynamically. The output of research is valued only insofar as it is original (a necessary, but, of course, not sufficient condition for acceptability). Academic discourse, then, is structurally dynamic. The academic may rely on traditional authority strategies by, for example, establishing originality only in terms of the empirical setting and not in terms of theoretical framework—replication studies would be of this form. However, work of the highest status must contribute to the development, the construction and/or discovery of the language of the discourse, which is to say, theory. This, of course, entails a destabilising of the institutionalised practice that affirms the two modes of authority action that I have referred to so far in this chapter. The third mode, referring to Figure 3.2, is charismatic authority and is predicated on the closure of the category of author and the opening of the category of practice. In establishing the originality of the analysis in this chapter (and in this book generally) I am, at least in some respects, attempting to deploy a charismatic authority action. I am served in this respect by the facility to refer to my own previous publications, establishing myself as an author of already accepted (and so publicly acknowledged as original) practice.

Naturally, there is a general level of resistance in the field to charismatic claims to originality because they must stand in competition with others. My work, then, must extend, even distort and transform the discourse, but I do not have free license. So how might this particular chapter be challenged? Well, on precisely the principles that are established in the terms of the public global discourse that I am referring to as mathematicoscience, though I have now moved higher up the academic ladder. So: have I deployed appropriate principles of exclusion in my engagement with the empirical and in the construction of my syllogisms; have I deployed an objective methodological apparatus with sufficient rigour to exclude subjective noise or distortion? My critic may point out, for example, that my sampling strategies are inadequate to my grandiose claims and that my analysis and argument are tendentious, rife with subjectivism. Within the context of the public global discourse of mathematicoscience my critic would be entirely justified as I will authoritatively affirm as the co-author of works on research methodology (Brown & Dowling, 1998; Dowling & Brown, 2009). Insofar as my chapter is recognisable in the public sphere, it can be recognised only as heresy. The physicist, Alan Sokal—whose gleeful assault on cultural studies will be discussed in Chapter 8—exemplifies the moral panic of the mathematico-scientists:

> In short, my concern over the spread of subjectivist thinking is both intellectual and political. Intellectually, the problem with such doctrines is that they are false (when not simply meaningless). There *is* a real world; its properties are *not* merely social constructions; facts and evidence *do* matter. What sane person would contend otherwise? And yet, much contemporary academic theorizing consists precisely of attempts to blur these obvious truths—the utter absurdity of it all being concealed through obscure and pretentious language. (Sokal, 1996, no page numbers in the WWW version)

It is the thrust of my argument, however, that the lance of my quixotic critic cannot penetrate me, precisely because it misses the point, which is as follows. All technologies—including mathematicoscience—are here being regarded as emergent upon the formation of alliances and oppositions in social action—they are the public visibility of these alliances. However we know from our respective experiences that the work that goes into social action is very substantially conducted in private—in the lavatories, not the boardroom. Furthermore, the opening up of private spaces to public scrutiny—ethnography, perhaps, or the ungendered toilets in *Ally McBeal* and the Belgo restaurant in London's West End—will simply resite the private, not eradicate it,[81] just as the zero-tolerance policing paving the way for the gentrification of London's Kings Cross produces assaults on hapless students in Bloomsbury. The private, in other words, is for the most part where, for good or bad, things get done.

Let me complete my schema for authority strategies. This has, of course, already been done in Chapter 3, but the move from two or three categories to a complete set of four is a crucial, if not entirely exclusive, aspect of my method, so a reprise at this stage seems timely. I have, in effect, introduced two variables, the category of author and the field of practice and each of these are binary nominal scales, open/closed. The product of these two variables gives rise to the space in Figure 3.2. It will be apparent that there are now four modes of action, three of which have

---

[81] *Ally McBeal*, see http://www.imdb.com/title/tt0118254/maindetails. The toilets in the Belgo restaurant actually have gendered sets of cubicles, but in a single space and with communal washbasins.

already been deployed in this chapter. The fourth, *liberal* mode, is essentially a mode of action in which authority is negated. In liberal mode, persons are interchangeable and practice is mutable. Piaget's (or Marx's) paradise, perhaps, but a mode of action that does seem to characterise the licence of a private audience: unless you intend or are required to respond to this book in public, then there are no necessary constraints on the way in which you read and make use of it (or choose not to). The book stands as a resource or reservoir of resources for recruitment by the audience and, in this aspect, the relationship between author and audience is one of exchange. But I will conclude the chapter by offering some suggestions.

This chapter, in a slightly different form, was originally written for an international collection, which is managed by an international editorial group. Those of us submitting chapters also had to submit to a peer review process and face the threat of required revision or exclusion. The structure of this practice—also a feature of the most respected academic journals—would appear to militate for some level of adherence to a public discourse which will include, as in this sentence, the genuflections of hedging, because the authority of our utterances must reside, bureaucratically, with the discourse, our mastery of which is yet to be finally affirmed. To read my analysis of the TIMSS test items as literal criticism within the field of the assessment of school science and mathematics would be to sublimate the chapter on the level of this public discourse. This would be to render it legitimately open to revision in respect of the necessary exclusion of subjectivity and, incidentally, tricky language which can only be obscuring the clarity (or fallaciousness) of its syllogisms. Interaction in this mode is the equilibration that I introduced in Chapter 3 (Figure 3.1). In this mode, an acceptable piece of work must contribute or potentially contribute to the coherence of public rationality, to which it stands in synecdochic relation. But if my overall analysis is persuasive (for whatever reason) then, as private intellectuals and teachers, we may be sharpening the sword of our own executioner.

Academic engagement does not always work like this. In the club mode of peer review (including the audiencing of papers at conferences and the recruitment of 'the literature' in our own papers) we may also be familiar with the facility to read or listen politely and with at least apparent interest and to withhold equilibrating action on the grounds that contingency insulates us from the other author. This mode is the exchange of narratives.

But the public discourse will not go away. Perhaps the arbitrary nature of public discourses may be made more apparent (or perhaps not) by the introduction of the third set of test items that is made available by clicking the frog on the TIMSS USA website. Perhaps surprisingly, perhaps not, this set of items is from the Civic Education Study (CivEd). The CivEd homepage notes that:

All societies have a continuing interest in the ways in which their young people are prepared for citizenship and learn to take part in public affairs. At the turn of this new century this has become a matter of increased importance not only in societies striving to establish or reestablish democratic governments, but also in societies with continuous and long established democratic traditions. (http://nces.ed.gov/surveys/cived/)

I will not offer an analysis of the CivEd text items. However, the 'International Fast Facts' box in the screen shot of the TIMSS USA home page that I have included as Figure 6.1 presents what is presumably a finding from the study:

> In 1999, about 90% of 9th-grade U.S. students reported that it is good for democracy when everyone has the right to express opinions freely.
> Year of the Data: 1999[82]

It would appear that the discourse of liberal democracy is a second key component of the public global technology alongside mathematicoscience. Jean Baudrillard (talking about Saddam Hussain and the first Gulf 'War') offers a rather different take on democracy:

> ... as with every true dictator, the ultimate end of politics, carefully masked elsewhere by the effects of democracy, is to maintain control of one's own people by any means, including terror. (Baudrillard, 1995, p. 72)

It's not altogether certain that the masking is everywhere very substantial.

Again, here is not the place to engage in an explicit critique—which would, in any event, be quixotic, a quixocritique—of liberal democracy as a universal aspiration and absolute good. All that I should do here is to point to the alignment of discourses associated with the TIMSS site. Alan Sokal would (should he consider an assault on this book to be worth the effort) no doubt berate me for making anything at all out of the juxtaposition of the language of democracy with the language of scientific rationality other than that, perhaps, they are *in fact* properly aligned: the one seeking the optimising of the exigencies of social organisation in the context of liberal values; the other seeking the optimising of our engagement with the empirical world in the face of imperfect knowledge. I am easily defeated in the public discourse that emerges out of social alliances that must overwhelm me. Indeed, even Sokal's far more celebrated public victims must often appear to be skulking back into the privacy of their arcane, alchemic worlds in the face of his dazzling crusade.

The invoking or the awareness of a public/private duality seems to provoke hegemonic or counter-hegemonic, metaphorical action, but to engage in this way is either to play the game of the dominant alliances or to falter. To the extent that the bureaucratised public technology constitutes the language by which expertise is defined, the traditional expert—insofar as their expertise stands in excess of the bureaucratically defined practice—or the charismatic or liberal innovator may participate only as heretics—and heretics always get burned eventually (in this world or a next).

---

[82] It is not helpful to provide a reference as this appeared in a box on the site, the contents of which vary.

I have deployed three of the modes of interaction introduced in Chapter 3: synecdochic equilibration; metonymic exchange of narratives; and metaphoric hegemony. The first two of these modes presume an alliance of similars—we all speak the same public language. They differ in that equilibration seeks a discursive closure whilst the exchange of narratives deploys contingency to avoid closure. Hegemony contrasts with both in recognition of the public/private partition. Here engagement is between disimilars. But like equilibration, the target is discursive closure. The product of the two variables, alliance (similars/disimilars) and target of discursive action (closure/openness) gives rise, once again, to the relational space shown in Figure 3.1. As with my analysis of authority action, I am left with a residual category. In this case, the category, pastiche, defines an interaction between disimilars—public/private—under conditions of discursive openness. I have offered corresponding tropes for the other modes. The characteristic trope for pastiche is catachresis (see Burbules, nd). I want to suggest that it is precisely in this mode that private action in non-bureaucratic mode is most productively elaborated. Here, apostasy in relation to the global public technology of mathematicoscience (and democracy) may be sustained whilst still recruiting from it that which may be of practical value in our local pursuits. We have, in other words, to recognise, that very few of us are going to change the world in any sense at all and that those of us who do may well not welcome the outcome; some people change the world, but not in ways that they themselves choose.

So what does this mean in the context of mathematics and science education? I ought, in righteous exchange mode, to say, 'I don't know,' but then, I'm a teacher. I suppose that it may well come down to paying close attention to the matter at hand and, in particular, to the nature of the local relations that will tend to dominate any given intervention or interaction. Very little will be served, I think, either by total submission to the hegemony of mathematicoscience or by opposition in quixocritique. The whole point of pastiche interaction is that the integrity of the participating discourses must be maintained—catachresis must not be permitted to degenerate into metaphor or, perhaps worse, the literal discursive identity of equilibration or exchange of narratives. As has been demonstrated by a wealth of sociological and sociolinguistic work,[83] the predisposition to accept public forms of discourse is itself emergent upon structuration that can be described in socioeconomic terms. As I have demonstrated elsewhere (in relation to school mathematics at least), public forms of discourse necessarily serve to recontextualise and transform and so subordinate private forms where the latter are introduced into the public domains of the former (Dowling, 1991b, 1995, 1996, 1998, 2001a). As the bureaucratised spokesperson of mathematicoscience the teacher may draw their students into their own game, but they will not solve any of the problems, address any of the concerns of their students insofar as these problems and concerns are constituted within localised, private discourses—and

---

[83] See, for example, Bernstein (1971, 1999), Bourdieu (1991), Bourdieu and Passeron (1977), Gee *et al* (2001), Hasan (1999), Heath (1986), Moss (2000)—though not all might concur with my formulation of their findings; see also Chapter 3.

one suspects that most of them are. Essentially, school is a very bad place to learn anything beyond how to survive as a school student (or teacher).[84] Yet, knowing all of this, my erstwhile[85] mentor, Basil Bernstein had this to say in 1971:

> It is an accepted educational principle that we should work with what the child can offer: why don't we practice it? The introduction of the child to the universalistic meanings of public forms of thought is not compensatory education—it is education. (Bernstein, 1971, p. 199)

Thirty years and two Gulf 'wars' on, you'd think we'd know better. But I fear not; *viva el Don*, it seems.

---

[84] Cf. Lave and Wenger (1991).

[85] And, despite all, fondly and gratefully remembered—see Dowling (1999, 2001b) and Chapter 4.

PEDAGOGY AND COMMUNITY IN THREE SOUTH AFRICAN SCHOOLS[86]

An iterative description

PAUL DOWLING & ANDREW BROWN

STARTING THE DAY

The Mont Clair High School assembly was held after the first two lessons. We entered from the back of the gallery of a large hall. Students were sitting in the body of the hall and on the carpeted steps of the gallery. We, together with some of the teachers, sat on chairs at the back of the gallery. We were all facing the stage. There were large, upholstered chairs on the stage, arranged in rows. A number of teachers and four or five senior students were sitting on these chairs; there was a desk in front of them and a lectern to one side of the stage. We were all told to stand. The principal, wearing an academic gown, walked onto the stage and stood behind the desk. He addressed the school, 'Good morning, school'. There was a mumbled response of 'Good morning, sir'. The principal announced the name of the 'today's song'. The words of the song were displayed by an overhead projector to a piano accompaniment. Some of the teachers appeared to be singing the song; the students and the other teachers either mumbled or mouthed the words.

At the end of the song, we all sat down and the principal introduced the deputy principal, who was to present the lesson. The deputy principal talked about the trouble in Kwa-Zulu Natal. 'What a sad situation in our country', the democratic principle is being undermined by unscrupulous and selfish people. In a democracy, we as individuals must be responsible for government. The deputy principal referred to a discussion about shoplifting that he had had with the manager of a security firm. Again, the emphasis was on individual integrity, I believe in what is right and good and I do it. Corruption in high places is only possible because there is corruption in low places. He appealed to the community of the school by

---

[86] Some additional footnotes have been provided by Jaamiah Galant and Ursula Hoadley and are identified by the appending of the initials of the authors in square brackets, thus '[JG&UH]'. These notes offer additional clarification and contextualisation.

reference to 'we of the Christian faith'. He read an extract from the Gospel of St John and a prayer that was introduced by 'Let us pray'.

Another teacher and a student read notices; a water polo team from Eton—'the most prestigious school in England'—was to play the Mont Clair side that afternoon. The deputy principal returned to talk about a current problem with theft. One of the workers had been dismissed; this may or may not be related to the problem. However, the pupil committee had requested that students should report any instance of another student looking into a bag other than their own. Any student about whom repeated reports were made would be investigated. The deputy principal read out the names of several students who have detention and others who had been given permission to wear long hair because they were to perform in the school play. The principal made a number of celebratory announcements regarding individual sporting and academic successes. Mont Clair students have obtained two out of only seven national scholarships for overseas study. Mont Clair students, the principal said, are so articulate and confident. The principal and teachers and students sitting on the stage left and the school was dismissed by a senior student.

***

It was the start of the school day at Siyafunda High School. The principal led us out of his office asking a member of staff on the way whether or not it was raining—it wasn't. The principal led us to a space between two of the school buildings where we stood against one of the walls. Another adult man (not a teacher) stood in front of us and a small group of members of staff stood at the side, mostly out of sight of the students. A number of students had already gathered in the space and were facing us; others joined them, filling up the space. There were about the same number of students as had been in the Mont Clair assembly hall, but we were outside; the assembly would have been cancelled had it been raining. We were waiting for the principal or the other adult to address the school, but neither of them did. Instead, a voice from amongst the mass of students started to sing in Xhosa. After a few words, the whole mass of students joined in in multipart harmony. The impact on us was visceral.

After the hymn, the man who had positioned himself in front of us read from the Gospel of St Matthew in a highly phatic manner. When he had finished, another voice from the student body began the chant the Lord's Prayer. As with the hymn, the whole school took up the chant in multipart harmony. Apart from us, everyone at the assembly had their eyes closed. Again, the impact was considerable.

At the end of the prayer, the principal gave out two notices. He introduced us, announcing that we would be tracking a particular standard seven class for the day and apologising that there had not been time to inform the pupil council. He said that he was sure that we would be welcomed. His second notice concerned a concert that was to be held on the following day. After this, we all left the assembly space.

***

The assembly at Protea High School also took place at the start of the day and was also held outside, this time in a quadrangle. It was the first day of the second term. The students had gathered in the space. There was a delay of approximately five minutes whilst the students were organised into lines and quietened down by those teachers who were present. The principal was standing on a podium and used a public address system. He instructed the students to take a few moments for private reflection. After a short interval, the principal referred to the new curriculum, which was to be introduced and about which he had just received information. The curriculum introduced a new role for the teacher and for the parents and for the pupil. The pupil is now the learner. The teacher is no longer the educator, but the facilitator. 'The responsibility now falls on your shoulders, your parents' shoulders. ... teachers do not have to do that; the responsibility lies with you and your parents.' The principal repeated this point a number of times. After this, the principal gave out a notice about uniform—pupils were allowed to wear tracksuits without 'tackies'[87] in the second term—and a reminder about the June examination in which it was very important that pupils should do well. He ended with 'I can see you're all glad to be back, for hard work'. There was general laughter in response.

REVISITING A STUDY IN THREE SOUTH AFRICAN SCHOOLS

I have a complex agenda for this chapter. The first objective is to get into publicly available print form something of a very brief piece of research that was carried out in the mid-nineties by Andrew Brown and myself. We have both always been well aware of its limitations, but we are, nevertheless, rather proud of it. The work gave us a short glimpse of pedagogic relations and practices in three very different schools within a society that was and, indeed, is only in the early stages of its emergence from the cruel apartheid regime. Three very different schools, but also three very good schools, by the accounts of others and by our own observations. I will try to indicate what *I* mean by 'good' at the end of the chapter. The three schools were located in three very different communities: the first, predominantly white and privileged; the second, at the opposite end of the economic spectrum, black and very severely disadvantaged; the third, a localised, but highly complex case of what I'm referring to as *class condensation*. We set out to explore how we might conceive of the relationship between the nature of pedagogic strategies that are deployed in a school by students and teachers, on the one hand, and the nature of the community that the school serves, on the other. A key source of our pride— until now celebrated mainly in private—was our sense that we had made some progress in this direction.

Now it's important to say up front that there is no claim here to have *discovered* some essential features of schooling in general, about schooling in South Africa, even about schooling in these three schools; this is not a forensics of schooling.

---

[87] 'Tackies' is a slang word equivalent to 'trainers', 'sneakers', etc.

Rather, the aim is to present a commentary that allows us to look at and interrogate pedagogy in these schools in a new way. The coherence of this commentary—such as it is—also provides a new mode of interrogation of pedagogy in other schools and sites.

I also want to present, in a more dynamic way than is usual, the iterative nature of analysis. All of the school data and the majority of the data relating to the three communities were collected by Andrew Brown and myself during two periods of three weeks in April 1996 and April 1997. The schools and their communities were all located in the Western Cape province of South Africa, a province that exhibits a unique demographic structure, some of the attributes of which will be described below. The initial analysis was also carried out by us between April 1996 and the Autumn of 1997. This is what is presented in the descriptions of the three assemblies in 'Starting the day' above and in the central sections of this chapter, between the end of this section and the beginning of the section, 'Technology, Text, Commentary'; *these sections are spoken, conventionally, in the first person plural and the use of tenses is appropriate to a text written (mostly) in 1997.* This section of the chapter and those from 'Technology, Text, Commentary' onwards are spoken in the first person singular and with a choice of tenses appropriate to writing in 2007. They have been generated out of my (Dowling's) revisiting of the work of nearly a decade ago. This revisiting has allowed me to establish the earlier work as the object of my own organisational language and produce a new commentary according to more explicit principles that are, themselves, developed out of the transaction. The next phase of the iteration would be to test out these principles in other settings in which the question of the relations between pedagogy and community are relevant. This phase remains, at this stage, programmatic.

I have received comments on earlier versions of this chapter (which were published on my website and presented in a number of settings in South Africa, the UK, and Japan). Some of these comments, in particular, those offered by Jaamiah Galant and Ursula Hoadley, have been extremely thoughtful and informed. I have not responded to everything that they have said in formulating this final version. An example may be helpful in clarifying the position that is being adopted here. Hoadley (personal communication) points out that social class is underplayed, particularly in respect of the 'African field' that, as she notes, is 'far from homogenous'. I do not dispute this. It may well be that a more extended study—and particularly one that moved more substantially beyond the school gates in terms of data collection—would have led us to conceive of social class and, indeed, ethnicity in a more developed way than we have here. However, we have tried to resist imposing categories on the data, but rather to allow it to speak to us and we hope that it has.

Furthermore, even had we conducted a far more extensive study, we would not—as, I hope, previous chapters in this book will have established—have been seeking to present a total description, but, as here, a view that emerges out of a transaction between a general method and a particular set of observations—a transaction between a problematic and an empirical setting. The outcome will be bound to upset at least some of those who identify with the South African settings and at least some of those who would expect sociology to take on a different form. Indeed, it already has. But this chapter does not set out to gainsay alternative, even contradictory accounts. Its pedagogic form should not be allowed to negate the exchange relation that is being encouraged between author and audience of this book. The questions that you are invited to answer are: does the method that is being introduced here have potential—in literal or heretical readings—for your own work; does the description of the Western Cape setting of a decade ago raise useful questions for other settings in the here and now, wherever and whenever that may be?

A STUDY OF THREE SOUTH AFRICAN SCHOOLS

Post-apartheid South Africa is, of course, still very young. The organisation of residential communities, in particular, remains substantially structured, in formal terms, by the apartheid 'racial' classifications. In apartheid South Africa, education was officially organised under these headings. Thus, the Department of Education administered 'white' schools; the Department of Education and Training (DET) administered 'black' schools; the House of Representatives (HoR) administered schools for the 'coloured' population (which comprises 60% of the population of the Western Cape Province); and the House of Delegates administered schools for the 'Indian' population.[88] Under the current government, all schools in the Western Cape are administered by the Western Cape Department of Education. All South African schools charge fees. However, the amount of the fee and, in consequence, the available facilities, vary dramatically between schools.[89] We shall describe the schools in our study and their referent communities below.

---

[88] The House of Representatives and the House of Delegates were separate assemblies 'elected' by the 'coloured' and 'Indian' population, respectively. It is important, however, to make clear that the 'elections' were a long way from what might be expected in most contemporary democracies. As Jaamiah Galant (personal communication) has emphasised: 'The HOR and HOD were created by the government of the day in the context of a very contested 'tricameral parliament' in the early 80s in which each population group was given a separate 'house' in parliament and a very small section of the 'Indian' and 'Coloured' population groups participated and supported this initiative. It has to be stated that these 'assemblies' were not elected by the general populace in a 'general free and open election'—we were still very much disenfranchised at the time, it was not a free vote. These so called elections were actively boycotted and 'Africans' were not given any vote. These officials were viewed by the majority of the non-white population as puppets of the apartheid regime—they had no constituencies.'

[89] Following the dissolution of the seventeen separate, and racially defined education departments under apartheid, a new system of school funding was established for all schools. The underlying principles of public education are those of a semi-private system, realised to different degrees depending on the capacity of the parent community to pay fees and make other contributions. Public schools have thus ended up on a continuum in terms of the extent of funding contributions via fees; their position on the continuum being largely relative to the economic level of the community they serve. In order to cross-subsidise poor schools from wealthier communities, schools have subsequently been divided into quintiles. The poorer quintiles receive a greater state subsidy than the wealthier schools. In 2007, the two bottom quintile schools, serving 40% of the school-going

(continued)

At this stage, we should simply indicate that one, Mont Clair High School,[90] is an ex-Model C school[91] serving a predominantly 'white' community. The second school, Siyafunda High School, is an ex-DET school in an African township. The third, Protea High School, is an ex-HoR school in a 'coloured' suburb.[92] Our data collection involved, firstly, student-shadowing for whole days. Three of us[93] shadowed Standard 7 (13-14-year-olds) and Standard 10 (16-17-year-olds) students. In addition, we interviewed 50 students in single-gendered groups of (generally) four. We also interviewed the Principals and several other teachers in each school. We also spoke with several officials in the Western Cape Department of Education. All of the interviews with the students were tape-recorded and transcribed. We used fieldnotes for interviews with the teachers and for observation. Here are the schools and their communities.

THE SCHOOLS AND THEIR COMMUNITIES

We are defining a 'community' as a definable site for communicative action, which is characterised by specific forms of social relations that are produced and reproduced in cultural practices that, in general terms, may or may not be specific to the site. In this conception, individuals are not contained by a single community, rather they routinely participate in a complex of communities which might be conceived as 'cover-sets' in Atkin's sense (1981). A school clearly constitutes a community, in these terms. However, the school also refers to and is referred to by other communities in which its students and staff participate. This will always result in a highly complex structure. For the purposes of analysis, we must, of necessity, produce a simplified description. We are suggesting that *there is some reason to believe that those elements of community structure that we are foregrounding in this chapter are of particular significance in respect of understanding the pedagogic practices of schools.*

---

population, were declared fee-free schools, with a state subsidy to compensate for the loss of fees. Differences in the capital that schools are able to raise and use for the employment of additional teachers and other services, however, remains highly unequal. [JG&UH]

[90] The names used here are fictitious.

[91] The term 'model C' refers to the former mode of state funding.

[92] The racial profiles of the student bodies in these schools have remained largely the same. Chisholm and Sujee (2007) show that since 2001, nationally there has been more movement of African learners into schools previously defined as Indian and Coloured, and that schools previously defined as African and White have remained largely so. Western Cape statistics are complicated by high incidence of the use of the classification 'other', hence the racial make-up of schools, according to Chisholm and Sujee, in the Western Cape is 38% white, 41% 'other', 3% African and 17% coloured in former white schools. In former coloured schools student numbers are 86% coloured, 8% 'other', and 6% African. The picture is further complicated in the Western Cape by the fact that some white schools on the border of former group areas have transformed wholly in terms of racial profiles of students. [JG&UH]

[93] We were assisted by Parin Bahl in the data collection.

Mont Clair High School

Mont Clair High School is located in a stunning setting in the Western Cape. It is very well appointed. It comprises a number of buildings, including a sports centre and purpose-built music accommodation. There are also specialised laboratories for science, art and design rooms, and a seminar room for large group teaching. The school has a swimming pool and sports fields. Every classroom is equipped with an overhead projector and every student has a textbook for each subject. The carpeted staffroom is furnished with upholstered armchairs and sofas as well as working areas and there are lunch and tea facilities for the staff. All of the students wear school uniform. There are approximately 900 students in the school and approximately 55 teaching staff. Most classes contain approximately 30 students. South African education is currently undergoing a process of rationalisation, which is designed to produce a more even distribution of teachers across all South African schools. Since the target student: staff ratio is 30:1, Mont Clair was scheduled to lose approximately 20 staff by the year 2000. However, the Parent Teacher Association decided to increase the fees from R3600 to R6000 per annum in order to maintain the status quo.

The students attending Mont Clair are predominantly from white, Protestant, middle class backgrounds. There are minorities of Jewish and Moslem students and very small numbers of Asian and African children.[94] Their parents are mostly in professional or managerial occupations. To a substantial extent, we can conceive of the Mont Clair students as the children of a globally distributed virtual community, which is, in abstract terms, the referent community of the school. The global nature of the virtual community may be enhanced by the tendency for 'white flight' from South Africa, following the installation of an ANC government. A number of the pupils indicated the possibility of their studying and/or working outside of South Africa in the future. French is an option on the senior school curriculum. The French teacher pointed out that French is an African language, although other non-South African African languages, such as Arabic, Portuguese and Swahili, were not on the curriculum.

In practice, the school draws its students not from a global, but from a more localised space, although it is considerably more widely distributed than the catchments of either of the other two schools. Nevertheless, even this more localised space is served by a number of schools that are in competition which each other. The principal told us that he had rejected a suggestion that the school should become a 'community school', but that he attempted to develop a community within the school.

The school markets a range of services. The curriculum is a service that is specialised to the school. Educational success is a principal regulator of entry into

---

[94] Unlike the situation at the other two schools described here, the demographics of the Mont Clair student population has changed considerably since 1997. It now has a ratio of white to non-white students close to 1:1; there has been minimal change in respect of teaching staff. See also footnotes 90 and 108.

occupations within the global virtual community, so that curricular provision as a service is an important purchase made by parents. The principal told us that most Mont Clair students enter the professions, although the current practice of 'affirmative action' had resulted in fewer going into medicine. The school also markets extracurricular activities in the form of sports and leisure activities. In general, these are not specialised to the school and such services are also provided by clubs, private tutors, and so forth. Nevertheless, in respect of these extracurricular activities, the school does provide one route into leisure networks that, like the school itself, constitute communities of the global virtual community. Parents are, we were told, very vocal in respect of monitoring the school's quality of service; the principal noted, for example, that he would expect to receive a delegation if the rugby team were not performing well.

Whilst it is clear that the students or their parents select the school, it is also the case that the school selects its students. In general, students are selected on the basis of their academic performances. Even siblings of current students would not necessarily obtain a place at Mont Clair and might be directed towards another school if their academic potential was not up to standard. [95]

Thus the school is accountable to its student/parent community in respect of its provision of curricular and extracurricular services. Correspondingly, the student/parent community is accountable to the school in respect of academic and ethical performance and payment of fees. Sanctions in regard of student breach of the academic code are predominantly restitutive. Failure to produce homework will result in detention; latecomers may also face detention and/or they may be denied access to the lesson for which they have arrived late (that is, the service is denied). Breach of the ethical code is, in general, regarded as the responsibility of the parents. Smoking results in parents being called in immediately. 'Serious' offences, such as those relating to drugs or theft will result in the student 'being asked to leave'. Bullying, we were told, was not a problem.

There is, then, a contractual relationship between the school and the student/parent, with a clear demarcation of responsibilities between them. In respect of the curriculum, the school is responsible for transmission, whilst the responsibility for acquisition lies clearly with the student. Both at the corporate level and at the level of the individual teacher, the school appears to adopt a professional comportment towards its curriculum service provision. The principal is developing a Total Quality Management approach towards the maintenance and enhancement of the school's performance and subscribes to *Managing Schools Today*. He runs regular workshops and was currently working on a presentation to the staff on the new curriculum document (National Department of Education, 1997) that outlined the new curriculum policy, *Curriculum 2005*. He told us that he believed that the new curriculum would act as an incentive to him and his staff to review and improve their performance. In respect of the emphasis, in the curriculum, on the role of the student as taking responsibility for their own

---

[95] Although circumscribed, schools are by law allowed to determine feeder areas. This has significant impact on the way in which the community is constituted. [JG&UH]

learning, there would appear to be a convergence with the code already in practice in the school.

Attention to the management of time and space appeared to be an important feature of classroom performances. The head of the mathematics department, for example, had organised the teaching on the basis of a combination of large group lectures and small group work, with students providing support for each other, together with individual tutorial work. The teacher of a Standard 7 geography class that we observed has arranged her classroom as in Figure 7.1.

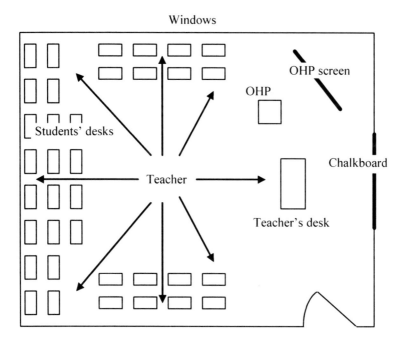

Figure 7.1. Classroom Layout in Mont Clair Geography Class

The organisation of the desks in these orientations was not peculiar either to this classroom or to Mont Clair. The room was also similar to all of the others at Mont Clair (but different from most of those in the other schools) in being provided with an overhead projector (OHP) and screen and in having its walls covered in (mostly professionally produced) posters. However, this room stood out in respect of the large space that the teacher had established in the centre of the room. This was the area in which she could perform and from which she could penetrate the students' spaces. The subject of the lesson was erosion. The teacher made use of physical action in illustrating various geological formations: waterfalls, potholes and so on. She arranged the class into groups of different sizes, combined groups and held plenary discussions. The groups were set tasks, which required them to list were working, the teacher moved around the class offering suggestions, often in the form of physical encodings. For example, in discussion with the 'water' group, she asked what was going to happen when there was a big rock in the river, gesturing with her hands to signify a waterfall, which the students recognised. Later, she asked the same group what would happen if there was a 'huge rock' and a hole forming in it, gesturing in a circular, drilling motion with her finger, 'what's it going to make? a ...'. One student suggested 'borehole', 'that's not quite right', 'a pothole', the teacher confirmed, 'a pothole'. The groups reported back in a plenary session at the end of the lesson. In the plenary, a student would give one of their suggestions, the teacher would summarise and then show the students an illustration from one of a number of books of photographs of geological formations. The teacher also asked the students if they knew of or had seen examples of these formations.

In this lesson, the students were required to decode the teacher's representations of geological knowledge. The teacher summarised these decodings introducing a certain amount of technical language and clarifying erosive activity. The pedagogic practice could be described as initiating an apprenticing of the students into geological discourse by drawing on their existing geological and proto-geological knowledge. She was transmitting the privileged discourse that the students were to acquire.

We observed that the teachers in Mont Clair were also available themselves as resources for interrogation by the students. During a Standard 10 history lesson, for example, the teacher was asked to compare her description of the practices of Nazi Germany with those of Stalin's Soviet Union. The teacher readily complied. In a Standard 7 English class, the teacher, who appeared to be very clearly in control of the class, was nevertheless challenged in respect of a perceived inconsistency in her application of her rule for the correct use of an apostrophe-s.

The contract between the school and the student/parent is, in a number of respects, an individualised one. It is true that, as we have noted, the school community itself (via the Parent Teacher Association) can and does hold the principal and his staff accountable for the quality of their service provision. Nevertheless, there is no contractual obligation on the part of the school to a client community greater than that constituted by the actual clients themselves. The referent global community is, as we have indicated, more appropriately conceived of as virtual. The substantive contract, certainly in respect of the transmission of the academic curriculum is between the teacher/school and the individual student/parent.

The individualised nature of this relationship appeared to be realised in the classroom. Teachers interacted with individuals as frequently as they interacted with the group. The Standard 7 English teacher was taking one of the classes that we observed for only the second time. She had arranged for each student to place on their desk a sign showing their name. Similarly, opposition was also privatised. In a Standard 7 mathematics class, the teacher appeared to avoid any interaction with two Asian boys. The boys spent most of the lesson talking quietly to each other with no reference to the content of the lesson. At one point in her exposition to the class the teacher said, 'I got stuck on this when I was at school and I was hopeless at algebraic graphs after that'. One of the two Asian boys said quietly to the other, 'So how do you know it now, then?' This was a novice teacher. At any given time, possibly less than half of the students appeared to be attending to her exposition. Nevertheless, although the non-attendants chatted to each other, this was maintained at a low level. We did not observe any attempts to communalise an expression of negative evaluation of this lesson.

As we have suggested, success in respect of the school curriculum regulates entry into the professional occupations, which constitute both the family origins and intended and actual destinations of many if not most of the students at Mont Clair. The students whom we interviewed all expressed the opinion that academic success was important. However, they also generally denied that the curriculum had any intrinsic value, thus one Standard 10 girl noted:

> It's purely, purely like just going, just getting through matric so you can get your piece of paper and say you've got this amount of whatever to get in, but once you're in, I mean, the work that you've done in matric or, like, learning something in geography is not going to help you if you want to go into advertising.

A Standard 10 boy:

> No, I don't think so, I don't think matric itself is important, um, I'm doing history for matric and French, but when I leave school I, I might use French to talk to people, but I'll never use my history again, I'll never use all sorts of things that I've learnt. Matric is probably mainly for developing skills, study skills, lifestyle skills, but matric is important to get into university and university is important to get qualified and the qualification gets you the job. So it's one of the steps, but actual matric, I don't think is effective at all.

Almost without exception, none of the students in any of the schools intended to go into teaching themselves. One possible explanation may be because the rationalisation programme in South African education had resulted in very substantial retrenchment of teachers in the Western Cape and there are very few jobs for newly qualified teachers wishing to remain in the province.[96] Ursula

---

[96] The programme of rationalisation is intended to move towards parity in respect of student:teacher ratio nationally. The Western Cape has a substantially lower average student:teacher ratio than the other provinces, so will experience a net outflow as teachers are relocated or 'take the [redundancy] package'. As we have noted above, Mont Clair would be scheduled to lose approximately 20 teachers were it not for the governors deciding, on the advice of the PTA, to raise the fees so as to maintain the current staffing. Siyafunda, which has an average of approximately 60 students per class on roll, but an attendance which rarely exceeds 45 per class, expected to increase its staff numbers by four. The head of mathematics told us that he did not expect this would have any significant impact. The class sizes at Protea are also approximately 40. However, this is in the context of an attendance rate much nearer to 100%. Protea expect to lose 19 teachers by the year 2000 with no possibility of increasing fees to compensate. As an oversubscribed school, Protea had, *(continued)*

Hoadley has suggested that this has partly contributed to a general lowering of the status of teaching, which:

> ... is spread across the entire population. So in 2000, there was only *one* South African black student in pre-service education in the Western Cape, and seriously dwindling numbers across other population groups. This is partly historical, that teaching and nursing are no longer the only, nor desirable, entry in the middle class for black people, but also relates to the perceived poor salaries and conditions of teaching, contributed to by the rationalisation and redistribution process. (Hoadley, personal communication)

Presumably, the curriculum would be attributed intrinsic value as the basis of teachers' professional services. The teachers appeared to value their academic and pedagogic knowledge and skills in these terms irrespective of how they might see these discourses as relating to activities beyond schooling. We spoke to the French teacher about her involvement with the professional association of French teachers. The Head of mathematics had been awarded a scholarship to study for a masters degree in mathematics education in the US.[97] He had also published articles and given presentations on his pedagogic strategies involving the use of different sizes of groups. The accounts teacher had produced his own textbook in photocopied form. He used this to supplement the official texts in his Standard 7 classes.

To summarise, then, we are proposing that the teacher-student relationship at Mont Clair can be described as individualised and contractual. The teacher provides a professional service in respect of the transmission of the curriculum. Curriculum and pedagogy constitute the discursive basis of the teacher's professional specialism, it marks them out within the professional division of labour. The school also contracts to provide extracurricular services relating to leisure and sporting activities. The student contracts to pay a fee and also to be responsible for acquisition of the curriculum and to behave in accordance with an ethical code. The core activity of the school community is the transmission and acquisition of the academic curriculum, success in which regulates entry to the professional region of the division of labour. This region has a global referential community that is virtual, because it does not define a coherent space for communicative action. Rather, it comprises a complex of 'cover-sets', of which the school community itself may be said to be one. Other such cover-sets include teachers' professional organisations, sporting associations, religious communities, and so forth.

---

according to the principal, been taking on additional student numbers in order to keep staff. As a result, the buildings were very crowded.

[97] He had taken up this scholarship in 1997 and was on sabbatical leave during the second year of our study.

Siyafunda High School

Siyafunda High School is situated in a township that largely comprises shacks of wood and corrugated iron. The residents of the township are generally socially located in the most subaltern class. There is comparatively little access to regular paid employment. There are large chain supermarkets and other stores in the township, but there is also evidence of a substantial informal economy in the areas (at least) of services and retailing. The population of the township is complex in terms of origins, but we were told by teachers and students of Siyafunda that there is a significant representation of migrants from rural areas, mostly outside of the Western Cape Province. On the basis of comments made by teachers, students and other informants, we inferred that the population is predominantly Christian and the church is regarded as very important. The population is multilingual, although Xhosa seems to be the dominant language.

We have described the referential community of Mont Clair as a virtual community. That of Siyafunda, however, can be constituted as a substantive community. The township constitutes a definite location, which is bounded, on different sides, by a major freeway, by open country, and by a dramatic change in architecture, from shacks to permanent housing. The majority of Siyafunda students live in this community.[98]

The community is to a considerable extent self-governing. One of our informants (we shall refer to him as Sivuyile) was chairman of his street committee. He told us that a 'street' generally comprised fifty householders, usually, but not necessarily, men. The street elects an executive committee and a chairman annually. This was currently Sivuyile's fifth year as chairman. Individuals or families wanting to move into the street have to submit an application to the committee, which (according to another informant) may take up references before deciding. One of us asked Sivuyile, 'What would happen if I asked to move into your street?' Sivuyile and his colleagues thought that this was quite an amusing idea, but said that it would probably be OK; they noted that they work with white people, so that there is no reason why they shouldn't live with them. The committee and meetings of the whole street also make decisions relating to law and order. An offender may be taken to the police station (also situated in the township).

In addition to the local community, there was also evidence of reference to a broader Xhosa virtual community. This was apparent in the responses of students, in particular, whose references to 'my people' clearly referred to such an entity. Entry into the Xhosa virtual community is regulated, for men, by male initiation. Sivuyile and his colleagues told us that the young men would have to go into the rural areas for this process. When they returned, they would be required to dress in a manner which marked them out from other members of the community for a period of time to be determined by their family, but which was generally about six

---

[98] Transport costs, which are generally not state subsidised, also constitute a *local* school community. [JG&UH]

months. During our observation in Siyafunda, we encountered two individuals who, we were told, were in this phase. They were both 'sharply' dressed in patterned trousers and jackets and large hats. One wore a large, floppy peaked cap, the other wore a round, green felt broad brimmed hat that we were told was the traditional form. Both of these individuals, and the latter, in particular, tended to keep to themselves.[99] We were told, by the Standard 10 pupils whom we interviewed, that these individuals kept to themselves because they felt embarrassed to be marked out in this way.

Siyafunda is located within the township, but is fenced off from it. The gates to the fence are locked during the school day to prevent students from leaving. The teaching rooms are contained in two rectangular, two-storey, brick-built blocks. There is also a small administration block and another building from which refreshments can be bought. All of the ground floor windows have iron bars fitted. There is a library, which houses a small number of books. The teacher responsible for the library—a responsibility that is additional to her teaching and for which she is not paid—was, at the time of our first visit, in the process of sorting the books onto the appropriate shelves. The classrooms are furnished with fewer desks and chairs than there are students in each class. There are few textbooks and we saw no overhead projectors. The staffroom has a bare floor, six tables and about the same number of plastic chairs, one or two of which we observed to be broken. Some of the students wear tracksuits with the school badge, others wear school blazers, some wear everyday clothes. There are approximately 1400 students registered at Siyafunda and approximately 40 teaching staff. Class sizes may be up to 50 or 60, although absenteeism is comparatively high. A Standard 7 class that we shadowed contained 44 students on that particular day. The Standard 10 classes are (as is the case in the other schools) much smaller.

The teachers live outside the township community in permanent housing in somewhat more affluent suburbs. A number of them drive to school, others come by bus. The teachers are thus partially alienated from the community. The basis for this alienation is their marginal entry into association with the white global virtual community via their educational success. Sivuyile told us that people who attained this kind of career generally leave the township and move into houses.

Most of the Standard 10 students with whom we spoke at Siyafunda envisaged moving on to some form of further or higher education and into a professional career. Matriculation constitutes a necessary condition for this move.[100] The students at Mont Clair viewed matric as a certification, rather than intrinsically valuable knowledge. The Siyafunda students, however, all expressed the view that

---

[99] We encountered these individuals on the first day of our 1997 visit to Siyafunda, but did not have the opportunity to talk to them or ask why they were dressed differently from the other students. Before our next visit, we described their dress and demeanor to a number of non-Xhosa informants and were told by all but one that they were gangsters.

[100] But not a sufficient one. Unless they can obtain a scholarship, students must finance themselves for the first year of their higher education course before they are eligible for a loan. Scholarships, such as the National Student Financial Aid Scheme are limited. [JG&UH]

the knowledge that they learned at school formed the basis for what was to follow, thus in an interview with Standard 10 boys:

AB   ... is matriculation important for the careers that you have chosen.

P1   Yes I think it is important because, to me I say the base of, if you got no matric you can't do anything because each, each, anything that I'm going to do, the base of it would be a matric. So I say it is important to have a matric and then going to do [...] The base is matric and then take your career and then [...]

...

AB   ... if I said that, OK, I've got some matriculation certificates here and I'll just write one for each of you and give them out.

P2   [...] it wouldn't count, you must have the base.

We want to suggest that this is consistent with a view of school knowledge as being associated, by these students, with a community beyond that of the township. A virtual community that is currently dominated by whites. As a Standard 10 girl put it:

OK, as I see now they are mostly white people who are doctors, so we have no chance to be doctors, like blacks, black people, they are not so much black people as white doctors, so I want to make that, I want, I want that to end and show them that we, as blacks, we can do that.

In Mont Clair, curricular knowledge specialises the teacher within the virtual community, which is the student's origin. In Siyafunda, the curriculum facilitates entry into the margins of this virtual community, which is the student's aspired destination. Furthermore, the Siyafunda students' evaluation of school knowledge is based upon evidence from the next stage in their career, for example, a Standard 10 girl:

I think it's important because when I heard some students were doing these things at tertiary level, they say they are not being taught like us so we don't know everything, so the other things that they do is they work from the low standard, standard ten [...] so I think matric is important, because you know what you are going to do when you go after [...]

It seemed that many of the teachers saw teaching as a transitional occupation *en route* to something more lucrative. The head of mathematics, for example, told us that he was working towards a career in medicine or, if that failed, in engineering. Almost all of the teachers at Siyafunda were very young.

We want to propose that the teachers are partially alienated from the township community. Nevertheless, they retain an obligation to it via their organic association with this particular community and/or with the Xhosa virtual community, and perhaps an African virtual community. As they are no longer fully a part of the township community, the nature of their obligation is defined, essentially, in terms of the transmission of their means of success—the academic curriculum. In addition, the community, acting via the pupil council recruits the teachers as instruments of moral regulation. This recruitment is similar to the community's recruitment of the police for a similar purpose. In the school setting, the pupil council have, a teacher told us, asked the teachers to use corporal punishment even though this is officially proscribed. Such punishment is carried out in private and generally administered to boys who have assaulted girls.

We suggest, then, that the principal form of the relation between the teacher and the pupil is one of obligation and that the nature of the teacher's responsibility is defined by their recruitment by the community as agents of the transmission of the curriculum and, to a lesser degree, as instruments of moral regulation. This relationship, however, is probably best described as one-to-many. That is, the teacher's obligation is to the community, rather than to individuals, which is the case in the contractual relationship at Mont Clair. We noted, for example, that the teachers rarely addressed or referred to any students by name, even when calling on individuals to respond to a question.

Whilst it is the teacher's responsibility to transmit the curriculum, it seems clear that the students take collective responsibility for its acquisition. We found evidence of a considerable amount of informal self-help grouping. Standard 10 students formed study groups. The teacher remains a resource for students in their acquisition of the curriculum. Thus the students whom we interviewed said that a good teacher was someone who would help you with any difficulties that you had with your work. A bad teacher, by contrast, doesn't turn up, or is drunk, or swears at or becomes angry with the students.

A dominant mode of lesson at Standard 7 illustrates the collective nature of acquisition. In this lesson form we describe the classroom as a site for the collective production and acquisition of the privileged text. The teacher was clearly the leader in this production and students are largely undifferentiated.

In leading the production of the text, a number of resources appeared to be available to the teacher. Firstly, the teacher must recruit their own knowledge of the privileged text to the extent that textbooks are unavailable. Where they are available, they may nevertheless be backgrounded. For example, a science teacher said that she had bought her own textbook. She did not, however, remove it from her bag at any point during the lesson. Secondly, the teacher may initiate a sentence to be collectively completed in a choral response. For example, the science teacher, pointing to a diagram on the chalkboard addressed the class with: 'These are said to be <u>ovules</u>'. The last word of the sentence was chorused by the class, the invitation for this chorus being indicated by a rising intonation. [101] Thirdly, the teacher may demand individual responses either in public or in private. In the private form, the teacher writes questions and incomplete sentences to be answered/completed by students in their exercise books. Publicly, the teacher may call upon an individual to answer a question. In each case, these individual

---

[101] This mode of pedagogic interaction in South African schools is described by Muller (1989).

responses affirm the acquisition of the privileged text. Fourthly, the teacher may make reference to a stock of common knowledge. Thus, the science teacher asked if the class had ever seen a 'bird sitting on a flower', ('yes'); the English teacher made reference to current South African national politicians in elaborating on the political structure represented in a play. Finally, although the official medium of instruction is English, the teacher can make use of Xhosa, which is the first language of most of the students and teachers. We noticed, however, that apart from the Xhosa lesson, Xhosa was used to elaborate upon interpretations, but was not incorporated into the privileged text itself. Other than in Xhosa and Afrikaans lessons, one principle of evaluation of the privileged text was that it should be in English[102].

In a number of the lessons that we attended the format could be described as follows. Firstly, the privileged text was collectively produced as a system of signs that was represented on the chalkboard. Secondly, the teacher wrote on the board a number of questions and incomplete sentences which constituted the 'classwork'. Thirdly, the teacher would move around the class offering assistance and, finally, marking the work. In the case of the geography lesson, for example, the privileged text consisted of a system of signs relating to maps. These signs included specialised terms and diagrams. In these lessons, the text was produced on the board primarily via the use of teacher exposition and the choral response. Students would actively assist in the completion of the chorus. Thus, if the response was not immediately forthcoming, an individual would offer a suggestion. If the teacher responded positively to the suggestion, the invitation to chorus was repeated and the whole class chorused the suggested expression. However, we observed that individuals offering suggestions in this way tended to do so whilst apparently drawing a minimum of attention to themselves. Sometimes the student ducked down, giving us the appearance of countering the individualising effect of their intervention by merging physically into the class. Students also assisted the individual written affirmation of the acquisition of the privileged text by sharing their answers with each other. For example, a student who had completed the written work in the Xhosa lesson passed her book to her colleagues who copied the answers into their own books. The teacher made no move to interfere with this.

We observed that chorused expressions were not confined to specialist terms. Hence these examples from the geography lesson: 'When the topographical map is

---

[102] In a response at a seminar at the Institute of Education given by Vivien de Klerk, I speculated that, under certain circumstances, it might be appropriate to understand the use of English within Xhosa-speaking communities in South Africa as dominated by style significations. In this respect, English use may be construed as similar to the use of Latinate or French expressions in European English. There is a resonance between this speculation and the finding that the privileged text in Siyafunda classrooms must be produced in English, whilst its content may be explicated in Xhosa. Thus there is a separation of mode of expression from content, with the former being dominated by style signification. That which is signified here is the academic genre. Academic success facilitates flight from the most dominated position; English—the language of the academic—was also seen as the language of the struggle in the sense of a symbolic language, rather than necessarily a functional language.

drawn a scale is <u>used</u>'; pointing at diagrams showing contour lines, 'They can be <u>close together,</u> or they can be <u>far apart</u>'. In this geography lesson, the teacher also made use of material texts. She used a single photocopy of an aerial photograph and a number of maps each of which were shared by up to four students.

This format—collective production of the privileged text followed by affirmation of its acquisition—comprised the lesson. In the Xhosa lesson, the sequence had been completed with fifteen minutes of the lesson still remaining. Some students had, in fact, completed the work and had it marked with thirty minutes of the hour-long lesson remaining. For the remainder of the period, the students talked to each other and to the teacher. No more pedagogic content was introduced as far as we could tell (none of us speaks more than a few words of Xhosa).

A mathematics teacher produced a variation on this lesson format. Her strategy was to put an algebraic expression on the board and ask for suggestions as to its simplified form. She collected several suggestions and asked students to indicate support for one or other of them. The proposers of the suggestions were asked to explain their answers and the class asked to indicate support or otherwise, 'Can he do it like that?' Through asking questions like this and making minimal use of the choral response, the teacher eliminated the idiosyncratic suggestions and established an expression of consensus on each of the examples that she used, writing the correct, answer—the privileged text—on the board. Thus this lesson was constructed as a series of very short privileged texts that were, again, collectively produced. In this case, the series extended for the whole of the time allotted for the lesson.

The mathematics teacher had participated on in-service training courses given by the Mathematics Education Project (MEP) at the University of Cape Town. She indicated that this was the origin of the strategy that she used in this particular lesson. We have no evidence regarding the form in which the strategy was presented by MEP. Nevertheless, it is clear that the form that it took in this lesson conformed with the dominant mode of operation of pedagogic practice which we observed in the Standard 7 classes.

One Standard 7 lesson was very different. This was an Afrikaans lesson. We were informed by the Deputy Principal (who had been promoted to principal when we visited the school in 1997) that this subject was generally resented by students and teachers at Siyafunda. Afrikaans, she said, was recognised as the language of the oppressor.[103] Furthermore, there were no occasions when students would make use of this language. The Deputy Principal said that there was a general pattern of failure in this subject throughout the school until students reached Standard 10, when they would pass Afrikaans, which they needed for matriculation.

The teacher that we saw was unusual in that Afrikaans was her own first language; this, we were told, would not be the case for most teachers of Afrikaans in this category of school. The Afrikaans teacher—who was also the class teacher

---

[103] This contrasts with English as the universal symbolic language of the struggle against apartheid.

of this particular Standard 7 class—employed a form of pedagogic practice that was highly energetic, highly dramatic and highly unpredictable. She was clearly very well-prepared. There was an exercise already on the board and she had prepared two worksheets for this class. There was also evidence of similar preparation in respect of other classes for that day and the room was heavily decorated with posters relating to Afrikaans and to biology—the teacher's other subject.

In all of the other classes, there was a clear space between teacher and students. Even when the teacher would move around the classroom, she would be standing and carrying a pen for marking, so that the division of labour between teacher and students was always apparent. The Afrikaans teacher, however, employed some strategies that questioned this division, but always ambiguously and always subject to sudden change. Thus, in an early interaction with an individual, she moved very close to him, putting her face very close to his and at the same level. He apparently answered her question incorrectly, because she reached behind her, took a ruler from another student's desk and struck the first student on the hand with it. A little later, she slapped another student on the back several times with her hands. Neither of these actions were sufficiently forceful to inflict pain. The effect appeared to be, however, to disorientate the students.

Throughout the lesson, the teacher would move very close to students, especially the boys, putting her arm around them and calling them 'darling' and 'sweetheart' and allowing them to whisper answers to her. She would also make sudden, unpredictable moves and call sharply on a number of students in turn to answer the same question. The teacher also made considerable use of exaggerated facial expressions, moving, again rapidly, between a broad smile and a cross look. The lesson itself was moved along at a very fast rate, with a sequence of distinct, well-planned tasks (some in the form of photocopied activity sheets) being introduced by the teacher. It seemed clear that no one in the room had any idea what the teacher might do next. This was particularly apparent in the way in which students would flinch at the teacher's sudden movements and the way in which they would attempt to privatise their interactions with her by whispering answers, which she might, and occasionally did, choose to make public.

There was no real possibility of the collective elaboration of this lesson, because the teacher was very effectively disrupting the community of the classroom. Each individual was individually, not collectively, subject to the teacher's charismatic authority, which was personalised by and in the teacher.[104]

---

[104] On the first day of our 1997 visit to the school, we were told by the principal (who had been the deputy principal in 1996) that the charismatic Afrikaans/Biology teacher would be leaving that day and that this was a considerable loss to the school. She told us that the teacher was one of the best teachers she had worked with and that she put everything into her teaching, even buying fish with her own money for dissection in biology classes. The school had been unable to make a permanent post available for her. Such a post had been offered by the principal of another local school. This principal had been the principal of Siyafunda in 1996.

The Standard 10 lessons that we observed at Siyafunda were directly concerned with the matric examination and generally consisted of the teacher or (in the case of a mathematics lesson) individual students rehearsing worked examples or summaries (such as the construction of the standard taxonomy of forms of settlement in a geography lesson). This might be described as an expanded elaboration of the classwork phase that we observed in most of the Standard 7 lessons. To this extent, we would suggest that there was an apparent continuity in pedagogic strategies. There was, however, an important shift in the social structure of the classroom as we moved from Standard 7 to Standard 10. Our observations of the Standard 7 classroom suggested a degree of horizontality in gender relations. The classroom was not ungendered; boys tended to sit with boys and girls with girls, for example. However, in general terms (and given our limited period of observation) there was no obvious hierarchy in respect of teacher-student or student-student interactions.[105] In an English lesson, for example, girls and boys were allocated parts to read in a play without any obvious regard to the gender of the respective character.

As far as we were able to tell, the individuals in Standard 7 came from approximately the same age cohort. However, by Standard 10, whilst the girls were all in the equivalent cohort (16-17 year-olds), there was a virtual absence of boys from this cohort. Rather, the boys were almost all two or more years older. The boys whom we interviewed told us that they thought that the average age of the boys in their class was about 22 years and that there was only one 17-year-old boy. One of our interviewees was, in fact, Sivuyile, the chairman of the street committee to whom we have referred above. Sivuyile was 34 years old and was married and had three children and was clearly a key member of the township community. Sivuyile had left school at the end of Standard 7 in 1980 because his family could not afford to keep him. He left home and worked for fourteen years, saving up to complete his schooling and higher education. Standard 10 at Siyafunda contains other returnees like Sivuyile (although we understood that he was the oldest student at that time) and also students who had repeated one or more years having failed to be promoted to the next Standard.

Thus, the Standard 10 class comprised approximately equal numbers of teenage girls and adult men. The hierarchical nature of the relationship between 'boys' and girls in this classroom was quite apparent. In particular, the teachers generally tended to address themselves to the boys and the boys tended to dominate the responses, sometimes to the complete exclusion of the girls. In a physics class, for example, the boys sat on one side of the room and the girls on the other. The male teacher stood on the boys' side of the class and directed his gaze at them during his exposition. A substantial proportion of a geography lesson was spent on a discussion in Xhosa between the female teacher and the boys with the girls remaining completely silent. The teacher told us that the boys had been telling her about the sizes of towns in the Eastern Cape as she was unfamiliar with that region.

---

[105] This horizontality was somewhat disturbed in the Afrikaans lesson that we describe above.

The female principal (in our 1997 visit) organised an English lesson as a discussion, mainly, about teenage pregnancy. She had asked the class for suggestions for the topic of discussion. The boys made a number of suggestions. As far as we were able to tell, the girls did not offer any suggestions. Nevertheless, the teacher presented 'teenage pregnancy' as though it had come from the girls. When she asked the class which of the suggestions should be taken up, she again selected 'teenage pregnancy' as that which had been chosen by the girls, although we did not see or hear any girl indicating this or any other preference. The ensuing discussion was dominated by the principal and the boys almost to the exclusion of the girls, despite the principal's attempts to involve them.

We observed that the girls were clearly actively involved in the lessons insofar as written work had been set. Their exclusion seemed to be from interactive participation. We asked a group of girls whether the boys or the girls did most of the talking in class. They told us that the boys did most of the talking, 'maybe because the girls are shy'. One of the girls said,

> Yes, some of them they talk too much in class, but when it comes to writing, we beat them.

The gendered hierarchy of the Standard 10 classroom clearly may have been related to its age structure. In any event, it would seem to be (re)productive of patriarchal relations within the school community and, potentially, beyond.

We suggest that, at Siyafunda, the teacher is alienated from the immediate community of the township, but retains an obligation to it by virtue of a mutual affiliation to a broader African virtual community. This obligation is to the collective rather than to individuals, so that the teacher-student relationship is characterised as one-to-many. The community recruits the teacher as transmitter of the curriculum as the means of their own alienation into an association with the global virtual community. In pedagogic action, the teacher must lead the collective in the production of the privileged text and affirm its authority. The community also recruits the teacher as an instrument of moral regulation. The teacher's authority is thus delimited and substantially bureaucratic in nature. In general, we observed no challenging or questioning of the teachers in respect of this authority. There was one exception to this to which we shall return later. The students claimed responsibility for the acquisition of the curriculum, although they retained an expectation that the teacher would serve as a resource in this respect.

It may be that this structure of classroom relations was distorted by the practice of the charismatic Afrikaans teacher who appeared to fragment the collective student relations and, by virtue of her constant and often privatised interrogation of individuals, to claim some responsibility for acquisition. On the basis of just a single lesson, it is inappropriate to draw firm conclusions. Nevertheless, the unique, charismatic nature of this teacher's authority was explicitly recognised by at least the two principals of the school whom we met.

Protea High School

Protea High School is situated in a suburb of single storey detached permanent housing and some multi-storey multiple housing. The suburb is localised, in contrast to the virtual referential community of Mont Clair. Unlike the Siyafunda township, however, the Protea suburb is economically far more diverse. The principal told us that some of his students live in informal settlements on the outskirts of the suburb. There is also a great deal of unemployment. On the other hand, professional and managerial workers also live in the suburb. We observed that, whilst most of the students walked to school, some were dropped-off in new-looking BMWs. In social class terms, the suburb clearly represents a highly unusual community, a *class condensation.*[106]

The inhabitants of the suburb were categorised by the apartheid regime as 'coloured'. According to the principal of Protea, there are two main groups, firstly, there are mainly Afrikaans-speaking families, commonly Christian and designated, by the apartheid regime as 'of mixed race'. Secondly, there are mainly English-speaking, Moslem families. Members of this latter group were said to be descended from Malay indentured labour. We were told that there was some correlation between ethnicity and social class, the Moslem community being overrepresented amongst the professional and managerial classes. We are not asserting any more, here, than that that was what we were told at the time and that this understanding, at least on the part of the principal, may have been significant in terms of pedagogic practice. As Jaamiah Galant has pointed out to us:

> ... the assertion that Moslems are largely descended from Malay indentured labour is true only for a small percentage of the Moslem population in the Western Cape and is regarded nowadays more as a 'myth' that attempts to mask the San heritage of the majority of the 'Coloured' Western Cape population—irrespective of religious group. (Galant, personal communication)[107]

By the evidence of some of our interviews with students, it is also clear that Afrikaans was a home language for at least some of the Muslims. What is clear, however, is that the physical catchment community of Protea is highly complex in class, religious and ethnic terms. Protea is a 'parallel medium' school in which students' parents opt for either the Afrikaans track or the English track. Although individuals acknowledged either Afrikaans or English as their first language, we observed that bilingual fluency was a common (although not universal) state, certainly amongst the teachers. The staff meetings that we attended, for example, were characterised by frequent code-switching by and between individual speakers. For the Moslem boys whom we interviewed, Afrikaans had definite connotations:

---

[106] Unusual, generally, but not in the Western Cape region.

[107] The San were the indigenous people of South Africa.

AB   And what you're saying is ... that English-speaking students get a better deal because

P1   The reputation, OK, like [another school in the area], most of the people there they speak Afrikaans. Now, um, ... I think it's associated Afrikaans with gangsterism and with er, and with the slum areas. So now they're coming here and they, and they already, when they come Afrikaans class already in the teachers mind, might be problems.

...

AB   ... presumably your parents made the decision that you went into the English language ... stream of the school rather than the Afrikaans speaking ... why did they make that decision?

P2   Um, I won't say it's a decision they made, in most households, um, both languages are used quite often, in my, especially in my household, um I don't speak English with my father, I speak Afrikaans with him, because Afrikaans is more of a stern language, so I would associate it with my father [...] so he'd speak more Afrikaans and my mother speak English to me.

P1   Um, because, you know there's this kind of ... this period where the, um, the so-called whites, like ruled and what mostly, um Afrikaans speaking whites. So, when, when, the, our fathers ... when we were born we're still in that era and so they thought, we'll try and break away from their regime by going to English class. You see, like, like, um, they ... they were prominent Afrikaans speaking, so they, we tried to break away from them by going over to English class, then, then, alright different from them, so, so that we could become stronger and have our own identity instead of the identity they tried to give us ...

...

P3   Because, er, English is a language that is spoken throughout the world and Afrikaans is only, er, um, South African, like a South African language, it's only spoken in South Africa, so that's probably also another reason why.

According to the Director of Education[108] for the province, the coloured population comprises 60 per cent of the population of the Western Cape. In our discussions with him and with other informants, it became clear that this population constitutes a complex arena of political divisions and alliances both internally and externally to itself. This population is, in a sense, sandwiched between the two virtual communities of the old white regime and the new African one and this is the basis

---

[108] The director is himself a member of the coloured population and is an ANC supporter working under a National Party administration.

of its unique form of condensation, which may well not last very long into the new political era. On the basis of our current data, we cannot attempt to understand the complexities of the suburban community. It does, nevertheless, constitute a substantive community and the teachers at Protea appear to stand in a particular relationship to and within it. We shall attempt to describe this relationship and its apparent consequences for the classroom.

The school itself comprises a complex of buildings, mostly two-storeyed, and is set in a large grassed area. There are no specialised classrooms, such as laboratories, so that students are shown videoed experiments in some science lessons. The school also arranges local field trips for practical work in science and geography. There is a small staffroom with armchairs, lockers and some desk space. All of the students wore school uniform. In most cases the uniform took the form of the school tracksuit.

The principal told us that, because of the organic nature of the relationship with the community, the school could not impose any form of selection upon its intake, even though it is heavily oversubscribed. Should he attempt anything of the kind, there would be a deputation of residents to the local ANC who would lobby the Department of Education, which would most certainly intervene.[109]

The number of students on role at Protea in 1997 was 1434 and the student:staff ratio was approximately 24:1. The largest class size is reportedly 47. Most classes contain about 40 students, although the Standard 10 teaching groups were smaller. Protea is scheduled to lose 19 staff under the rationalisation programme. However, it is also likely to reduce in student population because of its own overcrowding and because of spare capacity at other local schools. This would entail an even more substantial staff loss.[110]

Given the nature of the division of labour within the suburb, the teacher can be understood as a comparatively successful individual, having achieved professional status. At Protea, the teacher seems to be constituted as a guardian with respect to both the students and the community more generally, thus, the boys whom we

---

[109] The principal contrasted this with the situation of another school, which was in a 'white' area. Since the local population tended to send their children to other schools (such as Mont Clair), this school served a widely distributed, which is to say, virtual coloured community. Under these circumstances, the school had no organic association with a community as such and was able to operate selection and, as a result, produce greater matriculation success and so forth.

[110] On one of our visits in 1996, each lesson was shortened by fifteen minutes in order to allow additional time for a staff meeting to discuss the rationalisation proposals. The principal and staff invited us to attend the staff meeting, which ran for three hours. It is worth noting that there appeared to be general agreement that there was a need for rationalisation because of the extreme shortage of teachers in some parts of the country (some schools have student: staff ratios of up to 120:1). However, there was obvious concern about the likely outcome for Protea, which already had very large classes. The mechanisms of rationalisation were also having an impact on promotions and management. The principal and his deputies were all acting up from head of department level in 1996, although two of these appointments (including that of the principal) had been made permanent by 1997. A principal on a permanent appointment would have to re-apply for his job at a lower salary should the school reduce in size.

interviewed contrasted Protea with another school in a somewhat different location:

AB   OK, so there's a lot of sport being played here, um, a lot of activities that are around sport and things

P2   Yuh, that's, that's in our area, only in our area, I would say. You go furthest, further up you get the school, you get, like [the other school] then they don't have the same facilities, so they, instead of playing rugby on a weekend they'll ... stand on corners or go to a disco or do any nonsense, whatever. So they're not as fortunate as us.

AB   Right, and this is the school that has this effect, or is it the community that has the effect?

Ps   school

P1   Because, um, ... that area's like, how can I say this, um, ... slums, but is ... like gangsters and stuff that ... it's the flats, that's where, um, the gangsters coming to school, not really interested in sports, they have drugs and gangs with gang fights ... now the teachers are there, I would say, become despondent, then they just leave it at the beep teach the, day finish ... You'll see that at night when you come here, parking lot's full, the teachers, everybody's here, nightclasses and things, always happen, school always alive.

P   There's activities here.

PD   ... do any of the people you're talking about, any of the gangsters, if you like, do any of them come to this school?

P2   OK, here we have, you know, on the school we do have, you know, a couple of guys that want to be, you know, but not actually any serious cases where you can say, hey watch out for that guy, he's so-and-so, because he will be sorted out quick, cos, you know, the discipline here is quite strict over here. So, ... because ... someone who don't waste any time, if there's anything to be done, he goes to the police station and have it done. Now ... the majority of the population in that area, this, er, you know, up to gangsterism and stuff like that. But here it's more, um, sports, ... understand?

The nature of the relationship between the teacher and the student was illustrated by one teacher's description of another:

He's got such a good relationship with the kids ... he's like a brother to them ... he gets the best out of them ... no one else here really has that talent.
(transcribed from fieldnotes)

The teacher being described was also reported as performing driving duties for members of the community, so that the latter did not drive home after having consumed alcohol.

As is the case at the other schools, academic success is a condition of entry into certain occupations. However, unlike Mont Clair, this is not a necessary condition for entering the referent community, which is socially very diverse. Unlike Siyafunda, academic success is not a route out of the community, which can contain the professional and managerial occupations. The deputy principal informed us that over half of the teachers at Protea lived within the community and he himself had moved into it, although he originates from another suburb in the area. Teachers' curricular responsibilities entail the transmission of the curriculum as the means of their own success and as the route into professional occupations. However, insofar as the teacher-student relationship is appropriately described as guardian-ward, teachers also take considerable responsibility for the acquisition of the curriculum. Thus, there is frequent assessment and the teachers (especially those of Standard 7) deploy tactics to ensure that the curriculum gets into the books, as well as the heads, of the students. For example, considerable use is made of printed and photocopied notes. On a number of occasions, the principal emphasised the extent of the expenditure on photocopying.

There was also some use of the choral response mode, which we observed in Siyafunda, although, in our observations, it was far less common at Protea. We did note that the chorus became more extended in the Standard 10 lesson, thus the mathematics teacher said as he wrote on the board:

If DE is parallel to BC then ...

employing an upward intonation on 'then'. The students responded in chorus:

AB over AD is equal to AC over AE[111]

In general, we observed considerable use of community strategies by the teacher, both inside and outside of the classroom. For example, the deputy principal, in whose office we conducted out student interviews, needed to enter the room upon several occasions. Each time, he engaged in some form of banter with the students. Within the classroom, there was a great deal of smiling by teachers and students were addressed by their first names. In a Standard 7 English lesson, the teacher was encouraging students to suggest slang words that they used; at one point, she said:

... don't see me as the teacher ... remember that we are here to share.

There seemed to be very weak classification between the curricular and moral guardianship roles of the teacher, so that we observed an intrusion of the moral into the classroom. A Standard 10 English lesson, for example, began with an

---

111 These utterances were recorded on the board symbolically, thus: If DE $\parallel$ BC then $\dfrac{AB}{AD} = \dfrac{AC}{AE}$.

expression of disappointment on the part of the teacher over the students' behaviour in which alcohol had been brought onto the school premises.

The interrelationship between the moral and the curricular was particularly clear in a Standard 7 mathematics lesson. The teacher had collected students' books earlier in the day than had been expected and had discovered that most of the students had not completed their homework. She pointed to two piles of exercise books, one pile being about three times as high as the other. She indicated that the smaller pile comprised the books of those students who had completed their homework and the larger pile those of students who had not. She told the class that she felt that they had let her down, that she was providing work for them to do and that they were not taking advantage of it. The students in the room were silent during the teacher's admonition, mostly looking downwards rather than at the teacher. The teacher announced that the students who had not completed their homework would be punished by loss of marks and also they would have to do additional homework. The teacher then recruited some of the students who had completed the homework to put their answers on the board.

Despite the fact that many of the students hadn't completed their homework, it was still necessary for them to record the work in their books. As the students who had done the work were writing their answers on the board, the teacher told the others that they must do it quickly now, so that they could mark it.

It appeared that the mathematics teacher had initially established a differentiation in the class between the good students and the bad students. This was achieved through her display of the books, which was an anonymous differentiation, and her recruiting of good students to write on the board. This latter strategy identified at least some of the good students. At the start of the lesson, the teacher presented a very grave appearance, attenuated a little when she referred to the good students. During the course of the lesson, she became increasingly relaxed, so that, by the end of the lesson, the whole of the class had been rehabilitated. Right at the end of the lesson, however, the teacher returned to the homework issue, introducing the memory of shame, 'I'm really insulted'. She announced the additional, punishment homework and said that everyone should do it, even those who had done the original homework, because '... it will be good for you'. In what appeared to be a communal strategy, individual responsibility had been effectively equated with collective responsibility and the class, which had been divided at the start of the lesson, was reunited at the end. No student made any visible or audible objection.

Communal strategies were also employed more generally in punishment, which often made use of shaming. This was apparent in the mathematics lesson, but also in the public display of offenders, who would be made to work at desks in the quadrangle. The deputy principal told us that students would sometimes be made to stand in public places holding a notice indicating their offence.

It appeared, then, that the teacher-student relationship at Protea was much closer to a parent-child relationship than seemed to be the case at the other two schools. That is, it was a personalised relationship and its remit extended over a wide range of the students' lives. It would seem that the students were allowed comparatively limited space of their own in the school context. Possibly as a response to the extent of their perceived supervision, the students appeared to attempt to establish or at least to desire their own space. In general terms, we observed far more evidence of resistance in the classroom at Protea than at the other schools (although not to the point of a breakdown of discipline) and, in their characterising of good teachers, students whom we interviewed identified recognition or provision of such space as an important element, thus, a Standard 10 girl:

OK, a good teacher, OK, that would be someone, um, who's very objective, you know, sort of open to what you have to say about the subject, um, [...] will be open, if you come with your own idea, er, and, um, you know, it's not the norm, OK, that person should be open to it, maybe consider it and, um, sort of accept it then as part of what she's supposed to pass down to the rest of the class. And also somebody, um, who goads you to thinking for yourself rather than, say, 'now, um, I'll tell you the way it's done'. Somebody who will encourage you to think, you know, cos that's important. Cos otherwise you come here and your brain rots and you just take in so much rather than also figure out something for yourself.

A Standard 10 boy said

A teacher who can distinguish between when we work and when we can have fun. OK, if you work now, you work now, you can have fun later, but now you get this, you know those [...] work whole period and have no fun. So soon the children will start being, you know, [...] if we're on our way to class, 'Oh no, you're going to that teacher's class, now', they feel despondent, they don't feel relaxed in the classroom, or. So that's, I think that's the bad teacher, when, er, they just want to work. But if you have a teacher who can, can, um, divide, having fun now and just now we will work, then I'm sure the majority of the class will, OK, we're gonna work now we had our fun, or we work now, just now we have our fun, OK? So, there must be some freedom in the class as well, you can't just work all the time.

The Protea students were the only ones who expressed their evaluations of teachers in these kinds of terms.

To summarise, then, we are suggesting that the teacher-student relationship at Protea can be described as that of guardian-ward, as personalised and non-specialised in the sense that it seems to cover a wide range of aspects of the students' lives.

Having illustrated our descriptions of the relationships within the three communities and those between teachers and students at each of these schools, we will finally reconsider some of the key features of the three school assemblies that we described earlier.

RE-STARTING THE DAY

We have described the teacher-student relationship at Mont Clair as individualised and contractual. Teachers are specialists in respect of a curriculum area and its mode of transmission. The referent community of the school is, essentially, global and virtual. The curriculum constitutes the essential basis for students' entry into this community as adults. We propose that the school assembly is a site in which the corporate school can address the real community that constitutes the school and that, in doing so, it deploys two strategies which are consistent with the relationships that we have described.

Firstly, the school affiliates to its referent virtual community through affiliation to one of its cover-sets, that is, a particular form of Christianity. This potentially evokes resistance from non-Christian students. Indeed, one of the students whom we interviewed had been chairperson of the Students Jewish Association, which had made representations to the principal in opposition to the Christian form of the assemblies. However, the extent of this opposition appeared to have been limited and, indeed, this student did attend the assemblies.[112]

We would propose, tentatively, that this comparatively muted opposition is in accord with the comparatively muted participation in the religious component of the assembly by the student body as a whole, especially in the first year of our visits. We suggest that this form of institutionalised Christianity stands as a metaphor for any religious institution of the global virtual community. There is a sense, then, in which we can interpret affiliation to Christianity as an affiliation to the virtual community that constitutes the students' origins and intended destinations. Their active participation is not necessary for this to be effective as an identity-forming marketing strategy. Indeed, it may be that the comparatively strong classification between the school services and community religious activities, serves to inhibit active participation. In 1997, the introduction of a charismatic 'warm-up man' who gave a talk before the song, seemed to increase participation insofar as the singing was a little louder than we had remembered from 1996.

The assembly also incorporated another affiliation strategy through the reference to Eton school. This time, the affiliation was being made to a globalised icon of the virtual community rather than to one of its cover-sets.

The second strategy was a more or less direct marketing of the schools' services via the declarations of the academic and sporting successes of certain of its students which are distributed as the potential achievements of all of Mont Clair

---

[112] Because of the change in the demographics of the school student population (referred to in footnotes 92 and 94 above), the assemblies are now consciously 'inclusive' of the major religions. This entails the use of readings from the *Koran* and Imams invited to address the students. Arguably, however, the practice continues to constitute an affiliation to the virtual community that constitutes students' origins and intended destinations, because these are class rather than religiously based. I am grateful to Jaamiah Galant for this information.

students. The claim of the marketing strategy is that Mont Clair is providing a good service, which is worthy of the continued support of the students in the contract.

At Siyafunda, there is, again, a strong classification between school and community practices insofar as the former relate to the partially alienated teacher and the latter to the township community. The school itself appears to constitute a site for both modes of practice. Township community practices are elaborated in, for example, sports (which appear to be organised by the students during lunch breaks and after school) and choral singing. The assembly seems, in general, to be constituted as a township community practice. The teachers played little or no part in the religious component, even the reading being given by an individual who was clearly not a teacher. The participation in the songs and prayers was very substantial, especially in comparison to that in the Mont Clair assembly. An African informant from outside of this particular township told us that this was because 'we' take our religion very seriously. But our interviews with informants from the white Christian communities suggested that they also took their religion very seriously and, no doubt, sang loudly in church. We offer, by way of an explanation, the suggestion that at Mont Clair, the assembly was constituted as a school practice, which was thus differentiated from the substantive community practices of the church.

The secular component of the Siyafunda assembly was brief and served simply as an informational relay and clearly not the marketing strategy of Mont Clair. In the second year of our visits to Siyafunda, the Deputy Principal of 1996 had, as we have indicated, been promoted to the position of Principal. We observed that she seemed to be adopting a more participative and evaluative role in the religious component of the assembly. In particular, she shuffled her feet and swung her arms in time to the singing and, at its conclusion, announced that it had been great. This principal had also organised and manipulated the discussion on teenage pregnancy that we observed in a Standard 10 English lesson, an apparent attempt to lay claim to moral leadership in and of the collective. The result, in this lesson, was unenthusiastic and even mocking participation by the boys. This was the only occasion that we observed when a teacher was called into question. When the principal instructed the students to discuss 'sex' with their parents, one of the boys said that he didn't live with his parents—a common situation of which the Principal would certainly have been well aware. In our interview with the Principal she appeared to us to misrepresent the status of the girls, suggesting that they are just as active as the boys and that there were just as many older girls. However, her main interest seemed to lie in how we might arrange for her to visit London. This was not an unreasonable interest, given her open, enthusiastic cooperation with us in allowing access to the school; unhappily, it was an interest that we proved unable to satisfy.

If, in its assemblies, Mont Clair markets a service that is available, essentially on an individualised basis, Siyafunda is a site in which the collective recruits its educational leaders. Whilst the teachers stand in authority, they do so only as community servants. Attempts to turn the tables and establish charismatic leadership are, it seems made, but with uneven success. The Afrikaans teacher achieved success by radical individualising strategies. Arguably, this was necessary in the context of an apparently despised curriculum subject. The Principal, however, appeared eager to take on the collective as a whole. This may be seen as a worthy ambition for someone in her position—although the previous Principal did not seem to share it. But we might expect that such an already well-organised collective need do little more than shrug off such confrontation, or wait until it goes away.

Both Siyafunda and Mont Clair serve virtual communities that are united, in a sense, by, respectively, economic and political oppression and economic and political opportunity; a class very much in and for itself, in the township and its broader African field, and the organic solidarity of an entrepreneurial culture, insulated from the ravages of failure by the layers of underclass beneath it. Protea, by contrast, is sited within a *de facto* community that is always already riven by severe class and ethnic divisions and stratifications. The prison without walls of the Protea suburb condenses this diversity in a manner that may only hitherto have been found in frontier communities. Here, there is opportunity for success—though presumably filtered through the reproductive effect of a class society—but without the insulation from failure and in the context of objective cultural differentiation. The Mont Clair Principal can directly address his catchment community with a realistic sense of a unified audience and with a potentially effective marketing message. The Siyafunda teacher can recognise—or fail to recognise—their place as a community servant. But the Protea Principal confronts a motley congregation that has no unity other than the unity or, at least, equilibrium that he can establish. And so he does establish it. The Protea teacher—and the Principal *primus inter pares*— is the latest in a long line of community leaders celebrated in proudly displayed photographs of past generations of school staff.

The Protea teacher, it seems, deploys whatever resources may be at hand to decimate resistance and foster community, strategies most effectively illustrated by the Mathematics teacher, betrayed by her students. But the Principal does not have religion as a resource in his assemblies; both student and staff bodies are split between the Islamic and Christian faiths. We did not see an assembly during our time at Protea in 1996. *Curriculum 2005* (National Department of Education, 1997)—the policy introducing the new National Qualifications Framework—had been introduced in March 1997, immediately prior to our visit in April. When the Principal ascended his podium, his oration actually had the sense of the actor leaving the stage, 'The responsibility now falls on your shoulders, your parents' shoulders. ... teachers do not have to do that; the responsibility lies with you and your parents.' Such was the repeated message of the assembly, the community leader was no longer to lead. In interview, the Principal also spoke of his intention to retire in the not too distant future, though he appeared to be years, possibly even a decade or more short of his sixtieth birthday. On the face of it, placing responsibility for learning on the learner is entirely consistent with both the Mont Clair and Siyafunda communities within which the teacher stands as service provider and as community servant, respectively. In Protea, however, it seems to undermine fundamentally the *raison d'être* of the teacher as guardian; chivvying their wards out to fend for themselves.

TECHNOLOGY, TEXT, COMMENTARY

The limited extent of the data collection activity reported in this chapter disqualifies it as ethnography, by most interpretations of this approach. But then, Andrew Brown and I did not set out to conduct an ethnography; we lacked the resources, certainly in terms of time. We had a question: 'how can we describe the relation between pedagogic strategies deployed in a school, on the one hand, and the nature of the community that the school serves, on the other?' In attempting to address this question, we decided to go and have a look at what went on in three schools that had each been represented to us as very successful schools of their respective kind.

The operation of these schools on the days of our visits constituted the objects of our gaze; I want to say that we constituted them as a complex *text*. On these objects, this text, we deployed a range of research methodological strategies relating to, for example, sampling, data collection and data analysis. We also deployed theoretical resources in our analysis. These derived from our background knowledge of sociological and educational literature as well as from our own previous research. I want to refer to the apparatus of research methodology and theoretical resources as a *technology*. The outcome of the deployment of our technology on our text was the *commentary* that is provided above. This schema, *technology, text, commentary* is inspired by Jerome McGann's acts of *deformance*, introduced in Chapter 3, but I'll defer establishing the link until Chapter 8. The schema can, I want to maintain, be generally applied to any empirical research, but there will be variation in the relative emphasis that is placed on each moment of the schema. An ethnography is likely to place far more emphasis on the *text* in attempting to provide what Geertz (1973 (2000 Edn)), borrowing from Gilbert Ryle, 1968) refers to as 'thick description'. We might suppose that a good deal of quantitative research will place rather more emphasis on the *technology* moment. Certainly, counting is pretty much as radical a reduction of textual richness as is generally attempted. Certain approaches to literary criticism, by deploying a lightly explicated *technology* on a lightly represented *text*, perhaps place more emphasis on the *commentary*; Geoffrey Hartman's (1987) 'mildly deconstructive reading' of Wordsworth's ode—introduced in Chapter 5 comes to mind.

At the time that our data collection and analysis was carried out and the first and second versions of our commentary originally written—in 1996 and 1997—our *technology* was not very well developed and certainly not very explicit. Yet some interest was shown in our *commentary* at various presentations in South Africa and in the UK and by the editor of the *British Journal of Sociology of Education* that accepted our initial commentary, subject to some rather minor modifications; modifications that were never made, the paper never re-submitted, but published only on my own website (Dowling & Brown, 1996). The original ending to the second version, written by myself in 1997, was lost in a computer breakdown. I have included most of this version above together with a prosthetic termination of some 750 words, rendered possible by notes for a presentation that I gave at Chuoo University in Tokyo in September 2001. At this point and in this brief and belated conclusion, I shall try to firm up a little on my *technology* in a manner that is consistent with the general approach that is the central rationale of this book. In doing this, I shall highlight and somewhat and only in part organise the analysis of this second version, which now itself stands as my *text*.

I shall begin by observing that the students in these schools were either *individualised* or organised *collectively* by teacher and/or student strategies, whether in collaboration or in resistance. Thus the Mont Clair Standard 10 students' individual calling to account of their teachers contrasts with the general situation at Siyafunda in which the student collectivity was seen as recruiting the teachers as *community servants*. At the same time, the teacher might be constructed as a *recruit*—as in these two cases—or as a *leader*, as was commonly the case in Protea. The cross-product of the student and teacher variables gives rise to the relational space represented in Figure 7.2. The result is four categories of teacher identity and four categories of student identity that are organised in teacher/student pairs. I shall define a state of *identity equilibrium* as one in which teacher and students collaborate, or at least coincide, in their identity constructions. States of *disequilibrium* are those in which teacher and student identity constructions differ.

Student	Teacher	
	Recruit	Leader
Individualised	*service provider/client*	*guardian/ward*
Collective	*community servant/community member*	*general/footsoldier*

Figure 7.2. Teacher/Student Identity

Again, as is consistent with my method, my analysis does not fix particular settings in specified locations within this space. Much of the classroom interactions between Mont Clair students and teachers—especially in the Standard 10 classes— might be described as collaboration in the *Service provider/client* mode that was, therefore, sustained in equilibrium. This relates to what Bernstein (2000) refers to as the 'instructional discourse'. However, in terms of his 'regulative discourse'—in the Mont Clair assemblies, for example, as well as in the general disciplinary practices—there is evidence of *guardian* strategies, in the *individualising* of blame and praise.

Bernstein's (1996, 2000) analytic distinction between 'regulative' and 'instructional' discourses constitutes the former as the moral order. This discourse is, he claims, dominant. 'Instructional' discourse is concerned with the transmission of competences. Bernstein points out that this kind of distinction tends to be reified in educational research, as if there were entirely separate discourses. Similar kinds of differentiation are, of course, very familiar in the professional discourse of schooling. I recall, as a high school mathematics teacher, having to grade students separately on the basis of 'achievement' and 'effort'.[113] Bernstein's own view, however, is that there is only one discourse, but he seems, nevertheless, to want to maintain an analytic distinction. I introduced Bernstein's distinction in Chapter 4 and there is a little more on it in Chapter 8. Some of the data in this chapter does appear to challenge the usefulness of Bernstein's claim that 'there are not two discourses, there is only one' (Bernstein, 1996, p. 46) and also reveals the analytic binary, regulative/instructional to be perhaps unduly reductionist. The use of detentions and the denial of the service (students having to sit outside the classroom) in exchange for lateness at Mont Clair seems to be divorced from those aspects of the curriculum that are formally assessed in the matric, for example. The same would appear to be the case with the beating of boys who have assaulted girls in Siyafunda and the regulation of school uniform and clampdown on alcohol etc at Protea. On the other hand, there are clearly instances displaying strongly institutionalised modes of transmission/acquisition of the official curriculum. The collective production of the privileged text that was dominant at Siyafunda being an outstanding case in point, but also the Geography teacher's performance of the curriculum and orchestration of the class at Mont Clair and the use of the choral response mode in both Siyafunda and Protea.

Some kind of distinction seems to be called for. I am inclined to reject both of Bernstein's terms. I hope that it is clear from earlier chapters in this book that I am conceiving of subjectivity as having been/being achieved via the apprenticeship (explicit or otherwise) into a more or less strongly institutionalised practice. One is always a subject *of* something and that something may be academic discourse or body hexis or may be theorised as some kind of psychological or biological drive. The point is that being a subject *of* always entails being subject *to*, which is to say, it always entails a regulation on behaviour in some form or other. Instruction, as the transmission of competences, is, therefore, also tied up with the production of subjectivity (or potential subjectivity) and so also concerned with the regulation of behaviour. What does seem to be the case, is that these schools, through their regulatory practices, constitute a distinction between *disciplinary* and *non-disciplinary* practice. The former category relates to *specialised* areas of the curriculum—mathematics, geography, and so forth. The latter relate to what are constituted as *generalised* practices that are not *specialised* to particular curriculum areas—school uniform, religious and moral dispositions would be examples, here. In respect of each of these two dimensions of school practice, the school (at any given level of analysis) may seek to establish either pedagogic or exchange relations *vis-à-vis* its students. Taking the cross-product of these two variables produces the relational space for *regulatory strategies* in Figure 7.3.

---

[113] I also recall reflecting on the rather cruel irony that, whilst the most damning assessment would appear to be an E for 'achievement', but an A for 'effort', the highest praise would seem to be the reverse. Presumably, neither school nor parents would welcome either.

Disciplinary (specialised practice)	Non-disciplinary (generalised practice)	
	Pedagogic	Exchange
Pedagogic	*disciplinary regulation*	*disciplinary enquiry*
Exchange	*moral regulation*	*de-regulation*

Figure 7.3. Regulatory Strategies

We can exemplify these strategies from the schools data and, at the same time, explore the teacher/student identity modes in the three schools. *Moral regulation* strategies at Mont Clair entail the deployment of *guardian* strategies in the *individualising* of blame and praise in certain of the assembly practices and in terms of the general punishment regime—the withdrawal of instructional services, detentions and so forth. There is also evidence of the strategy of the *general* in the *collective* identification of the whole school with various high profile institutions, the government, the church, English public schools and so forth. The use of the 'warm-up man', the 'song', the hierarchical organisation of senior students, teachers, Deputy Principal and Principal, the trappings of academia and so forth are also strategy of the *general* deployed by or on behalf of the Principal *vis-à-vis* the school as a whole. The success of the strategy of the general in terms of the establishing of an identity equilibrium was clearly patchy. But, as marketing strategies—and moral regulation may also be constituted as a marketing device—rather than substantive community leadership moves, they might be understood as functioning in marking out the fictional identities of imagined communities (cf. Anderson, 1991). It may not matter if the students do not really think of themselves as *footsoldiers* in a moral crusade; a virtual identity may be more readily accepted than a substantive one.

The subject lessons at Mont Clair clearly involved *disciplinary regulation* in, for example, the performance of the geography teacher. Here, the mode of activity of the class as well as the knowledge content were well-orchestrated by the teacher. The general context of the disciplinary curriculum at Mont Clair established a service provider teacher identity, so we might speculate (in the absence of additional data) that the geography teacher's disciplinary regulation was constituted as a part of this *service* and would be accepted, which is to say, an identity equilibrium would be sustained, so long as it proved to be effective. There was some evidence of disequilibrium in the classrooms of the novice mathematics teacher and a teacher of Xhosa. Here, we might question the perceived adequacy of the service.

Other aspects of the Mont Clair disciplinary curricular service are more appropriately interpreted as *disciplinary enquiry*. The openness of the teacher to student interrogation would be an example. Clearly, there would be (probably tacit) limits on student behaviour, but this does at least represent a shift towards more of an *exchange* mode in respect of non-disciplinary, generalised student engagement.

Evidence of *de-regulation* was comparatively sparse at Mont Clair and, perhaps was limited to the relaxing of the general strategies relating to presentation under very special circumstances, such as the granting of permission for boys performing in a particular school play to wear their hair longer than would normally be permitted.

At Siyafunda, the prevalent condition seemed to be an equilibrium, *community servant/community member* mode in relation to all apparent regulatory strategies, though moral regulation was not generally in evidence. In general, teachers were recruited as community servants in disciplinary regulation (the leading of the collective construction of the privileged text), in disciplinary enquiry (teachers would be available to study groups), and in de-regulation, in which the 1996 Principal was almost a guest at the assembly and it was the students, not the Principal, who required teachers to beat moral offenders. There were, however, local deviations. The Standard 7 Afrikaans teacher's individualising and leadership strategies in respect of disciplinary regulation were not only consistent with the guardian/ward mode, but seemed to be very effective in establishing this as an equilibrium state. By contrast, the 1997 Principal's attempts to deploy the strategy of the general in the assembly and in the class on teenage pregnancy seemed either to be collectively ignored by community members or, occasionally, individually resisted by dissatisfied clients. The teenage pregnancy discussion took place in what was scheduled as an English lesson, where the appropriate regulatory strategy seemed generally to be disciplinary regulation, but here seemed to be shifting towards moral regulation, a strategy apparently unacceptable in this setting.

The dominant identity mode at Protea is a fairly stable guardian/ward mode operating within strongly pedagogic non-disciplinary practice. There was resistance; the maths teacher's students had not, after all, done their homework. But whilst this is clearly a resistance to authority, it is not necessarily to be interpreted as a resistance to identity; the equilibrium of the guardian/ward mode was very quickly re-established. The students' evaluations of their teachers is also not inconsistent with a stable guardian/ward mode, especially as these tended to be directed precisely at the teachers' ability to discharge their guardian role in encouraging the students to work—disciplinary regulation. As has been mentioned, one teacher in particular—another mathematics teacher—volunteered to drive locals to football matches in a minibus so that they would not be tempted to drive themselves after drinking. This teacher had extended the guardian/ward mode well beyond the school gates and into the wider community. We did not meet this teacher at Protea, as he was seconded to work at the University of Cape Town, where we did meet him. It is perhaps particularly moving that this young teacher, as a Moslem, took an ethical stand against drinking alcohol. This guardian was well aware of the 'frailties' of his wards and readily forgave them; their protection was far more important, but this was offered in exchange mode and so de-regulation. Other teachers spoke in admiration of this man, constituting him as, perhaps, the ideal teacher identity for Protea.

Of all the schools, Protea exhibited the most coordinated identity structure. Perhaps the only routine directed at a collective student body was the insistence on uniform. This is the strategy of the *general* in constituting a recognisable army—moral regulation. However, the students' general acceptance of this was probably also more in keeping with the guardian/ward mode; teacher and students constructing different identity structures that contingently produced a stable outcome. A more austere uniform policy may have shattered this. As the commentary on the Protea assembly suggests, the new education policy, *Curriculum 2005*—by apparently constituting the teacher as a recruit rather than a leader—was received by many (not all) of the teachers as a potential threat to their *guardian* identity.[114] The Principal's utterances at the assembly—'The responsibility now falls on your shoulders, your parents' shoulders. ... teachers do not have to do that; the responsibility lies with you and your parents'—might be interpreted as a half-hearted attempt to foment collective resistance to an external authority, but this seems a little less plausible than its understanding as sigh in the face of anticipated anomie.

CONCLUSION: THE COMMUNITY SCHOOL?

I said at the beginning of this chapter that I would give some indication as to what I mean by referring to these schools as 'good' schools. To try to get at this, I want to report briefly on an EdD thesis in which Rod Cunningham (2004) explored the potential of a complexity approach to school effectiveness. In the thesis, Cunningham takes issue with conventional approaches to school effectiveness/improvement which often seem to propose the possibility of a more or less continuous state of improvement that might be achieved via the deployment of generalisable strategies that may be imposed, top-down, or evolved, bottom-up. These approaches also have a tendency to focus their attention on management and on teaching. Cunningham's first point of departure was to place his own focus on learning. Consistent with the complexity approach, he placed an emphasis on local activity rather than on utopian states; we might recall that this was Forrest Gump's recipe for success, paying attention only to the matter at hand (see Chapter 3). Cunningham looked at different levels within school activity: student-student; student-teacher; teacher-teacher; teacher-manager; manager-local education authority; and so forth. In Cunningham's approach, there was no presumption that practices at each level either would or should be consistent. On the basis of interview data relating to each level, Cunningham produced two 'attractor states' as follows:

Research—Process Attractor
- authority is with the author or shared

---

[114] The retrenchments and relocations expected as a result of a national redistribution of teacher resources also generated a good deal of anxiety, as might be expected, and this economic threat may have been seen as rather more urgent than the identity issue.

- levels of negotiation are high
- collaboration is viewed positively
- solutions to problems are generalised and it is expected that new solutions will emerge.
- practices are consistently applied
- similar patterns emerge across level

Adopt—Content Attractor
- authority is with others
- levels of negotiation are low
- collaboration is viewed positively
- solutions to problems are generalised and are largely taken from elsewhere.
- practices are consistently applied
- similar patterns emerge across levels

(Cunningham, 2004)

These are very different states. The first involves the local generation of good practice in a research mode at all levels. The second state involves the importing of good practice from other levels, described by Cunningham as the 'adopt-content' attractor. One of Cunningham's schools complied with the conditions of the 'research' attractor and the other with those of the 'adopt' attractor. Both of these schools were 'successful' according to more conventional criteria. A third school— less 'successful'—did not conform to either pattern. This study, like our study of the three South African Schools, was a very small-scale study and so raises questions—presents a mode of interrogation—rather than a blueprint for excellence. Indeed, the latter would run counter to the methodology adopted in both Cunningham's study and that conducted by Andrew Brown and myself. But Cunningham's study does suggest that attending to consistency across levels may be worthwhile.

Cunningham's 'attractor states' do not, of course, necessarily entail specific teacher/student identities in the terms constituted in Figure 7.2. But the equilibrium achieved by a convergence of teacher and student identities, service provider/client, guardian/ward, community servant/community member, and general/footsoldier, would suggest a continuity across levels (ie teacher-teacher, student-student), perhaps resonating with the last pair of conditions in each of Cunningham's 'attractor states'. This is not to say that a 'good' school is one that can be defined by only a single teacher/student identity. Indeed, the identity pairs vary to some degree across the practices of at least two of the South African schools. If we look at Siyafunda, in particular, whilst the prevalent equilibrium was in the community servant/community member mode, the Standard 7 Afrikaans teacher's class quite clearly worked as guardian/ward, suggesting, perhaps, that where charismatic authority strategies are effectively deployed, identities are mutable. Identity modes may also vary between different regulatory strategies as is illustrated in the Mont Clair setting. However, there may be contingent limits on this. The 1997 Siyafunda Principal's attempts to deploy the strategy of the general and to shift towards moral regulation did appear to result in disequilibrium.

Nor am I suggesting that identity equilibrium should be regarded as a sufficient condition for a 'good' school. Whilst there was general stability in the service provider/client identities in Mont Clair, it did seem to be the case that one or two of the teachers (only one or two) were not, at that time, providing a particularly good service. We might, rather, think of identity equilibrium—perhaps equilibria, accounting for possible variation across regulatory strategies—as a necessary (but not sufficient) condition for a 'good' school. This would call into question the wisdom of the attempt, apparent in *Curriculum 2005*, to delimit the range of identity models—by constructing the teacher as a recruit—across all schools. Where the available models do not include ones that are consistent with that achieved within a particular school (and in relation to particular regulatory strategies), we might not be surprised if the transition to the new regime resulted in the disruption of the equilibrium. The analysis here suggests that the greatest threat in terms of identity was to Protea, though, of course, it is always possible that government initiatives may be ignored, thwarted or recontextualised.

But it's a little more complicated that this—or, perhaps a little simpler. This study set out to explore the possibility of describing the relationship between pedagogic strategies deployed in a school, on the one hand, and the community that the school serves, on the other. In this second phase analysis, I have, so far, focused exclusively on pedagogic identities and their stability or instability as mapped across the range of regulatory strategies. I have suggested that equilibrium might be interpreted as a necessary condition for school quality. What is less important, as with Cunningham's 'attractor states', is around which particular modes identity stabilises. However, the first phase commentary above proposes a substantial coherence between the structure of the community and the structure of student and teacher identities in these three schools.

The virtual community that is served by Mont Clair resonates somewhat with the culture of 'active individualism' in Mary Douglas's (1996b) 'cultural theory'— to be discussed briefly in Chapter 8 (see Figure 8.1). Here, the individual is weakly incorporated into a weak structure. Authority, in this cultural mode, is affirmed by individual entrepreneurial initiative. Insofar as the symbolic capital (cf Bourdieu, 1991) of schooling qualifications are perceived as legitimate currency within this culture, student initiative is appropriately directed at obtaining the best possible service from the teacher. The interests of the teacher—a junior member of this virtual community—are best served by providing a good service. At the level of classroom interaction in respect of disciplinary practice, the teacher stands in legitimate traditional authority. This mode closes both the practice—here, the disciplinary practice—and the author—here, the teacher—as qualified to transmit it. The relationship between teacher and student is, in its most legitimate form, pedagogic in terms of this disciplinary practice, that is to say, the author/teacher may legitimately retain control over the principles of evaluation of instructional texts. This is the case even where, as in disciplinary enquiry, there is an exchange relation in respect of the manner of engagement by the student with the instructional text. The teacher is thus in authority, but this authority is potentially limited by exchange relations in the non-disciplinary practice and, presumably, by exchange relations pertaining to the evaluation of objective measures of success, most particularly examination results. At Mont Clair, teachers and students, though individualised, are all motivated by the same ambition, the provision and receiving of a high quality schooling service, so that the service provider/client identity pair is optimal in the context of the virtual community of 'active individualism'. Naturally, both the Principal and the students in general have an interest in excluding bad clients, provided that they constitute a manageably small proportion of the school population. Where disciplinary authority is minimised—that is, where relations in this respect are exchange—non-disciplinary practice is most likely to be in pedagogic mode, constituted as a legitimate identity equilibrium in guardian/ward mode in respect of moral regulation. The 'attractor state' at Mont Clair, then, seems to enable a switch between disciplinary regulation and disciplinary enquiry, where the disciplinary practice is foregrounded, and guardian/ward, where it is not. To the extent that the teacher is *in loco parentis*, which is to say, that a part of the service that the virtual community buys is one of childcare, then the nature of this complex attractor state would seem to be appropriate.

The Siyafunda community seems to fit best with Douglas's (1996b) 'conservative hierarchy', which consists of strongly incorporated groups with complex hierarchies. Here, authority is affirmed by collective and rule following action. Advancement is clearly on the basis of individual effort, but in the context of a supportive community—study groups, for example, were common at Siyafunda. It is in everyone's interests that individuals succeed in order to reproduce the pool of, shall we say, organic intellectuals (Gramsci, 1971; Connell *et al*, 1982) as well as to advance the interests of the community as a whole through the achievement of influential positions within the national and international sphere now that the ending of the apartheid era would permit such upward mobility. The teachers at Siyafunda commonly saw themselves on their way to bigger and better positions in administration or, after they had saved enough for the next phase of their education, in the higher professions. *En route*, however, they were recruited to leadership roles in the school. Here, the teacher is, again, installed in a position of traditional authority as community servants in respect of the disciplinary practice. Non-disciplinary practice is, at least in some respects, de-regulated in the sense that the teacher is subordinated to the bureaucratic authority of the community in being required—against the regulations—to administer corporal punishment. At the same time, this subordination to the general bureaucratic authority of the community in general, establishes the teacher in bureaucratic authority *vis-à-vis* the offending individual. The 'attractor state'—an identity equilibrium of community servant/community member—was disturbed only by the charismatic practices of the Afrikaans teacher, who successfully maintained a guardian/ward equilibrium and the hegemonic moves of the 1997 Principal in an apparent attempt to establish moral regulation where either de-regulation or disciplinary regulation would have been expected by the students/community.

The Protea community is rather more problematic in the complexity of its class and ethnic structure. I have insufficient data to make confident statements about it, but some speculation is perhaps warranted. During the apartheid regime, individual advancement was largely restricted to advancement within the coloured community itself, giving rise to positions for community leadership. The teachers at Protea presented themselves in this kind of role, both in the school and, at least in some cases, beyond its gates. As a senior community member, the position of teacher is not consistent with the service provider that is the legitimate role of the junior community member at Mont Clair. Nor is it consistent with the even more junior position of community servant as at Siyafunda. The substantive lack of unity in the structure of the community generally seems unlikely to be consistent with the general/footsoldier identity equilibrium in the absence of some external motivating force (physical, economic, charismatic) and, indeed, tends to place the student in a more individual relationship to teachers and other potential sponsors (including, presumably, senior family members etc). The guardian/ward identity equilibrium, then, would seem to be the only sustainable mode—the 'attractor state'. Protea was the only one of the three schools in which we found no substantial evidence of any of the other modes in operation. This situation places the Protea teacher in traditional authority within a pedagogic relation to the student in respect of both disciplinary and non-disciplinary practices, so that we would expect to see very limited evidence of de-regulation. Perhaps the only instances that were hinted at were in the student expectations that the 'good' teacher would allow time for 'fun', though this might also signal an approval of what was perhaps better interpreted as the successful deployment of a charismatic strategy in the context of disciplinary regulation. The authority mode is generally traditional insofar as the teacher is associated with the closed disciplinary and non-disciplinary practices by virtue of their own qualities and knowledges that have enable them to reach the community leader position.

| Community | Leadership Relations | |
	Exchange	Pedagogic
Individualised	*service provider/client*	*guardian/ward*
Collective	*community servant/community member*	*general/footsoldier*

Figure 7.4. Leader/Follower Identity

Given the potential to align identity equilibrium states in schools with community structure illustrated by this, admittedly rather speculative (in the absence of adequate ethnographic data) description, we might re-label the table presented in Figure 7.2 to give the more general schema for leadership identities in Figure 7.4. I have labelled the variable defined by the columns of the table as leadership relations and scaled it exchange/pedagogic. The rationale should be clear from the description above. Service providers and servants, whilst in pedagogic relations with their clients/communities in respect of their professional competencies, are recruited by these clients/communities, who/which ultimately retain control over the principles of evaluation of their performances. Guardians and generals, by contrast, can stand as such only to the extent that they retain this control themselves.

Douglas suggests that her four cultural types—of which two have been introduced here—are mutually inconsistent, which is to say that none can 'flourish in the conditions predicated for any of the others' (Douglas, 1996b,p. 42); this tendency towards essentialising will be questioned in Chapter 8. South Africa, in the immediate post-apartheid era, is probably unique in many ways, not least in the structure of its various communities in the Western Cape and elsewhere. It may be that the virtual community served by Mont Clair is approximated in other regions of privilege, such as that defined by the clientele of the English Public Schools.[115] It is less clear that the Siyafunda or Protea communities have obvious equivalents. My guess is that the communities served by, for example, inner city schools in Europe or the US are rather more complex, structurally, and rather less appropriately described as 'communities', lacking the legacy of an oppressive, racist regime to hold them—historically by force—together. If this is the case, then it may be even less appropriate to think, generally, in terms of monolithic identity equilibrium states that match the school to its community. Rather, the school might strive to respond to the more diverse identity constructions of and in its fragmented catchment. This may be too much to ask. Clearly, we hope that South Africa moves rapidly away from the extremes of inequality and oppression that characterised apartheid and that are still its legacy. It may be that the end of the 'good' school will be a price that will just have to be paid.

***

As I have indicated at the beginning of this chapter, what is produced here—two commentaries and a simple technology—is not being presented as a discovery about the nature of these schools and certainly not a discovery about the Western Cape of South Africa. It is, rather, an iterative analysis. The first commentary was achieved via the transaction between, on the one hand, a fairly loosely defined (in theoretical, though not research methodological terms) technology and, on the other, a data text—the visits to the Western Cape by Andrew Brown and myself. The second commentary arises out of the transaction between a somewhat more explicit analytic technology—an aspect of the organisational language that is being presented in this book—and the first commentary as its text. Whilst the language of

---

[115] The so-called English public schools are, in fact, high status, high fee-paying private schools and include Eton College, the school mentioned in the Mont Clair assembly.

the commentaries is presented in conventional, 'realist'—even forensic—terms, what I am offering is a construction that, at least to some degree, includes some directions for further constructions, its method. New constructions may be achieved by following and by developing, or indeed critiquing, this method. Whilst none of these constructions should be understood as blueprints for concrete social action, they can ask some searching and potentially productive questions.

The general approach—*constructive description*—that I am introducing in this book is to be distinguished from other methods associated with qualitative analysis—ethnography, ethnomethodology, grounded theory, analytic induction, and so forth. Essentially, the method and the organisational languages that it generates are inspired by successive engagements with the empirical. In being so inspired, it constitutes commentaries on the settings that it encounters. What it does not do is lay claim to the enduring truth of these commentaries and this is why it is particularly suited to iteration. Its deployment does the same kind of thing that surveys do; it raises questions that, if its done well, would have been unlikely to have been formulated in the absence of this deployment; it shows the setting in a new light. Furthermore, to the extent that the method encourages the use of such data as is available, rather than insisting on the thickest of possible description, its use is appropriate for studies of any scale, rather like the experimental method in quantitative research, though without necessitating the manipulation of the empirical and generally understood within the frame of a rather different epistemology.

KNOWERS' ARK/A SHIP OF FOOLS?

PAUL DOWLING & SOH-YOUNG CHUNG

HAGGLING VOICES: AN OVERTURE

Recall a TV commercial for Barclaycard in which Rowan Atkinson played a bungling secret agent—Richard Latham—who was always outdone by his calmly efficient assistant, Bough (Henry Naylor). In one of the ads, Latham attempted to haggle in the vernacular with an apparently Tuareg carpet seller, to little avail. 'You're very fluent, sir', remarked Bough (and we're drawing on Dowling's memory for the dialogue). 'We are both fluent, Bough', Latham replied, 'unfortunately, in different languages'. A lot of this goes on in the academic field. Here is an attempt to haggle over the truth.

> All accounts have, first, to theoretically construct the world they go on to describe in various ways and, in principle, be able to demonstrate non-tautologically [...] that the world is in fact as such. What voice discourses suppress is the manner in which they covertly exempt themselves from the condition they prescribe and hold to be true for everyone else. This exemption is always a form of the basic contradiction of relativism. The truth that all truths are relative must exempt itself in order to be true; there is *one* truth that is *not* relative: the truth that all truth is relative. But then, of course, it is not true that all truth is relative. Positions that deny that anything can be 'in fact' the case (because what is the case is only ever so from a particular perspective) implicitly suppress the claim that it is *in fact* the case that the world is thus and, furthermore, can be shown to be so. In fact, we know full well that it is not! (Moore & Muller, 1999, p. 201)

Here is an example of what we are going to refer to as (following Harold Bloom—see below) a *misreading* or a *misprision*. We intend this to be a positive act that enables us to establish our own position. So, in our misreading, we might summarise Moore's and Muller's argument in this extract as follows:

1. All accounts of the world have a duty to demonstrate, not just assert, their conformity with that world.
2. Voice discourses claim that all truth is relative.

3. The claim that all truth is relative is a claim to the truth and is therefore relative within voice discourse.
4. Therefore voice discourses are self-contradictory.
5. However, they conceal this by 'covertly' exempting their own truth claim as an object of itself.
6. And, anyway some truths are not relative because they meet the requirement of 1 above.

1 is a moralising of research. But it is more than that. What would it mean for an account to conform to a world other than itself? First of all, the account will be a form of text (discourse) that is other than the other world (largely non-discursive), so there must be principles that facilitate translation between the non-discursive and the discursive, to affirm validity and reliability. Ultimately, there is going to be some uncertainty, here, because there is clearly nothing that can mediate unproblematically. In other words, there is always space for doubt and dispute and absolutely no telling how big that space is. And what is meant by 'the world', anyway, are we talking about perceptions or do we mean something else, something that putatively lies behind perceptions and is in some sense their cause?

2-5 is the standard attack on relativism. It exhibits a questionable understanding of propositional logic. But let's put the situation like this. We have a schema that asserts that all claims to truth are defined by the discourse within which they are made. That clearly includes truth claims being made by our own schema. And this schema also accepts that there are others that establish that truths are not relative to the schema; it does not necessarily contradict such positions (as Moore and Muller seem to think it does), it merely questions their helpfulness in some instances.

6 This is simply an assertion. Interestingly, it seems to be tantamount to an empirical claim that simply negates a theoretical claim: voice discourse claims that all truths are relative, but *in fact* some truths are not relative. This is rather odd.

Now an alternative to the schema that we have proposed above, would be explicitly to exclude the truth claim of a voice discourse (ie that all truth claims are relative) as a possible object of itself. There is nothing wrong with that: this is simply a proposition that operates on all members of a set of which it itself is not a member. A plausible principle of exclusion might be to define possible objects as members of the set of all truth claims that do not define the conditions of their existence in terms of social relations of power. In effect, this would be to constitute a metadiscourse that stands in judgement, as it were, of all others. This is what Moore and Muller are accusing voice discourse of doing, except that they claim that this is being done 'covertly', rather than explicitly. Following their own principle in 1, they should demonstrate this rather than simply assert it. But, in fact, it seems to us that 1 is precisely itself a metadiscourse that stands in judgement over all others. Whether it too excludes itself from its own range of objects depends upon whether Moore and Muller are able to justify their claim about voice discourse; we shall return to voice discourse later. As far as we can see, they have, themselves, produced no close textual analysis that would seem to be required in order to establish the validity of their claims either that the category that they are calling 'voice discourse' does claim that there are no kinds of truth claim that are not relative or that it *covertly* exempts itself from this set. We shall also return later to consider such apparent indifference to the empirical.

THE THREE Rs OF ANTI-POSTMODERNISM

Haggling over the truth sometimes gets rather heated. In particular, realists—who explicitly consider that it is crucial to postulate some kind of world that is independent of our knowledge of it, but that is, in some sense, the condition of this knowledge—can often be drawn to using sarcasm and insults when referring to their opponents. Here is Rom Harré and Michael Krausz on Richard Rorty:

> 'Facts', for him, are 'sentence-shaped things', a charming if shallow metaphor. One might be tempted to think that the world helps us to decide between say, 'Strychnine is poisonous' and 'Strychnine is nourishing'. (Harré & Krausz, 1996, pp. 202-203)

And in reference to Goldstein's argument to the effect that 'existence is relative to the equipment available' (*Ibid.*, p. 122):

> Does a relativist seriously expect us to suppose that the potsherd dug up in an archaeological excavation was not there all along waiting to be found? Would its ontological status have been different if it had been lying on the surface for millennia, glanced at each day by passing shepherds? (*Ibid.*, p. 123)

And here is the physicist, Alan Sokal—who was introduced, briefly, in Chapters 1 and 6—in a footnote, smugly casting aside another line of relativist thought:

> By the way, anyone who believes that the laws of physics are mere social conventions is invited to try transgressing those conventions from the windows of my apartment. I live on the twenty-first floor. (Sokal, 1996, no page nos. in the version on Sokal's site)

For Harré and Krausz and for Sokal—and apparently for Moore and Muller as well—whilst our ways of knowing the world may be problematic, uncertain, subject to critique and revision and so forth, the idea that we can simply dismiss the existence of such a world that has real, material effects on our lives makes a nonsense of our ways of life. Rorty's (1979) contention that 'facts' are constituted sociolinguistically and that there is no direct link between 'truths' that are established in this way and the way 'the world really is' clearly irritates Harré and Krausz, but it's not clear that they are fairly representing him, here. We suspect that it is no more likely that Rorty would agree to a strychnine supper than any non-suicidal relativist would be likely to take up Sokal's offer. We doubt, also, that there would be much support amongst even suicidal relativists for the idea that the archaeologist's trowel spontaneously materialises that which it only apparently uncovers.

A better way of understanding these positions might be that, rather than actively denying the existence of the world, they are claiming simply that reflection upon a world that is independent of our knowledge is of no particular value in the pursuance of such knowledge. Categories, such as 'strychnine', 'poisonous', 'nourishing', are not considered to refer to entities that exist as such, but are constructed in the discourses of (amongst others) the natural sciences. Furthermore, the ways in which they are constructed in these discourses is likely to be rather different from the ways in which they are constructed elsewhere. Even within western science, poisons can be, in some sense, nourishing when used in the context of chemotherapy, and nitroglycerin is a poison as well as an explosive, yet is routinely medically prescribed as a vasodilator for patients under threat of heart attack. Similarly, the 'facts' constructed by passing shepherds are likely to be very different from those constructed by archaeologists on encountering the potsherd and, to an extent anyway, this difference is constituted in the divergence of their instruments—the archaeologists' tools designed to preserve the integrity of certain kinds of objects; those of the shepherds designed to preserve the safety and well-being of others. Sokal does add a parenthetic comment in his footnote:

> (P.S. I am aware that this wisecrack is unfair to the more sophisticated relativist philosophers of science, who will concede that *empirical statements* can be objectively true—eg the fall from my window to the pavement will take approximately 2.5 seconds—but claim that the *theoretical explanations* of those empirical statements are more-or-less arbitrary social constructions. I think also this view is largely wrong, but that is a much longer discussion.)
> (Sokal, 1996, no page nos. in the version on Sokal's site)

Easy to say. Given that we accept that few would accept Sokal's offer to test out levitation as an alternative to gravitation, all that he is doing with this sarcasm is demonstrating that he has not understood what he has read; this is not a misreading, it is misrecognition. The paper in which his footnote appeared is an 'afterword' to a paper that he had managed to have published in the journal, *Social Text*. The original paper was intended as a parody of the genre. This is from the 'afterword':

> Like the genre it is meant to satirize—myriad exemplars of which can be found in my reference list—my article is a mélange of truths, half-truths, quarter-truths, falsehoods, non sequiturs, and syntactically correct sentences that have no meaning whatsoever. (Sadly, there are only a handful of the latter: I tried hard to produce them, but I found that, save for rare bursts of inspiration, I just didn't have the knack.) I also employed some other strategies that are well-established (albeit sometimes inadvertently) in the genre: appeals to authority in lieu of logic; speculative theories passed off as established science; strained and even absurd analogies; rhetoric that sounds good but whose meaning is ambiguous; and confusion between the technical and everyday senses of English words. (N.B. All works cited in my article are real, and all quotations are rigorously accurate; none are invented.)
>
> But why did I do it? I confess that I'm an unabashed Old Leftist who never quite understood how deconstruction was supposed to help the working class. And I'm a stodgy old scientist who believes, naively, that there exists an

external world, that there exist objective truths about that world, and that my job is to discover some of them. (If science were merely a negotiation of social conventions about what is agreed to be "true", why would I bother devoting a large fraction of my all-too-short life to it? I don't aspire to be the Emily Post of quantum field theory.)

But my main concern isn't to defend science from the barbarian hordes of lit crit (we'll survive just fine, thank you). Rather, my concern is explicitly *political*: to combat a currently fashionable postmodernist/poststructuralist/ social-constructivist discourse—and more generally a penchant for subjectivism—which is, I believe, inimical to the values and future of the Left. (Sokal, 1996, no page nos. in the version on Sokal's site)

We wonder just what kind of genre Sokal considers himself to be writing in here. Steven Ward reports on a similar kind of politically-motivated condemnation by two other scientists:

In their condemnation, Gross and Levitt portray scientists as the good and virtuous defenders of rationality protecting themselves from the onslaught on the evil and misguided people of postmodern and feminist irrationality. They accuse academic groups that critique science as being guilty of 'intellectual dereliction' [...]. From now on Gross and Levitt advise scientists to be on the guard against the erosion of scientific rationality wherever it may occur. Scientists are encouraged to attend seminars given by nonscientists about science in order to set the record straight. They are invited to scrutinize the tenure decision of science critics and evaluate the science education curriculum at their respective universities to make sure it has not been infiltrated by anti-scientists [...]. Gross and Levitt's critiques go so far as to argue that if the humanities faculty were to walk out of an institution such as MIT, that the science faculty could manage to put together a respectable humanities program. On the other hand, if scientists were to walk out, the humanists would be unable to carry on the science curriculum [...]. (Ward, 1996, pp. 49-50)

Here, the politics are not coming from the same direction (the 'left'), but the rancour is still there, as is the claim that the scientist is quite capable of doing (or, in Sokal's case, successfully imitating) the work of the 'humanists'. Why are Gross and Levitt so concerned about what non-scientists think about scientific activity? Ward suggests that the daggers of their relativist critics cut to the heart of scientists' faith in scientific realism and that it is this faith that is indispensable to their activity as scientists. Not all scientists, it seems, share this faith, here is Stephen Hawking in his first lecture in his debate with Roger Penrose:

I take the positivist viewpoint that a physical theory is just a mathematical model and that it is meaningless to ask whether it corresponds to reality. All that one can ask is that its predictions should be in agreement with observation. (Hawking & Penrose, 1996, pp. 3-4)

Though Roger Penrose, Hawking's co-author in this book does take the realist view. Hawking doesn't seem to come in for the same kind of treatment as non-scientist *anti-realists*, why is this? Well, possibly, Hawking is able to be very successful at doing what other scientists do without the need for faith in the real. So he is not in any sense attacking science, just doing it. Presumably, then, Gross and Levitt see a more material danger in the assaults of the 'humanists'.

Alan Sokal doesn't see any substantive threat to science—'we'll survive just fine, thank you'—but does see a material danger to leftist political action in the 'postmodernist/poststructuralist/social-constructivist discourse'. Essentially, this seems to be because it is a weapon that backfires along the lines of the argument that Moore and Muller make about voice discourses in 2-5 above. This being the case, its seductive powers must be resisted. The seduction presumably lies in the explicit challenges to prevalent patterns of domination and oppression that are made in much of the work that these critics are challenging. Michael Young makes a similar point in the context of educational studies:

> ... there could be serious consequences if, during their training, intending teachers learn not only that all curriculum knowledge is socially constructed, but that it inevitably reflects the values and interests of the dominant class. For example, it could appear to follow that the same claims to objectivity could be made for the everyday mathematics of the street market as are made for the mathematics of the text book. From a postmodernist perspective, the only difference between the two types of mathematics would be that the latter reflects the dominant perspective shared by professional teachers and mathematicians. The limited scope, beyond a very specific set of contexts, of street or what has become known as ethnomathematics, can be easily forgotten. This kind of sociological approach to mathematics can undermine the curriculum rationale for teaching formal mathematics at all. The issue is, of course, not just concerned with mathematics; it applies to all curriculum subjects. If, in literary studies, students learn that there are no criteria for claiming the superiority of Jane Austen over *Neighbours* or *Home and Away*, then the only basis for selection of texts for the English literature curriculum that we are left with is the white middle-class biases and prejudices of teachers or curriculum policy-makers, on the one hand, or what students want, a kind of consumer approach, on the other. It is the possibility that a sociological view of knowledge might actually influence the ways that teachers think about how and what they teach that makes the knowledge question so much more problematic in the sociology of education than in intellectual fields such as cultural and literary studies, which are far more insulated from any practice external to themselves. (Young, 2000, pp. 528-529)

Writing with Rob Moore a year later, Young gives us some indication of why he thinks that Jane Austen should be considered to be superior to *Neighbours* or *Home and Away*:

There are good reasons why we still want people to read Jane Austen's novels, which are not weakened by the narrow community that she wrote about. Her novels are situated in time and context, but they are also timeless in the issues that they explore. One can make a slightly different kind of argument for keeping Newton's laws of motion and Mendeleev's Periodic Table on science syllabuses; both are examples of knowledge that remains powerful and transcends its origins in a particular social context. (Moore & Young, 2001, p. 450)

Michael Young seems to have travelled some considerable distance since the publication of his seminal collection, *Knowledge and Control*, in 1971 (and why not). Moore and Young are arguing for what they refer to as a social realist approach[116] that grounds objectivity in the practices of legitimate communities or networks of experts—so that which physicists as physicists regard as 'true' is 'true'. This view, they claim, stands opposed to 'postmodern theories'. Oddly, a similar kind of claim can also be made by a prominent 'postmodernist' literary critic, here is Stanley Fish:

I assert, and assert without contradiction, that post-modernist accounts of how disciplines come into being are correct, but that such accounts, rather than telling us that disciplines are unreal tell us just how disciplines came to be as real and as productive as they are. (Fish, 1995, p. x)

Part of the problem for Moore, Muller and Young is that they seem, more or less, to equate 'postmodernism' and 'voice discourse' with a textbook by Usher and Edwards (1994), again displaying a certain indifference to the empirical world in which they would find a far more diverse—indeed, contradictory—field of discourse. It seems to us that the central concern of those who explicitly or implicitly adopt realist positions is that research performances, or other performances that are important to them, have some referent beyond themselves that underwrites their value. Insofar as contemporary scientists tend to view science as progressive, then some version of realism might be necessary in order to ground this claim. Stanley Fish wants to establish that there is a thing that is the legitimate practice of literary studies. Self-confessed 'old Leftists', like Alan Sokal, need to be able to establish that there is a thingness about the working class that really is oppressed and that leftist political strategy really can be effective in liberating it. Michael Young wants teachers to be able to believe that Jane Austen really is superior to *Neighbours* and *Home and Away*. For at least some of these, it seems necessary to counter anything that appears to undermine the possibility of anything having any kind of necessary value beyond itself. Their criticism is often characterised by rhetoric, as in the condensation of 'postmodernism' onto Usher and Edwards or this scandalous instance of displacement by Michael Young, referring to the 'debunkers of epistemology':

---

[116] Deriving from the later work of Émile Durkheim and others. As I pointed out in Chapter 1, historian Robert Alun Jones (1999) interprets Durkheim's social realism as a political strategy.

Fundamentally flawed ideas persist because they have powerful social functions in society. Such ideas may, like fascism and racism, have a function for certain groups in society generally. (Young, 2000, p. 524)

Rhetoric, Realism and Rancour: the three Rs of antipostmodernism.

BERNSTEINIAN VOICES

The sociologists cited above—Moore, Muller and Young—in various ways recruit the work of Basil Bernstein. Bernstein was, of course, a theorist of considerable and continuing significance in the sociology of education in the UK and elsewhere, yet, as Sally Power (2006) suggests, the deployment of his theory in informing empirical work is very rare. Power argues that there are a number of factors contributing to this. During his lifetime, Bernstein had a tendency to police the ways in which his work was used, ironically deterring followers. Much of his work was also badly written and often self-contradictory (though many of us are guilty of this). Most crucially, though, and despite his own loud protests to the contrary (for example, in Bernstein 1995) his theorising generally emerged from mere glances at the empirical and subsequently spun off into complex configurations of increasing distance from anything that might be legitimately interpreted as data. His most bizarre flight of fancy, perhaps, is his essay, 'Thoughts on the Trivium and Quadrivium' (in Bernstein, 1990), but his own work is full of fictional 'data' and very light indeed on sustained or close analysis of anything 'real' (see Chapter 4 and Power, 2006), he left that to others.

On a number of occasions, Bernstein repeated to Dowling the aphorism, 'from high enough up everything looks the same'. This was his strategy and this is precisely the strategy of grand theory: the theory that describes everything must eliminate all detail, must be very high up indeed. But the metaphor breaks down to the extent that, the viewpoint from the ascending balloon, unlike that of the abstracting theorist, remains constant in terms of the nature of its gaze; it is simply moving farther away, losing resolution. Bernstein, however, hovers in the theoretical stratosphere holding the lens that is, oddly, the abiding degree zero of all of his work and that is most clearly present in the categories, classification and framing, the lens that establishes a determining opposition, between/within. Chapter 4 presents a fundamental critique of this opposition that grounds it in a decoupling of space and time, the re-coupling of which renders the between as necessarily predicating and predicated of the within. This can be obscured only by ignoring slippage between levels of analysis. Bernstein's classification is established in his hovering above the unroofed school, framing by his entering the classroom, like a fictional team-working of De Certeau's (1984) strategies and tactics. But our suspicions are raised as we notice that the values (+/-) of classification and framing always seem to ride in tandem; neither Bernstein nor his disciples tend to alter their position very much.

Now, one area in which Bernstein has been highly and productively influential is in the 'cultural theory' of Mary Douglas (1996a, 1996b), referred to in Chapters

4 and 7. The origins of cultural theory lie in Douglas's recruiting and recontextualising of Bernstein's restricted/elaborated code and positional/personal family system schemas that was presented in the first edition of Douglas 1996a, published in 1970. Figure 8.1 represents the version of Douglas's schema that appears in her more mature work (Douglas, 1996b).

Douglas claims that there are 'four distinct kinds of culture, no one of which can flourish in the conditions predicated for any of the others' (Douglas, 1996b, p. 42) and these are represented by the italicised categories in the four lower righthand cells of Figure 1, conservative hierarchy, dissident enclave active individualism, and backwater isolation. Here is how she introduces them in *Thought Styles*:

> ... one [conservative hierarchy] is based on hierarchical community, and so in favour of formality and compartmentalisation; one [dissident enclave] is based on equality within a group, and so in favour of spontaneity, and free negotiation, and very hostile to other ways of life; one [active individualism] is the competitive culture of individualism; and fourth [backwater isolation] is the culture of the isolate who prefers to avoid the oppressive controls of the other forms of social life. Any choice which is made in favour of one is at the same time a choice made against the others. The choices are made by the subjects of our study, and it is not our place to let personal preference between alternative ways of living bias the discussion. (Douglas, 1996b, p. 42)

	Incorporation	
Structure	Weak	Strong
Complex	*backwater isolation*	*conservative hierarchy*
Weak	*active individualism*	*dissident enclave*

Figure 8.1. Mary Douglas's 'Cultural Theory' (modified from Douglas, 1996b, p. 43)

Like Bernstein, Douglas also introduces pedagogic examples that are not explicitly sourced in terms of empirical data. However, she also provides a wealth of real stuff, from her own observation and that of others. Her theory also transforms—though not to any great extent—as it encounters new contexts and endeavours to accommodate to them. The theory certainly seems productive in generating Douglas's narratives, revealing diverse cultural settings in ways that, we can readily believe, would not have been possible without it. But the only information that we have of these cultural settings—from the unfamiliar worlds of the Mbuti and the Hazda to more commonplace (to us, anyway) decisions between conventional and complementary medicine or on tableware—is what Douglas provides for us. Examining our own practices through the eyes of her apparatus presents an agnosiac vision that fails to recognise who and what either of us is, diffracting each of us in its 'grid and group'.[117] One would never accuse Douglas of paying scant regard to the empirical, but her essentialising strategy (there are 'four distinct kinds of culture, no one of which can flourish in the conditions predicated for any of the others'), by aspiring, in effect, to grand theory, achieves the same result. So, we can recognise ourselves in all of her cultural modes and cannot confine ourselves to any one of them, even within a particular region of either of our lives—say that relating to our workplaces. This difficulty is also, we think, apparent in respect of the uneasy fit of the Mont Clair and Siyafunda communities into their closest approximating cultural modes (see Chapter 7). By interpreting Douglas's cultural theory as generative of what Lyotard (1984) referred to as *petits récits*, we are able to see ourselves in new ways and describe our practices as cultural complexes, but only at the expense of this necrotising grand theory—perhaps not such a great loss.

INTRODUCING A MISREADING

Douglas's cultural theory theorises states of being: one is either strongly or weakly incorporated—one cannot be both (or, presumably, neither)—and structure is either complex or weak—here, the relationality is weaker, but we must assume that these two are mutually exclusive. Such a rigid frame either works or it shatters under empirical engagement. Another Bernsteinian, Karl Maton, provides another rigid frame, but one that possibly offers more in relation to the direction in which we wish to proceed in this chapter. We shall consider, first, an article that Maton co-wrote with Rob Moore. Moore is the main author of this article, which is perhaps better interpreted as a development of Bernstein than of Maton's own language, although the latter is clearly present. Then we shall explore some of Maton's own work and progress through it to our own position.

We are not, however, haggling over the truth. We feel that we have rattled the cages of some of the authors whom we have mentioned above (and we shall rattle some more), loosening, just a little, the binding of their ontological faith from their theoretical and empirical interests, giving license to the play of, shall we say (why not), constructive positivism. We appreciate, however, that the faithless will never convince the faithful, so we do not present a reading of their work, but rather a misreading and here we are taking our lead from one of the fields that Moore and Maton define.

Harold Bloom argues in his seminal work, *The Anxiety of Influence: A Theory of Poetry* (1973), that all strong poets must struggle to find their own space for originality by liberating themselves from the influence of the poetry that has inspired them. The liberation entails '*misprision*' or *misreading* of the earlier poets. To misread, a poet imagines a space left by the incapacity of the prior poet. In this

---

[117] Douglas (1996a) uses the expression, 'grid and group' in relation to her earlier construction.

sense a strong poem is always a form of misreading, which at the same time becomes influence:

> Poetic Influence—when it involves two strong, authentic poets,—always proceeds by a misreading of the prior poet, an act of creative correction that is actually and necessarily a misinterpretation. The history of fruitful poetic influence, which is to say the main tradition of Western poetry since the Renaissance, is a history of anxiety and self-serving caricature, of distortion, of perverse, wilful revisionism without which modern poetry as such could not exist. (Bloom, 1973, p. 30)

As a poem is always misreading of another poem, its meaning can only be understood by engaging with reading that poem's misreading of other poems. Bloom, therefore, argues that a poem is not a single entity conveying meaning. Rather, meaning arises between poems rather than within a single poetic text: then, a poem is not the text, but the reading or yet another misreading.

We are not writing poetry. But neither are we writing mathematics, a practice that, according to Moore and Maton, is characterised by a very strong grammar (more of this later). In sociology—as in poetry, but unlike mathematics, perhaps—there is a lot of room for interpretation. Our fascination with the prior work that summons our attention is at the same time our anxiety that our desire has already been articulated or gainsaid and our fear of seeing our 'inner struggle as being mere artifice' (Bloom, 1973, p. 65). To acquire a clear space for our creation, we have to misread this prior work. Our reading, therefore, is resistant to the reification of theory and finds itself most productive when seeing through the intertextuality of misreadings. In this sociological misreading, we deploy the translucent technology of research methods to light the way in.

OUR MISREADING OF BERNSTEIN

Moore and Maton (2001) provide an account of the 'knowledge structure' of literary studies conjoining an analytic framework, invented by Maton, with their own misreading of Bernstein. We shall need, before proceeding much further, to discuss both Bernstein and their interpretation of him. Taking cultural studies as his empirical field, Maton (2000) has generated an account of knowledge in terms of the principles whereby its claims are legitimated. He proposes two 'modes of legitimation': 'knowledge mode' and 'knower mode':

> These refer to a distinction between legitimating educational knowledge by reference to procedures appropriated to a discrete object of study (the knowledge mode), or personal characteristics of the author or subject (the knower mode). (Maton, 2000, p. 155)

Moore and Maton also take up Bernstein's (1996, 1999, 2000) theorising of 'vertical knowledge structures' (see Chapter 4), which, firstly, distinguishes between hierarchical and horizontal forms:

A vertical discourse takes the form of a coherent, explicit, systematically principled structure, hierarchically organized, *or* it takes the form of a series of specialized languages with specialized modes of interrogation and specialized criteria for the production of texts. (Bernstein, 1996, p. 171)

Bernstein then distinguishes between strong and weak 'grammars':

It might be useful here to make a distinction within horizontal knowledge structures, distinguishing those whose languages have an explicit conceptual syntax capable of 'relatively' precise empirical descriptions and/or of generating formal modeling of empirical relations, from those languages where these powers are much weaker. The former I will call strong grammars and the latter weak grammars. It is important to add here that 'strong' and 'weak' must be understood as relative within horizontal knowledge structures. From this point of view, economics, linguistics and parts of psychology would be examples of strong grammar. Mathematics would also be considered a horizontal knowledge structure as it consists of a set of discrete languages, for particular problems. Thus, mathematics and logic would be regarded as possessing the strongest grammers [sic], although these languages, for the most part, do not have empirical referents nor are they designed to satisfy empirical criteria. Examples of weak grammars would be sociology, social anthropology, and cultural studies.

The strong grammars of horizontal knowledge structures (excluding mathematics and logic) often achieve their power by rigorious [sic] restrictions on the empirical phenomena they address. For example, the formal precision of transformation grammar arises out of the exclusion of meaning from its concerns; whereas Halliday's systemic functional grammar addresses meanings as the fundamental focus of the grammar and is a much less tidy system. (Bernstein, 1999, p. 164)

Now, it is interesting that Bernstein identifies strength of grammar with explicitness of conceptual syntax and, thereby, it seems, with the level of precision of empirical descriptions. It is not entirely clear whether this level of precision refers to accuracy, validity or reliability or some combination. Yet nor is it clear that an explicit conceptual syntax in and of itself enables any of these. It is of course open to empirical question just how much of mathematics as an academic practice is constituted by formal language. Livingston (1986), for example, engages in an ethnomethodological analysis of Gödel's inconsistency theorem, arguing that mathematical procedures are (and, indeed, must be) open to interpretation. Certainly some forms of proof are widely considered to be superior to others in terms of elegance or some other judgement of value. Nevertheless, there probably is general agreement amongst mathematicians that even less highly regarded forms of proof can still generate certain truth, thus:

... when Appel and Haken completed a proof of the 4-color map theorem using a massive automatic computation, it evoked much controversy. I interpret the controversy as having little to do with doubt people had as to the veracity of the theorem or the correctness of the proof. Rather, it reflected a continuing desire for human understanding of a proof, in addition to knowledge that the theorem is true. (Thurston, 1994, p. 162)

The strong syntax of the formal languages of mathematics in principle enables consensus amongst mathematicians as to whether or not a string of symbols is well-formed or not. Insofar as we might regard a proof as a single string (this is taking some licence, of course), then proof in mathematics closes on certainty in terms of the validity of its claims (theorems). But mathematical systems are, in general, closed systems (like the Mastermind game introduced in Chapter 1) and do not, as Bernstein realises produce 'precise empirical descriptions', nor do they, of themselves, generate 'formal modeling of empirical relations'. In general, mathematics is not an empirical game[118] (although, of course, inspiration for new mathematics may come from anywhere). Mathematical systems must be recruited by empirical practices—including *school* mathematics (see Dowling, 1998)—in the constructing of models.

Dowling (1994, 1998) has introduced an organisational schema for describing the strategies that are involved in one discourse describing another. This schema has been partly introduced in various chapters in this book, but will be elaborated more fully here. In considering text relating to any given practice, Dowling makes an analytic distinction between *expression* (signifiers) and *content* (signified) and considers each in terms of the level of institutionalisation of the text (or textual element) in terms of the practice under consideration. So, here is a mathematical string that consists of strongly institutionalised expression (algebraic and logic symbols) and content (what it means, in the context of a mathematical text, rather than, say, in this text):

$$2(P) \equiv (\exists x)(\exists y)[P(x).P(y).x \neq y.(z)(P(z) \supset z = x \vee z = y)]$$

We can decode this as:

... there are two Ps if and only if there are x, y such that x is P and y is P and x is not the same thing as y and for all z, if z is P then z is the same thing as x or z is the same thing as y ... (Benaceraf & Putnam, 1983)

The decoded version still comprises strongly institutionalised content, but the strength of institutionalisation of the expression has weakened a little, because some of the formal language has been replaced by natural language—it *could* have been decoded differently. The string and its decoded version are definitions of the number 2. Here are two other strings:

$$x = 2 \text{ (where } x \text{ is the number of hens in a coop)}$$

There are two hens in that coop.

---

[118] See Dowling (2001a).

The first of these retains the strongly institutionalised expression, at least in part, of the original string, but now refers not to a mathematical object, but to hens. The second loses all of the strongly institutionalised mathematical expression. These four strings illustrate Dowling's four domains of action shown in Figure 8.2.

	Content (signifieds)	
Expression (signifiers)	I^+	I^-
I^+	esoteric domain	descriptive domain
I^-	expressive domain	public domain

$I^{+/-}$ represents strong/weak institutionalisation.

Figure 8.2. Domains of Action

So, insofar as pure mathematics does not constitute empirical referents (and we are not making a strong empirical claim that this is the case; it clearly depends on how you delimit pure mathematics), it is confined to the lefthand side of the table. *School* mathematics, however, might be described as recruiting to its *esoteric domain* regions of mathematical activity, which are then used in the mathematising of the world to create descriptive and *public domains* (see Chapter 6 for some examples).[119] School mathematics, then, does constitute empirical referents (to do with shopping etc). But the 'precision' of the statements that it makes about these referents does not so much depend upon the strength of the esoteric domain syntax, as on the strength of the syntax of the *gaze* whereby non-mathematical objects are consumed by mathematical language as *descriptive domain* text. By and large, this syntax would seem not to be explicit. We might say that school mathematics has no explicit methodology in its constitution of its descriptive and public domains. The descriptive and public domain school mathematical illustrations in Chapter 6 seem very familiar to mathematics teachers only because such examples are repeated over and over again in the enactment of school mathematics. In terms of its gaze, school mathematics is characterised by low discursive saturation (DS^-) as this is defined in Chapter 4.

Sociology, on the other hand, tends to have rather more explicit, DS^+ methodologies (see, for example, Brown & Dowling, 1998), but, because their internal languages are not formalised as are those of either mathematics, *per se*, or of the esoteric domain of school mathematics, we might say that the 'precision' of their empirical claims is rather weaker. On the other hand, other fields of

---

[119] This personification of school mathematics is clearly not quite right. It would be better, perhaps, to refer to the subject of school mathematics (for example, *qua* school mathematics teacher). The 'recruiting' of mathematics is also something of a simplification, although school mathematics certainly involves/involved recontextualisation from mathematics *per se* (see Dowling, 1998). However, these small fictions perhaps allow us to avoid losing the argument in the obfuscation of pedantry.

practice—physics, for example—would seem to be characterised by comparatively explicit (DS$^+$) syntaxes in both their internal languages and their gaze, whilst we might concede that literary studies in general (though of course there is considerable variation within this field [120]) might be described as exhibiting comparatively tacit (DS$^-$) syntaxes internally and in terms of the gaze (which is to say, the principles determining the constitution of its objects). Considering, in this way, the level of discursive saturation of internal and external syntaxes, gives rise to the relational space in Figure 8.3.

External syntax (gaze)	Internal syntax	
	DS$^+$	DS$^-$
DS$^+$	*metonymic apparatus*	*method*
DS$^-$	*metaphoric apparatus*	*fiction*

DS$^{+/-}$ represents strong/weak *discursive saturation*.

Figure 8.3. Grammatical Modes

In terms of the categories presented in Figure 8.3, physics (as we've described it) resembles a *metonymic apparatus*, school mathematics a *metaphoric apparatus*, literary studies a *fiction* and sociology a *method*. Pure mathematics, insofar as it remains a closed game, cannot be seen in this space because it lacks the dimension of a gaze. We might imagine, however, that at least some original work in mathematics is inspired from beyond the field of mathematics itself, generating an *expressive domain* of action. Under such circumstances, mathematics joins *school* mathematics as a metaphoric apparatus. Indeed, as with all of the relational spaces presented in this book, Figure 8.3 constitutes a field of strategy. The analysis of any empirical instance at any given level of analysis might be expected to reveal a more complex situation than is suggested by these summaries of whole fields.

MISRECOGNITION OF EVIDENCE

Bernstein's simple weak/strong comparison is a metaphoric apparatus and so misrecognition will often tend to go unnoticed. Our own misreading of this apparatus, however, recontextualises its internal syntax by rendering it two-dimensional. We can now return to Moore and Maton, who argue that the constituency of the knowledge of the field of literary criticism is based on knower mode, therefore exhibiting weak grammars, while the field of mathematics is based on knowledge mode, exhibiting strong grammars. Using Maton's definitions (quoted above), this entails that literary criticism is legitimated in terms of the

---

[120] Literary theory in various forms and New Criticism would quite clearly exhibit more explicit syntax than, say, Leavisite or post-theoretical criticism.

'personal characteristics of the knower' and, to the extent that this is an appropriate description, this constitutes literary criticism as fiction, in our terms. Mathematics, on the other hand, is legitimated 'by reference to procedures appropriated to a discrete object of study', which would seem to constitute it as a *metonymic apparatus* and so more like physics (that, interestingly, Bernstein describes as a hierarchical knowledge structure). We shall deal with literary criticism first.

The first thing that our misreading of Moore and Maton's study will establish is a range of problems with their engagement with their empirical field. Their description of the empirical field, 'literary criticism' as a 'field of intellectual production', then, begins to lack precision. Literary criticism clearly takes place in various institutionalised forms, two of which are journalism and the university.[121] However, to imagine that the focus of their study is literary criticism in the university would not be presumptuous since the central source of their evidence, *The Sense of an Ending*, by Frank Kermode (1967),[122] is clearly addressing literary scholars in academia (and was originally presented as a series of lectures in 1965). Even within the university, however, to take a single work as definitive, even illustrative, of a whole field of practice is unduly reductionist, given the diverse regions of intellectual production in the field—research journals, conferences, lectures, etc—not to mention the diversity within any given region.

A second difficulty is the absence of any adequate empirical data in support of most of their claims about literary studies as a practice. Their claim, for example, about the generational conflict between members of the field causing complete breaks in the history of the field and incommensurability between different intellectual traditions are provided without any empirical referents. This invites us to look at a few journals. These exhibit diverse ways in which academic alliances are formed and it is not difficult to see that senior members and junior members appear in the same journal, constituting a form of continuity in an aspect of literary studies. For instance, many journals are founded on intellectual allegiance to literary authors, such as *Shakespeare Quarterly*, *Conradian*, *James Joyce Quarterly*, and so forth, and contributors to these journals are from different generations and theoretical interests. Here, the continuity of literary criticism is maintained through the establishment of canonicity in respect of specific authors. Another major principle is the literary genre, whence *Poetry Review*, *Modern Fiction Studies*, etc. Contributors to *Conradian* and *James Joyce Quarterly* are all potential (and sometimes actual) contributors to *Modern Fiction*.

Forms of alliances take place in various ways and they are not exclusive to one another. Furthermore, examination of works cited within any given article tends to show that the formulation of argument essentially rests on prior work. These alliances may be of similars or of disimilars and the target of action may be discursive closure or openness, so that all of the modes of interaction that were

---

[121] Note the important distinction, made by Bourdieu, between intellectual field and academic field in *Homo Academicus* (1988).

[122] In this chapter we refer to the 2000 edition, to which an Epilogue has been added, but no other noteworthy changes seem to have been made.

introduced in Chapter 3—hegemony, equilibration, exchange of narratives, pastiche—(see Figure 3.1) are possible and, at a lower level of analysis, alliances and oppositions will, of course, emerge within the formal alliances indexed by the journals. This, however, is precisely interaction within discourse, and that is not possible under conditions of incommensurability.

In an earlier paper by Maton on cultural studies (2000), Maton explains that he is:

> ... analysing educational knowledge in terms of the claims made on behalf of intellectual fields by their members. Such 'languages of legitimation' represent the claims made by actors for carving out and maintaining intellectual and institutional spaces within education, i.e. the proclaimed *raison d'être* that provides the conditions of existence for intellectual fields. When actors make claims on behalf of their field (or specific positions within it), they are also proposing a ruler for participation within the field and proclaiming criteria by which achievement within this field should be measured. (Maton, 2000, p. 149)

What is noticeable is the proximity between the data and the research question. The data that Maton recruits to analyse the knowledge structure of cultural studies are, primarily, the descriptions of cultural studies produced by those who are engaged in cultural studies. Why does Maton restrict himself to this metadiscourse, rather than putting his question to the routine products of the field? In effect, his shift between discourse and metadiscourse ventriloquises the former.

This ventriloguising is ironically amplified in Moore and Maton's analysis of literary criticism. As we have mentioned, their principal referent is the work by Frank Kermode.

> A characteristic of this form of intellectual field is its tendency towards proliferation and fragmentation into ever-smaller knower communities. Indeed, Kermode's starting point was Harold Rosenberg's (1962) description of *The Tradition of the New*—reports of the field's rebirth were occurring so often that it had become a tradition. With each new break proclaimed, the new epistemic community of privileged knowers becomes smaller, as each new knower brings with them a new object of study, with knower membership defined by increasingly hyphenated descriptions of identity and membership—to paraphrase Michael Ignatieff, a narcissism of ever smaller differences. Thus the move to weaken grammar tends to recur episodically, breaking the knowledge structure down into its constituent parts [...] (Moore & Maton, 2001, pp. 169-70)

But what was Kermode doing?

> It is not expected of critics as it is of poets that they should help us to make sense of our lives; they are bound only to attempt the lesser feat of making sense of the ways we try to make sense of our lives. This series of talks is devoted to such an attempt ... (Kermode, 2000 edn., p. 3)

His general response to this:

> Men [sic], like poets, rush 'into the middest', *in media res*, when they are born; they also die *in mediis rebus*, and to make sense of their span they need fictive concords with origins and ends, such as give meaning to lives and to poems. The ends they imagine will reflect their irreducibly intermediary preoccupations. They fear it, and as far as we can see always have done so; the End is a figure for their own deaths ... (Kermode, 2000 edn., p. 7)

Moore and Maton quote this extract that appears on the same page:

> When we survive, we make little images of moments which have seemed like ends; we thrive on epochs. Fowler observes, austerely that if we were always quite serious in speaking of 'the end of an epoch' we should live in ceaseless transition; recently Mr. Harold Rosenberg has been quite seriously saying that we do. *Scholars are devoted to the epoch.* (Moore & Maton, 2001, p. 168, original in Kermode, 2000 edn., p. 7; emphasis and final stop added by Moore & Maton)

Moore and Maton have added the emphasis to the final six words and have also added a stop in place of Kermode's comma, after which, in Kermode's publication, we find:

> ... and philosophers—notably Ortega y Gasset and Japsers—have tried to give the concept definition. (Kermode, 2000 edn., p. 7)

'Philosophers', not literary critics, and then:

> The matter is entirely in our own hands, of course; but our interest in it reflects our deep need for intelligible Ends. We project ourselves—a small, humble elect, perhaps—past the End, so as to see the structure whole, a thing we cannot do from our spot of time in the middle. (Kermode, 2000 edn., pp. 7-8)

Kermode is back to the point he made earlier: the sense of an ending is a necessary human solace. The book/series of lectures proceeds to reveal the ways in which a sense of an ending can be established in even the apparently most open of literary works. Kermode's book is subtitled, *Studies in the theory of fiction*, and this is exactly what it is. Not, in other words the metadiscourse that Maton recruited in his earlier study, so, according to our reflection on that work, an appropriate (if not necessarily representative) empirical object. Ironically, however, they seem to be treating the work as if it were metadiscourse. There is no doubt that the field of literary studies tends to generate apocalyptic metadiscourse; Bergonzi (1990), Ellis (1997), Fish (1995), Hilfer (2003), Kernan (1990), and Schwartz (1997) are a few examples; Rosenberg (1962) is not, the author having been, predominantly, an art critic.[123]

So Moore and Maton misrecognise Kermode's book as metadiscourse and Rosenberg as an academic literary critic. The inference that Moore and Maton make on the basis of these misrecognitions is that literary discourse is constituted as a series of apocalyptic fractures privileging the personal characteristics of the knower over the object of study to the extent that the grammar of the practice is weakened. This, of course, does not follow; there is no reason why an idiolect cannot be characterised by strong grammar in terms of its internal or external language or both, unless one makes the additional assumption that strong grammar is not achievable within the span of the life cycle; it is not clear whether or not Moore and Maton are making this assumption.

Moore and Maton's rendition of data poses another problem when we consider their analysis of the field of mathematics, which they describe as exhibiting strong grammars; and recall that we have argued that this statement in itself is an undue reduction of the field and that it may be more appropriate to refer to mathematics as predominantly a metaphoric apparatus. The data that Moore and Maton recruit is Hoffman's (1999) account of Fermat's Last Theorem in his biography of the mathematician Paul Erdos. They argue that the story of the theorem represents

> ... an epistemic community with an *extended* existence in time and space, a community where the past is present, one in which the living members interact with the dead to produce contributions which, when living members die, will be in turn the living concern of future members ... (Moore & Maton, 2001, p. 172)

Whereas in the knower mode:

> The legitimate language is held to be specialised to the knower, and in turn is said to specialise the object of study; only the privileged knower's 'gaze' may access the object of study. In other words, it is possession of the specialised sensibility, typically restricted to a social-temporal category of knower, which is the purported criterion for membership of the field—the means of socialisation into its principles of organisation is social rather than epistemic. (Moore & Maton, 2001, pp. 172-173)

For the knowledge mode of mathematics:

> ... the object (or problem) is held to specialise the language (procedures) required to access knowledge of the object, and this in turn is held to specialise knowers; that is, it is possession of the specialist language which is the purported criterion for membership of the field and the means of inculcation into its principles of organisation. (Moore & Maton, 2001, p. 173)

---

[123] Although there are chapters on poetry in Rosenberg's work, it would be quite perverse to take it as in any sense representative of academic literary criticism.

The source of evidence, this time, is even less appropriate; Kermode is a literary critic and Harold Rosenberg an art critic; Hoffman, however, is certainly not a mathematician; he is a journalist, author and broadcaster and has been the publisher of the Encyclopaedia Britannica. Hoffman's is a metadiscourse that is constituted by an outsider's gaze.

Indeed, the kind of unity across space and time represented by, so Moore and Maton claim, the longevity of Fermat's Last Theorem, is also to be found in literary studies, which, in the twenty-first century, still produces discourse on Milton and Shakespeare—and Aristotle still gets a mention now and again. The point that we are making is not that literary studies and mathematics are the same kind of practice—clearly they are not—but, rather, that Moore and Maton are imposing on these fields totalising characters that are generated by the application of a very simple metaphoric apparatus—hierarchical/horizontal knowledge structure, weak/strong grammar, knower/knowledge mode of legitimation—to inappropriate texts. Furthermore, their lack of a method—especially in terms of the weakness of their validity claims—suggests that, even if they were confronted with more appropriate data, they may not be able to hear it speak. Referring to the natural sciences and also presenting his agenda for the social sciences, Bruno Latour asserts that:

> Objectivity does not refer to a special quality of the mind, an inner state of justice and fairness, but to the presence of objects which have been rendered 'able' (the word is etymologically so powerful) to object to what is told about them ... (Latour, 2000, p. 115)[124]

For us, when Moore and Maton claim that,

> The knower mode problematises communication between different groups of knowers within the field (in this case between past and present members) resulting in a restricted epistemic community. Although each segment or language of the knowledge structure is cohered by shared socio-cultural dispositions (values, aspirations, beliefs), cohesion and communication between segments is at best uncertain and fragile. (Moore & Maton, 2001, p. 169)

The object, in this case, literary studies, does object; here is Stanley Fish:

> When I use words like 'institution' or 'community' I refer not to a collection of independent individuals who, in a moment of deliberation, choose to employ certain interpretive strategies, but rather to a set of practices that are defining of an enterprise and fill the consciousnesses of the enterprise's members. Those members include the authors and speakers as well as their interpreters. Indeed they are all interpreters: when Milton puts pen to paper

---

[124] Note the resonance with the utterance of William Morris quoted in Chapter 3, 'You can't have art without resistance in the materials' (quoted by McGann, 2001, p. 54).

he no less than those in his intended audience is a reader of his own action. (Fish, 1995, p. 14)

Here is an 'institution' or 'community' that includes at least ten generations and we have already illustrated the objection of the object to the decimation of its contemporary community by referring to the structure of journals in the field.

THEORETICAL EXCESS/EMPIRICAL PAUCITY

Again, just as Bernstein's categories, classification and framing, are conjoined (see Chapter 4), so too are key dimensions of Moore and Maton's metaphoric apparatus: knower mode, it seems, entails weak grammar and knowledge mode entails strong grammar; the degree of explicitness of syntax is, it seems, implicated in the principles of object-knower relation. Not only do we have a redundancy, here, but it would seem that knower mode practices can have no facility for its own reproduction; new members of such alliances, it would seem, simply stream through the academy unimpeded—a ship of fools indeed.

Moore and Maton seem to be ready for this assault in their introduction of what they present as the epistemological analogue of Bernstein's pedagogic device (itself a misreading (not a misrecognition) by Bernstein of Chomsky's language acquisition device—see Chapter 4):

The epistemic device is thus the *precondition* of knowledge production; without the epistemic device, there is no means of establishing the basis of knowledge claims. As we show, the epistemic device is also the means, through its realisation in differing modes of legitimation, whereby the knowledge structure and grammars of intellectual fields are maintained, reproduced, transformed, and changed. Whoever owns or controls the epistemic device possesses the means to set the structure and grammar of the field. This is also to say that the device is the object, the means, and the stakes of struggles within intellectual fields. (Moore and Maton, 2001, p. 161)

They are eager to head-off the kind of criticism that has been made of the pedagogic device in Chapter 4:

Bernstein, for example, has had to repeatedly emphasise the distinction between educational knowledge codes and the distributive, recontextualising and evaluative 'rules' regulated by the pedagogic device (which are the *resources* for codes). Such confusions reflect an empiricist tendency to substantialism, that is, to asking *where* the device may be seen, rather than *when*. Crucially, such postulated generative principles are realised not in space, but in time. One sees, as it were, the *effects* of the device, rather than the device itself. (Moore & Maton, 2001, p. 161)

Here we have a literal reading of Bernstein in respect of their ability to separate time and space (see Chapter 4). Again, we have the postulation of an object that cannot object. What the device entails is that the legitimation mode and strength of grammar of practices may change. Moore and Maton introduce an imaginary struggle in which the field of sociology is transformed from a field of intercommunicating *perspectives* to one of incommensurable *paradigms*, thus shifting from knowledge to knower mode. But wherein would reside the incommensurability of the paradigms? Difficult to answer—an imaginary object is certainly in no position to object—but possibly not in the personal characteristics of their respective knowers, suggesting not a knower mode, but knowledge mode, in Maton's terms. Incommensurability itself is a condition that we would tend to reject, here is a stunning metaphor reported by Gayatri Spivak:

> I think now of the improbable hero of [Mahasweta Devi's] novel, "Pterodactyl, Pirtha, and Puran Sahay": a pterodactyl, discovered in a tribal area in the modern state of Bihar. It could not be kept alive, although the journalist and the child wanted to feed it. The look in its eyes could not be understood. The child drew its picture on the cave wall. The latest entry into that collection of figures, mute guest from an improbable and inaccessible past, before the origin of paleonymy or archaeology, guardian of the margin, calling for but not calling forth the ethical antiphone, measures for me the risk of obliterating the rift between the narrow and the general in the name of a merely liberal politics. (Spivak, 1996, p. 167)

Literally:

> Especially in cultural critique, the event of political independence can be automatically assumed to stand in between colony and decolonization as an unexamined good that operates a reversal. As I am insisting, the new nation is run by a regulative logic derived from a reversal of the old colony from within the cited episteme of the postcolonial subject: secularism, democracy, socialism, national identity, capitalist development. There is however a space that did not share in the energy of this reversal, a space that had no firmly established agency of traffic with the *culture* of imperialism. Paradoxically, this space is also outside of organized labor, below the attempted reversals of capital logic. Conventionally, this space is described as the habitat of the *sub*proleteriat or the *sub*altern. (Spivak, 1996, p. 164)

Here is incommensurability, indeed, but at the necessary expense of total exteriority—is this what Moore and Maton (or Kuhn (1970), come to that) intend, or do they simply reject a relational sociology that would render exteriority (and so incommensurability) invalid? No matter, this is a misreading.

The epistemic device refers to the possibility of the transformation of structure and grammar, which, as we have pointed out, entail each other in this paper by Moore and Maton. Since this possibility has been realised only in the imaginary in their paper, it seems to us to have a somewhat nostradamic quality. But it also tends to fetishise knowledge in what we consider to be an unhelpful way. By referring to qualities of knowledge, the device proposes knowledge—literary, mathematical—as a level of analysis that can in and of itself be grasped and analysed. Any text that can even plausibly be associated with a field of practice—a very loose and non-technical term, in our usage—can, it would seem, be read as revealing a feature of the whole field—just as a tissue sample from any part of the body will betray its unique DNA pattern. This field feature can be transformed and when it is (whenever that may be) we will surely see the radiance of the device. We consider that it is more helpful to deploy a method that is sensitive to the possibility of complexity within and across levels of analysis to produce a description that charts rather than totalises a terrain.

A KNOWER'S CASE

We introduced the epistemic device as a potential drag on the unimpeded streaming of knowers through the knower mode region of the academy, but its insubstantial, mythical nature renders it unsuitable to the purpose. We shall, then, return to the empirical and consider a critical case within the field of cultural studies. Here is Maton's description of the procession of knowers, which we need to quote at some length:

> The mode of legitimation represented by cultural studies is the knower mode, comprising actors claiming to represent the interests of a social group outside academia, as in the notion of 'giving voice to'. Knower modes base their legitimation upon the privileged insight of a knower, and work at maintaining strong boundaries around their definition of this knower—they celebrate difference where 'truth' is defined by the 'knower' or 'voice'—i.e. they exhibit strong classification and strong framing of the social relation. Such discourses are legitimated on the basis of the inability of existing educational knowledge to articulate the voice of this previously silenced knower. However, once a knower mode has succeeded in carving out an institutional or intellectual position within higher education, it is likely to become the most prone to the same legitimating strategy; it is difficult to deny new voices what one has claimed was denied to one's own. Such a strategy thus tends to evoke its own disrupter, a new voice—'interruptions interrupted' as Brunsdon [...] characterises feminist work in cultural studies—enabling a procession of the excluded.
>
> If such developments are considered over time, then as each new voice is brought into the academic choir, the category of the new privileged knower becomes ever smaller, each being strongly bounded from one another, for each voice claims its own privileged and specialised knowledge inaccessible to other knowers. The range of knowers within the intellectual field as a whole thus proliferates and fragments, each client knower group having its own representative. For example, this may begin with 'the working class'; then, as the category of the working class fragments under the impact of the procession of the excluded (as the knower's ability to speak for other voices is critiqued), it may develop as follows:

Class:	the working class
Gender	working-class men
Race:	white, working-class men
Sexuality:	white, heterosexual, working-class men
	London-bred, Oxbridge-educated, white heterosexual men of working-class origin in their late twenties currently living in Leicester

And so on, until you reach ... me.

(Maton, 2000, pp. 161-162)

'Karltural Studies'? Again, argument seems to be being made on a 'stands to reason' basis: 'it is difficult to deny new voices what one has claimed was denied to one's own'—surely, this is rationalism, not sociology. The particular route that Maton has selected to reach himself is also interesting, not only because of the particular information that it provides about him (more than he says, perhaps), but because there is a break in it. Can we legitimately say that 'Oxbridge-educated [...] men of working class origin' is a subset of 'working class men'? If so, then any notion of class mobility goes out of the window. But the move is crucial as we shall argue.

Our search for an instance of cultural studies work whose author represents a social group as limited as possible has led us to Handel Wright's (2003) essay, 'Cultural studies as praxis: (making) an autobiographical case'.[125] As the title indicates, the paper is articulated in terms of personal experience, so that it is plausible to delimit the category of knower to a membership of one—that is, after all, at least part of the intention of case study. The central aspect of the author's personal experience recruited in the essay is the complexity of the identity generated by the continuous migration into various socio-cultural contexts. The complexity entails:

> ... identification as African and transition from Africanness to blackness (and overlapping of the two); being located in the contradictory space of the third world in the first world that is the Appalachian region of the USA; being located in the centre that is the US academy but undertaking work at the dual margins of cultural studies that are African cultural studies and cultural studies in education ... (Wright, 2003, p. 810)

Wright claims that he has chosen the autobiographical approach deliberately because its empirical specificity is expected to create more effective and efficient argument for his advocation of cultural studies as praxis:

> Rather than simply make generalized recommendations of and exhortations about cultural studies as praxis, my amended project is a more personal exploration of the source and rationale for my recommendations, the role experience and identity have played in my attraction to, relationship with and

---

[125] Maton has published with Wright: see, for example, Maton and Wright (2002).

conception of cultural studies, as well as how I position myself and am positioned as a teacher, especially a postcolonial African migrant teacher of cultural studies in the USA. (Wright, 2003, p. 809)

The basic structure of argument of the essay might be summed up as follows:

1. Formulation and exploration of the African identity through literature.
2. Engagement with cultural studies as experiencing the complication of identity.
3. Engagement with the conception of identity as an object of academic activity.
4. (Re)theorisation of the concept of identity in relation to and cultural studies.
5. Application of the theory in the teaching and proposition of cultural studies as praxis.

The ways in which Wright has engaged with cultural studies in personal terms, which has entailed his coming to terms with the complexity of his identity, substantiates the argument.

However, what allows the author to establish his argument, not simply as a personal proposition, but as an attempt to reconfigure or 'engender' the discourse of cultural studies as praxis, has not so much to do with the authenticity of his personal experience as to do with the successful academic possession of the personal via the gaze of cultural studies. Wright brings identity, previously his personal problematic, into cultural studies, reclaiming it as a 'pivotal aspect' (p. 811) of cultural studies, drawing upon already existing discourses:

Rather than seeing postmodernist and poststructuralist critiques of essentialist identity politics as reasons to consider identity *passé*, if not dangerously limited and limiting, I view them as providing caveats that press us to articulate more nuanced conceptualisations of identity and emphasize its strategic deployment (e.g. Gayatri Spivak's [...] notion of strategic essentialism, Stuart Hall's [...] assertion that identity is still useful if deployed strategically, and David Blades [...] nautical strategy of tacking back and forth between the modernist/humanist and the postmodernist). (Wright, 2003, pp. 811-812)

Having established identity as the central problematic of cultural studies, he, then, recruits identity as a tool to critique cultural studies for its theoreticism, which, he argues, tends to decentre the marginalised subject by dissolving the political agenda. This in turn is used to justify his re-introduction of identity via the personal case as a significant 'intervention' being located in the same context as 'the feminist and black intervention at CCCS', evoking the Women's Studies Group and Paul Guilroy. Wright's critical engagement of cultural studies via his personal situation results in a theoretical category that he labels 'black ambivalent elaboration', attributing the main inspiration for the term to Homi Bhabha's 'ambivalence' and Gramci's '*elabore*'. This new standpoint enables him to engage with cultural studies in particular relation to black subjectivity, which leads him to a re-thinking of cultural studies in terms of empirical praxis, especially in an educational context, and this is located within the web constructed with names from Raymond Williams to Paul Willis to Patrick Brantlinger to Trinh Minh-Ha.

The essay lists 84 references and contains about 150 citations within the text. What authorises the personal experience as a legitimate part of the argument—to be published alongside essays such as 'Cultural studies at Birmingham: the impossibility of critical pedagogy?' (Gray, 2003) or 'Intellectual spaces of practice and hope: power and culture in Portugal from the 1940s to the present' (Pina, 2003)—is the space that the author contrives with the 150 citations and its clear signalling of its institutional identity. Wright is the only knower with respect to the personal experience, but to be a contributor to the journal, so to the configuration of cultural studies, he must be *The Snow Man* 'And have been cold a long time' (Wallace Stevens, 2001, see Chapter 1) within his own life and, crucially, within the academic field of cultural studies. Furthermore, it is precisely the latter that must be recognised by the academy in order that it might award Wright the skeptron of peer review acceptability. Wright the knowledgeable culturalist must recontextualise Wright the experienced knower just as biographical (as opposed to autobiographical) sociologists must recontextualise the data from their fieldwork; there is quite generally and generally quite deliberately an uncertainty about the location of legitimacy as it shifts between sociologist and informant.

Wright argues, further, that:

> I speak autobiographically and to my experience, not in an attempt to claim the authority of authenticity-precisely the opposite. [...] I speak autobiographically here in an effort to avoid the pitfalls of overgeneralization, assumed authenticity and authority and the various burdens of representation in cultural studies. In my case, given that both my collective identity and the areas of cultural studies I work on are distinctly underrepresented (in both senses of the word), there is the danger that my account may be taken up variously as the authentic and authoritative representation of blacks, Africans, black cultural studies, African cultural studies or cultural studies in education. (Wright, 2003, pp. 809-810)

The accusation seems to be that regions of cultural studies practice do indeed constitute their representations of nominal groups on the basis of the organic origins of the voices producing such representations—'knower mode', apparently. But the authority of the knower is conferred by the cultural studies field in constituting that which might stand as a legitimate nominal group. Wright's highly localised referent group is precisely that which may not so stand; the 'or' in the final sentence of the above extract is indeed telling.[126]

---

[126] Wright's concern about potential overgernalisation is not a singular response. Francis Mulhern, for example, argues that cultural studies tends to generate a 'metacultural discourse':

(continued)

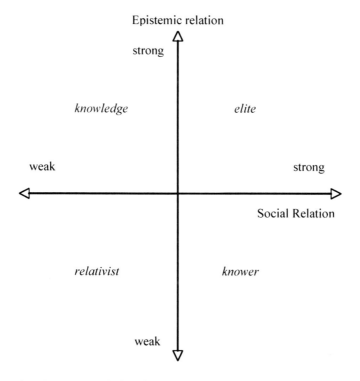

Figure 8.4. 'Legitimation Codes of Specialisation' (Adapted from Maton, 2006, p. 54)

Wright's essay, then, exhibits both a strong 'social relation' (his relationship to his own sociocultural location and history) and a strong 'epistemic relation' (his relationship to cultural studies 'knowledge', in Maton's terms). Maton's analytic schema as presented in Moore and Maton (2001) and in Maton (2000), which constructs only two modes of legitimation, knowledge mode defined by strong epistemic relation and weak social relation, and knower mode defined by weak epistemic relation and strong social relation, is unable to locate Wright's essay.

... in which 'culture' addresses it own generality—that is, the whole domain of meaning— and historical conditions of existence. Its fixed impulse is to displace politics as a form of social authority in the name of true and truly general authority, or 'culture'. (Mulhern, 2000, pp. 181-182)

This view of cultural studies would seem to question Maton's generalisation of the field as operating in knower mode.

	Social Relation	
Epistemic Relation	weak	strong
strong	*knowledge mode*	*autoethnographic mode*
weak	*nomad mode*	*knower mode*

Figure 8.5. Modes of Legitimation

However, Maton's two dimensions do provide for a more complex schema, as he himself clearly realises and exploits in Maton (2006). Maton presents this space—representing his 'legitimation codes of specialisation'—in terms of vertical and horizontal axes, thus constituting four quadrants as in Figure 8.4. This gives rise to four codes: elite, knowledge, relativist, and knower. Surprisingly, perhaps, this schema would identify Wright's paper, as interpreted by us, as elite code. In our initial engagement with Maton's schema, we posited alternative terms, which we have shown in Figure 8.5, in which we have reverted to the style of presentation of relational spaces that is preferred in this book. We identify Wright's strategy as *autoethnography*. It may be productive to juxtapose this identification with Clifford Geertz's description of another tug of war, this time in anthropology, that was introduced in Chapter 1:

> The clash between the expository conventions of author-saturated texts and those of author-evacuated ones that grows out of the particular nature of the ethnographic enterprise is imagined to be a clash between seeing things as one would have them and seeing them as they really are. (Geertz, 1988, p. 9)

He argues that clash, however, is not so much about constructing and describing the relation between the observer and the observed as about 'constructing texts ostensibly scientific out of experience broadly biographical' (*Ibid.*, p. 10). He is marking the distinction between ethnographer as an observer in fieldwork and as an author of an ethnography:

> However far from the groves of academe anthropologists seek out their subjects—a shelved beach in Polynesia, a charred plateau in Amazonia; Akobo, Meknes, Panther Burn—they write their accounts with the world of lecterns, libraries, blackboards, and seminars all about them. This is the world that produces anthropologists, that licenses them to do the kind of work they do, and within which the kind of work they do must find a place if it is to count as worth attention. In itself, Being There is a postcard experience ('I've been to Katmandu—have you?'). It is Being Here, a scholar among scholars, that gets your anthropology read ... published, reviews, cited, taught. (Geertz, 1988, pp. 129-130; ellipsis in original)

Wright's autoethnography is perhaps not so very different. In respect of his claim to be the legitimate author of a life-narrative, he must rely on the 'being there' mode, the knower mode. But for this life-narrative to be constituted as legitimate cultural studies discourse, the specific life must be constituted as being of legitimate interest to that discourse and its mode of representation must be consistent with the generic form of that discourse. In other words, 'being here', in the academy, is a prior condition for his 'being there' to be of any consequence. This is precisely why Maton's break in his procession of knowers from 'working class men' to 'Oxbridge-educated [...] men of working class origin' is so telling.

DEFINING AND STRATEGIC SPACES

Maton's use of axes, complete with arrows, suggests that he wants to consider variation in strength of relation—epistemic, social—as exhibiting a higher level of measurement than the nominal variables that have been introduced in the relational spaces in this chapter and throughout this book. Indeed, his recruitment of this kind of graph, with intersecting line axes, suggests ratio scales with absolute zeros. This is necessary—as it seems to be necessary for Bernstein in respect of his insistence that strong and weak grammars are always relative terms—because Maton is totalising fields of practice rather than, as we are attempting to do, identifying strategies within fields. Thus Wright's paper is located somewhere in the first quadrant—the elite quadrant. Yet we would want to identify at least two legitimising strategies in Wright's work. The first identifies him as an authentic practitioner of academic cultural studies—in the referential space established by his citations and bibliography, which also establishes his own case as significant. The second strategy establishes him as the unique informant in respect of a field of data—his own life. Both strategies close the category of author—only someone knowledgeable in cultural studies and then only Wright himself may publish the paper. The first strategy, however refers to a closed field of practice—it has to be recognisably cultural studies. The second opens the field considerably, this is a unique case that is yet to be institutionalised by any field. Openness/closure of the category of author and of the field of practice are precisely the variables defining the modes of authority action space that was introduced in Chapter 3 as Figure 3.2. For convenience, we reproduce it here as Figure 8.6.

	Field of Practice	
Category of author	Open	Closed
Closed	*Charismatic*	*Traditional*
Open	*Liberal*	*Bureaucratic*

Figure 8.6. Modes of Authority Action

In terms of this schema, Wright is deploying traditional and charismatic authority strategies. Indeed, if he is to get his work published in a refereed, academic journal, he is more or less constrained to deploy both of these strategies. Traditional authority (if the strategy works) establishes him as a legitimate member of an academic community and his work as a legitimate product within that community; charismatic authority establishes his work as original. Indeed, the placing, by the producers of the journal, of the name of the journal and volume and issue number etc on the first page of Wright's paper is a bureaucratic authority strategy that simply asserts that the article that begins on this page is legitimate. The fourth category, the liberal strategy, is the denial of authority, which, of course, cannot be legitimately asserted (though it is often asserted illegitimately)— to do so would be an act of irony. There is nothing that is necessarily incoherent or contradictory in the deployment of multiple strategies.

By contrast, Maton's totalising strategy—'the internal—discursive language of legitimation of cultural studies exhibits a knower mode' (Maton, 2000, p. 157)— does tend to suggest that legitimating strategies within the region defined that diverge from this mode are, in some sense, disruptive or contradictory. It also suggests that, once the code has been identified, it might be appropriate to hunt around for a cause. This, in fact, is precisely the move that he makes in his examination of the school music curriculum (Maton, 2006a,[127] 2006b), charting changes in the code from knower mode, in the primary school, through knowledge mode in early secondary to elite mode at 16+. Again, the data sources that he draws on are very slender (in this case, music curriculum documents).[128] Maton's example of the basis for establishing the code of GCSE music as elite is an examination syllabus statement that,

> Edexcel pupils are required to include a solo musical performance which is assessed for being both 'accurate and fluent' and 'an expressive performance that is generally stylish', with equal emphasis on technical accuracy and personal interpretation—an élite code. (Maton, 2006b, p. 55)

There does not seem to be anything here that indicates that 'personal interpretation' necessarily indexes a strong 'social relation' any more than does the questionnaire item intended as an indicator, 'You need to have "natural ability" or a "feel" for it' (Maton, 2006a, p. 17). There is no reason to suppose that 'natural ability' is *generally* held to be socially distributed (for example, on the basis of social class), nor that 'personal interpretation' or 'feel' may not be acquired in the context of acquiring a DS⁻ practice. Nevertheless, GCSE music is characterised by Maton as elite code and this is subsequently the basis of hypothesis:

> ... one hypothesis from the study of curriculum documents is that the élite code of GCSE Music may reflect a dominant view of professional music among actors in higher levels of education, such as universities and

---

[127] Maton (2006a) appears to be an earlier version of Maton (2006b) and is published on Maton's website. The earlier version seems to have been edited down for the book publication, though the reference given at the head of the former is that of the latter.

[128] Sampling strategies and research design are rather important if one intends to essentialise or totalise a practice, which one must do if, as Maton seems to want to do, one is to identify generative contradictions. We, however, are adopting the iterative approach that was described in Chapter 7.

conservatoires; distinguishing between professional, élite performers combines exacting standards of both technical proficiency and sensibility and this may shape the nature of qualifications in Music at lower levels of the educational system … (Maton, 2006a, p. 19)

'Elite' performance is an expression commonly used in the media to denote the very highest international level of performance—often in sport—and this seems to resonate with Maton's use of it in this last extract. The only link to the social relation seems to be via a metaphorical jump to C.P. Snow's *Two Cultures* lecture (Snow, 1964). We might suggest that it really is about time sociology concentrated on method rather than fiction; but then, this is a misreading.

CONCLUSION: FROM VOICE TO METHOD

Chapter 2 introduced Jerome McGann's (2001) proposal for critical work as 'deformance'. There is an appeal, here, for the term that we have used in this chapter, misreading, because McGann suggests rather more structure, a small increase in the level of discursive saturation and an increase also over the terms treachery and heresy that were used in Chapter 4. In Chapter 2, the 'doubled gap' that opens in the interpretive process was itself interpreted as a gap between *scientia*—in McGann's case, digital technologies—and analysis, and between analysis and *poiesis*—the painting as text. We can now deform/misread this to produce the schema in Figure 8.7, in which the category, commentary, provides for the doubled gap. Any analysis, then, involves the bringing to bear of a technology on an object *text*, producing a commentary; this was the schema introduced in Chapter 7. There is a sense in which this schema might, itself, be construed as a technology, equivalent to McGann's deployment of Photoshop filters upon digitised paintings. We are not subscribing to McGann's realism—we do not need faith to produce interesting commentary—our game is constructive description, not discovery.

The schema in Figure 8.7 produces distinctions between the actions of the knowers and knowledges that have been introduced in this chapter and others. For example, insofar as Stanley Fish (1995) considers himself and Milton to be engaging in the same activity, because literary work and literary criticism constitute, for Fish, the same discourse, then text and commentary coalesce. Fish's technology—asking questions, such as, what does this text mean—is a productive device. New historicists, such as Louis Montrose, whom Fish is opposing in his book, deploy technologies that articulate Marxist, Foucauldian and postmodern influences that generate political commentaries of literary works, thus maintaining a distinction between the three elements of Figure 8.6.

There are differences between the technologies of Fish and Montrose to the extent that the syntax of the internal language of Montrose's technology, is comparatively explicit (DS$^+$), that is, it constitutes an explicit theory of the relationship between the nature of the social and political configuration in a given era and the literature that is generated in that era and, as such, it is not only productive, but a pedagogic device (though not in Bernstein's sense). We might consider that the syntax of the external languages of both are not explicit (DS⁻): Montrose's technology is, in the language of Figure 8.3, a metaphoric apparatus, that of Fish a fiction.

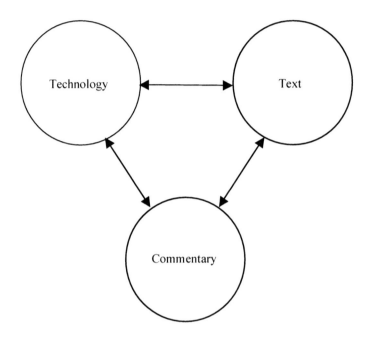

Figure 8.7. Schema of Interpretation

The Bernsteinians discussed in this chapter generate a more or less explicit (DS⁺) internal language. The categories, classification/framing, strong/weak grammar, strong/weak social/epistemic relation, epistemic device or course derive, at some point, from reflection upon empirical texts, but they are constituted as essential features of the sociocultural, thus Maton insists, in respect of his modes of legitimation, that:

> These concepts do not represent ideal typical models of educational knowledge, but highlight an *analytical* distinction between two modes of legitimation that are always and everywhere coexisting and articulating within educational knowledge, i.e. they are ever-present and competing *principles* of legitimation. As such, they represent a repertoire. The lack of empirical examples given in these definitions is thus intentional, for their realisations as *languages* of legitimation are a function of the context. The structuring relations of power and control inhering within specific empirical

contexts will condition which features of these modes are enabled and realised—which parts of the repertoire become voiced. (Maton, 2000, p. 157)

However, as we have illustrated in this chapter, the methodological principles that are deployed by these authors in recognising instances of their theoretical categories are not explicit, often not easily comprehensible. These Bernsteinians, in general, are working with a technology that we can describe as a metaphoric apparatus. There is, incidentally, nothing essentially wrong with this unless one accepts Latour's challenge to produce a form of objectivity that constitutes objects able to object. We do not subscribe to Latour's realism, either, but accept his challenge because it opens us to the voice of the empirical. Moore's, Muller's and Young's apparent decision to totalise 'postmodernism' by reference to a single textbook certainly does not constitute an openness to the empirical. Many of us (see, for example, Wheale, 1995) would find the term 'postmodern' very difficult to close down on and the attempt rather pointless. Moore and Maton's reliance on and their particular misrecognition of a single work in literary studies and a biography written by a non-academic and non-mathematician to grasp literary studies and mathematics, respectively, in terms of their analytic categories, also does not give much room for these objects to object. To be sure, Maton (2000) does, in his analysis of cultural studies, work with a far larger number of texts and, in his consideration of the school music curriculum (2006a, 2006b) presents what is only a preliminary part of a larger project that was underway. However, the syntax of the external language does not refer only to sampling strategies, but also to the reliability of their interpretation; it is this, primarily, that we have called into question, here.

It may be (though we cannot be sure) that it is precisely their insistent embracing of the metaphysical—the ontological, the unobservable, the real—that holds these Bernsteinians to their theoreticism—ironic, of course. It is our claim in this chapter and, indeed, the claim made in this book as a whole, that, even though it may be heresy, letting go of this faith can encourage us, like Forrest Gump (Chapter 3), to concentrate on the matter at hand, which is to say, on our construction of an organisational language out of a dialogue between existing methodological principles and empirical texts. The discussion of this method will be summarised in Chapter 9.

SOCIOLOGY AS METHOD

SOME DIVISIONS AND A DISMISSAL

Some years ago I received a report—verbal or email, I can't remember which—of an interaction during a presentation given by Basil Bernstein at the University of Cape Town. Basil had been talking about boundaries. A member of UCT staff—someone I'd met during my visits to South Africa between 1993 and 1997—made the comment that Dowling had said that there was no such thing as a boundary. Basil's response (as close as I can recall from the report): 'Really, and I have been labouring for the whole of my academic career under the impression that there is.' Wonderful reply, I've always thought. For Bernstein, boundaries establish what can be put together, what must be kept apart. But, as I argued in Chapter 4, for me, boundaries are problematic because they inhibit relationality. So, I like to ask, 'where is the boundary between the North and South poles of a magnet?' Boundaries always seem to me to abandon theory at the level of the empirical. Of course my movement is restricted by a locked door, but what theoretical work does the concept of a boundary as such do in Bernstein's schema? It's a metaphor, a term borrowed from the empirical field and without theoretical development; metaphors have weak principles of recognition; Bernstein's language of description, as I have misread it, is a metaphoric apparatus; it is characterised by DS^+ internal syntax, but DS^- external syntax; its gaze is myopic.

What I have been labouring to achieve for the whole of my, rather shorter, academic career has been the engineering of theory and commentary, rearranging the deck chairs on the Titanic after first having established that we are sinking without hope of salvation. This has, indeed, involved putting things together, pulling other things apart, forming, maintaining, destabilising alliances and oppositions. As a result, there are a lot of dehiscences in this book, but no boundaries.

The most fundamental division, perhaps, is that of author/audience. This is undermined by my Barthesian reference to text-as-work/text-as-text and, indeed, by my claim to have produced an exchange text, to be (earnestly or heretically) written by my audience. Yet I have to construct an authorial voice if I am to call attention to myself in a way at all likely to be successful in forming new alliances—autopoietic action recruiting the structural linkages between us, writer and reader. So each chapter in this book raises what I have considered to be key questions for sociology, for educational studies (possibly for some other fields as well) and offers possible responses to these questions that cohere in a general approach—constructive description—and in an organisational language that I think I shall now call *social activity method* (SAM); after all, in my terms, it isn't a theory, though the commentaries that it produces are perhaps appropriately tagged as such.

In Chapter 1 I drew a distinction between discursive practices, on the one hand, and what I constituted as the mythical region of 'things as they are', on the other. This is not a dehiscence in the social; it is the imagining of a substantial, but unobservable realm that holds the sociocultural to account. I have no argument with the philosophers who constitute their discourse in this way, but I find it unhelpful in sociology and educational studies, where it often seems to serve as a reservoir of alibis for incomplete or incoherent method or theory. This mythologising is the work of forensics. Attention should, rather, be paid to the discourse itself. The manner in which this is to be performed, in my general approach, is precisely in the establishing of analytic partitionings in the sociocultural. This is the *constructive description* that I have elaborated in Chapter 4. Constructive description involves, initially, distinguishing between *theoretical* and *empirical texts*. This is not an essentialising of these categories, but an organising of one's workspace—autopoiesis. Organising subsequently proceeds deductively, from the theoretical side, and inductively, form the empirical, to constitute, at the heart of the schema in Figure 4.2, a set of theoretical propositions and an organisational language. As with all theory, all explicit methodology, this is a simplification, of course, and a little of the complexity is returned to the practice via the practical strategic space, also introduced in Chapter 4 and recruited in Chapter 5 (see Figure 4.5).

In Dowling and Brown (2009) (see also Brown & Dowling, 1998) constructive description is recontextualised as the establishing of a dehiscence between a theoretical and an empirical field; the former resolved via a process of specialising to a problematic and thence a specific problem; the latter via a localising to a particular empirical setting and, ultimately, a set of findings. The relationship between the problem and the findings is described in terms of the category, validity: do the findings address the problem enabling a conclusion? The discourse of research methods is constituted as the technology that facilitates this re-suturing of the initial theoretical/empirical dehiscence. In the present work, the original schema for constructive description as constituted in Figure 4.2 has also been recontextualised as the technology/text/commentary schema that was introduced in Chapter 1, but not finally established until Chapter 8—see Figure 8.7.

These four schemas, represented in Figures 4.2, 4.5, 8.7 and in Dowling and Brown (2009)[129] are compatible, but emphasise different aspects of constructive description; the schema in Figure 8.7 is probably most appropriate in respect of the dominant discourse of this book, in which diverse texts are engaged. Similarly, the schema in Figure 4.2 is perhaps more appropriate where there is an extended

---

[129] See Figure 9.1 in Dowling and Brown (2009); Figure 8.1 in Brown and Dowling (1998).

engagement with a single text, as in Dowling (1998) and that in Figure 4.5, where the focus is on a practice rather than a text. The schema as realised in Dowling and Brown (2009) is probably most appropriate in reflecting on issues of research methodology, but that's just the way I see it; this is an exchange text.

If the author/audience division is most fundamental, then that between teacher and student is primaeval—the birthing of audience/student from the womb of author/teacher that establishes a potential new voice. That there is always a tension between reproduction of self—vegetative reproduction—and reproduction of recontextualised (misread) self—sexual reproduction, which always involves intercourse of one form or another—ensures that this birthing is always painful, generally for all participants. The chapters in this book have introduced a range of euphemisms for this birthing: deformance, treachery, heresy, misprision, misreading. These are my terms for the relationship between my discourse and those of my theoretical antecedents; none of them (I hope) constitute misrecognition—that is not birthing, it's assault. The theoretical antecedent and the empirical must both be given fair audience unless, of course, the speaker is in a position that is beyond learning. These divisions—real (things as they are)/discourse (things as they are described), author/audience, technology/text (shall we say), theoretical/empirical, teacher/student, new voice (heretical student)/antecedent voice (abandoned teacher)—are always constituted on behalf of the first term such that the second term is always an instance of it. The claim, by the exponents of forensics, that the first of these divisions—real/discourse—underpins all of the others is, of course, rejected here as an act, not of misreading or misrecognition, but dismissal; the rest is constructive description.

QUESTIONS AND ANSWERS

Chapter 2 introduced two key questions. Firstly, how might we conceive of the relation between social action and things as they seem (having dismissed the need to consider things as they are). My answer here is, firstly, to understand social action as consisting in autopoietic action directed at the formation, maintenance and destabilising of alliances and oppositions. However, social action cannot, in general, engineer these alliances and oppositions (much as it may try); to paraphrase Foucault, what people don't know is what what they do does (see Dreyfus & Rabinow, 1982, p. 187). Then, what what they do does constitutes the structure that is emergent upon autopoietic cultural action. This, however, is not a generative structure, but epiphenomenal and available to us only via our structural linkage with each other's material expressions, immediate (such as speech) or sedimented (such as writing). Epiphenomenal structure-as-work is thus available for us to recruit as structure-as-text into our further autopoietic social action; patriarchy does not so much cause dress codes in Rajasthan as emerge from social action, to be available for recruitment in what might subsequently be described as patriarchal practices or in opposing or undermining such practices; we can choose sides once positions appear.

The second key question introduced in Chapter 2 is something like this, in concrete terms: how is it possible to constitute a sociological analysis of a, say, thirteenth century Florentine painting? My answer presents two strategic moves. Firstly, we must bound the text, which is to say, we must decide on the limits of our textual data. My decision, in this case, followed that of Hodge and Kress (1988), so that the data included the image itself and some information about its authorship and the place and time of its production. The second strategic move is to constitute the text as an instance of a suitable sociological organisational language. Here I chose Durkheim's language, because that had also been recruited by Hodge and Kress. This general strategy is consistent with constructive description, which always constitutes the empirical as instances of the theoretical, texts as instances of analytic technologies and so forth.

In Chapter 3 I have moved from Durkheim's complex sociology to my own, far simpler organisational language. I asked, in effect, what are some of the consequences of my 'theory of the sociocultural', that is, that it consists of the autopoietic formation, maintenance and destabilising of alliances and oppositions? A very light and in no sense original 'theory' that was probably inspired (how can one be sure) by Laclau and Mouffe (1985), but, doubtless had other theoretical antecedents as well. Nevertheless, the 'theory', such as it is, does sensitise us to look for certain kinds of social action: interaction, of course, and also authorising strategies; potential partners in an alliance must exhibit sufficient strength to make an alliance worthwhile, but sufficient vulnerability to make it possible; a consideration of the modality of interaction (see Figure 3.1) and authority (Figure 3.2) is clearly going to be crucial. The negotiation of authority in interaction (and in any utterance that anticipates interaction—this book, for example) is constituted in the author/audience nexus and the play between pedagogic and exchange relations; this is also introduced in Chapter 3, though it was adumbrated in the preceding chapters.

Chapter 4 is, as I pointed out in Chapter 1, in many ways the central chapter in the book. It renders explicit the conditions and nature of my departure from the forensic sociology of Basil Bernstein. Its central question is, how does one discourse read—which is to say, recontextualise—another? In answer I offer the schema of domains of practice that, in fact, was the original starting point of my organisational language, though it is not fully elaborated in this volume until Chapter 8 (see Figure 8.2). The schema was developed, inductively, in the analysis of a school mathematics scheme, not published in its complete form until Dowling (1998), but presented in various forms throughout the 1990s. However, there was (and is) also a deductive motivation for this scheme. Essentially, for alliances to be recognisable (and there's little point in thinking about the sociocultural in this way otherwise), then they must institutionalise a practice, they must constitute esoteric domains. Such esoteric domain must be more or less opaque to each other; that which constitutes a legitimate utterance, for example, is constituted differently as one moves between domains and these differences are greater the stronger the institutionalisation of the field of practice. There is, in other words, no direct entry to the esoteric domain of one alliance from the esoteric domain of another or from the weakly institutionalised practices of the everyday (weak institutionalisation that is achieved by the misrecognition of locally nuanced practice as idiosyncratic, rendering invisible corresponding local alliances). I therefore postulated that alliances must also constitute regions of weakly institutionalised practice as pedagogic portals; this is the public domain. A further deductive move was to consider separately the institutionalisation of expression and content of practice, giving rise to the fourfold relational space in Figure 8.2—more on this space later.

Chapter 4 also raises a second question concerning the differentiation of practice between and within an alliance. Here, the differentiation in level of institutionalisation is considered in relation to the level of discursive saturation of the practice, the result is given in Figure 4.5. In contrast with the domains of practice schema, The differentiation between strong and weak institutionalisation in the schema in Figure 4.5 constitutes what might be interpreted as a public/private differentiation, resonating with the distinction between the limitations on public authorial authority, on the one hand, and private audience authority, on the other, discussed in Chapter 3 in relation to hypertextual media. The contrast points to a difference in levels of analysis. The public domain weakly institutionalises expression and content in relation to esoteric domain, but this relationality might be interpreted as strongly institutionalised at a higher level of analysis. I will elaborate on this in a development of the use of the domains of action space below. The challenge for would-be innovators in an alliance is to market their private idiolects and tricks. Success here would enable them to force into the public sphere of discourse and skill. The central action in producing this book is clearly an attempt at such marketing.

Chapter 5 represents another act of misreading, more treachery. The work of my colleague, Gunther Kress, has been very influential, very productive, in the development of SAM, but I need also to depart from his forensic semiotics. In Kress (1993) he challenged Saussure's proposition that the linguistic sign is arbitrary, arguing that, on the contrary, the bringing together of a specific signifier and a specific signified is always motivated and this motivation is constituted by the sociocultural location of the sign-maker. Stated thus, then what is needed for the analysis of texts is not, primarily, a semiotic grammar, but a sociological theory of motivation. Durkheim provides this (in a sense, though not at the level of the individual) and this was the point of my re-analysis of the Cimabue work in Chapter 2. The other departure that I want to make from Kress's language is to use the term text where he tends to use sign and this is the basis for my misreading in Chapter 5. In this misreading I have dismantled Kress's semiotic grammar and recontextualised it as a social grammar of textual modes (Figure 5.5). The grammar constituted by my relational space is social in that it is clearly (and, in Chapter 5, explicitly) articulated with the distinction between pedagogic and exchange strategies as a reservoir of motivated resources. Register/repertoire coding strength might be construed as a misreading of strength of institutionalisation or discursive saturation or even domains or action—it resonates with each of these, but does not coincide with any.

The other dimension in Figure 5.5 facilitates the mythologising of the chronotope as a synchronicity or, alternatively, a diachronicity. In Bernstein's work this has already been achieved and cemented into his language in the fundamental organisational categories of classification and framing, forcing us to confuse or conflate distinct levels of analysis. In my schema, the synchronising strategy of an index or a contents list might be constituted as an exchange strategy that asserts that the entire text is co-present and available for the imposition of audience principles of reading and evaluation, like a supermarket. The diachronising sequencing of the chapters, as is being attempted in the present Chapter, is a pedagogic strategy: despite appearances, there is a linearity to my message that you may want to take into account.

Chapter 5, more than any other, calls into question the value of an all-out drive for coherence in an organisational language (though I presented it as a temporary criterion in Chapter 2). Equilibration—internally and externally—is an important theoretical strategy, but total coherence (and let's pretend such a state is achievable) terminates both as the sclerotic language necrotises the world. This, of course, is called bigotry. So I am content, for now, simply to note the resonances between register/repertoire coding strength, institutionalisation, discursive saturation and domains of action and allow to remain the slight variation in nuance between the various ways in which I have established public/private divisions within this book. This is something that I've learned (slowly) since the production of my doctoral thesis. One of the examiners remarked, fairly early on in the viva (memory serving in lieu of fieldnotes), 'you have left us no way into or out of the thesis other than those that you have provided for us'; I've never been entirely sure whether this was intended as a positive or a negative comment, but I take the point. All that I require is that the degree of disequilibrium be sufficiently small to avoid as sense of jarring within the organisational language.

Chapter 6 involved a revisiting of a paper that I had written nearly twenty years ago, in which I attempted to establish the technological phenomena as signifiers for the globally developing division of labour. In the present work I have looked at a different technological phenomenon, mathematicoscience. This globally public discourse, I have argued, constitutes bureaucratic forms of legitimate relationship to the empirical—via the excision of the subjective—and the legitimate form of argumentation—linearity, syllogism—that must be exhibited in public debate. The global public discourse of democracy constitutes the bureaucratic form of legitimate governance. Again, there is the theme of a partitioning of the sociocultural into public and private spheres. Here, private discourse is rendered illegitimate in the context of the global public forms; it is not possible to challenge rationality or democracy unless one is truly outside of the system (and which of us is?) But private discourse is not thereby rendered impotent; its effectiveness is determined by the context of its elaboration, by the nature of the local topography of alliances and oppositions within which it operates. Both the powerful and the powerless operate in private. [130] Chapter 6 recruits both the authority schema (Figures 3.2 and 8.6) and the interaction schema (Figure 3.1), illustrating their potential in mapping fields of action. In respect of the latter, the strategy of pastiche is offered as generative, perhaps, of the 'gift' that the globalised system cannot return—a moral form of terrorism (though Baudrillard (2001) might claim that such a form is no terrorism at all).

Chapter 7 is the only chapter that has focused on a sustained empirical investigation. However, whilst I hope that the commentary that is offered will be of interest, in and of itself, this was not the principal motive of the chapter. Rather, my motive was to illustrate the potential of iteration in constructive description in respect of both the development of commentary and the development of the organisational language. If the question, how much data is needed for analysis to begin is put to this chapter, the answer that it offers is, not very much. Although the actual amount of data that Andrew Brown and I gathered was certainly not trivial, it must be regarded as meagre in relation to the usual expectations of (for example) ethnographic work, especially given that the empirical field with which we were concerned was potentially so extensive.

In re-visiting this South African study, SAM has been developed in respect of three relational spaces, two of which—teacher/student and learner/follower identities in Figures 7.2 and 7.4—are closely related. These schemas emerged, mainly inductively from the data itself. The third space maps pedagogic regulatory strategies. This schema represents a dismantling and reformulation of Bernstein's regulatory/instructional analysis of pedagogic discourse. The commentary that is produced in this chapter is, of course, a commentary on schooling in the Western Cape province of South Africa at a particular time, but it is openly a commentary produced by a particular technology and so does not foreclose on alternative commentaries. Rather than define schooling in this context, it maps and interrogates it in a way that may prove productive in respect of other contexts. In particular, it offers a perspective on how we might conceive of a 'good school'— without negating more conventional approaches—in terms of identity equilibrium, which state may take different forms in different aspects of the school activity. The study has, in a sense, been re-re-visited by the inclusion of several footnotes written by Jaamiah Galant and Ursula Hoadley as a kind of author/audience dialogue.

Chapter 8 was a return to primaeval heresy, now as a misprision or misreading, in a re-engagement with forensic realists and, in particular, the Bernsteinians. There is a sense in which it shouldn't matter if sociologists, or even physicists, want to hold on to some sense of the really real—things as they are—any more than it should matter (as far as their research is concerned) whether or not they hold to a religious conviction or support a particular football team or are fans of a particular T.V. soap opera. In strongly institutionalised practices, such as physics seems largely to be, the impact of realist faith may well be minimal. In less

---

[130] Please excuse the breach of faith in the use of power as something possessed; I want to offer a quotable.

strongly institutionalised fields, such as sociology and educational studies, however, it does sometimes seem that faith in forensics can sustain a certain casualness towards the empirical in favour of theoreticism or its *alter ego*, empiricism. This is clearly a very different kind of forensics from the version prepresented in currently popular T.V. shows (but then that's T.V.)

In respect of the domains of action schema that is presented in its complete form in Chapter 8 (see Figure 8.2), it is important to point out that neither the esoteric domain, nor the public domain are constituted as 'things as they are'. The esoteric domain is the practice in its own language, so to speak. The public domain is, using the same metaphor, the practice speaking the language of another practice, but according to its own principles. The schema of authority strategies (Figures 3.2 and 8.6) is arrived at, in this chapter, via a dismantling and reconstruction, through an intermediate stage, of Maton's forensic scheme of modes of legitimation. A key new relational space is introduced in the grammatical modes schema in Figure 8.3. This apparatus is the response to Bernstein's forensic dichotomy of strong/weak grammar that also bears on his distinction between internal and external languages. The result presents Bernsteinian sociology as characterised predominantly as a metaphoric apparatus and my sociology as a method, thus, I hope, justifying the title of this book. Finally, the chapter also elaborates on the technology/text/commentary interpretation of constructive description that, as I've suggested above, probably works best for the way in which SAM has been introduced and recruited in this book.

The above is, I suppose, an attempt to describe how I read my own book. In the penultimate section of its final chapter I want to provide some brief illustrations of how SAM might be and is being taken forward in different contexts, making reference, in the main, to the work of some of my research students and my own thinking. Some of the latter is very speculative, at this stage, and it is included in order to provide an open conclusion to the book as a whole—perhaps partly in response to the examiner's comment that I referred to above.

DEVELOPMENTS (SOME MORE TENTATIVE THAN OTHERS)

The domains of action schema

In the discussion above I have made reference to the two ways in which the category, institutionalisation, has ramified in the book. In one branch, the strong institutionalisation of a practice is seen to constitute public and private regions of practice. This is most obviously the case with the institutionalisation of the global public discourse, mathematicoscience, that is analysed in Chapter 6. Here, I argued that public dialogue is, effectively, held to account by this public discourse, effectively privatising alternative modes of confronting the empirical and alternative forms of argumentation. The other branch distinguishes between a strongly institutionalised—in terms of expression and content—esoteric domain and a weakly institutionalised public domain, with the descriptive and expressive domains established as intermediate forms generated by considering expression and content separately. I suggested above that this apparent dichotomy might be resolved by considering different levels of analysis.

In research, currently underway, on the construction of the school mathematics and modern foreign languages curricula in the UK, Jeremy Burke (working papers) has extended the domains of action schema (Figure 8.2) to that shown in Figure 9.1, which, for the purposes of clarity, employs a different form of table layout. The capitalised, outer field might be constituted as the field of discourse that constitutes, shall we say, school mathematics. I have, here, produced no analysis of this field (though this is being done by Burke), but we might speculate that it would reasonably include policy discourse and the pedagogic recontextualisation of educational research that, together, constitute the school mathematics curriculum, including the nature of its esoteric domain gaze and the construction of the public domain. In this schema, then, we can interpret the public domain of school mathematics, weakly institutionalised at the level of curriculum delivery— that is, the public domain is presented as being concerned with non-mathematical practice—but strongly institutionalised at the level of curriculum construction.

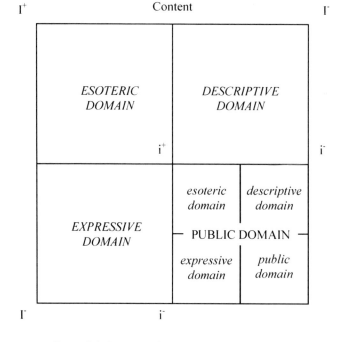

Figure 9.1. Domains of Action at 2 Levels of Analysis

Indeed, it might be helpful to consider policy discourse as constituting recontextualised educational discourse as its own public domain and educational discourse, in turn, constituting school mathematics as its public domain, giving rise to three levels of analysis as shown in Figure 9.2 (I have left out labelling to avoid producing an unduly cluttered diagram). What we have, in Figures 9.1 and 9.2 is, in effect, a reformulation of Bernstein's pedagogic device (see Chapter 4) that constitutes a method of analysis rather than operating as a metaphoric apparatus. Crucially, the fields at all levels of analysis are interpreted as emergent structure. Figure 9.1 does not, in other words, represent the regulation of the school mathematics curriculum (or of mathematicoscience) by the state or by some global alliance or, indeed, by educational research or any other regulatory or causal structure. Structure is always to be interpreted as emergent upon autopoietic action and that action must be studied in order to produce structure, which is, of course, the product of the analysis. We are doing constructive description, here, not forensics.

The constructions in Figures 9.1 and 9.2 also potentially provide a way of thinking about the distinction that I made in Chapter 1 between the apparently strong internal and external institutionalisation of the natural sciences and the weak internal and external institutionalisation of the social sciences and educational studies, in particular. Thus, whilst Figure 9.1 might provide the basis for a description of research in the natural sciences, we will need an alternative configuration for the social sciences and the humanities.

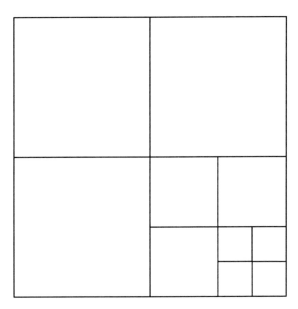

Figure 9.2. Domains of Action at 3 Levels of Analysis

In the course of his research into high school economics, Russell Dudley-Smith (working papers) has considered the way in which different discourses in the social sciences—economics and sociology, say—have a tendency to produce competing commentaries on the social, which is to say, they recontextualise social discourse differently. He produced the diagram in Figure 9.3 to describe this; again, some of the labelling has been omitted. In this new schema, the romanised domains represent the domains of one discourse and the italicised domains, those of another. The two configurations in Figures 9.1 and 9.3 might now be interpreted as a reformulation of the kind of distinction that Bernstein was making in referring to hierarchical (Figure 9.1) and horizontal (Figure 9.3) knowledge structures. Again, Burke's and Dudley-Smith's constructions constitute a method rather than a metaphoric apparatus. If we were to think of the social sciences and humanities in terms of Figure 9.3, then given that there are, in each case, many more than two competing discourses, the field as a whole might be imagined more as in Figure 9.4. Following on from the discussion in Chapter 8, I think that this is rather a more appropriate way of thinking about the social sciences and humanities than as a series of more or less incommensurable languages. The point here, I think, is that the public domains of competing discourses are never incommensurable (insofar as incommensurability is an operationalisable term) if they are understood as ways into the discourses—each must be, to a degree, recognisable by the others.

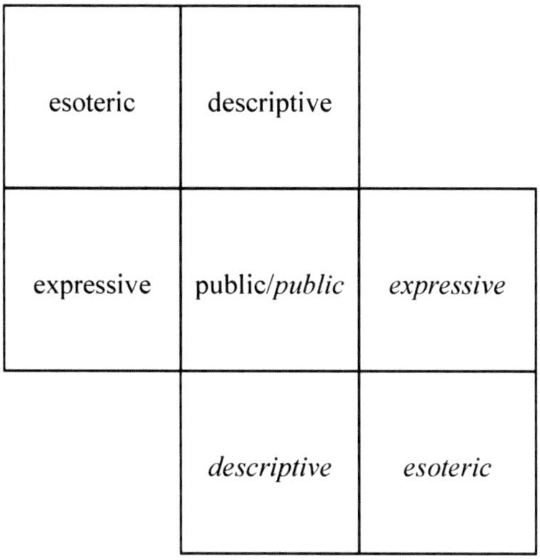

esoteric	descriptive	
expressive	public/*public*	*expressive*
	descriptive	*esoteric*

Figure 9.3. Competing Discourses

Again, it is necessary to emphasise that all of these geometrical structures are being interpreted as ideal typical states. It may well be that analysis will produce a description of literary studies or mathematics, say, as in certain aspects, exhibiting the kind of structure illustrated in Figure 9.1 and, in others, that of Figure 9.4. Furthermore, the analysis of a field of practice (at any level of analysis) is only one aspect that is currently available or that might be developed in SAM. It does not, for example, address the issue of grammatical mode, which is schematised in Figure 8.3.

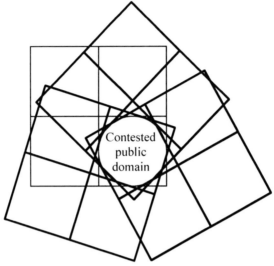

Figure 9.4. Public Domain Contested by 4 Discourses

Before leaving the domains of action schema, I want to sketch another application of it that occurred to me and to Colin McCarty, who is researching the pedagogic use of computer games. It arises out of a reflection on how one might go about playing a new game. I shall illustrate using *Tomb Raider II* (I'm ashamed to admit, one of only very few computer games I've ever played). The game itself (which I've also introduced in Chapter 3) is produced as an amalgam of electronic hardware and a game program that I'm going to refer to as the game's esoteric domain, probably produced in C_{++} and an assembly language, by a substantial team of diversely specialised game programmers. Despite an ancient BSc in physics, I have no direct access to either the hardware innards of my computer or to the game program that would enable me to figure out directly what is going on when I play the game; the esoteric domain, defined in these terms, is a complete mystery to, I suspect, most (though certainly not all) players.

I do have access to a Graphic User Interface (GUI) and a keyboard. The former appears to me as a polyhedral environment in which an avatar performs various movements as I manipulate the keyboard. I can make sense of this GUI, though I am a little concerned that I can't allow the avatar sit down while I'm thinking what to do next. This is the game's public domain. Now the way that I played the game was to formulate—either by experiment or cheating (i.e. using a walkthrough)—rules that enabled me to associate precise keyboard movements with predictable outcomes on the screen. Many of these rules were, as I recall, highly localised, for example, identifying a precise point in an action when a particular keystroke has to be made in order to achieve a particular result. A few were more general, for example, compiling a repertoire of avatar actions (with associated keyboard action) that may provide solutions to recurring problems, such as there being no apparent way out of a room and so forth.

What I am doing in compiling these rules (idiolect—see Figure 4.5) and repertoires (tricks—see Figure 4.5) is attempting to represent esoteric domain principles in the language of the public domain, which is to say, I am generating an expressive domain commentary on the game. This, of course, is not the only way to play the game, as I mentioned in Chapter 3, but it is, arguably, one way to learn to play it. Presumably, experienced and successful game players may generate a far more extensive set of rules and repertoires that operate over a wide range of games to constitute the esoteric domain of a game playing practice, as distinct from a game authoring practice, thereby generating a new structure of domains of action. To the extent that the new structure is institutionalised across a game playing alliance, then the idiolect and tricks become discourse and skills (Figure 4.5).

The domains of action schema might be used in a similar way to describe interactions between individuals and groups. When someone addresses me, they have access to aspects of meaning relating to their utterance that are not accessible to me—this, in a sense, might be described as their esoteric domain. One strategy that is available to me is to interpret the utterance in terms of my own esoteric domain of thought, resulting in the struggle illustrated in Figure 9.3, whether or not the struggle is actually recognised as such at the time; this is misrecognition, if unselfconscious, misprision if explicit; in the doctor's surgery, it's called diagnosis and in the school classroom, assessment. Alternatively, I might attempt to learn about my interlocutor, by producing an expressive domain—learning, perhaps. Construed in this way, Figure 9.3 also provides a map for hegemonic pedagogic action, which, if successful, involves the movement of the apprentice from one esoteric domain to the other via a contested public domain and the descriptive and expressive domains of the hegemonising activity.

More relational spaces

Having explored some of the potential of the domains of action schema, I want to introduce briefly one or two other SAM schema. The first provides a map of strategies relating to the delimitation and expansion of the descriptive power of an activity. The schema is given in Figure 9.5.

The most obvious way in which this schema has already been recontextualised and deployed is in Dowling and Brown (see also Brown & Dowling, 1998). Here, the formulation of constructive description was, as I have indicated above, as the establishing and subsequent re-suturing of a dehiscence in the sociocultural to produce theoretical and empirical fields. The theoretical field is interpreted as a field of principled discourse and the delimiting move to produce, first, a problematic and, ultimately, a research problem is on of *specialising*. The empirical field, on the other hand, is understood as a field of, shall we say, exemplary practices. Even where the empirical setting involves a discourse—say medical practice—its own principles are, ultimately, to give way to those of the theoretical field and the result is a DS⁻ field. The delimiting move to an empirical setting and thence to a set of findings is described, therefore, as *localising*. We further argued that the process of *generalising* to a broader population (in the case of quantitative research) or to a broader empirical field of processes etc is achieved via the discourse of research methods. Now, we might have added that some forms of expansion of an activity may also be achieved via *articulation*. Here, I am thinking of the way in which the field of anthropology might be considered to expand via the accumulation of localised studies. I shall not expand further on the deployment of this schema—that is being left as programmatic.

| Discursive Saturation | Pedagogy | Power | | Repertoire |
		Delimit	Expand	
DS⁺	principles	*specialise*	*generalise*	discourse/competence
				ideolect/performance
DS⁻	exemplars	*localise*	*articulate*	skill/competence
				trick/performance

Figure 9.5. Expanding and Delimiting Strategies

The schema in Figure 9.6 provides a modality of discursive comportments that, I think, opens up a more revealing space than the commonplace, modernist/postmodernist kind of distinction. I have made the distinction between forensics and constructive description in Chapter 1 and subsequent chapters of this book. But perhaps that, also, is not the whole story. Forensics operates on the basis of a two level world: there is the world of the discourse and there is the world of 'things as they are'. However, there would seem to be a difference between, on the one hand, a comportment that seeks to *discover* things as they are (even if this is understood, ultimately, to be a forlorn quest) and, on the other, a comportment that seeks to replace 'things as they are' with 'things as they really are'—*critique*. The distinction seems to me to be one that might be caught by the opposite vectors, *territorialisating* and *de-territorialising*. A similar distinction might be made in respect of the other of forensics, which I am here referring to as *construction*, which operates on a shallow, single level world, concentrating only on the discourse. *Constructive description* seems to me to be predominantly characterised by territorialising. On the other hand, *deconstruction* seems to be an appropriate term for de-territorialising construction (sic). Again, empirical practices are likely to display more than one comportment; my presentation in this book probably exhibits all four, unless, that is, the audience interprets everything in the light of my formulation of constructive description.

	Vector	
	Territorialising	De-territorialising
Forensics	*discovery*	*critique*
Construction	*constructive description*	*deconstruction*

Figure 9.6. Discursive Comportment

I next want to introduce two schemas that were developed by Natasha Whiteman (2007) in her research into two online fan communities. Silent Hill Heaven (SHH) is a community of fans of the series of video games, *Silent Hill*; City of Angel (COA) was a community of fans of the T.V. series, *Angel*. The first of Whiteman's schemas, shown in Figure 9.7, arose out of her consideration of the ways in which fans displayed what she referred to as 'nostalgia' (see also Whiteman, 2005, in press):

> When used in relation to media products and audiences, 'nostalgia' typically refers to some interest in classic or 'retro' texts. [...] I propose a move beyond such everyday conceptualisations of nostalgia, towards thinking of nostalgia relationally. This involves the consideration of the ways in which the fans on SHH and COA express their affiliation to, and longing for, their favoured objects. I will argue that the varying emphases in their moves - particularly in responses to challenges to the stability of their objects (for example the release of new material)—enable the marking out of analytical distinctions between differing modes of nostalgia within these settings. This broadening move resonates with recent work on the translation and localisation of videogames for different markets, which suggests a consideration of the essential elements of a videogame that must be maintained as it is carried across cultures [...]. Whilst extending the use of the term in this way, I do not want to lose the ways in which 'nostalgia' is already loaded with meaning. The idea of homesickness, longing or memory for a past state, for example, is retained, with the notion of homesickness particularly significant for the discussion of SHH which is to follow. (Whiteman, 2007, p. 150)

As with the other SAM schemas, Whiteman's nostalgia schema takes the cross-product of two binary, nominal variables, the first of which distinguishes between two modes of desire:

> The first involves a desire to return to a fixed textual universe, either to repeat the same experience or a return to the universe to explore it. In this context, change to the universe (or the way that the universe is experienced) provides disappointment. The second contradicts these desires, celebrating the development of the object. (*Ibid.*, p. 154)

Whiteman refers to these 'chronotopic' modes as 'synchronic' and 'diachronic', respectively. The second variable distinguishes between orientation to external (to the fan) and internal (by the fan) authorship.

Chronotope	Comportment	
	External	Internal
Synchronic	*repeat*	*explore*
Diachronic	*spectate*	*mod*

Figure 9.7. Modes of Nostalgia (from Whiteman, 2007)

Whiteman describes the *repeat* and *explore* modes in the second extract above. The explore mode in the context of a game might involve a desire to explore the virtual environment rather than necessarily conform to what are perceived as author expectation of how the game 'ought' to be played. *Spectators* and *modders* are both looking for development in the game world. The distinction is that the latter is looking to make their own modifications to the game environment, rather than waiting for 'official' developments. The schema clearly presents a more complex conceptualising of nostalgia than the everyday use of the term and clearly has potential for deployment in a far wider range of settings: think about the activities of politicians, managers, teachers, ...

The second of Whiteman's schemas that I want to introduce is particularly interesting in that it involves a misprision of Goffman's (1990 Edn) contrast of the 'sincere' and 'cynical' belief of an actor in their own action. Whiteman distinguishes between fans maintaining a *suture* with their object of fan identification—let's say, the fourth game in the *Silent Hill* series, SH4—and those establishing a rupture. Here is an unhappy fan of the series who seems to have taken a dislike to SH4, in particular:

[...] We are supposed to empathize with this character who can't escape his supernaturally sealed apartment ... fine ... yet he can't even shoot out a window or yell through a hole in his neighbor's wall? Okay sure, I'm sure the windows are bullet-proof and Henry's voice wouldn't make it through the wall to Eileen's apartment. This is a minor complaint on my part, but it's merely the feather that broke the camel's (or the franchise's) back. And another thing, the ghosts that appear later on in the apartment are extra cheap. The main place where your health could be recovered is now just another opproutunity for the game to take another cheapshot at your health guage. And it's my understanding that it's even worse if you accept the shabby doll ... which I fortunately sidestepped, courtesy of Gamefaqs. Thanks a lot Konami. (quoted in Whiteman, 2007, p. 162; typos etc. in the original post)

This fan is establishing a series of local *ruptures* with the game on the basis of a *suturing* with alternative worlds. Their complaint about Henry not being able to shoot out a window or shout to neighbour—and, indeed, the 'explanations'—seem to be evaluating the game against, shall we say, the 'real world' (although bullet-proof apartment windows are a bit far fetched). The fan's complaint at cheap ghosts and a 'cheapshot at your health g[au]ge' seem to compare the game with, not so much the 'real world', but an ideal game. It is as if the fan is unpinning themselves from identification with the game by these local identifications with alternative worlds. Here is the response to the above post from another fan:

> You seem to be angry at the game for not allowing you to escape the room. Well, that isn't the point of the game. The point of the game is to be trapped. Your complaining about this is like someone saying, "Why can't I just use a machine gun to shoot the Goombas in **[Super]** Mario? It's stupid to jump on them." The point of the game isn't to shoot the Goombas, it's to stomp on them. Stop complaining about things that were never meant to be in the game in the first place. [...] As for not yelling through the wall to Eileen, I think at that point Henry probably realizes that it's pointless. (Quoted in Whiteman, 2007, p. 162)

In contrast to the first poster, the respondent is identifying, *suturing* with the game world, creating a separation with the 'real world', which is not, here, considered to be a relevant frame of evaluation. Note, however, that, in the final sentence of the response, there is a certain ambivalence, a concession, perhaps, though this might also reasonably be understood as an interpretation within the game world.

Move	Power	
	Local	General
Suture (1)	*involve*	*reside*
Rupture	*estrange*	*alienate*
Suture (2)	*involve*	*reside*

Figure 9.8. Suturing and Rupturing Identification (adapted from Whiteman, 2007)

Both fans are pointing at *local* instances within the game. However, the articulation (see Figure 9.5) of local instances by the first poster extends the power of the identification, constituting a *general* rupture with the game. Bringing together the two variables, suturing/rupturing move and local/general power produces the schema in Figure 9.8. The table has been slightly modified from Whiteman's original: the central, rupturing move row has been shaded to highlight the reflective symmetry of the table in this row. If we think of the suture (1) row as representing a suture with the game world, then the rupture move is established via suture (2), which is a suture with the 'real world' or an ideal game world.

The configuration in Figure 9.8 might be interpreted as an alternative way of conceptualising the schema of competing discourses in Figure 9.3. A move from suture (2) via rupture (with discourse (2)) to suture (1) might describe an apprenticeship into, in the example from Whiteman's work presented here, the game world, the move in the opposite direction, an objectification of the game world. I have also considered these kinds of moves in terms of pedagogic and exchange relations. The former maximises the level of agency attributed to the author and the latter maximises the level of agency attributed to the audience. However, there is, in each case room for variation in the level of subjectivity (or potential subjectivity) attributed to the other position—audience, in the case of pedagogic relations, author, in the case of exchange relations. This schema is presented in Figure 9.9.

In Dowling (1998) I described apprenticeship as the (re)production of subjectivity. This involves the apprentice moving via the public and expressive domains (Figure 8.2) into the esoteric domain of the hegemonising discourse (Figure 3.1). In terms of the schemas introduced in this chapter, it is now possible to describe this in terms of the hegemonised discourse by retaining the form of Figure 8.2 in Figure 9.3, or in terms of Whiteman's identification schema in Figure 9.8. The distinction is in terms of whether emphasis is being placed on the practice itself or on the identification strategies of the apprentice.

	Level of Subjectivity Attributed to Unauthorised Position		
Relations/Authority	High	Low	Zero
Pedagogic/Author	*apprenticeship*	*dependency*	*objectification*
Exchange/Audience	*marketing*	*routine*	*compliance*

Figure 9.9. Distribution of Subjectivity in Pedagogic and Exchange Relations

In fact, in Dowling (1998), I distinguished between three modes of pedagogic action. The first mode is apprenticeship and characterised the principal textual strategies deployed in school mathematics texts aimed at 'high ability' students. The second mode, *dependency* was deployed mainly in texts aimed at 'low ability' students. The potential subjectivity of dependents was reduced compared with that of apprentices via their exclusion from the esoteric domain of school mathematics or by the reduction of the level of DS of the esoteric domain by, for example, the use of procedures rather than principles; the student was, in terms of textual strategies, rendered dependent on the, largely, public domain instructions in the text, having no access to the esoteric domain principles whereby the instructions are generated. Further, since the public domain is constituted as a recontextualisation—from the student's point of view, a distortion, to a greater or lesser extent—of the practical experiences of the students (shopping etc), the dependent student is presented with a quasi-apprenticeship into a mythical practice.

In addition to apprentices and dependents, the mathematics texts also constructed a wide range of *objectified* positions. In many cases, these represented neither author nor audience positions, police officers, a man building a wall, a geologist, and so forth. In a few cases there were categorical statements about the audience position that were not open to negotiation. These cases represent the *objectification* of unauthorised positions in which zero subjectivity is attributed.

As illustrated in Figure 9.9, we can conceive of a similar variation in the attribution of subjectivity to the author in the context of exchange relations. It is difficult to envisage a situation in which a text is constructed so as to impose absolutely no constraints on its audience. This is not to say that a text must in effect constrain its audience, only that in its construction this seems to be a necessity. An announcement such as 'Please tell me what to do' perhaps comes closest to what is labelled in Figure 9.9 as *compliance*. A rather greater subjectivity is attributed to, say, the supermarket that claims to be able to satisfy all of its customer needs, but that imposes *routines*—in terms of its own layout as an operational matrix, queuing at the checkout and so forth—in terms of how this may be achieved. I have already suggested that my intention in the production of this book is to produce an exchange text, but at the same time, I am also recruiting devices—attempts at rational argument, for example—that serve as *marketing* strategies in potentially biasing audience response. The complete schema in Figure 9.9 now supplements those in Figures 8.2, 9.3 and 9.8 in terms of the ways in which we might think of and map empirical instances of pedagogic action. Again, further development is being left as programmatic in this final and distinctly speculative chapter.

I shall introduce, very briefly, two more schemas. The first of these is part of work that is underway by Soh-young Chung, my co-author in Chapter 8. In reviewing a range of books that, in various ways, identified a crisis in literary studies, Chung devised two binary variables. The first distinguishes between the perspective that is being adopted in reviewing literature, is it an *intrinsic* view from within the practice of production of literature, or an *extrinsic* view. For example, Stanley Fish (1995) opposes the new historicist theorists for, amongst other things, potentially endangering the continued existence of literary studies, which, for Fish, is essentially the same field of practice as that in which literary production occurs: literary studies, conducted properly, produces literature. Tony Hilfer (2003), on the other hand, sees literary studies as concerned with exploring and revealing the meaning in literature, so that the literary work is constituted as the object of a practice that is extrinsic to it.

Chung's second dimension distinguishes between, for example, Fish's (1995) view that the value of literature—which includes literary studies—is intrinsic to itself and Alvin Kernan's (1990) contention that literature cannot be dissociated from other cultural practices and social structure and, to that extent, its value is, at least in part, extrinsic to itself. The combination of the two variables then gives rise to the schema in Figure 9.10.

	Value	
Perspective	Intrinsic	Extrinsic
Intrinsic	*reproductive*	*accommodating*
Extrinsic	*curatorial*	*instrumental*

Figure 9.10. Perspective/Value Schema

Chung thus identifies Fish's (1995) work as predominantly *reproductive*, Kernan's (1990) as *accommodating*, Hilfer's (2003) as *curatorial* and constitutes an *instrumental* strategy that seems to fit with Michael Bérubé's (1998), *The Employment of English*.

Finally, then a schema that constitutes a misreading of another method, that of Pierre Bourdieu (1984). I am including this at the end of the book not as a claim to develop Bourdieu's work, but rather as a small strategy—a tactic—of alliance in sociology as method, which is how I tend to think of Bourdieu's sociology as well as my own. In conducting his research for works such as *Distinction* (1984) and *Homo Academicus* (1988) Bourdieu deploys a complex sociological and statistical apparatus as a heuristic tool in iterative explorations of the sociocultural. I want to suggest—and here is not the place to argue this in any detail—that Bourdieu's heuristic sociology is, in at least some respects, characterised by the grammatical mode *method* (Figure 8.3), which is the mode in which I see SAM as predominantly operating. So the schema in Figure 9.11 is, I suppose, a wa(i)ve in Bourdieu's direction.

	Orientation to Economic Capital	
Orientation to Aesthetic Capital	Economy	Spending
Low	*necessity*	*opulence*
High	*asceticism*	*haute couture*

Figure 9.11. Aesthetic Modes

The distinction between *economy* and *spending* as opposite orientations to economic capital, does not necessarily relate to the amount of economic capital available from the perspective of an objective observer. The figure of the wealthy individual who displays economy is very familiar, as is that of the comparatively impoverished person who seems to spend in excess of what they can objectively afford, in localised instances or generally. The other dimension is rather more tentatively offered because it postulates a unidimensional aesthetic to which orientations may be either *low* or *high*. There is clearly scope for development here, but in a general way, it does distinguish between the individual who, for example, prioritises economy (which might be taken to be some articulation of cost, durability, etc) at the expense of any aesthetic consideration as such—the aesthetics of *necessity*—from the person who will go out of their way to acquire what to them is aesthetically appropriate, but within their budget—the refashioning of secondhand clothes that Bourdieu (1984) describes, perhaps—the aesthetics of *ascetics*. Alternatively, the low/high aesthetic orientation distinguishes between the spender who is concerned to get exactly the *haute couture* clothing and the spender aiming only at a display of *opulence*. Of course, the two economisers might end up with the same items as might the two spenders; the schema is concerned with strategies, not outcomes.

The final schema—introduced in Dowling, 2007—is another misreading of Bourdieu. This relational space (Figure 9.12) stands as a development, for my own purposes, of Bourdieu's (1991) forms of capital, which I have never really understood. Not understood, because I can't seem to make much productive use of the term 'exchange' in the context of cultural capital being exchanged for economic or social capital, nothing, apparently, being given up in the transaction. Nor can I take seriously the idea of aggregating different forms of capital, or even that of capital, other than economic capital as measurable at higher than the ordinal level. So I find this,

> The social space can be described as a multi-dimensional space of positions such that each actual position can be defined in terms of a multi-dimensional system of co-ordinates whose values correspond to the values of the different pertinent variables. Agents are thus distributed, in the first dimension, according to the overall volume of the capital they possess and, in the second dimension, according to the composition of their capital—in other words, according to the relative weight of the different kinds of capital in the total set of their assets. (Bourdieu, 1991, pp. 230-231)

puzzling; what is the concept of 'dimension', here? Clearly, it works for Bourdieu and, generally used very loosely, has worked for many others (even myself, upon occasion), but I really need something rather more direct. I want to approach a related conceptual space from another point in Bourdieu's work, the dialogic of embodied and objectified culture introduced in *Outline of a Theory of Practice* (1977); I shall use this as one dimension of my new space. For the second dimension I shall distinguish between a focus on *practice* or on *relations* in pedagogic activity, for my purposes here, concentrating on the acquirer side. The schema is presented in Figure 9.12.

In elaborating this space, I shall refer back to the work on three South African schools that was introduced, iteratively, in Chapter 7, specifically, to the differences between the ways in which students at Mont Clair and Protea schools, on the one hand, and Syafunda, on the other, confronted curriculum content. In the former two schools, students saw the acquisition of the content of the curriculum as motivated by its facility in respect of achieving a pass at the matric examination. This having been achieved, the school curriculum could, in a sense, be left behind. Siyafunda students, by contrast, seemed to constitute a continuity between school knowledge and that which lay beyond it, such that the former was seen as a necessary condition—the base—of the latter. There was an exception to this at Syafunda in the case of Afrikaans. This language—seen as the language of the oppressor—was unpopular and students had no context for its use, nor could they foresee any such context in their futures. We were told that—other than in the class of the charismatic Afrikaans/biology teacher whom we introduced—students would put no effort at all into their Afrikaans studies and would fail annual examinations up to the point of matric, when cramming would enable them to pass. Students whom we met and observed in the three schools deployed different behaviours in respect of learning: the Mont Clair students—particularly the more senior ones—seemed often to take control of their learning, whilst those at Protea and Siyafunda seemed to be more dependent upon the leadership of the teacher. However, their strategies in respect of the evaluation of the curriculum were patterned differently. Mont Clair and Protea students and Siyafuynda students in the context of Afrikaans valued the *symbolic* objectification of curriculum practice, whilst Siyafunda students generally valued the embodied curriculum practice as *habitus*. Clearly, all recognised that acquisition was necessary, but valuing the curriculum exclusively in terms of its symbolic objectification in the form of a matric diploma predicts a point in the future at which the acquired habitus might be dispensed with.[131]

Culture	Acquirer Focus	
	Practice	Relations
Embodied	*habitus*	*hub*
Objectified	*symbols*	*network*

Figure 9.12. Acquirer Strategies

Thus far I have concentrated on the *practice* category of *acquirer focus*. The other category is *relations*, which, again, may be privileged by the local culture in *embodied* or *objectified* form. Where relations are embodied, then, as with embodied practice, they are being valued, by the acquirer, in and for themselves. We might suppose that this would be the form of many (certainly not all) kinship relations, romantic relations, and relationships between friends as friends. The term *hub* is used to describe this strategy, because we might imagine the acquirer standing at the centre of a collection of family, lover(s), friends and so forth, relating to each individually (though they may, of course, also stand in relationships with each other). This may well be a simplification of any particular

---

[131] Clearly, I am stretching the use of the term *habitus* here.

case, but the image is intended only to motivate the metaphor, hub, which is to be distinguished from the strategy that values a relation in terms of what it might provide access to, in other words, where the relation is valued for something other than itself. Some instances of this kind of relation may be one-to-one. An example would be robber-to-robbed. Insofar as a single robber may constitute relations with multiple victims, the 'topography' of the situation would resemble the hub image, but the terms are only metaphors and not intended to capture the structure of all cases. The general case of the objectification of relations is the *network*, in which one relation provides access to another and so forth. One might imagine that the professional robber would need to establish such a network in order to maximise the profit from their activity and minimise the risk of capture by the police; then again, they may just be rapt in the act of robbery—a hub strategy.

I have resorted to imaginary data on lovers and robbers in order to introduce the relation category of acquirer focus in Figure 9.12. I have, I realise, complained about the use of such strategies by other authors (see, for example, Chapter 4); *mea culpa*. But this is a speculative, final chapter, so I'm behaving badly (again, probably). So a little more speculation: it seems possible that there are broadly similar opportunities for the deployment of hub strategies at all three of the schools that I've referred to here, though this will depend upon, amongst other factors, the amount and nature of private time enjoyed by students. Equally, there may be similar opportunities for networking at the three schools. However, it seems likely that networking will operate differently in each setting. Insofar as the expected career trajectory of the Mont Clair students targets a globally distributed virtual community, then the potential economic value of networking strategies may well exceed that of strategies deployed by Siyafunda students by an order of magnitude (more bad behaviour), but may be no less important to the students for all that. A Standard 10 girl whom we met at Siyafunda asked us if we could help her get into medical school; clearly a networking strategy, and one that may have paid off: we mentioned to a South African university contact that we had been very impressed by her erudition, the contact passed this tip onto the medical school and, I am led to believe, they followed it up. As I mentioned in Chapter 7, the Siyafunda Principal during our second year of data collection asked us if we could get her an invitation (and presumably funding) to visit London; another networking strategy— unfortunately, not as successful. We were not the targets of networking strategies at either of the other schools, which, unlike Syafunda, were already implicated in communities that included high socio-economic status groups.

As I've pointed out, the schemas in Figures 9.11 and 9.12 are misreadings of Bourdieu: they are not Bourdieu's sociology (whoever would think they were?) This is so, not least, because they are not—at least, not directly—concerned with social class. Nor are they concerned with people's actual choices, but with the strategies that they might deploy. In conducting interviews, one would be interested not so much in *what* the interviewee preferred or valued, but in *why*— rather more difficult to access, perhaps (but, of course, I'm drifting into forensics). The schemas are, in any event, offered only as theoretical resources that might be worth deploying, exploring, dismantling, misreading.

DEEP WATER: NO SWIMMING ALLOWED

Very little attention has been given, in this book, to the conventional concerns of sociology, social class, gender, ethnicity, disability; I am expecting to be vilified for this—vilified, not criticised; the latter would seem to entail that I might have something so say, however distorted. It's not that I am unconcerned with the grotesque degree of inequality that one finds almost wherever one looks, at whatever level of analysis; I most certainly am agonised by material suffering, wherever it occurs (and sometimes it occurs here). But most of it I can't fix at all—or even contribute to its fixing; some—very local stuff—I might be able to ameliorate a little. On leaving the Peace Museum in Nagasaki I was approached by one of a group of college students conducting some interviews for their school magazine. Would I agree to be interviewed (in English)? Yes, of course.

"What do you think you can do for World Peace?"

"Absolutely nothing whatsoever."

"*Eeee!*"

"But I can be polite to the sales assistant in *Takashimaya*."

"*Aa, soo desu ne. Wakarimashita.*"

Patronising, of course (I'm sorry), but it makes the point.

Don't you find it appalling when sociologists, educationalists alibi their erudite academic activities by suggesting that they can improve a world that lies beyond their control, beyond even their influence? I have found that I can make a good deal of use of my sociology in my teaching (identifying the esoteric domain and routes to it is always a useful exercise) and in other aspects of my life. Not to direct my actions, but to interrogate them, to organise them—it's an organisational language. I feel that the result has been beneficial and I hope this has benefited others (but which ones?) as well as myself, though maybe not (maybe): the desire to help others is never enough; actions designed to help others may be too much.

I live next door to a couple of docks. Around about the place there are a number of signs that draw attention to them. One reads, 'Deep Water: No Swimming Allowed'. Now I've always found this to be rather odd and am frequently tempted to alter it to, 'Deep Water: No Drowning Allowed'. Indeed, if you're swimming, it doesn't really matter how deep the water is: all that matters is the surface; provided, of course, that you can swim well and that you can keep it up indefinitely. Constructive description is all surface; perhaps that's why I've never really inhabited Ryle's (1968)/Geertz's (1973) expression 'thick description'. For me, description is always the thinnest that it is possible to be: two-dimensional. Description, then, proceeds by establishing dehiscences in the surface and suturing them in the developing and deploying of an organisational language—SAM. The language is never complete, never fully coherent, so there is always scope for transaction between schematic moments as well as with the empirical. Naturally, I am sensitised to the familiar dimensions of social inequality, but I don't need to dive beneath the surface of the sociocultural to find them. I understand them as emergent structure, patternings on the surface field of autopoietic action. At this point, the geometrical metaphor begins to strain because it seems to suggest that we would need to escape from the surface in order to see the patterns. Perhaps a relational network in multidimensional space would be a better concept for the sociocultural, though dehiscences and suturings don't seem to work quite so well now. This is always the problem with metaphorical apparatuses: they always do too much and too little work.

So, just one more, to return myself close to where I started—with Jeff Vass and the Titanic. Walking along the River Thames one morning I noticed a sign on a rack holding a lifebelt.

To Save a Life
Do not interfere with this equipment

"Just think", I suggested to Jeff, who was with me at the time, "at this very moment we are saving a life, probably two lives." And it suddenly occurred to me that almost no one in the world was interfering with the equipment and would be unlikely ever to do so. So many lives saved. Surely our immortality is assured— just as long as this equipment remains undisturbed.

A SHOOTING IN HIROSHIMA

Hiroshima bears some thinking about. The city has constituted its corporate image as the city of peace—rather more strongly so than Nagasaki, I thought (though there are plenty of symbols of peace there as well, in and around the museum). There is a roughly triangular area in the centre of Hiroshima with one apex at the Aioibashi bridge which was the target for the bombardier of the Enola Gay, the warplane agonisingly named for the pilot's mother. Aioibashi bridge is itself at the junction of two rivers (Hiroshima is on a delta) and in between the rivers is the Peace Memorial Park with the Peace Memorial Museum and Peace Boulevard (having Peace Bridge and West Peace Bridge at either end) forming the final side of the triangle. Inside the park is a Pond of Peace, a Flame of Peace, a Peace Memorial Post, a Peace Clock Tower, and so on; a park of many peaces. Near the Aioibashi bridge and on the opposite side of the river from the park is the A-Bomb Dome: the remains of one of the only buildings to have been left standing in the city immediately after the bombing—the Hiroshima Prefecture Industry Promotion Hall. Outside of this area, the city looks much the same as any other in Japan (apart from the substantial number of bridges and the flat reclaimed land that are consequences of the locating of the city on the delta), that is, a confusion of advertising signs—some illuminated, others not—power cables, architectural diversity, people and traffic. The sublime tidiness within the confusion and the presence of kanji and kana distinguish it as specifically Japanese.

The point of entry to the museum (entry is, unlike almost everywhere else, especially the shrines and temples, very cheap) is to a video and sombre music that can be heard throughout. Thence to a room at the centre of which are two models of Hiroshima—one before, one after—surrounded firstly by a video reconstruction of the bombing and, outside that, a ring of posters including images and text depicting the city before the bombing and the events that led up to it. Dominating this part of the museum is a macabre model of the A-Bomb dome that you can walk inside. The text is surprisingly neutral. There is no 'we-ness' in the text that affiliates the authorial voice to Japan. It is the voice of a disinterested commentator that presents the Japanese state as oppressive of its own people and aggressive against others. Almost everyone in the vicinity, it seems, was suffering as a result of Japanese militarism.

the Manchurian incident of 1931 was taken as an opportunity to start a 15-year war with China … in December 1941, Japan ignited the Pacific war with a surprise attack on Pearl Harbour in Hawaii and a subsequent attack on the Malay peninsula. (*Spirit of Hiroshima*, guide book)

The reasons for the bombing of Hiroshima are presented as logical and emotionally detached: to bring the war to a close before the USSR entered the game so as to limit Soviet influence in Asia afterwards; to test the bomb in a real war situation and measure effects on buildings and civilians (Hiroshima was, for a variety of reasons, ideally suited for this purpose). Up the stairs to more posters and glass cased exhibits of the immediate and delayed effects of the bombing, further stairs to posters and exhibits revealing the current state of the nuclear age and, finally, the activities of the mayor and other Hiroshima dignitaries in speaking for peace and nuclear disarmament.

In the next room is the shop selling a range of books and souvenirs of the city and museum at surprisingly low prices. The cadential shop might be the end of the exhibition, but it isn't. A further room, very dark, combines exhibits and limited text that close-in on the personal and local damage: exhibits of the clothes that children had been wearing together with their brief and pitiful stories; skin and fingernails that detached from the hands of one boy and that were retained by his mother to show his father; the shadow of a woman who had been sitting on the steps of a bank waiting for it to open; the tricycle of a boy that had, originally, been buried with him by his father; the lunchbox of another. And then bits of bomb material and warped iron doors and roof tiles. Next, a one-hundred-and-eighty degree turn to the opposite side of the building and the final room that runs parallel to the darkened room. This room is well lit has seating and includes recorded commentaries and some drawings and paintings by survivors of the bombing. The room windows out onto the Peace Memorial Park and is in a straight line with the flame of peace and the A-Bomb dome.

This is the chronicle of my first visit to the museum in 2001; let me recast it in the form of my own apprenticeship into the ironies of weapons of mass destruction.

At the centre of the city/museum is the constitution of the 'tragedy' as a unique site of apprenticeship into a microcosm of what might befall us in the context of a dangerous contemporary configuration. 'We' have arrived at this point from various directions. The museum dissolves blame in a primeval agentic soup in marking out the trajectories towards the tragedy: Japan's militarism is a consequence of economic decline, this leads to its stimulation of U.S. belligerence which ineluctably led to the dropping of the bomb. In establishing the trajectories towards the tragedy, the museum incorporates both generalising and localising strategies. The former are constituted as the message of the voice of the disinterested historical narrator; there is no agency in Hiroshima or in the U.S. Agency is restricted to objectified voices of historical characters, the Japanese government and so forth. Localising strategies are established in, for example, the message of the photographer; the latter being almost automatically placed in an objective position in the representational photography.

The narrative moves on to the construction of the tragedy itself as event. Again agency is effaced. Again there is the deployment of generalising and localising strategies. Hibakusha (the victims of the after-effects of the radioactivity released by the bomb as well as the immediate victims) are represented visually and in terms of their possessions—the wristwatch that stopped at precisely 8:15, for example. Research into the condition of the hibakusha is explicated in some detail as is the relationship between the damage done to victims and their distance from the hypocentre.

From here, the narrative moves into the phase of reconstruction and the ironic reinvention of the city as a unique site of knowledge—It is important, I think, that references to Nagasaki are almost entirely eliminated from the museum—and activity in educating the world having, by the industry of its people (the same industry that they showed before the event in prosecuting warfare) narrowly escaped from the hell that, if we fail to learn, is the potential destiny of all of us. The facility for pedagogy is extended in the shop, which stocks piles of books as well as photographic reminders for us to purchase (at actually very reasonable prices—my *Spirit of Hiroshima* was a mere 1000 yen (£5)).

The discursive domination of generalising strategy gives way to the localising strategies constituted by individual stories of, first, the dead and—having rotated through one-hundred-and-eighty degrees to return from the near dead—and then the living. Whilst hearing the latter voices we are able to gaze out at the symbol of a future of peace growing out of the past of destruction that both originate at the centre of Hiroshima. The line from the A-Bomb dome near the hypocentre of the bombing to the museum conjoins opposing vectors; what we learn from the destruction, what we learn from the narrative must surely both lead us towards the Flame of Peace at its centre and at the centre of the garden.

Near the Flame of Peace stands a monument to Sasaki Sadako. A girl who died of leukaemia at the age of 13 having been born shortly after the bombing. During her illness, she tried to make one thousand origami cranes, the achievement of this task being believed to effect a cure. It failed. Nevertheless, Sadako's sad story of hope has been concretised in the monument around which are strewn chains (and the occasional collage) of origami cranes (presumably all consisting of a thousand paper birds) that have been sent by children from all over Japan and other countries. From time to time, young girls photograph each other in front of the monument—they giggle and make the conventional 'v' sign with both hands. This sign—it would seem an almost automatic response by young Japanese girls to the lens of a camera, wherever they are—is not the Churchillian victory, but apparently an emblem of peace.

On past the Monument and the Flame of Peace, over the bridge to the A-Bomb dome itself. In front of the scaffolded ruin a young Japanese father is taking a photograph of his family—the obligatory tourist shot. The mother is holding her baby in her arms.

"Chotto matte"—"wait"—yells her other child, a boy of maybe five or six. He crouches slightly with one foot thrust forward and the other back and carefully aims the toy rifle that he is holding directly at his father.

"Shoot."

EYELESS IN GINZA

A trip to the local supermarket involves a walk or cycle ride through Kishine Koen. Early in the morning, the park is full of power-walkers and joggers, practitioners of Tai Chi and the occasional tennis-star-*manque* competing against a wall. Later in the day mothers pushing baby-carriages, children on bicycles and elderly men flying model aircraft take over. Later still and, in early Spring, *hanami* parties under the cherry blossom. A few of these go on into the night, until the beer and *sake* run dry, otherwise, darkness clears the park until the arrival of the first joggers.

The supermarket is on the far side of a crossroads at the corner of the park where the marshal arts centre rests above a small lake bordered by *sakura*. The crossroads is regulated by traffic lights—*shingo*. I wait obediently for my turn and recall the day, a year or so ago, when the lights went out—*shingo no go*. I emerged from the park into chaos. Nothing was moving apart from six police officers waving furiously and blowing whistles and shouting angry and contradictory instructions to bemused and very stationary drivers.

I stood and watched the Kishine Cops for ten minutes. Then another police car arrived. I was not entirely clear how it had managed to thread the traffic jam, but there it was. Two more officers had arrived. But these looked different. Their colleagues were not shabby, by any means, but the newcomer's uniforms—a different design—gave the impression of having been pressed and starched only moments before their arrival and their pristine white cotton gloves positively gleamed in the sunshine. The six originals retreated to their own vehicles, exhausted. But before they had started their engines, their replacements had the junction back in perfect operation—Yokohama boogie-woogie.

Back in the UK, I tend to find that traffic at broken-down traffic-lights passes almost as well as it does when the lights are working—sometimes better—until the police arrive; thenceforth bedlam. In Japan, it would appear that they have a traffic-lights-broken-down division, wonderful. It's almost a pity that Japanese traffic-lights almost never break down.

Japan, it would seem, is a society that privileges the strongly coded over the weakly coded and this is nowhere more visible than when the system belches, in the hiatus between the engagement of subsystems; traffic lights give way to traffic-light-broken-down police. Sometimes the system refuses to budge. Japan is the only place in the world where the kitchen of an up-market restaurant has refused my request (on health grounds) that they substitute fresh fruit for the sugary dessert on the set menu. Even asking for the ketchup to be omitted from a morning-set at

Narita airport sometimes presents problems. Trains famously run to perfect time, gliding into the station as the minute hand clicks to the appointed minute; this is not like clockwork, it is clockwork. Ever since an inexperienced driver crashed a train by driving too fast in order to try to keep to the timetable, the trains seem to glide into the station exactly one minute late (perhaps it's my imagination). But the *shinkansen* management have no answer to snow in Kyoto, the mid-point between Tokyo and Hiroshima. The *shinkansen* cannot run through snow, but clear weather on either side of Kyoto should allow a shuttle service with conventional train connections, not possible: most of the travellers will have reserved seats; this cannot be managed using an ad hoc timetable. True to Saussurean principles, though, the 12.19 in from Shin Osaka remains the 12.19 even when it arrives five hours later after the snow has been cleared. Tragically, sarin gas set loose on the Tokyo subway in 1995 was also a gift that the system could not return as Murakami Haruki's (2000) interviews with victims of the attack so poignantly reveal. But the system recovers.

In the supermarket perfectly stacked shelves neatly display perfect packages containing appropriate-sized portions of vegetables. Cabbages are available in quarters or halves or whole, for the large family; tiny polystyrene trays each contain what one suspects is precisely the same number of fresh peas. Fish is similarly gift-wrapped—just how can salmon and tuna be cut into such perfect cuboids—as is meat—the only time you ever get to find out what a whole chicken looks like is at Christmas when there may be one or possibly two on the shelf (the fishmonger in the *chikadou* at Yokohama Station didn't really expect anyone to buy a whole tuna for ¥318.000 (around £1500), but if he didn't pin a price on it people would keep asking what it would cost if they wanted to buy it). Above all, everything is clearly divided into Japanese and foreign produce (the latter at maybe one-third of the price of the former).

On the face of it, then, the region of the uncodified is a dangerous space to be avoided if at all possible. But perhaps this is a too simple. During another walk in Kishine Koen—this time *en route* to the subway station on the corner on the other side of the lake—I am reminded of something else that I've noticed before. It's the middle of the day so the park is dominated by women and young children. I am walking quite briskly along the wide path at the top end of the park, gaining on a small, elderly woman hand-in-hand with a young boy—her grandchild, maybe. Then, without any obvious (to me) warning, they turn to the right to walk across the path, crossing just in front of me. They're not moving very fast, but I'm very close and I have to execute an emergency stop to avoid skittling them over. Neither of them had looked around to see if another pedestrian or even a cyclist might be occupying the lane that they chose to cross. A little irritated, I stride on past the children's playground area at the top of the steep slope down to the entrance to the station. Here, another young boy, this time on his own and on a bicycle, rides straight across the path and onto the grass, again cutting directly in front of me. Again, not as much as a glance in my direction. I perform an emergency *henka*, this time.

I've seen something like this on a Los Angeles freeway some years before. I found myself (without entirely remembering how I got there) in five lanes of bumper-to-bumper automobiles all doing exactly 70 miles per hour and with exits occurring apparently randomly either on the inside or outside of the carriageway: how on earth do you get off? I had visions of running out of gas before I could figure it out. I needed a miracle and one happened. A large sedan on an inside lane signalled right and pulled immediately into the next lane and then the next until it reached the outside in time for the exit. At each lane change the solid line of cars had parted to allow the sedan passage. I tried it. It worked almost as smoothly as a junction operated by the Yokohama traffic-lights-broken-down police. In both Kishine Koen and L.A. it might appear to the observer that the traffic was invisible to the individual or vehicle making the manoeuvre and that it could be relied upon to remain invisible.

On to the subway and to Yokohama main line station. This is a Sunday, so the place is absolutely heaving—Yokohama Station always seems to be busiest on Sundays. Here, there are literally thousands of people walking in every possible direction, but this is no Brownian motion. Paths cross smoothly without any abrupt changes in pace or direction and without a single collision—not even a brushing of bags *en passant*. Naturally, I am a bit of a foreign body in the fluid as I appear to dummy my way through the crowd, but awkward as my staccato moves might look, they fail to generate the slightest eddy. The really surprising thing is that no one appears to be paying the slightest attention to anyone else. It's as if they can navigate on peripheral vision and they're all doing it except me. What's more, I've noticed that if I walk straight ahead without looking where I'm going, then people will move aside faintly rippling the flow. I can't keep it up for long, though, it induces in me far too much anxiety and I quickly revert to clumsy ducking and diving.

The sense of invisibility carries on into the trains as well. My Japanese girlfriend recently passed on a question that had been put to her by a colleague. The colleague is a bilingual Japanese American now living in Tokyo and teaching at one of its universities. Why is it, he had asked, that we see so much putting-on of make-up by women travelling on trains these days; it never used to be like that? Some imaginary sociology was called for. The separation of home and workplace, of course, establishes a private-public delineation. Both of these spaces will be strongly coded in terms of who is permitted to do and say what under what circumstances and, in particular, in terms of relations between individuals. The regulation of the latter will certainly be coded, in Japan, in spoken and body language. The between space is, in this sense, relatively uncertain, relatively weakly coded or, at least, open to alternative codings.

If invisibility is the prevalent code here, then it is unsurprising to find a well, if casually, dressed man in his sixties dangling from the handrail in the subway train. He might do much the same thing in Kishine Koen when he interrupts his power-walking for a spot of arm-stretching. In the park, though, the iron frame is installed for precisely that purpose and not to assist stability in the event of an earthquake—not an infrequent event in the Kanto area. Nor is it surprising that absolutely no one at all pays any mind to the mentally disturbed young man who dances and shrieks at his reflection in the glass of the train door, or that another young man—very sharply dressed—appears to feel quite comfortable to stand in front of a mirror on the wall of Kishine Koen subway station and finalise his coiffe before scrutinising the inside of his mouth and nose. Once in the train, the working man sitting next to me feels perfectly free to ogle openly the centrespread in a sex-mag; again, no one is looking.

Alternative coding on the railways has been available to men for some time, of course, but is perhaps a more recent feminine space. Two of the Japanese expressions for wife place her in the house: *kanai* might literally be rendered as 'inside the house' and *okusan* might be 'the person who resides at the back of the house, where wives and family sleep (though an alternative might connote treasure). Another two expressions—*tsuma* and *nyoubou*—might both connote something supplementary or decorative and this might resonate with the coding for women in their undifferentiated space outside of the private domain. Regionalisation of this space arises with women's increasing economic activity so that they too have access to alternative public codings and, in particular, to the invisibility of railway travel. Hence the increase in cosmetic incidents, visible only to a non-native. Unhappily, this invisibility is symbolic rather than material. The Yokohama City mayor has found it necessary to provide women-only carriages on the subway during rush-hour travel in an effort to counter sexual assaults by men in sardine-tin conditions. Nevertheless, there is the appearance of a kind of cultural autism; not only no eye contact, but a general facility to look at no one at all even on a crowded train—unless, of course, it is introspection within a group of travelling companions.

So a young couple and a magazine are able to occupy a row of three *shinkansen* seats in a stuffed non-reserved car. Their two-year-old daughter is playing on the floor in front of the father. Standing in the crowded aisle next to them is another couple, rather older and taking turns to carry a somewhat heavier child who would be trampled on this part of the floor. To offer the spare seat would naturally be to admit to breaking the taboo on visibility. Even pre-coded objects—the elderly, the infirm, the pregnant or child-carrying—seem frequently to be invisible so that the silver-coloured 'priority seats' on the JR trains are often occupied by young and apparently fit businessmen asleep or engrossed in *manga*. It is of some note that foreigners are allowed to be visible, just occasionally; I have been openly stared at by an elderly bucolic man, perhaps on a rare trip to the city, and offered a seat (me, not my Japanese, female companion) by an urbane gent who must have had at least ten years on my age and, of course, fellow foreigners exchange furtive glances. Generally, though, I am as invisible as everyone else. Foreigners, of course, can 'see' the invisible. The Japanese American colleague of my girlfriend also reported overhearing very intimate conversations that would never, he asserted, take place on an American train.

Outside, the invisibility continues. No one holds a door open for anyone else (or, apparently, expects a door to be held open for them). Three schoolgirls practice a dance routine In Yokohama Park. They set up their audio system at a point where there are unlikely to be too many passers-by, but they seem completely unfazed by my presence

But the spell of invisibility can be broken and a more formally coded interaction inaugurated. Asking directions works effectively. The response to "sumimasen" (excuse me) is a smartly uttered, "hai", from everyone from a policeman to a school student to a parked motorcylist to a vagrant. It doesn't always work quite like this with foreigners, whose spoken Japanese seems sometimes to be almost wantonly misrecognised. For natives, though, a coded space is easily and quickly established. Eruptions that are less easily accommodated within the public coding system remain invisible. No one intervenes to arrest the young pickpocket as he runs from his victim who shouts after him in the Yokohama supermarket—a rare event indeed. So the sellers of *The Big Issue* (recently introduced in Osaka but making a holiday appearance in Ginza) are dressed in smart denims, outclassing the more conventional street vendors in Tokyo and very different from the assortment on the Tottenham Court Road.

Japanese tour groups are recognized all around the world, but joining a coach trip in Hokkaido brings new insights. We are together—mostly on the coach—for two days, yet interaction between parties is minimal. At one point the tour guide organises a paper-scissors-stone competition with a large dried fish as the prize for the winner. Each party must nominate one participant (I nominate my girlfriend). There is much laughing, but no commiserating or congratulating or even conversation between the parties, which each relate separately to the guide like spokes to their hub. The overnight stay is at an *onsen* hot spring baths. I refrain, preferring a bottle of *sake* and a book in our room (I take a solo shower every morning and communal bathing is not really my thing and the water is very, very hot). Everyone else, though, rushes for the pools. The genders are kept apart, but other than that, everyone goes in together. When my Japanese girlfriend recently accompanied a group of freshmen undergraduates to an *onsen* 'camp' for a weekend, she stayed dry until students' lights out; communal nudity with unseeing and unseen strangers is one thing, but in coded public—unthinkable. Once out of the baths our tour companions descend to the hotel restaurant dressed only in *yukata*—light cotton *kimono*—and sit with their respective parties on separate tables; one doesn't make friends in the bath.

Oddly, there is a sort of parallel of the visible-invisible code in the Japanese language. The name of my local park, Kishine Koen can be written in *hiragana*—a kind of alphabet: き is ki as in kit; し is shi as in ship; ね is ne as in net; こう is koo—take the co from cot and sustain it without changing the vowel sound; え is e as in net; and ん is the consonant n, so きしねこうえん is ki-shi-ne-koo-en. If I were to read Kishine as if it were English (as perhaps you did when you began this essay), then I might come up with something like ki-shine—just two syllables, because the final e merely imposes on the pronunciation of the second 'i' distinguishing its sound from that of the first 'i'. But in Japanese, *hiragana* generally have no phonetic impact on any other in the word; し is always pronounced in pretty much the same way irrespective of the characters around it. Where there are phonetic changes (particular consonant combinations, for example) then this is recorded in the spelling or by the addition of a diacritic mark.

The one partial exception in this example is こう. These two *hiragana* would be separately rendered ko (as co in cot) and u (as a very short oo with the lips held back), but here form a combination. There are a few other examples of such companions (and they are all consistent in their phonetic behaviour). For the most part, though, *hiragana* are largely invisible to one another.

However, the name of the park would be more likely to be written in the more arcane *kanji*—the Chinese characters that predominate in written Japanese—thus, 岸根公園. Here, the four *kanji* are pronounced kishi, ne, koo and en respectively and might be translated as river bank, root, public, garden—so, park by the river. But each of these *kanji* might be pronounced in at least one other way depending upon the combination in which it is involved. Thus 根気 is pronounced kon-ki, ne has become kon. Not only that, but 根気 means perseverance or patience and doesn't have any obvious (to me) connection with root. *Kanji* 'see' each other; *hiragana* are mutually invisible, perhaps.

I'm told that business in Japan has to be conducted, at least initially, face-to-face with no mediation, not even a telephone and certainly not a computer. Perhaps the codes that establish visibility are more difficult to enact in a mediated environment. This seems to benefit the Tokyo rail and subway networks that can carry businessmen to and from meetings with their customers all day. Again there is a kind of analogy elsewhere, this time on the TV. Japanese television advertisers are very inventive with their use of moving image editing techniques; I particularly like the one with the girl running along on the surface of the water in a lake and tripping over a boat when she is hailed by a guy on the shore. News and documentary programmes, though, often appear almost technophobic. Information is presented on cardboard charts that are held in place by the commentator who might tear off a sticker to reveal a baseball championship draw and so forth. I was enthralled by the demonstration of baseball hitting techniques that involved a polystyrene ball that could be moved along a track connected to an oversized bat. The ex-hitter expert slid the ball along its track manually to demonstrate a possible trajectory. The ads, of course, are playful and not to be taken too literally, unlike the baseball (live American major league in the daytime—Ichiro for the Seattle Mariners or Matsui for the New York Yankees). Virtuality, it seems, entails invisibility.

Now Japan is not the first place that I have encountered something that looks like a culture of autism. Tesco in Surrey Quays is another place. But here, the apparent oblivion to the actual or potential presence of others tends to be rather intrusive most commonly realised in the form of trolleys and or gossiping shoppers blocking entire aisles. For the most part, self-indulgent behaviour in Japan seems to be non-intrusive unless, that is, you happen to be a staring foreigner who doesn't know and can't work out the rules (or a sociologist who (invisibly, of course) ignores them). Not absolutely always: whilst taking a tourist snapshot at the Imperial palace in Kyoto I was very forcefully shoved out of the way by a very small old woman who wanted to speak to a police officer who was standing behind me. I have also been admonished by another elderly woman on the Kyoto subway for sitting with my legs crossed (not advised in crowded Tokyo, but on this occasion in the old capital the old woman, myself and my girlfriend were the only passengers in the entire carriage). I have been asked, at a bus stop, if I needed any assistance. I have been invited to conversation by an old-soldier in a tracksuit who recited the words of the Japanese national anthem translated into English and then German and announced that, studying at the Imperial University in Kyoto shortly after the second world war, he had read John Stewart Mill and this had converted him from a militarist to a liberal. He also wanted to look at the book I was reading, but gave up when he admitted that the English was too difficult for him. Of course, I am very visibly not Japanese. But on the same bus I saw a young girl give up her seat to an old woman—both apparently Japanese—and my Japanese girlfriend was also engaged in conversation by the same old soldier and has, herself, been roughly pushed aside as she spoke with a subway ticket collector by a very small old man who wanted to show his pass. It may or may not be a coincidence that all of these incidents happened in Kyoto, which is in the Kansai region of the country (a region whose people are widely stereotyped by Tokyo denizens). It should also be said that Kyoto is a small city that receives rather more than its share of tourists, both Japanese and international.

Nevertheless, for the most part, the codes seem to operate quite consistently here. That which is readily codified by the system is codified and receives the appropriately codified response; that which cannot be codified is invisible. And, for the most part, that which cannot be codified is the intrusion of the private into the public. The unruly *wagamama* of personal desires and habits can happily coexist with the only apparently all-encompassing system of smooth regulation and ritualized language that is stereotypical Japan. And where system and lifeworld touch then the former will ensure the continued invisibility of the latter as the bubblegum is scraped from the station floor in almost the same instant that is spat there. "Shitsurei shimasu"—"I am going to be rude"—says the waitress as she interrupts my conversation to place dessert in front of my dining partner (in Japan it seems that you really can have your cake and eat it).

This is, of course, a condition that is very worthy of preservation. It is oddly consistent with the common attitude to 'returnees' here. These are Japanese and, in particular, Japanese schoolchildren, who have spent time living abroad after which they return to remain in Japan. Reportedly, these kids often have a very hard time with bullying in school, often by exclusion. What they might acquire outside Japan, of course, is an eyesight for the invisible. Such acquisition would render them uncodable—not Japanese/not foreigners—and in danger of invisibility where the code is visibility. A common defense, I'm told, is the avoidance of talking about experiences outside of Japan, even feigned inadequacy in the English classroom by students who may have acquired fluency in an Anglophone country.

Basil Bernstein, my former mentor, claimed that the very worst fate was to be ignored. Yet he was a man who didn't take at all kindly to criticism—on those aspects of our identities in which we place greatest private investment perhaps none of us do. His claim, provoking as it is, is not to be generalised. Even as a foreigner, I feel private and safe in busy Ginza and in Kishine Koen, whichever shift is on. By contrast, my native London feels dangerous and eyes burn into me from every direction. The real question, though, is, which comes first? Commentaries are often (usually) written as if they provide insights into the objects of their analysis. It is perhaps more appropriate to see the commentary as the reference of an object text or field to an analytic system of which it thereby stands as an instance. Now this is not to claim pure structuralist subjectivity: the analytic system is not entirely closed, but is able to learn from its encounters; the commentary is the product of a transaction. The commentator produces their commentary in her or his own developing self-image. The eyes of the sociologist project their descriptive systems onto their objects but are constantly searching for what is initially invisible to them and in accommodating to the light, the descriptive systems transform, they are voyeuristic.

The eyes of the Japanese system may be innocent of this particular pathology, but if they are, it can only signify the stasis of a system that is doomed to reproduce itself; a cool, clone death, however economically productive it might be. My glimpse of my own invisibility, walking through the park, is an insight into the dilemmas that dominate my existence. I can hide away at home or I must intrude where I am not welcome and will not be greeted; I can play the game or I will not be seen and, either way, I will not be seen. My mentor was, it seems, wrong: the only fate that awaits us is to be ignored; we are all eyeless and everywhere is Ginza.

Well, that's the pessimistic version. Another day and another walk in the park. It really is a glorious spring day—sunshine, low twenties—I walk to the supermarket for provisions, forget to buy bottles of cold green tea and happily walk back to repair my error. I buy two small bottles to drink in the park as well as the large bottle for the fridge.

POSTFACE

Inside another cave

The next day I'm in a very different cave. The first one had been dark and seedy, cigarette butts in the bin, old wooden floor, creaky wooden stairs, opening out onto the main street. Today's cave is bright and *tatami* floored. This cave also has hot, public baths. But I have a private room. On the other side of a fairly conventional hotel bathroom, there is a large, rectangular, stone-lined hole in the floor, which is filling with hot water direct from the spring—about sixty degrees, I guess. But I also have a cold-water tap, so I can set the bath temperature to thirty-seven degrees—just right. And although the bath penetrates the space of the balcony, only trees—lots on the other side of the stream and one *sakura* growing through the balcony—take any interest in occupants of the bath. Here, I can soak and read philosophy and sip *nihonshu* and theorise. Next time I visit the other cave I'll have more to say.

GLOSSARY

The terms in this glossary are, mostly, defined as they are specialised by my organisational language. In some instances in the book some of these terms will be used in non-specialised ways; I hope that the context will make clear the use in each case.

Accommodating see *perspective/value schema.*

Acquirer focus, see *acquirer strategies* schema.

Acquirer Strategies

The *acquirer strategies* schema, like the *aesthetic mode* schema, derives from a misreading of Bourdieu's forms of capital; it also misreads his concept *habitus*. *Culture* may relate to *practice* or to *relations* and the *acquirer* may *focus* on these as *embodied* (or to-be-embodied) by or may focus on their *objectified* forms. Practice is embodied as *habitus* and objectified as *symbols*. Relations are embodied in *hub* mode—where the acquirer stands, metaphorically, at the hub of a set of 1-1 relations that are each valued in and for themselves—and objectified as a *network*, in which any given relation is valued in terms of that to which it can provide access.

Action

Action, or *social action*, is to be understood as a move that is *strategic* in the sense of serving, potentially, to establish, maintain or destabilise an *alliance* or *opposition*.

Activity

An *institutionalised* practice that is associated with a particular *alliance*. Note that both *activity* and the *alliance* are *emergent* structures.

Aesthetic mode

The *aesthetic mode* schema, like the *acquirer strategies* schema, derives from a *misreading* of Bourdieu's forms of capital. It is proposed that orientation to economic or cultural capital may be high or low, independently of each other, high and low orientation to economic capital being referred to as *spending* and *economy* respectively. Where orientation to aesthetic capital is low, the *aesthetic mode* is *necessity* (*economy*) or *opulence* (spending); where orientation to aesthetic capital is high, the *aesthetic mode* is *asceticism* (*economy*) or (*haute couture*). The schema is presented in Figure 9.11.

Alienate see *identification.*

Alliance

An emergent structure, but also a motive posited by *SAM* for all social *action*. An *alliance* is to be associated with a particular *activity*.

Anxiety

Proposed as the pathology that is resonant with the *liberal authority* mode.

Apprenticeship, see *subjectivity.*

Articulating, see *power.*

Asceticism, see *aesthetic mode.*

Authority, see also *interaction mode*.

Authority is claimed by or attributed to the authorial voice in *pedagogic relations*. The *authority* schema (Figures 3.2 and 8.6) allows *authority* to be claimed/attributed in terms of a closure of the category of *author* and/or a closure of the category of *practice*. *Traditional* authority *strategies* close both categories: only the suitably qualified may speak only in respect of that for which they are qualified, *charismatic authority strategies* close the category of author, whilst leaving open the category of *practice*: only the (self-)nominated may speak. *Bureaucratic authority strategies* open the category of author, whilst closing the category of *practice*: whoever holds the relevant office may speak in respect of the remit of the office. *Liberal authority strategies* leave both categories open, thus locating *authority* with the audience: this constitutes *exchange relations*.

Autoethnographic mode, see *Legitimation modes*.

Autopoiesis

Autopoiesis, or 'self-making', allows me to think of the subject of *action* as the product of that *action* and other *actions*. The subject may be defined at any level of analysis—the individual, the group, sub-individual. What constitutes the subject, then, is the pattern of more or less stable *alliances* and *oppositions* that is emergent upon *action*.

Bureaucratic authority, see *authority.*

Charismatic authority, see *authority.*

Chronotope, see *nostalgia modes.*

Chronotopic strategy, see *textual modes.*

Class condensation

This expression refers to the social structure of the Protea *community* that is described in Chapter 7, but potentially extends to areas of gentrification-in-progress in London, for example, and also to frontier contexts. It refers to a context in which a residential *community* exhibits the full range of social classes that participate in the life of the *community*. Clearly, the extent to which this marks a *community* depends upon the level of analysis being applied; we might expect, for example, that all national territories in effect exhibit *class condensation*; it will depend also on the representation of different class factions (does one member of parliament or one medical practitioner living in a shanty town establish the *community* as a *class condensation* in any useful way?) The expression is, therefore, underdeveloped here and may be used only comparatively.

Client/service provider, see *leader/follower identity.*

Collectivising, see *leader/follower identity.*

Commentary, see *technology/text/commentary.*

Community, see also *leader/follower identitiy.*

'A definable site for communicative action, which is characterised by specific forms of social relations that are produced and reproduced in cultural practices that, in general terms, may or may not be specific to the site. In this conception, individuals are not contained by a single community, rather they routinely participate in a complex of communities ...'

Community servant/community member

Compliance, see *subjectivity.*

Comportment, see *nostalgia modes.*

Construction, see also *discursive comportment.*

> *Construction* refers to an approach that claims no more than an attempt at semantic organisation, in contrast with *forensics*, which claims to reveal or attempt to reveal 'things as they are'.

Constructive description, see also *discursive comportment.*

> The *constructive description* schema is presented in Figure 4.2. It constitutes the general methodological approach of which *SAM/SAT* is a particular method. Essentially, *constructive description* inaugurates a *dehiscence* in the *empirical* world between *empirical* texts and *theoretical* texts. The transaction between the *theoretical* and the *empirical* generates an internal language—comprising a reading of the *theoretical* texts and a set of theoretical propositions—and an external language—consisting of an *organisational language* and a description of the *empirical* texts. Were total coherence to be achieved in the *empirical/theoretical* transaction, this would effect a suturing of the original *dehiscence.*

Critique, see *discursive comportment.*

Culture, see *acquirer strategies* schema.

Curatorial see perspective/value schema.

Deconstruction, see *discursive comportment.*

Deformance, see also *heresy, misprision, misreading, treachery.*

> This is an expression introduced by Jerome McGann (*op. cit.*) to signify, in effect, any transformation performed on an artistic text. His examples include Emily Dickinson's suggestion that, if one is failing to make headway with a poem, one might try reading it backwards; another is his use of a Photoshop filter on a digitised image of Rossetti's *Blessed Demozel*. Here, the term is used along with *heresy, misprision, misreading and treachery* to signify a knowingly transformative reading of an antecedent work. These expressions contrast with *misrecognition*, which the knowing irony is (apparently) absent.

Dehiscence, see *constructive description.*

Delimiting power, see *power.*

Dependency, see *subjectivity.*

Depression

> Proposed as the pathology of the *traditional authority* mode.

De-regulation, see *regulatory strategies.*

Descriptive domain, see *domains of action.*

De-territorialising, see *discursive comportment.*

Diachronic, see *nostalgia modes.*

Diachronising, see *textual modes.*

Disciplinary/non-disciplinary practice, see *regulatory strategies.*

Disciplinary enquiry, see *regulatory strategies.*

Disciplinary regulation, see *regulatory strategies*.
Discourse, see *practical strategic space*.
Discovery, see *discursive comportment*.

Discursive comportment

Forensics or *construction* may each be deployed with a *territorialising* or a *deterritorialising vector*, which is to say, the attempt may be to establish a discursive territory or to dismantle one. The resulting *relational space* comprises four *discursive comportments*: *discovery* (*territorialising forensics*); *critique* (*deterritorialising forensics*); *deconstruction* (*deterritorialising construction*); and *constructive description* (*territorialising construction*).

Discursive saturation (*DS*)

Practices are distinguished in terms of the extent to which strategies are deployed that establish or tend to establish discursively available principles. *Practices* exhibiting such strategies are described as high *discursive saturation* (*DS$^+$*); *practices* exhibiting predominantly tacit principles of regularity are low *discursive saturation* (*DS$^-$*).

Domains of action

The *domains of action* schema is presented in Figure 8.2. It establishes four domains where the form of expression (signifiers) and content (signifieds) may each be strongly or weakly *institutionalised* ($I^{+/-}$) in/by a *text* or *texts*. The *esoteric domain* constitutes the most strongly *institutionalised* region of a *practice* and can be realised only where expression and content are both I^+. The *public domain* is realised by *texts* in which expression and content are both I^-; *texts* of this form provide a way in to the *practice*. The *descriptive domain* is realised by I^+ espression and I^- content; within mathematics, for example, this is the domain of the mathematical modelling of non-mathematical contexts. The *expressive* domain is realised by I^- expression and I^+ content, for example, where non-mathematical terms are used as metaphors for mathematical content—an equation, for example, being represented by a balance.

Economy, see aesthetic mode.

Elaborated description

This expression was introduced in Brown and Dowling (1998) and refers to the need in qualitative analysis, in particular, to elaborate on why/how it is that a section of data—in an interview transcript, or an instance of observed behaviour, etc—is being interpreted as an instance of a particular concept.

Embodied, see *acquirer strategies* schema.

Empirical

In *constructive description*, the *empirical* is established strategically as constituting local instances and events in contrast with the *theoretical*, which is constituted as general claims, statements, debates. Metaphorically, the *theoretical* is the library, the *empirical* is that which lies beyond, though, clearly, one might regard a library as an *empirical setting*.

Empirical field

This expression was introduced in Brown and Dowling (1998) to signify the widest *empirical* context having to do with a particular area of research interest, for example, the teaching and learning of school mathematics, as an *empirical field*, would comprise all of the classrooms and texts that constitute instances of it.

Empirical setting

The *empirical setting* is a *localising* of the *empirical field* that is achieved by methodological strategies relating to, for example, research design and sampling, data collection and data analysis strategies as well as contingencies.

Epistemological Paradox

This term was introduced in Brown and Dowling (1998) to refer to the claim that making one's experience explicit is of necessity a transformation of it.

Equilibration, see *interaction mode*.

Esoteric domain, see *domains of action*.

Estrange see *identification*.

Exchange action

An *exchange action* is one in which the author of the action locates or seeks to locate *authority* with its audience.

Exchange of narratives, see *interaction mode*.

Exchange relations

Exchange relations between author and audience locate *authority* with the audience.

Exchange text

An *exchange text* is on in which the *authority* is located with the audience voice.

Expanding power, see *power.*

Explore, see *nostalgia modes*.

Expressive domain, see *domains of action*.

Fiction, see *grammatical modes.*

Field

This term is not being used technically here and its use is thus to be distinguished from, for example, that by Bourdieu.

Findings

This expression was defined in Brown and Dowling (1998) as the summaries of relations between indicator variables and so the *empirical* correlate of the research problem.

Forensics, see also *discursive comportment.*

I am using this term, metaphorically, to refer to a claim in sociology or in educational studies to be revealing or attempting to reveal 'things as they are'. This approach is contrasted with *construction*, which claims only to be an attempt at semantic organisation.

Guardian/ward, see *leader/follower identity.*

Gaze, see *grammatical modes.*

General see: *identification; leader/follower identity.*

General/footsoldier, see *leader/follower identity.*

Generalising, see *power.*

Grammatical modes

It is postulated that *institutionalised practices* may constitute a *gaze* whereby they establish other practices as objects, which is to say, as instances of themselves; the productivity of this *gaze* is the *public domain*. *Institutionalised practices* may therefore be considered in terms of internal and external syntaxes. A *metonymic apparatus* is a practice exhibiting DS^+ in both internal and external syntaxes; a *fiction* exhibits DS^- in both; a *metaphoric apparatus* displays DS^+ internally and DS^- externally; a *method* has DS^+ external syntax and DS^- internal syntax. The schema is presented in Figure 8.3.

Guardian/ward, see *leader/follower identity*.

Habitus, see *acquirer strategies* schema.

Haute couture, see *aesthetic mode*.

Hegemony, see *interaction mode*.

Heresy see also *deformance, misprision, misreading, treachery*.

A self-consciously transformative reading of an antecedent work. *Heresy* is contrasted with *misrecognition*.

Hub, see *acquirer strategies* schema.

Hysteria

Proposed as the pathology of the *charismatic* mode of *authority*.

Identification

This schema has been devised by Natasha Whiteman (see Figure 9.8). *Identification* may be established by *suturing* or by *rupturing moves*. The former constitutes an *identification* with a specific *activity*, the latter establishes a *rupture* with that *activity* via a *suture* with another *activity*; pointing out the lack of realism of a film, for example, would constitute a *rupture* with the film via a *suture* with an aspect of 'the real world'. Both *suturing* and *rupturing moves* may vary in terms of *power*, which is to say, the extent to which they refer to *local* or *general* aspects of the activity. Thus *suture* may *involve* (*local*) or *reside* (*general*) and *rupture* may *estrange* (*local*) or (*alienate*).

Identity equilibrium

Identity equilibrium is established where teacher and student or leader and follower collaborate or coincide in their identity constructions. See Figures 7.2 and 7.4.

Idiolect, see *practical strategic space*.

Individualising, see *leader/follower identity*.

Informational decoupling

The relationship between author and audience is, in general, being understood as one of *structural coupling* and *informational decoupling*. The *structural coupling* is necessary if, shall we say, data is to be transferred between author and audience. However, insofar as we may regard information as meaningful data, no information is transmitted, because meaning can be attributed only on the basis of an *organisational language* and this is always the unique property of the subject; that is, author and audience must, to a degree, deploy distinct *organisational languages* and so must *misrecognise* each other to greater or lesser effect.

Institutionalisation

Institutionalisation is a regularity of *practice* emergent upon *autopoietic action.*

Instrumental see perspective/value schema.

Interaction mode

An *interaction* constitutes a form of *alliance* that may be one of similars or of disimilars. In either case, the *target of discursive action* may be closure or openness. Thus, where an *alliance* of similars targets discursive closure, the *interaction* is described as *equilibriation,* where it targets openness, the *interaction* is an *exchange of narratives*; where an *alliance of disimilars* targets closure the *interaction* is *hegemony,* where it targets openness, it is *pastiche.* The schema is presented in Figure 3.1.

Involve see *identification.*

Knower mode, see *Legitimation modes.*

Knowledge mode, see *Legitimation modes.*

Language of description

This is a term introduced by Basil Bernstein that I have previously used. I now refer to *SAM/SAT* as an *organisational language* because I want to distance it from any notion of a pre-existing dichotomy of the form, describer/described; in my conception, we only ever (re)organise the space that we inhabit.

Leader, see *leader/follower identity.*

Leader/follower identity

This schema is presented in Figure 7.4. Strategies relating to leader/follower relations may be *exchange* or *pedagogic* and *community*/community strategies may be individualised/*individualising* or collective/*collectivising.* The relational space thus generated constitutes *leader/follower identities* for an individualised *community* as *service provider/client,* where *leadership relations* are *exchange,* and *guardian/ward,* where they are *pedagogic.* The corresponding identities for a collectivised *community* are *community servant/community member* and *general/footsoldier.* This schema is specialised to *teacher/student identity* in Figure 7.2, where the teacher is either a *recruit* (*exchange* relations) or a *leader* (pedagogic relations).

Leadership relations, see *leader/follower identity.*

Legitimation modes

This schema, in Figure 8.5, is derived from a *misreading* of Karl Maton's 'legitimation codes' *en route* to the *Authority* schema. Figure 8.5 reveals the relational space that results from allowing Maton's categories, 'social relation' (relationship to sociocultural location and history) and 'epistemic relation' (relationship to the knowledge), to be strong or weak, independently of each other. The *autoethnographic mode* obtains where both categories are strong and the *nomad mode* where both are weak. *Knowledge mode* obtains where the 'epistemic relation' is strong and the 'social relation' is weak and *knower mode* where the opposite is the case.

Liberal authority, see *authority.*

Local see *identification.*

Localising, see *power.*

Mapping, see *textual modes.*

Marketing, see *subjectivity*.

Mathematicoscience

I have defined *mathematicoscience* as a public, global discourse, established in and by the public forms of school mathematical and scientific discourse, that defines that which can stand as a legitimate form of argumentation (the mathematical moment) and that which can stand as a legitimate form of relationship to the empirical (the scientific moment).

Metaphoric apparatus, see *grammatical modes*.

Method, see *grammatical modes*.

Metonymic apparatus, see *grammatical modes*.

Misreading, see also *deformance, heresy, misprision, treachery*.

This term, along with *misprision*, is taken from Harold Bloom, who describes the way in which a poet must constituted a *misreading of another poet* in order to make space for her/himself. Here, of course, the context is not necessarily poetry. *Misreading* is contrasted with *misrecognition*.

Misrecognition

An apparently (or, of course, putatively) unknowingly transformative reading of an antecedent work.

Misprision, see also *deformance, heresy, misreading, treachery*.

This term, along with *misreading*, is taken from Harold Bloom, who describes the way in which a poet must constituted a *misreading of another poet* in order to make space for her/himself. Here, of course, the context is not necessarily poetry. *Misprision* is contrasted with *misrecognition*.

Mod, see *nostalgia modes*.

Moral regulation, see *regulatory strategies*.

Mythologising

Mythologising is the action of *forensics* in laying claim to a state of 'things as they are' that is generative of things as they seem to be. It is generally achieved as the reification of a theoretical construction.

Necrotising

The danger of all theorising is that it achieves a level of consistency and completeness in itself—a sclerosis—to the extent that it is unable to learn and can do no more than convert what it confronts into repetitions of itself. A prime example would be the system of the natural numbers, whence the necrotising power of statistics.

Necessity, see *aesthetic mode*.

Network, see *acquirer strategies* schema.

Nostalgia modes

This schema, devised by Natasha Whiteman, is presented in Figure 9.7. The first dimension of this schema resonates with the *chronotopic strategy* of the *textual modes* schema and relates to the construction of the *chronotope* as either fixed—synchronic—or dynamic—*diachronic*. Nostalgia in the *synchronic* mode entails a desire to return to a universe either to *repeat* and experience or to *explore* a world. The distinction between these two *strategies* is constituted by a difference in *comportment*: the *repeat strategy* is constituted by an orientation to an external authorship: the subject of the *action* is constituted as the passive audience of an external author; the *explore strategy* constructs a more active audience. The corresponding *strategies* constructing a *diachronic chronotope*— a dynamic universe—are *spectate* and *mod*: the former strategy constructs the audience as a spectator of a changing scene; the latter entails the active modification of the scene—audience as author.

Nomad mode, see *Legitimation modes*.

Objectified, see *acquirer strategies* schema.

Objectification, see *subjectivity*.

Obsession

This is proposed as the pathology of the *bureaucratic mode* of *authority*.

Opulence, see *aesthetic mode*.

Organisational language

There is clearly a sense in which this expression is pleonastic: organisation is what language does, though its use can disorganise as well (see *discursive comportment*). I use *organisational language* to say what kind of thing *SAM/SAT* is in a manner that emphasises its *constructive* rather than its (inevitable, to a degree) *forensic* nature,

Orientation to aesthetic capital

Orientation to economic capital

Opposition

An emergent structure, but also a motive posited by *SAM* for all social *action* in the sense that the formation of an *alliance* of necessity entails the formation of one or more *oppositions*.

Operational matrix

A technology—a regularity of practice—that incorporates, non-discursively, the principles of its own deployment: a supermarket and the World Wide Web would both be examples.

Painting, see *textual modes*.

Pastiche, see *interaction mode*.

Pedagogic action

A *pedagogic action* is one in which the author of the action retains or seeks to retain *authority*.

Pedagogic relations

Pedagogic relations between author and audience locate *authority* with the auhtor.

Pedagogic text

A *pedagogic text* locates *authority* with the author.

Perspective/Value schema

This schema has been devised by Soh-young Chung. *Perspective* refers to the position that is adopted in reviewing literature that may be intrinsic or extrinsic to the practice of literary studies. The other dimension of the schema distinguishes between positions that locate the *value* of literature and literary studies as intrinsic or extrinsic to itself. The strategies that are constituted by the schema are: *reproductive*, intrinsic *perspective* and *value*; *accommodating*, intrinsic *perspective*, extrinsic *value*; *curatorial*, extrinsic perspective, intrinsic *value*; and *instrumental*, extrinsic *perspective* and *value*. See Figure 9.10.

Power

Strategies may tend to *delimit* or *expand* the descriptive *power* of an *activity*. DS^+ strategies thus *specialise* or *generalise*; DS^- strategies *localise* or *articulate*. (See also *identification*).

Practical strategic space

This schema is introduced in Figure 4.5 and distinguishes between DS^+ and DS^- *practices* at different levels of *institutionalisation*, formal (I^+) or informal (I^-). DS^+/I^+ practices are referred to as *discourse*; DS^-/I^+ practices as *skills*; DS^-/I^- practices as *tricks*; and DS^+/I^- practices as *idiolect*.

Practice

This term is not being used in a specialised way here. It is being taken to refer to *action* that is *institutionalised*, which is to say, exhibits some degree of regularity. There is a sense in which *practice* might be interpreted as a *langue* where *action* is *parole*, though the relation between the former and the latter is one of emergence rather than generation. See also *acquirer strategies* schema.

Printing, see *textual modes*.

Problem

This is the term used in Brown and Dowling (1998) for the most highly *specialised* region of the *theoretical field*. The *problem* may generally be formulated as the research question or as the conclusion.

Problematic

This term is used in Brown and Dowling (1998) for the subset of the *theoretical field* that directly concerns the concepts entailed in the *problem*.

Public domain, see *domains of action*.

Public/private

Strategies constituting *alliances* and *opposition* may clearly differentiate *public* and *private* spaces. It is postulated—for example, in Chapter 6—that it is generally in *private* rather than *public* spaces that *action* can be effective, though this will depend on the extent to which any given *private* sphere can *articulate* with others.

Recontextualisation

This is a term that is used by Basil Bernstein and is also used here, but with a less specialised meaning. In general, it refers to the way in which one *practice* regards another.

Recruit, see *leader/follower identity*.

Register coding, see *textual modes*.

Regulatory strategies

This schema is presented in Figure 7.3. It is proposed that the school distinguishes between *disciplinary practices* that are *specialised* to particular regions of the official curriculum—mathematics, science, geography, and so forth—and *non-disciplinary practices* that are *generalised* across the curriculum—including the ethics of school uniform and general behaviour. *Strategies* in either category may be *pedagogic* or *exchange*. Where both *disciplinary* and *non-disciplinary practices* are *pedagogic*, the *regulatory strategy* is one of *disciplinary regulation*; where they are both *exchange*, the strategy is *de-regulation*. *Disciplinary enquiry* is the *strategy* where only *disciplinary practices* are *pedagogic*, *moral regulation* that where only *non-disciplinary practices* are *pedagogic*.

Relational space

A distinguishing strategy of *SAM/SAT* (though not one that is unique to it) is the generation of a *relational space* via the cartesian product of two binary variables. The variables originate in *empirical* observation, but are subsequently *theoretically* defined to produce the characteristic 2x2 tables that give rise to four ideal types (my use of this term representing a *misreading* of Max Weber). Upon return to *empirical* observation, any given context may be mapped synchronically and diachronically using the *relational space*.

Relations, see *acquirer strategies* schema.

Repeat, see *nostalgia modes*.

Repertoire coding, see *textual modes*.

Reproductive see perspective/value schema.

Reside see *identification*.

Routine, see *subjectivity*.

Rupture see *identification*.

Scribing, see *textual modes*.

Servant/community , see *leader/follower identity*.

Service provider/client, see *leader/follower identity*.

Sign

A moment of an already established, which is to say, *mythologised*, system; *mythologised* because establishing a system as such is interpreted as a structuralist closure. A *sign* is to be distinguished from a *text*, which is an *articulation* of *signs*.

Skill, see *practical strategic space*.

Social action, see *action*.

Social Activity Method (SAM)

The *organisational language* that is presented in this book was referred to previously (in Dowling, 1998, for example) as *Social Activity Theory*. It is clearly *theoretical*, in the way that this term has been defined here. However, the schema of *grammatical modes* presented in Figure 8.3, appropriately identifies it as a *method*, whence the name change.

Social Activity Theory (SAT), see *Social Activity Method*.

Sociocultural

I am using this term to refer to the general *empirical field* that is constituted as the object of sociology.

Specialising, see power.

Spectate, see *nostalgia modes*.

Spending, see aesthetic mode.

Strategies of the general, see *leader/follower identity*.

Strategy

All *action* is being interpreted as *strategic* in respect of the formation, maintenance and destabilising of *alliances* and *oppositions*. This statement is, in a sense, the fundamental theoretical proposition that constitutes the internal language of *SAM/SAT*. It is important to emphasise, therefore, that that which constitutes a *strategy* is that which is established as such in the action of *SAM/SAT* and not necessarily that which is conceived of as a strategy in the mind of the strategist.

Structural coupling, see *informational decoupling*.

Subjectivity

The schema in Figure 9.9 distinguishes between three levels of subjectivity, high, low and zero, in *pedagogic* and *exchange* relations. Where relations are *pedagogic*, high *subjectivity* establishes the *apprenticeship* of the audience, which is to say, the audience is a potential author. Low *subjectivity* establishes audience *dependency*. *Objectification* denies subjectivity and so excludes the objectified 'subject' as either audience or author. Where relations are *exchange*, high author *subjectivity* is constituted by *marketing*, whereas low author *subjectivity* is established by *routine*; zero *subjectivity* establishes the author as *compliant*.

Suture see *identification*.

Symbols, see *acquirer strategies* schema.

Synchronic, see *nostalgia modes*.

Synchronising, see *textual modes*.

Target of discursive action, see *interaction mode*.

Teacher/student identity, see *leader/follower identity*.

Technology/text/commentary

This schema of interpretation is represented in Figure 8.7. The category, *technology*, is the analytic apparatus that constitutes meaning out of the *text* that it takes as its object, thus generating a *commentary*. In the context of this book, the *technology* is *SAM/SAT*.

Territorialising, see *discursive comportment*.

Text, see *technology/text/commentary*.

Text-as-work

This expression is taken from Roland Barthes. It is an ideal category, referring to the text prior to its reading.

Text-as-text

This expression is taken from Roland Barthes. It is the pragmatic category that refers to the text as read.

Textual modes

This schema (in Figure 5.5) derives from a *misreading* of Gunther Kress's multimodality approach to the analysis of text. Its first dimension distinguishes between *synchronising* and *diachronising chronotopic strategies*. The former will tend to make multiple elements of a text available at the same time (for example, a roadmap), whilst the latter will tend to highlight a sequence (for example, a novel). The second dimenstion distinguishes between strong and weak *register* or *repertoire coding*. Strong coding entails that selections will be reliably repeated, whilst weak coding will give rise to a greater or lesser degree of variation between selections. *Diachronising* may be *printing* (strong coding) or *scribing* (weak coding); *synchronising* may be *mapping* (strong coding) or *painting*.

Theoretical, see *empirical*.

Theoretical field

The *theoretical field* was introduced in Brown and Dowling (1998) to refer to the widest category of general statements having to do with a particular research interest. For example, the theoretical field of mathematics education would comprise all research, professional and official literature on or plausibly relating to mathematics education, but it would probably exclude specific instances of mathematics education, such as textbooks or specific classrooms or lessons etc, which would constituted the *empirical field*.

Traditional authority, see *authority*.

Treachery, see also *deformance*, heresy*, misprision, misreading*.

Treachery is the knowingly transformative reading of an antecedent work and is contrasted with *misrecognition*.

Trick, see *practical strategic space*.

Value see perspective/value schema.

Vector, see *discursive comportment*.

Virtual community

In this book, I have used the expression *virtual community* not to refer to the internet or other means of distance communication, but where a *community* that is or that seems to be being referenced extends substantially beyond the practical range of communicative participation of any of its participants. Such *mythologisings* of *community* are not uncommon; we, for example, familiar with such expressions as 'the gay community' and so forth.

REFERENCES

Aarseth, E. (1994). Nonlinearity and literary theory. In G. P. Landow, *Hyper/text/theory* (pp. 51-86). Baltimore: The John Hopkins University Press.

Aarseth, E. (1997). *Cybertext: Perspectives on ergodic literature.* Baltimore: The John Hopkins University Press.

Aarseth, E. (1999). Aporia and Epiphany in *Doom* and *The Speaking Clock*: The temporality of ergodic art. In M.-L. Ryan, *Cyberspace, Textuality: Computer technology and literary theory.* Bloomington, Indiana University Press.

Adlam, D. S. (1977). *Code in context.* London: Routledge & Kegan Paul.

Anderson, B. (1991). *Imagined communities: Reflections on the origins and spread of nationalism.* London, Verso.

Association of Teachers of Mathematics (1979). Submission of evidence to the committee of enquiry into the teaching of mathematics in schools. *Mathematics Teaching* (89).

Atkin, R. (1991). *Multidimensional man.* Harmondsworth, Penguin.

Austin, K. (1975). How do you play master mind? *Mathematics Teaching* (71).

Babbedge, T.S.R. *et al* (2005). Can a photometric redshift code reliably determine dust extinction. *Monthly Notices of the Royal Astronomical Society, 361*(2), 437-450.

Bann, S. (1995). History as competence and performance: Notes on the Ironic Museum. In F. Ankersmit and H. Kellner, *A new philosophy of history.* Chicago: University of Chicago Press.

Barthes, R. (1973). *Mythologies.* London: Paladin.

Barthes, R. (1981). Theory of the text. In R. Young, *Untying the text: A poststructuralist reader.* London: RKP.

Baudrillard, J. (1993). *Symbolic exchange and death.* London: Sage.

Baudrillard, J. (1995). *The Gulf War did not take place.* Sydney: Power Publications.

Baudrillard, J. (2001). The spirit of terrorism. *Le Monde.* 2nd November 2001. Available at http://www.egs.edu/faculty/baudrillard/baudrillard-the-spirit-of-terrorism.html.

Bayatt, A. S. (1991). *Possession: A romance.* London: Vintage.

Beck, J. & M. F. D. Young (2005). The assault on the professions and the restructuring of academic and professional identities: A Bernsteinian analysis. *British Journal of Sociology of Education, 26*(2), 183-197.

Becker, B. & J. Wehner (2001). Electronic networks and civil society: Reflections on structural changes in the public sphere. In C. Ess, *Electronic networks and civil society: Reflections on structural changes in the public sphere* (pp. 65-85). Albany, NY: State University of New York Press.

Benaceraf, P. & H. Putnam (Eds.) (1983). *Philosophy of mathematics: Selected readings.* Cambridge: CUP.

Bergonzi, B. (1990). *Exploding English.* Oxford: Clarendon.

Bernstein, B. B. (1971). *Class, codes and control: Theoretical studies towards a sociology of language.* London: RKP.

Bernstein, B. B. (Ed.) (1973). *Class, codes and control, Volume II: Applied studies towards a sociology of language.* London: Routledge & Kegan Paul.

Bernstein, B. B. (1977). *Class, codes and control: Towards a theory of educational transmissions.* London: RKP.

Bernstein, B. B. (1990). *Class, codes and control volume IV: The structuring of pedagogic discourse.* London: RKP.

Bernstein, B. (1995). Code theory and its positioning: A case study in misrecognition. *British Journal of Sociology of Education, 16*(2), 3-19.

Bernstein, B. B. (1996). *Pedagogy, symbolic control and identity.* London: Taylor & Francis.

REFERENCES

Bernstein, B. B. (1999). Vertical and horizontal discourse: An essay. *British Journal of Sociology of Education, 20*(2), 158-173.

Bernstein, B. B. (2000). *Pedagogy, symbolic control and identity* (2nd edition). New York: Rowman & Littlefield.

Bernstein, B. *et al* (Eds.) (2001). *Towards a sociology of pedagogy.* New York: Peter Lang.

Bérubé, M. (1998). *The employment of English: Theory, jobs and the future of literary studies.* New York: New York University Press.

Bhaskar, R. (1997). *A realist theory of science* (2nd edition). London: Verso.

Bhaskar, R. (1998). *The possibility of naturalism* (3rd edition). London: Routledge.

Bloom, H. (1973). *The anxiety of influence: A theory of poetry.* New York: Oxford University Press.

Bloomfield, A. (1987). Assessing investigations. *Mathematics Teaching* (118).

Bolter, J. D. (2001). *Writing space: Computers, hypertext, and the remediation of print.* Mahwah: Lawrence Erlbaum Associates.

Bourdieu, P. (1977). *Outline of a theory of practice.* Cambridge: CUP.

Bourdieu, P. (1984). *Distinction: A social critique of the judgement of taste.* London: RKP.

Bourdieu, P. (1988). *Homo Academicus.* Cambridge: Polity.

Bourdieu, P. (1990). *The logic of practice.* Cambridge: Polity.

Bourdieu, P. (1991). *Language and symbolic power.* Cambridge: Polity Press.

Bourdieu, P. & J.-C. Passeron (1977). *Reproduction in education, society and culture.* London: Sage.

Bowman, J. (2001/2006). Performance art defined. Retrieved 06/03/07, from http://members.tripod.com/~jackbowman/perfdefn.htm.

Brown, A. J. & P. C. Dowling (1998). *Doing research/reading research: A mode of interrogation for education.* London: Falmer Press.

Burbules, N. C. (n.d.). Web literacy: Theory and practice of reading and writing hypertext. http://mroy.web.wesleyan.edu/webliteracy/linktropics.htm.

Cheshire, J. (2000). The telling or the tale? Narratives and gender in adolescent friendship networks. *Journal of Sociolinguistics, 4*(2), 234-262.

Chisolm, L. & M. Sujee (2007). Tracking racial desegregation in South African schools. *Journal of Education, 40,* 141-160.

Chouliaraki, L. & N. Fairclough (1999). *Discourse in late modernity: Rethinking critical discourse analysis.* Edinburgh: Edinburgh University Press.

Chung, S-Y. (2005). Towards methodology. Working Paper available from the author.

Chung, S-Y., P. C. Dowling, *et al* (2004). (Dis)possessing literacy and literature: Gourmandising in Gibsonbarlowville. In A. J. Brown & N. Davis, *The World Yearbook of Education 2004: Digital technology, communities and education.* London: Routledge.

Cockcroft, W. *et al* (1982). *Mathematics counts.* London: HMSO.

Collier, A. (1994). *Critical realism: An introduction to the philosophy of Roy Bhaskar.* London: Verso.

Collins, J. (2000). Bernstein, Bourdieu and the new literacy studies. *Linguistics and Educationl. 11*(1), 65-78.

Connell, R. W., D. J. Ashenden, *et al* (1982). *Making the difference.* Sydney: Allen & Unwin.

Cooper, B. & M. Dunne (1999). *Assessing children's mathematical knowledge: Social class, sex and problem-solving.* Milton Keynes: Open University Press.

Crotty, M. (1998). *The foundations of social research: Meaning and perspective in the research process.* London: Sage.

Crystal, D. (2003). *English as a global language.* Cambridge: Cambridge University Press.

Cunningham, R. B. (2004). *The application of a complexity model to the analysis and development of learning.* EdD Thesis. London: Institute of Education, University of London.

D'Ambrosio, U. (1989). On ethnomathematics. *Philosophia Mathematica, 2-4*(1), 3-14.

Davison, D. M. & K. W. Miller (1998). An ethnoscience approach to curriculum issues for American Indian student. *School Science and Mathematics.* May 1998. http://findarticles.com/p/articles/mi_qa3667/is_199805/ai_n8806623/pg_1.

de Certeau, M. (1984). *The practice of everyday life.* Berkeley: University of California Press.

Deleuze, G. & F. Guattari (1984). *Anti-Oedipus: Capitalism and schizophrenia.* London: Athlone.

Deleuze, G. & F. Guattari (1987). *A Thousand Plateaus: Capitalism and schizophrenia.* Minneapolis: University of Minnesota Press.

Derrida, J. (1978). *Writing and difference.* London: RKP.

Dick, P. K. (1972). *We can build you.* London: Vintage.

Donaldson, M. (1978). *Children's minds.* Glasgow: Fontana/Collins.

Douglas, J. Y. (1998). Will the most reflexive relativist please stand up: Hypertext, argument and relativism. In I. Snyder, *Page to screen: Taking literacy into the electronic era.* London: Routledge.

Douglas, J. Y. (2001). *The end of books—Or books without end? Reading interactive narratives.* Ann Arbor: University of Michigan Press.

Douglas, M. (1970). *Natural symbols: Explorations in cosmology.* Harmondsworth: Penguin.

Douglas, M. (1996a). *Natural symbols: Explorations in cosmology* (second edition). London: Routledge.

Douglas, M. (1996b). *Thought styles: Critical essays on good taste.* London: Sage.

Dowling, P. C. (1989). The contextualising of mathematics: Towards a theoretical map. *Collected Original Resources in Education, 13*(2).

Dowling, P. C. (1990). The Shogun's and other curricular voices. In P. C. Dowling and R. Noss, *Mathematics versus the National Curriculum.* Basingstoke: Falmer.

Dowling, P. C. (1991a). A dialectics of determinism: Deconstructing information technology. In H. McKay, M. F. D. Young & J. Beynon, *Understanding technology in education.* London: Falmer.

Dowling, P. C. (1991b). The contextualising of mathematics: Towards a theoretical map. In M. Harris, *Schools, mathematics and work.* London: Falmer.

Dowling, P. C. (1994). Discursive saturation and school mathematics texts: A strand from a language of description. In P. Ernest, *Mathematics, education and philosophy: An international perspective.* London: Falmer.

Dowling, P. C. (1996a). Baudrillard 1 – Piaget 0: Cybernetics, subjectivity and the ascension. http://homepage.mac.com/paulcdowling/ioe/publications/dowling1996/index.html.

Dowling, P. C. (1996b). A sociological analysis of school mathematics texts. *Educational Studies in Mathematics, 31,* 389-415.

Dowling, P. C. (1998). *The sociology of mathematics education: Mathematical myths/pedagogic texts.* London: Falmer.

Dowling, P. C. (1999). Basil Bernstein in frame: "Oh dear, is this a structuralist analysis", Presented at School of Education, Kings College, University of London, 10th December 1999. http://homepage.mac.com/paulcdowling/ioe/publications/kings1999/index.html.

Dowling, P. C. (2001a). Reading school mathematics texts. In P. Gates, *Issues in mathematics teaching.* London: Routledge-Falmer.

Dowling, P. C. (2001b). Basil Bernstein: Prophet, teacher, friend. In S. Power *et al.* (Eds.), *A tribute to Basil Bernstein 1924-2000* (pp. 114-116). London: Institute of Education.

Dowling, P. C. (2001c). School mathematics in late modernity: Beyond myths and fragmentation. In B. Atweh, H. Forgasz & B. Nebres, *Socio-cultural research on mathematics education: An international perspective.* Mahwah: Lawrence Erlbaum.

Dowling, P. C. (2004). Language, discourse, literacy: Stability, territory and transformation. In M. Olssen, *Culture and learning: Access and opportunity in the curriculum.* Greenwich, CT: Information Age Publishing.

Dowling, P. C. (2006). *Research and the theoretical field,* Online MRes Module. London: Institute of Education. Available at: http://homepage.mac.com/paulcdowling/ioe/rtf/rtf.pdf

Dowling, P. C. (2007). Quixote's science: Public heresy/private apostasy. In B. Atweh *et al,* *Internationalisation and globalisation in mathematics and science education.* Dordrecht: Springer.

Dowling, P. C. (2007). Social organising. *Philosophy of Mathematics Education Journal, 21,* 1-27. Available at: http://www.people.ex.ac.uk/PErnest/pome21/index.htm

Dowling, P. C. & A. J. Brown (2006). The divorce of schooling and research: Towards a reconciliation in teacher education. Preparing Teachers for a Changing Context—An international conference, 3-6

REFERENCES

May 2006. Institute of Education, University of London. http://homepage.mac.com/paulcdowling/ioe/publications/dowling%26brown2006/divorce.pdf

Dowling, P. C. & A. J. Brown (2009). *Doing research/reading research: Re-interrogating education*. London: Taylor & Francis.

Dowling, P. C. & R. Noss (Eds.) (1990). *Mathematics versus the National Curriculum*. London: Falmer.

Dreyfus, H. L. & P. Rabinow (1982). *Michel Foucault: Beyond structuralism and hermeneutics*. Brighton: Harvester.

Durães, C. (2001). *Disability in American film*, M.A. Dissertation. London: Institute of Education, University of London.

Durkheim, É. (1951). *Suicide: a study in sociology*. London: RKP.

Durkheim, É. (1984). *The division of labour in society*. Basingstoke: MacMillan.

Eco, U. (1976). *A theory of semiotics*. Bloomington: Indiana University Press.

Eco, U. (1984). *Semiotics and the philosophy of language*. Basingstoke: MacMillan.

Eco, U. (1989). *Foucault's pendulum*. London: QPD.

Ellis, J. M. (1997). *Literature lost: Social agendas and the corruption of the humanities*. New Haven: Yale University Press.

Fairclough, N. (1995). *Media discourse*. London: Edward Arnold.

Fish, S. (1995). *Professional correctness: Literary studies and political change*. Cambridge, MA: Harvard University Press.

Fleck, L. (1981). *Genesis and development of a scientific fact*. Chicago: University of Chicago Press.

Flude, M. & M. Hammer (Eds.) (1990). *The Education Reform Act 1988: Its origins and implications*. London: Falmer.

Foucault, M. (1972). *The archaeology of knowledge*. London: Tavistock.

Foucault, M. (1977). *Discipline and punish: The birth of the prison*. London: Penguin.

Foucault, M. (1980). *Power/knowledge*. Brighton: Harvester.

Freud, S. (1973). *New introductory lectures on psychoanalysis*. London: Penguin.

Gee, J. P., A-R. Allen & Clinton, K. (2001). Language, class, and identity: Teenagers fashioning themselves through language. *Linguistics and Education, 12*(2), 175-194.

Geertz, C. (1973, 2000 edn.). *The interpretation of cultures*. New York: Basic Books.

Geertz, C. (1988). *Works and lives: The anthropologist as author*. Cambridge: Polity.

Gerdes, P. (1985). Conditions and strategies for emancipatory mathematics education in undeveloped countries. *For the Learning of Mathematics, 5*(1), 15-20.

Gerdes, P. (1988). On culture, geometrical thinking and mathematics education. *Educational Studies in Mathematics, 19*(2), 137-162.

Giddens, A. (1984). *The constitution of society: Outline of the theory of structuration*. Cambridge: Polity.

Goffman, E. (1974). *Frame analysis*. New York: Harper.

Goffman, E. (1990). *The presentation of self in everyday life*. Harmondsworth: Penguin.

Gray, A. (2003). Cultural studies at Birmingham: The impossibility of critical pedagogy? *Cultural Studies, 17*(6), 767-782.

Halliday, M. A. K. & C. M. I. M. Mathiessen (2004). *An introduction to functional grammar*, third edition. London: Arnold.

Haraway, D. J. (1991). A cyborg manifesto: Science, technology, and socialist-feminism in the late twentieth century. In D. J. Haraway, *Simians, cyborgs and women: The reinvention of nature*. London: Free Association Books.

Harker, R. & S. A. May (1993). Code and habitus; Comparing the accounts of Bernstein and Bourdieu. *British Journal of Sociology of Education, 14*(2), 169-178.

Harré, R. & M. Krausz (1996). *Varieties of relativism*. Oxford: Blackwell.

Hartman, G. (1987). *The unremarkable wordsworth*. London: Methuen.

Hasan, R. (1999). The disempowerment game: Bourdieu and language in literacy. *Linguistics and Education, 10*(1), 25-87.

Hawking, S. & R. Penrose (1996). *The nature of space and time*. Princeton: Princeton University Press.

Hayles, N. K. (1999). *How we became posthuman: Virtual bodies in cybernetics, literature and informatics.* Chicago: University of Chicago Press.

Heath, S. B. (1986). Questioning at home and at school: A comparative study. In M. Hammersley, *Case studies in classroom research.* Milton Keynes: Open University Press.

Hebdige, D. (1988). The bottom line on planet one: Squaring up to the face. In *Hiding in the light: On images and things.* London: Routledge.

Heidegger, M. (1962). *Being and time.* London: SCM Press.

Hilfer, T. (2003). *The new hegemony in literary studies: Contradiction in theory.* Evanstone: Northwestern University Press.

Hodge, R. & G. Kress (1988). *Social semiotics.* Cambridge: Polity.

Holland, E. W. (1999). *Deleuze and Guattari's anti-Oedipus: Introduction to schizoanalysis.* London: Routledge.

Hunter, I. (1994). *Rethinking the school: Subjectivity, bureaucracy, criticism.* St Leonards: Allen & Unwin.

Illich, I. (1973). *Deschooling society.* Harmondsworth: Penguin.

Johnson-Eilola, J. (1998). Living on the surface: Learning in the age of global communication networks. In I. Snyder, *Page to screen: Taking literacy into the electronic era.* London: Routledge.

Jones, R. A. (1999). *The development of Durkheim's social realism.* Cambridge: Cambridge University Press.

Joyce, M. (1992). *Afternoon, a story.* Cambridge, MA: Eastgate.

Joyce, M. (1995). *Of two minds: Hypertext, pedagogy and poetics.* Ann Arbor: The University of Michigan Press.

Joyce, M. (1998). New stories for new readers: Contour, coherence and constructive hypertext. In I. Snyder, *Page to screen: Taking literacy into the electronic era.* London: Routledge.

Joyce, M. (1999). Beyond next before you once again: Repossessing and renewing electronic culture. In G. E. Hawisher and C. L. Selfe, *Passions, pedagogies and 21st century technologies.* Logan: Utah State University Press.

Joyce, M. (2001). *Othermindedness.* Ann Arbor: The University of Michigan Press.

Kaplan, N. (2000). Literacy beyond books: Reading when all the world's a web. In A. Herman and T. Swiss: *The world wide web and contemporary cultural theory.* New York: Routledge.

Kaprow, A. (2003). "Happenings" in the New York scene. In N. Wardrip-Fruin & N. Montfort, *The new media reader.* Cambridge, MA: MIT Press.

Kauffman, S. (1995). *At home in the universe: The search for the laws of self-organization and complexity.* New York: Oxford University Press.

Kermode, F. (1967/2000). *The sense of an ending: Studies in the theory of fiction.* New York: Oxford Univesity Press.

Kernan, A. (1990). *The death of literature.* New Haven: Yale University Press.

King, R. (1976). Bernstein's sociology of the school—Some propositions tested. *British Journal of Sociology of Education, 27*(2), 430-443.

Kogan, M. (1978). *The politics of educational change.* Glasgow: Fontana/Collins.

Kress, G. (1993). Against arbitrariness: The social production of the sign as a foundational issue in critical discourse analysis. *Discourse and Society, 4*(2), 169-191.

Kress, G. (2003). *Literacy in the new media age.* London: Routlege.

Kress, G. & T. van Leeuwen (1996). *Reading images: The grammar of visual design.* London: Routledge.

Kuhn, T. (1970). *The structure of scientific revolutions.* Chicago: University of Chicago Press.

Lacan, J. (1977). *Écrits.* New York, W.W. Norton.

Laclau, E. & C. Mouffe (1985). Hegemony and socialist strategy: Towards a radical democratic politics. London: Verso.

Landow, G. P. (1997). *Hypertext: The convergence of contemporary critical theory and technology (Parallax—Re-visions of culture and society).* Baltimore: The Johns Hopkins University Press.

REFERENCES

Latour, B. (2000). When things strike back: A possible contribution of 'science studies' to the social sciences. *British Journal of Sociology*, *51*(1), 107-123.

Latour, B. & S. Woolgar (1979). *Laboratory life: The social construction of scientific facts*. Beverly Hills: Sage.

Lave, J. *et al* (1984). The dialectic of arithmetic in grocery shopping. In B. Rogoff and J. Lave, *Everyday cognition: Its development in social context*. Cambridge, MA: Harvard University Press.

Lave, J. & E. Wenger (1991). *Situated learning: Legitimate peripheral participation*. Cambridge: Cambridge University Press.

Lévi-Strauss, C. (1972). *The savage mind (La pensée sauvage)*. London: Weidenfeld & Nicholson.

Livingston, E. (1986). *The ethnomethodological foundations of mathematics*. London: RKP.

Luria, A. R. (1976). *Cognitive development: Its cultural and social foundations*. Cambridge, MA: Harvard University Press.

Lyotard, J.-F. (1984). *The postmodern condition: A report on knowledge*. Manchester: Manchester University Press.

McGann, J. (2001). *Radiant textuality: Literature after the world wide web*. New York: Palgrave.

Manovich, L. (2001). *The language of new media*. Cambridge, MA: MIT Press.

Mason, J. (1978). On investigations. *Mathematics Teaching, 84*.

Mason, J. *et al* (1982). *Thinking mathematically*. London: Addison-Wesley.

Maton, K. (2000). Languages of legitimation: The structuring significance for intellectual fields of strategic knowledge claims. *British Journal of Sociology of Education, 21*(2), 148-167.

Maton, K. (2006a). On knowledge structures and knower structures. Available at http://www.cheeps.com/karlmaton/pdf/Knowerstrs.doc

Maton, K. (2006b). On knowledge structures and knower structures. In R. Moore, M. Arnot, J. Beck & H. Daniels, *Knowledge, power and educational reform: Applying the sociology of Basil Bernstein*. London: Routledge.

Maton, K. & H. K. Wright (2002). Returning cultural studies to education. *International Journal of Cultural Studies, 5*(4), 379-392.

Miles, A. (2001). Realism and a general economy of the link. *Currents in Electronic Literacy*. Fall 2001 (5). http://www.cwrl.utexas.edu/currents/archives/fall01/fall01/miles/index.html

Moon, B. (1986). *The 'new maths' controversy: An international story*. Lewes: Falmer.

Moore, R. & K. Maton (2001). Founding the sociology of knowledge: Basil Bernstein, intellectual fields, and the epistemic device. In A. Morais, M. I. Neves, P. B. Davies & H. Daniels, *Towards a sociology of pedagogy: The contribution of Basil Bernstein to Research* (pp. 153-182). New York: Peter Lang.

Moore, R. & J. Muller (1999). The discourse of "voice" and the problem of knowledge and identity in the sociology of education. *British Journal of Sociology of Education, 20*(2), 189-206.

Moore, R. & J. Muller (2002). The growth of knowledge and the discursive gap. *British Journal of Sociology of Education, 23*(4), 627-637.

Moore, R. & M. F. D. Young (2001). Knowledge and the curriculum in the sociology of education: Towards a reconceptualisation. *British Journal of Sociology of Education, 22*(4), 445-461.

Moss, G. (2000). Informal literacies and pedagogic discourse. *Linguistics and Education, 11*(1), 47-64.

Moulthrop, S. (1995). Rhizome and resistance: Hypertext and the dreams of a new culture. In G. P. Landow, *Hyper/text/theory*. Baltimore: The John Hopkins University Press.

Moulthrop, S. (1999). Misadventure: Future fiction and the new networks. *Style, 33*(2), 184-203.

Mulhern, F. (2000). *Culture/metaculture*. London: Routledge.

Muller, J. (1989). "Out of their minds": An analysis of discourse in two South African Science Classrooms. In D. Roger & P. E. Bull, *Conversation: An interdisciplinary perspective*. Clevedon, PA: Multilingual Matters.

Murakami, H. (2000). *Underground: The Tokyo gas attack and the Japanese psyche*. London: The Harvill Press.

Murray, J. H. (1997). *Hamlet on the Holodeck: The future of narrative in cyberspace*. New York: The Free Press.

Myers, G. (1992). Textbooks and the sociology of scientific knowledge. *English for Specific Purposes,* *11*(1), 3-17.

National Department of Education (1997). *Curriculum 2005: Lifelong learning for the 21ˢᵗ Century.* Pretoria: NDE.

Ong, W. J. (1982). *Orality and literacy: The technologizing of the world.* London: Routledge.

Penrose, R. (1997). *The large, the small and the human mind.* Cambridge: Cambridge University Press.

Piaget, J. (1972). *The principles of genetic epistemology.* London: RKP.

Piaget, J. (1980). *Opening the debate. Language and learning: The debate between Jean Piaget and Noam Chomsky.* M. Piattelli-Palmarini. London: RKP.

Piaget, J. (1995). *Sociological studies.* London: RKP.

Pina, Á. (2003). Intellectual spaces of practice and hope: Power and culture in Portugal from the 1940s to the present. *Cultural Studies, 17*(6), 751-766.

Polya, G. (1946). *How to solve it: A new aspect of mathematical method.* Princeton: Princeton University Press.

Power, S. (2006). Basil Bernstein: Directions for empirical research. Fourth International Basil Bernstein Symposium, Rutgers-Newark. 6-9 July 2006.

Power, S. *et al* (1998). Schools, families and academically able students: Contrasting modes of involvement in secondary education. *British Journal of Sociology of Education, 19*(2), 157-176.

Rorty, R. (1989). *Contingency, irony and solidarity.* Cambridge: Cambridge University Press.

Ryan, M.-L. (1999). Cyberspace, virtuality, and the text. In M.-L. Ryan, *Cyberspace, textuality: Computer technology and literary theory.* Bloomington, IN: Indiana University Press.

Ryle, G. (1968). The thinking of thoughts: What is "Le Penseur" doing?' *University Lectures, 18,* from http://lucy.ukc.ac.uk/CSACSIA/Vol14/Papers/ryle_1.html.

Schwartz, R. B. (1997). *After the death of literature.* Carbondale & Edwardsville: Southern Illinois University Press.

Searle, A. (2001). Whiteread's reminder of modernist ideals defies sentimentality. *The Guardian,* 5/06/2001.

Shayer, M., D. W. Küchemann, *et al* (1992). The distribution of Piagetian stages of thinking in British middle and secondary school children. In L. Smith, *Jean Piaget: Critical assessments. Volume 1.* London: Routledge.

Sirc, G. (1999). "What is composition ...?" After Duchamp (Notes toward a general teleintertext). In G. E. Hawisher & C. L. Selfe, *Passions, pedagogies and 21st century technologies.* Logan: Utah State University Press.

Snow, C. P. (1964). *The two cultures: And a second look.* Cambridge: Cambridge University Press.

Sohn-Rethel, A. (1973). Intellectual and manual labour. *Radical Philosophy, 6,* 30-37.

Sohn-Rethel, A. (1975). Science as alienated consciousness. *Radical Science Journal, 2/3,* 63-101.

Sohn-Rethel, A. (1978). *Intellectual and manual labour: A critique of epistemology.* London: MacMillan.

Sokal, A. D. (1996). A phycisist experiment with cultural studies. *Lingua Franca, 62-64.* Available at http://www.physics.nyu.edu/faculty/sokal/lingua_franca_v4/lingua_franca_v4.html.

Sosnoski, J. (1999). Hyper-readers and their reading engines. In G. E. Hawisher & C. L. Selfe, *Passions, pedagogies and 21st century technologies.* Logan: Utah State University Press.

Spivak, G. C. (1996). More on power/knowledge. In D. Landry & G. Maclean, *The Spivak reader.* New York: Routledge.

Stevens, W. (2001). *Harmonium.* London: Faber & Faber.

Sunnen, P. (2000). *Making sense of video games: A textual analysis of Tomb Raider II.* MA dissertation. available at http://homepage.mac.com/paulcdowling/ioe/studentswork/sunnen_diss.pdf.

Symonds, W. C. (2004). America's failure in science education. *Business Week Online.* http://www.businessweek.com/technology/content/mar2004/tc20040316_0601_tc166.htm.

Thurston, W. P. (1994). On proof and progress in mathematics. *Bulletin of the American Mathematical Society, 30*(2), 161-177.

Tyler, W. (1988). *School organisation: A sociological perspective.* London: Croom Helm.

REFERENCES

Usher, R. and R. Edwards (1994). *Postmodernism and education.* London: Routledge.
Vygotsky, L. S. (1978). *Mind in society: The development of higher psychological processes.* Cambridge, MA: Harvard University Press.
Vygotsky, L. S. (1986). *Thought and language.* Cambridge, MA: MIT Press.
Ward, S. C. (1996). *Reconfiguring truth: Postmodernism, science studies, and the search for a new model of knowledge.* Lanham: Rowman & Littlefield.
Walkerdine, V. (1982). From context to text: A psychosemiotic approach to abstract thought. In M. Beveridge, *Children thinking through language.* London: Arnold.
Warschauer, M. (1999). *Electronic literacies: Language, culture and power in online education.* Mahwah, NJ: Lawrence Erlbaum Associates.
Wheale, N. (Ed.) (1995). *The postmodern arts.* London: Routledge.
Weber, M. (1964). *The theory of social and economic organization.* New York: The Free Press.
Weber, M. (1968). *Economy and society.* New York: Bedminster Press.
Wenger, E. (1998). *Communities of practice: Learning, meaning, and identity.* New York: Cambridge University Press.
Whiteman, N. (2005). Homesick for Silent Hill: Fans' negotiation of textual identity in responses to *Silent Hill 4: The Room.* Playing the past: Nostalgia in video games and electronic literature. Presentation at 1st Annual Conference, Gainesville, Florida, March 18-19, 2005 (Proceedings).
Whiteman, N. (2007). *The establishment, maintenance, and destabilising of fandom: A study of two online communities and an exploration of issues pertaining to internet research.* PhD Thesis. London: Institute of Education, University of London.
Whiteman, N. (in press). Homesick for Silent Hill: Modalities of nostalgia in fan responses to *Silent Hill 4: The Room.* In L. Taylor and Z. Whalen, *Playing the past: History and nostalgia in videogames.* Nashville: Vanderbilt University Press.
Wolf, L. (2002). An environment that encouraged change. *IDB América.* Available at http://www.iadb.org/idbamerica/index.cfm?&thisid=353&pagenum=2.
Wright, H. K. (2003). Cultural studies as praxis: (Making) an autobiographical case. *Cultural Studies, 17*(6), 805-822.
Young, M. F. D. (Ed.) (1971). *Knowledge and control: New directions for the sociology of education.* London: Collier-Macmillan.
Young, M. F. D. (2000). Rescuing the sociology of educational knowledge from the extremes of voice discourse: Towards a new theoretical basis for the sociology of the curriculum. *British Journal of Sociology of Education, 21*(4), 523-536.

FILM AND TELEVISION

Ally McBeal (TV, 1997-2002, various directors)
Babette's Gaestebud (1987, Gabriel Axel, dir.)
Being John Malkovich (1999, Spike Jonze, dir.)
Emma (1996, Douglas McGrath, dir.)
Forrest Gump (1994, Robert Zemeckis, dir.)
Lost in Translation (2003, Sofia Coppola, dir.)
Possession (2002, Neil LaBute, dir.)
Pulp Fiction (1994, Quentin Tarantino, dir.)
Russian Ark (2002, Aleksandr Sokurov, dir.)
The Usual Suspects (1995, Bryan Singer, dir.)
Timecode (2000, Mike Figgis, dir.)
Truly, Madly, Deeply (1991, Anthony Minghella, dir.)
Short Cuts (1993, Robert Altman, dir.)
Star Trek: The next generation (TV, 1987-1994, various directors)

OTHERS

Silent Hill 1-4. Konami Digital Entertainment Inc.
Super Mario Bros. Nintendo.
Tomb Raider II: The dagger of Xian. 1997. Core Design. Eidos.

INDEX

Aarseth, Espen, 60
Accommodating. *See* Perspective/Value schema
Adlam, Diana, 91
Aesthetic mode
  asceticism, 247
  haute couture, 247
  necessity, 247
  opulence, 247
Aggleton, Peter, xii
Alienate, 243
Allen, Anna-Ruth, 92
Alliance
  disimilars, 46, 47, 59, 147, 208
  similars, 46, 47, 59, 147, 208
Alliances and oppositions, 12, 13, 17, 21, 23, 24, 26, 35, 42, 43, 46–48, 53, 56, 58–60, 62, 64, 65, 75, 93, 105, 107, 109, 119, 120, 122, 126, 144, 147, 208, 209, 227, 229–232, 236, 239, 246
Altman, Robert, 52, 57
Anderson, Benedict, 183
André, Carl, 53, 57
Anthropology, 9, 13, 21, 204, 220, 240
Antitheorists, 13, 14
Anxiety. *See* Authority: liberal
Appel, Kenneth, 204
Apprenticeship, 244, 254
Aristotle, 212
Arnot, Madeleine, xiii
Articulating, 95, 240
Asceticism. *See* Aesthetic mode
Association of Teachers of Mathematics (ATM), 100
Atheism, 57
Atkin, Ron, 154
Atkinson, Rowan, 193
Attractor states, 185, 187
Atweh, Bill, xii, 12
Austen, Jane, 198, 199
Austin, Keith, 5
Authority, 50–65
  bureaucratic, 52–54, 56–58, 60, 62, 63, 127–130, 132, 142, 143, 146, 169, 188, 222, 232
  charismatic, 50–53, 56, 59, 60, 62, 63, 66, 130, 143, 146, 167, 186, 221
  liberal, 54, 59, 62, 65, 145, 146, 222
  Liberal, 58
  traditional, 53, 56, 58, 60, 62, 63, 66, 96, 127, 128, 143, 146, 187, 189, 221

Autoethnographic mode. *See* Legitimation modes
Autopoiesis, 12, 13, 23, 24, 38, 39, 41, 42, 50, 55, 60, 105, 106, 119–121, 126, 227–230, 236, 250
Axel, Gabriel, 54, 57
Babbedge, T.S.R., 3, 6, 13
Bahl, Parin, xi, 5, 154
Bann, Stephen, 41
Barthes, Roland, 16, 18, 40, 86
Baudrillard, Jean, 25, 51, 80, 84, 146, 233
Beck, John, xiii, 105
Becker, Barbara, 128
Benaceraf, Paul, 205
Bentham, Jeremy, 15, 45
Bergonzi, Bernard, 210
Bernstein, Basil, xi, xii, 4, 11, 27, 29, 32, 33, 35–38, 40–42, 69–84, 86–95, 104–107, 121, 126, 147, 148, 181, 182, 200–205, 207, 208, 213, 221, 227, 230, 232–234, 236, 237, 264
  classification, 27, 32, 33, 76–81, 87, 93, 106, 118, 126, 200, 213, 215, 224, 232
  framing, 27, 32, 33, 76–81, 87, 93, 106, 121, 200, 213, 215, 224, 232
  grammars, 204
  hierarchical knowledge structure, 88, 106, 208, 212
  horizontal discourse, 90, 94, 105, 106
  horizontal knowledge structure, 106, 204, 212
  instructional discourse, 82
  invisible pedagogy, 33, 78, 84
  pedagogic device, 82, 84, 213, 236
  pedagogic discourse, 82, 84
  positional/personal families, 201
  regulative discourse, 82
  speech codes, 29, 89–93, 106, 201
  vertical discourse, 88, 94, 106, 204
Bérubé, Michael, 246
Bhabha, Homi, 217
Bhaskar, Roy, 6–8
Bible, 55, 57
Bishop, Alan, xii
Blades, David, 217
Bloom, Harold, 74, 193, 202
Bloomfield, Alan, 100
Bolter, Jay David, 60–63
Boltzman, Ludwig, 37
Borges, Jorge Louis, 122
Boundaries, 76–81
Bourbakiism, 126

Bourdieu, Pierre, 22, 24, 62, 80, 93, 94, 130, 147, 187, 208, 246, 247
Bowman, Jack, 19
Brannen, Julia, xii
Brantlinger, Patrick, 218
Bravenboer, Darryll, ix
Brown, Andrew, x, xii, 12, 16, 20, 48, 75, 95, 98, 141, 144, 149, 151, 152, 180, 186, 190, 206, 228, 229, 231, 233, 239
Brunsdon, Charlotte, 215
Bryman, Alan, 95
Burbules, Nicholas, 147
Bureaucratic. See Authority
Burke, Jeremy, ix, 235, 237
Burke, Kenneth, 109
Byatt, A.S., 54
Charismatic. See Authority
Cheshire, Jenny, 92
Chisholm, Linda, 154
Chisholm, Lynne, xii
Chomsky, Noam, 84, 213
Choral response, 164–166, 174, 182
Chouliaraki, Lilie, 49, 117
Christianity, 55
Chronotope, 242
Chronotopic strategy, 110–114
Chung, Soh-young, ix, x, xi, 1, 10, 11, 55, 63, 120, 193, 245, 246
Cimabue, Cenni di Pepo, 11, 28, 34–39, 49, 66, 231
City of Angel, 241
Civic Education Study (CivEd), 133, 145
Class condensation. See also Social class
Classification. See Bernstein, Basil
Clinton, Katharine, 92
Cockcroft, Wilfred, 100
Coleridge, Samuel Taylor, 1–4, 13, 16
Collectivising, 181, 183, 189
Collins, James, 90
Commentary, 9, 11–14, 20, 49, 50, 75, 180, 190, 191, 223, 228, 233, 234, 264
Community, 149–191
    African virtual community, 163, 169
    class condensation, 170
    community servants, 178, 181, 184, 188
    globally distributed virtual community, 155, 156, 160, 162, 177
    substantive community, 161
    Xhosa virtual community, 161, 163
Community servant/community member. See Teacher/student identity
Competence, 82, 84, 95, 97, 93–106, 98, 100, 109, 120, 121, 128, 182, 240
Compliance, 244, 245
Comportment, 242

Computer mediated communication (CMC), 78, 80
Connell, Robert William/Raewyn, 188
Construction, 240
Constructionism, 48
    social constructionism, 7
Constructive description, 11, 12, 14, 48, 66, 86, 87, 106, 191, 223, 228, 229, 230, 233, 234, 236, 239, 240, 241
Constructivism, 27, 62, 197, 198
Cooper, Barry, 99, 126
Critique, 240
Crotty, Michael, 48, 130
Crystal, David, 129
Cunningham, Rod, ix, 185
Curatorial. See Perspective/Value schema
Curriculum
    as technology, 126
    linearity, 11
Curriculum codes
    collection, 32
    integrated, 32
Cybernetics, 23, 48, 55, 58
D'Ambrosio, Ubiritan, 129
Daniels, Harry, xiii
Davies, Zain, x
Davison, David, 129
de Certeau, Michel, 23, 94, 99, 200
de Cervantes, Miguel, 125
de Fermat, Pierre, 211, 212
de Klerk, Vivien, 165
de Liefde, Peter, xii
de Saussure, Ferdinand, 51, 80, 231
Deconstruction, 240
Deduction, 86
Deformance, 47, 48, 50, 52, 59, 66, 74, 180, 223, 229
dela Volpe, Galano, 47
Deleuze, Gilles, 12, 23, 126
Dependency, 244
Depression. See Authority: traditional
De-regulation, 183, 184, 189
Derrida, Jacques, 40, 80
Descriptive domain. See domains of action
De-territorialising, 240
Devi, Mahasweta, 214
Diachronic, 242
Diachronising, 110–114, 118, 119
Dick, Philip K., 25, 50, 51, 57
Dickinson, Emily, 47
Disciplinary enquiry, 183, 184, 187, 188
Disciplinary practice, 182
Disciplinary regulation, 183, 184, 188, 189
Discourse, 95, 96, 93–106, 231, 239
Discovery, 240
Discursive comportment, 240

Discursive saturation (DS), 86, 94, 99, 100, 102, 104, 105, 93–106, 120, 121, 206, 207, 223, 231, 232
Division of labour, 28, 29, 34–36, 78, 79, 120, 125–128, 160, 167, 172, 232
Domains of action
  descriptive domain, 206, 234, 239
  esoteric domain, 4, 9, 81, 96–100, 134–137, 139, 206, 230, 231, 234, 235, 238, 239, 244, 250
  expressive domain, 206, 207, 234, 239, 244
  public domain, 3, 4, 8, 9, 12, 13, 81, 93, 99, 135, 137, 139, 140, 147, 206, 231, 234, 235, 237–239, 244
Douglas, Jane Yellowlees, 60, 62–64
Douglas, Mary, 32, 76, 187, 190, 200–202
Dowling, Paul, 4, 8, 11, 12, 16, 20, 23, 25, 40, 48, 55, 56, 63, 65, 69, 76, 79–81, 83, 86, 93, 95, 98, 99, 117, 118, 126, 128, 129, 135, 137, 139, 144, 147–149, 152, 180, 193, 200, 205, 206, 227–230, 239, 244
Dreyfus, Hubert, 229
Duchamp, Marcel, 27, 50, 62
Dudley-Smith, Russell, ix, 236, 237
Dunne, Mairead, 99
Durães, Cecilia, 52
Durkheim, Émile, 9, 28, 29, 31–39, 42, 66, 76, 125, 199, 230, 231
Eco, Umberto, 38, 40, 94
Educational studies, 9, 13, 74, 125, 198, 227, 228, 234, 236
Edwards, Richard, 199
Elaborated description, 98
Ellis, John, 210
Emergence, 23, 24, 35, 42, 43, 65, 93, 98, 105–107, 120, 121, 125, 126, 128, 129, 132, 134, 142, 144, 147, 229, 236, 250
Emin, Tracy, 63
Empirical
  empirical field, 20, 21, 37, 40, 48, 203, 208, 227, 228, 233, 239, 240
  empirical objects and encounter, 86
  empirical setting, 20, 21, 97, 143, 152, 228, 239, 240
Ensor, Paula, x
Epiphenomena, 24, 229
Epistemological fallacy, 6–8
Epistemological paradox, 98
Epistemology, 6–8, 23, 25, 42, 43, 48, 59, 69, 70, 72, 118, 191, 199, 213
Equilibration, 23, 58. See also Interaction mode
Erdos, Paul, 211
Escher, Maurits Cornelis, 122
Esoteric domain. See Domains of action

Estrange, 243
Ethnomathematics, 7, 129, 198
Ethnoscience, 129
Exchange action, 84, 87
Exchange of narratives. See Interaction mode
Exchange relations, 84, 97, 119, 128, 145, 182, 187, 188, 230, 244, 245
Exchange text, 66, 227, 229, 245
Explore, 242
Expressive domain. See domains of action
Fairclough, Norman, 49, 50, 117
  discourse, 49
Fiction, 10, 14, 77, 207. See also Grammatical mode
Field of practice, 37, 50, 51, 53, 54, 144, 208, 215, 221, 230, 237, 245
Findings, 228
Fish, Stanley, 130, 199, 210, 212, 223, 245, 246
Fleck, Ludwik, 72, 93
Flude, Michael, 56, 128
Forensics, 3–6, 11–14, 22, 26, 42, 50, 66, 74, 151, 191, 228–231, 233, 234, 236, 240
Forrest Gump, 52, 54, 55, 57, 59, 185, 225
Foucault, Michel, 40, 71, 80, 94, 125, 142, 229
Fractal quality, 24, 39, 42, 43, 87
Framing. See Bernstein, Basil
Freud, Sigmund, 42, 80, 94
Galant, Jaamiah, ix, x, 149, 152, 153, 170, 177, 233
Gaze, 8, 11, 17, 21, 35, 39, 49, 66, 69, 81, 83, 93, 99, 200, 206, 207, 217, 227, 235
Gee, James, 92, 147
Geertz, Clifford, 9, 13, 180, 220, 250
General/footsoldier. See Teacher/student identity
Generalising, 95, 96, 240, 254, 255
Genre, 49, 57, 113, 165
Gerdes, Paulus, 7, 8
Giotto di Bondone, 35–37
Globalisation, 126, 130, 134, 142
Globalising, 129
God, 16, 21, 35, 36, 55, 56, 125
Gödel, Kurt, 204
Goffman, Erving, 74, 242
Goldstein, R.L., 195
Gramci, Antonio, 218
Grammatical mode
  fiction, 207, 208, 223, 224
  metaphoric apparatus, 207, 211–213, 224, 225, 227, 234, 236, 237, 251
  method, 207, 223, 234, 236, 237, 246
  metonymic apparatus
Gramsci, Antonio, 188
Gray, Ann, 218

Gross, Paul, 197, 198
Guardian strategies, 183
Guardian/ward. See Teacher/student identity
Guattari, Félix, 12, 23, 126
Guilroy, Paul, 217
Haihuie, Samuel, ix
Haken, Wolfgang, 204
Hall, Stuart, 217
Halliday, Michael, 29, 84, 87, 109, 120, 121, 204
Hammer, Merrill, 56, 128
Happenings, 17–20
Haraway, Donna, 76
Harker, Richard, 75, 106
Harré, Rom, 195
Hartman, Geoffrey, 109, 180
Hasan, Ruqaiya, 89, 147
Hashimoto, Yuko, ix
Haute couture. See Aesthetic mode
Hawking, Stephen, 197
Hawkins, Peter, 90
Hayles, N. Katherine, 13, 22, 23, 26, 48, 55, 58, 60, 114
Heath, Shirley Brice, 147
Hebdige, Dick, 25, 26, 27
Hegemony, 13, 146, 147, See also Interaction mode
Heidegger, Martin, 110
Heller, Joseph, 18
Hepworth, Barbara, 53
Heresy, 59, 74, 76, 82, 84, 93, 106, 121, 125, 144, 146, 153, 223, 225, 229, 233
Hierarchical knowledge structure. See Bernstein, Basil
Hilfer, Tony, 210, 245, 246
Hoadley, Ursula, x, 149, 152, 160, 233
Hodge, Robert, 28, 29, 32–40, 42, 49, 230
Hoffman, Paul, 211, 212
Holland, Eugene, 126
Horizontal discourse. See Bernstein, Basil
Horizontal knowledge structure. See Bernstein, Basil
Humanities, 4, 13, 88, 130, 197, 236, 237
Hunter, Ian, 80
Hussain, Saddam, 146
Hypertext, 60, 62, 132, 140
Hysteria. See Authority: charismatic
Ideal types, 13, 87
Identification, 243
Identity. See teacher/student identity
Identity avatars, 75
Identity equilibrium, 181, 183, 187–190, 233
Ideology, 51, 82
Idiolect, 42, 93–106, 121, 211, 231, 239
Ignatieff, Michael, 209
Illich, Ivan, 41

Individualising, 181, 183, 184, 189
Induction, 86
Inequality, 250
Informational decoupling, 24, 41, 43
Institute of Education, ix, xii, 65, 96, 97, 114–117, 143, 165
Institutionalisation, 4, 9, 10, 13, 23–25, 35, 39, 41, 42, 58, 67, 76, 81, 84, 86, 95–99, 105, 106, 120–122, 126–128, 132, 135, 136, 142, 143, 182, 205, 206, 208, 221, 230–236, 239
Instrumental. See Perspective/Value schema
Interaction mode
  equilibration, 46, 59, 145, 147, 209
  exchange of narratives, 46, 145, 147, 209
  hegemony, 46, 48, 59, 66, 147, 188, 209, 239
  pastiche, 13, 46–48, 50, 65, 147, 209, 233
International Association for the Evaluation of Educational Achievement (IEA), xiii, 129, 130
Invisible pedagogy. See Bernstein, Basil
Involve, 243
Islam, 56
Japan, ix, x, 9, 47, 52, 152, 250, 253–264
Japsers, Karl Theodor, 210
Jesus, 55
Johnson-Eilola, Johndan, 63, 64
Jones, Robert Alan, 9, 199
Jonze, Spike, 51, 57
Joyce, Michael, 60, 62, 63, 132
Judaism, 56
Julie, Cyril, x
Kaplan, Nancy, 60, 117
Kaprow, Allan, 18, 19, 21, 54
Kauffman, Stuart, 25–27, 37, 39
Kelly, Dermot, ix
Kennedy, John F., 53, 79
Kermode, Frank, 86, 208–212
Kernan, Alvin, 210, 246
King, Ronald, 83
Knower mode. See Legitimation modes
Knowledge mode. See Legitimation modes
Knowledge, fetishising of, 214
Kogan, Maurice, 128
Koran, 56, 57, 177
Krausz, Michael, 195
Kress, Gunther, x, 11, 28, 29, 32–40, 42, 49, 61, 109, 110, 112–115, 117, 118, 230, 231
Kuhn, Thomas, 72, 214
LaBute, Neil, 54, 57
Lacan, Jacques, 40, 75, 80, 126
Laclau, Ernesto, 110, 230
Landow, George P., 60
Language of description, 41, 71, 84, 86, 227
  external language, 86

internal language, 86
Lapping, Claudia, x
Latour, Bruno, 4, 212, 225
Lave, Jean, 56, 70, 83, 99, 100, 148
Le Courbusier (Jean-Claude Jenneret), 50
Leader, 181
Leader/follower identity, 189
    community servant/community member,
        189
    general/footsoldier, 189
    guardian/ward, 189
    service provider/client, 189
Legitimation modes, 220
    autoethnographic mode, 220
    knower mode, 203, 207, 211–215, 218–
        220, 222
    knowledge mode, 203, 207, 211–214, 219,
        220, 222
    nomad mode, 220
Leont'ev, Aleksei N., 65
Level of analysis, 5, 23, 24, 42, 52, 55, 59, 75,
    78, 79, 81, 86, 87, 106, 120, 126, 182, 200,
    207, 209, 214, 215, 231, 232, 235, 236,
    237, 250
Lévi-Strauss, Claude, 80, 94
Levitt, Norman, 197, 198
Lévy-Bruhl, Lucien, 94
Liberal. See Authority
Liberal democracy, 146
Literary criticism, 180, 207–209, 211
Literary studies, 11, 60, 86, 198, 199, 203,
    207, 208, 210, 212, 223, 225, 237, 245
Literary theory, 207
Livingston, Eric, 204
Localising, 95, 240, 254, 255
Locke, John, 109
Lotman, Yuri, 94
Luria, Alexander, 94
Lyotard, Jean-Francois, 202
Mace, John, xii
Magritte, René, 53
Makoe, Pinky, x
Manovich, Lev, 22, 25, 27
Manzoni, Piero, 50, 51, 52, 57
Mapping, 110–114
Marketing, 244, 245
Marx, Karl, 51, 52, 69, 80, 125, 145
Mason, John, 100
Mastermind (game), 5–6, 13, 87, 205
Mathematicoscience, 118, 142–144, 146, 147,
    232, 234, 236
Mathematics, 6, 7, 8, 12, 79, 81, 83, 93, 95,
    105, 98–106, 126–130, 132, 134–137,
    139–142, 145, 147, 197, 198, 203–207,
    211, 212, 225, 230, 235–237, 244, 245
    as formalised discourse, 142

Mathematics education, 12, 98–106, 126–148
Mathematics Education Project (MEP), 166
Mathiessen, Christian, 109, 120, 121
Maton, Karl, xiii, 86, 105, 202, 203, 207–216,
    219–225, 234
Maturana, Humberto, 23
May, Stephen, 75, 106
McCarty, Colin, ix, 238
McGann, Jerome, 47, 48, 53, 59, 60, 61, 63,
    74, 180, 212, 223
McGrath, Douglas, 54
Mechanical solidarity, 28, 29, 32, 33, 35, 36,
    66
Mendeleev, Dmitri, 199
Metaphoric apparatus. See Grammatical mode
Method. See Grammatical mode
Methodology, 8, 38, 70, 84, 86, 93, 95–98,
    140, 144, 180, 186, 206, 228, 229
    general methodology, 48
Metivier, Joanne, ix
Metonymic apparatu. See Grammatical mode
Meyer, George, 19
Miles, Adrian, 60, 62
Miller, Kenneth, 129
Milton, John, 212, 223
Minh-Ha, Trinh T., 218
Misprision, 59, 74, 193, 202, 229, 233, 239,
    242
Misreading, 59, 74, 106, 193, 196, 202, 203,
    207, 208, 213, 214, 223, 229, 231, 233,
    246
Misrecognition, 74, 75, 106, 196, 207, 213,
    225, 229, 231, 239
Mod, 242
Mode of interrogation, 20, 48, 186
Mondrian, Piet, 37
Montrose, Louis, 223
Monumentalising, 51, 52
Moon, Bob, 83, 126
Moore, Rob, xiii, 86, 105, 193, 194, 195, 198–
    200, 202, 203, 207–214, 219, 225
Moral regulation, 81, 164, 169, 183–185, 187,
    188
Morris, William, 53, 212
Moss, Gemma, 147
Mouffe, Chantal, 110, 230
Moulthrop, Stuart, 60
Mulhern, Francis, 218, 219
Muller, Joe, x, 105, 164, 193, 194, 195, 198–
    200, 225
Murakami, Haruki, 258
Murray, Janet, 60
Myers, Greg
Mythologising, 8, 9, 11, 14, 16, 17, 19, 26, 27,
    39, 41, 42, 54, 97, 110, 122, 215, 228, 232,
    244

National Centre for Educational Statistics (NCES), 129, 131, 132
National Department of Education, 156
Natural science, 132, 134–137, 139–141, 147
  as formalising discourse, 142
  exclusion of subjectivism, 136–137
Natural sciences, 4–7, 9, 13, 26, 88, 130, 145, 196, 212, 236
Naylor, Henry, 193
Necessity. *See* Aesthetic mode
Network analysis, 87
New Criticism, 207
Newton, Isaac, 199
Nietzsche, Friedrich, 119
Noh, Yun-chae, x
Non-disciplinary practice, 182
Noss, Richard, 56, 128
Nostalgia modes, 242
Objectification, 244, 245
Obsession. *See* Authority: bureaucratic
Ong, Walter J., 110
Operational matrix, 142, 245
Opulence. *See* Aesthetic mode
Organic solidarity, 28, 29, 32, 33, 179
Organisational language, 8, 11–15, 24–28, 34, 36–39, 41–43, 46, 48, 50, 59, 65–67, 86, 87, 106, 114, 119, 121, 152, 190, 191, 225, 228, 230, 232, 233, 250
Orientation to aesthetic capital. *See* Aesthetic mode
Orientation to economic capital. *See* Aesthetic mode
Ortega y Gasset, José, 210
Painting, 110–114
Paltrow, Gwynneth, 54
Panopticon, 15, 45, 80
Parry, Michael, 1, 3, 13
Parsons, Talcott, 84
Passeron, Jean-Claude, 130, 147
Pastiche. *See* Interaction mode
Patriarchy, 16, 21, 45, 66, 169, 229
Pedagogic action, 56, 81, 84, 87, 106, 107, 132, 169, 239, 244, 245
  exemplars, 240
  principles, 240
Pedagogic device. *See* Bernstein, Basil
Pedagogic discourse. *See* Bernstein, Basil
Pedagogic relations, 80, 84, 96, 107, 119, 128, 132, 151, 182, 187, 189, 190, 230, 244
Pedagogic strategies, 95
Pedagogic text, 66
Penrose, Roger, 4, 198
Performance, 93–106, 109, 121
Perspective (intrinsic/extrinsic), 246
Perspective/Value schema, 246
Philosophy, 7, 8, 13, 47, 126

Physics, 4, 5, 82, 83, 127, 140, 195, 207, 208, 233
Piaget, Jean, 23, 57–59, 80, 94, 141, 145
Picasso, Pablo, 53
Pina, Álvaro, 218
Poiesis, 47, 48, 223
Polya, George, 100, 101
Positivism, 197, 202
Postmodernism, 8, 26, 40, 48, 52, 61–63, 195, 197–199, 217, 225, 240
Poststructuralism, 198, 217
Power
  delimiting, 240
  expanding, 240
  general, 243
  local, 243
Power, Sally, xii, 83, 200
Practical strategic space, 95–107
Principles of evaluation, 66, 80, 84, 87, 119, 128, 130, 187, 190
Principles of realisation, 75, 77, 96
Principles of recognition, 75, 77, 96, 98, 100, 227
Printing, 110–114
Problem, 228, 239
Problematic, 228, 239
Progress in International Reading Literacy Study (PIRLS), 130
Public domain. *See* Domains of action
Public/private, 98, 130, 132, 134, 135, 144–147, 231, 232, 234
Putnam, Hilary, 205
Qualitative research, 98
Quantitative research, 98
Rabinow, Paul, 229
Readymade, 27, 50
Realisation rules. *See* Principles of realisation
Realism, 5, 6, 8, 9, 13, 38, 71, 191, 195, 197–199, 223, 225, 233
  anti-realism, 8, 9
  critical realism, 6–9
  naive realism, 8, 9, 25, 27
  social realism, 4, 9
Recognition rules. *See* Principles of recognition
Recontextualisation, 8, 32–34, 39, 50, 59, 64, 69, 76, 81–87, 93, 106, 126, 147, 187, 206, 218, 228–231, 235, 237, 239, 244
Recruit, 181
Rees, Mary, ix
Register coding, 110–114, 231, 232
Regulatory strategies, 182, 184, 186, 187, 233
Relational space, 59, 147, 181, 182, 207, 231, 234
Relativism, 7, 25, 62, 194–197, 220
religion, 55

Religion, 28, 55, 56, 130
Repeat, 242
Repertoire coding, 110–114, 231, 232
Reproductive. *See* Perspective/Value schema
Reside, 243
Rorty, Richard, 41, 195
Rosenberg, Harold, 209–212
Rossetti, Gabriel Dante, 47, 61
Routine, 244, 245
Rupture, 242, 243
Ruskin, John, 47
Ryan, Marie-Laure, 26, 27, 61, 62
Ryle, Gilbert, 180, 250
Said, Edward, 54
Sasaki, Sadako, 255
Schooling
    as structurally conservative, 143
Schopenhauer, Arthur, 28
Schwartz, Richard, 210
Science. *See* Natural sciences
Science education, 4, 12, 126–148
Scientia, 47, 48, 223
Scribing, 110–114
Searle, Adrian, 50
Secondary Mathematics Learning
    Experiment/Experience (SMILE), 127
Service provider/client. *See* Teacher/student
    identity
Shakespeare, William, 212, 223
Shayer, Michael, 141
Silent Hill Heaven, 241
Silverman, David, 19
Simpson, Homer, 19, 66
Singer, Bryan, 52, 57
Sirc, Geoffrey, 27, 62
Skill, 93–106, 121, 231, 239
Snow, Charles Percy, 223
Social action, 35, 46, 65, 84, 126, 144, 191,
    229, 230
Social Activity Method (SAM), 228
Social Activity Theory (SAT), 13
Social class, 90, 99, 152, 222, 250
    class condensation, 151, 170
Social science, 4, 9, 13, 25, 26, 38, 88, 212,
    236, 237
Social structure, 15, 24, 29, 33, 35, 45, 91, 93,
    245
Sociocultural, 12, 13, 43, 45, 51, 56, 65, 67,
    69, 84, 106, 120, 125, 219, 224, 228, 230–
    232, 239, 246, 250, 251
    dehiscing, 45, 46, 48, 228, 239
Sociology, 5, 8, 9, 11–13, 16, 17, 21, 26, 28,
    32–36, 38, 42, 50, 66, 69, 72, 74, 86, 98,
    106, 114, 117, 119, 121, 147, 153, 180,
    198, 200, 203, 204, 207, 214, 216, 223,

227, 228, 230, 231, 234, 236, 246, 250,
    259
Sogang University, x
Sohn-Rethel, Alfred, 94
Sokal, Alan, 7, 8, 144, 146, 195–199
Sosnoski, James, 132
South Africa, x, 12, 73, 139, 227, 233
South Korea, xi
Specialising, 81, 95, 96, 239, 240
Spectate, 242
Speech codes. *See* Bernstein, Basil
Spivak, Gayatri, 214, 217
Stevens, Wallace, 1–3, 10, 13, 14, 218
Strategy of the general, 183–185, 187
Structural coupling, 23, 24, 41–43
Subjectivism, 48, 136–137, 144, 145, 197
Subjectivity, 2–4, 10, 23, 43, 48, 50, 75, 107,
    118, 182, 218, 244, 245, 264
    distribution of subjectivity, 244
Sujee, Mohammad, 154
Sunnen, Patrick, 64
Suture, 242, 243
Suzuki, Atsuko, ix
Symonds, William C., 129
Synchronic, 242
Synchronicity, 112, 232
Synchronising, 110–114, 119, 122
Systemic Functional Linguistics (SFL), 121
Takase, Kimiko, x
Takase, Mitsuki, x
Tarantino, Quentin, 52, 57
Target of discursive action, 147
Teacher/student identity. See also
    Leader/follower identity
    community servant/community member,
        181, 184, 186, 188
    general/footsoldier, 181, 186, 189
    guardian/ward, 181, 184–186, 188, 189
    service provider/client, 186
    Service provider/client, 181
Technological determinism, 12, 46, 118
Technology, 14, 15, 17, 26, 45, 48, 60, 61–63,
    65, 66, 80, 94, 95, 118, 125–130, 132, 134,
    142, 144, 146, 147, 180, 181, 190, 203,
    223–225, 228–, 233, 234
Territorialising, 240
Text
    art-as-work, 18
    as instance of an organisational language,
        42, 43
    bounding the text, 17–21, 20, 41, 43, 49
    c.f. sign, 110–111
    city-as-work, 17
    empirical text, 50, 86, 228
    exchange. *See* Exchange text
    object text, 50

pedagogic. *See* Pedagogic text
privileged text, 164–166, 169, 182, 184
technology/text/commentary, 180–181, 190, 223, 228, 234
text-as-text, 16, 18, 24, 41, 86, 95, 227
text-as-work, 16, 18–20, 24–27, 41, 43, 86, 95, 227
textual modes, 110–114
theoretical text, 86, 228
Theory
  engineering of theory, 227
  grand theory, 200–202
  metatheory, 26, 27, 42
  theoretical dualism, 49
  theoretical field, 20, 21, 36, 37, 40, 48, 49, 86, 228, 239, 240
  theoretical objects and discovery, 86
  theory as necrotising, 43, 105, 122, 202
Things as they are, 2, 3, 9, 10, 13, 14, 220, 228, 229, 233, 234, 240
Thurston, William, 205
Tomb Raider II, 64, 238
Tourist discourse, 15
Traditional. *See* Authority
Treachery, 59, 76, 106, 107, 223, 229, 231
Trends in International Mathematics and Science Studies (TIMSS), xii, 118, 129–142, 145, 146
Triangulation, 7
trick, 93–106
Trick, 95, 121, 231, 239
Tu, Yueh-Lin, ix
Tyler, William, 83
University

as structurally dynamic, 143
University of Cape Town, x, 166, 184, 227
University of the Western Cape, x
Usher, Robin, 199
Value (intrinsic/extrinsic), 246
van Leeuwen, Theo, 112
Vass, Jeff, xi, 1, 12–14, 251
Vector, 241
Vertical discourse. *See* Bernstein, Basil
Vygotsky, Lev, 56, 58, 65, 94
Walkerdine, Valerie, 94
Wallinger, Mark, 51
Ward, Steven, 197
Warschauer, Mark, 77, See
Weber, Max, 51–53, 142, 143
Wehner, Josef, 128
Wenger, Etienne, 56, 70, 83, 148
Wheale, Nigel, 225
Whiteman, Natasha, ix, 55, 63, 118, 241, 242, 243, 244
Whiteread, Rachel, 50–52, 57, 63
Wilderspin, Samuel, 80
Williams, Raymond, 218
Willis, Paul, 218
Wolf, Laurence, 129
Woolgar, Steve, 4
Wordsworth, William, 180
Wright, Handel, 216–218, 220, 221
Yanasei, Takashi, ix
Yonsei University, x
Young, Hugo, 54
Young, Michael F.D., 105, 198–200, 225
Zemeckis, Robert, 52, 57

Lightning Source UK Ltd
Milton Keynes UK
UKOW021638270112

186200UK00005B/25/P